The Fibre Channel Consultant Series

Fibre Channel over Ethernet (FCoE)

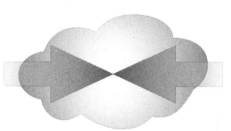

Robert W. Kembel

NIA

Be sure to check out the other books in the Fibre Channel Consultant series:

Fibre Channel A Comprehensive Introduction	ISBN 978-0-931836-10-7
Fibre Channel Switched Fabric	ISBN 978-0-931836-11-4
Fibre Channel over Ethernet (FCoE)	ISBN 978-0-931836-12-1
Fibre Channel Arbitrated Loop	ISBN 978-0-931836-13-8

ISBN: 978-0-931836-12-1

Published by:

Northwest Learning Associates, Inc.
12 Water Street
Hingham, MA 02043
781-626-4746, Fax: 781-626-4751
email: info@nlabooks.com
Visit our web site at www.NLAbooks.com

Printed in the United States of America

20 19 18 17 16 15 14 13 12 11 10 9 8 7 6 5 4 3 2 1

Contents

Section I. Introduction and Concepts

Section II. FCoE Technology

Section IV. Reference Information

List of Figures

List of Tables

Foreword

Current data centers usually deploy up to three different network technologies for different applications: Ethernet for LAN and IP traffic, Fibre Channel for networked storage, and, in some cases, when high performance computing is deployed, Infiniband for inter-process communications. The resulting system is expensive and difficult to manage because it requires multiple cabling systems and components, each associated with a different management framework.

A major trend in the information technology industry is achieving I/O consolidation, (i.e., the ability to transport multiple data-center traffic types over a converged network technology). I/O consolidation enables maintaining the advantages of each existing traffic type while minimizing the costs to build and manage a data center. With I/O consolidation a single cabling system and infrastructure can be used for all data center needs, reducing the number of components and simplifying the associated management structures.

A successful I/O consolidation strategy needs to consider that Fibre Channel is the preeminent technology used today for storage networking, while Ethernet is the dominant technology used for IP and LAN traffic. Trying to achieve I/O consolidation without Ethernet or Fibre Channel is doomed to failure. For this reason, previous attempts at I/O consolidation had limited success (e.g., Infiniband tried to replace Ethernet, or iSCSI attempted to replace Fibre Channel).

A significantly more interesting approach is the one provided by FCoE (Fibre Channel over Ethernet), defined by the FC-BB-5 working group of the INCITS T11 Technical Committee. By carrying Fibre Channel frames in Ethernet frames, FCoE achieves I/O consolidation over an Ethernet infrastructure without diminishing any existing Fibre Channel storage networking capabilities. Thus, FCoE is naturally compatible with the two current dominant technologies.

A consolidated Ethernet network with FCoE allows:

- fewer adapters and switch ports;
- reduction and simplification of cabling;
- absence of gateways;
- less power and cooling needs; and
- overall reduced costs.

For these reasons FCoE has been the focus of extraordinary industry interest since its inception. Today the FCoE standard is complete, products are available, and deployments are underway.

FCoE requires Ethernet links to be enhanced to provide the same level of service as a Fibre Channel link (i.e., no frame loss in the presence of congestion). Understanding FCoE requires a knowledge of both Fibre Channel and of the enhancements that make Ethernet links lossless.

This book provides the reader with a thorough explanation of the FCoE protocol and its implications for the world of computing. It presents a summary of the Fibre Channel and Ethernet architectures, the benefits of FCoE, and a set of suitable configurations and deployment scenarios. It then dives into the technical details, discussing the architectural models of FCoE, the way in which Fibre Channel frames are mapped into Ethernet frames, and the addressing structure used by FCoE. Finally, it elaborates on the FIP control protocol, that allows FCoE to be seamlessly integrated in the existing Fibre Channel environments, and on the extensions needed for Ethernet to be lossless.

Robert Kembel, the author of this book, has been active in the T11 Fibre Channel standards technical committee for many years. He develops and conducts seminars on Fibre Channel fundamentals, Fibre Channel Arbitrated Loops, and Fibre Channel Fabrics to engineers, managers, support personnel and marketers at various companies. Robert participated to the activity of the T11 FC-BB-5 working group, where FCoE has been developed. As chair of the FC-BB-5 working group, I have appreciated Robert's insightful contributions to the development process. Now, you have a chance to gain the benefits of Robert's experience in the building of this exciting new technology. With his book, Robert provides a comprehensive FCoE picture that will be meaningful for years to come, with the advent and diffusion of FCoE based I/O consolidated data centers.

Claudio DeSanti
Distinguished Engineer, Cisco Systems
T11 FC-BB-5 & FC-BB-6 Chairman

Preface

Fibre Channel over Ethernet (FCoE) burst upon the data center storage scene in April of 2007 with a joint press release issued by ten of the leading companies in the storage industry. Since that initial press release, FCoE has generated an extraordinary amount of discussion and controversy within the industry. The purpose of this book is to examine the FCoE technology and provide an understanding of the reasons behind its development and ultimate applications.

Just as Fibre Channel rode the way of Storage Area Networking and brought an entirely new paradigm to storage attachment, FCoE is riding the wave of the converged data center Ethernet (DCE). The realization of a converged data center network will fundamentally change the storage landscape and open the storage market to new ideas, architectures and products.

Because FCoE is based on both Fibre Channel and Ethernet, an understanding of both of these technologies is required to fully understand FCoE. It is not the intent of this book to cover those technologies in depth. The companion books in the Fibre Channel Consultant series already provide a thorough discussion of the Fibre Channel technologies and protocols. Similarly, there are many excellent books that already cover Ethernet. This book targets the marriage of those two technologies and explains how FCoE leverages the advantages of both technologies as the storage component of a converged data center Ethernet.

Robert W. Kembel

1. What is FCoE?

In today's world, many servers are connected to the Internet or a corporate intranet and external storage (some servers may also connected to other servers within a clustered environment). An example of a server with utilizing three different external interfaces (one for each type of communication) is shown Figure 1-1 on page 1. While this figure shows a single adapter of each type, keep in mind that multiple adapters of a given type may be used to provide higher performance or redundancy.

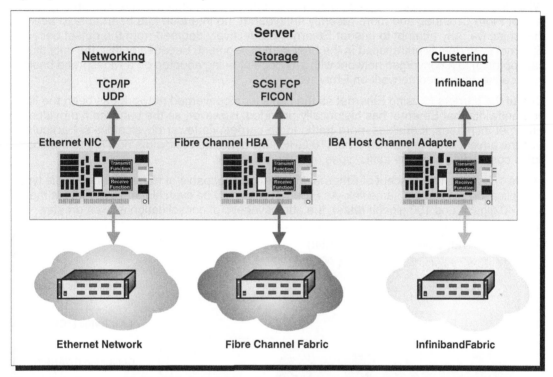

Figure 1-1. Server with Multiple Interfaces

The network connection to the Internet or intranet is usually provided by Ethernet with a server having one or more Ethernet Network Interface Cards (NICs) as needed to provide the required bandwidth and redundancy.

The external storage connection may be provided by a number of different interface types, including the Small Computer System Interface (SCSI) bus, Serial Attached SCSI (SAS), or Fibre Channel (FC). For small to medium size configurations, the SCSI bus or SAS is commonly used. Within the datacenter environment, Fibre Channel is the predominant interface. Again, multiple Host Bus Adapters (HBAs) may be used to provide higher bandwidth or redundancy.

When a server is part of a clustered environment, the server may use either the network interface or external storage interface to provide the inter-server communications or it may use a dedicated interface such as InfiniBand (IB).

1.1 The "Converged" Data Center Network

There has been a long-standing desire to consolidate the different types of application traffic onto a single, converged network. Consolidation offers numerous immediate benefits in terms of costs, power and cooling, infrastructure complexity and ease of management.

While the idea of a converged network has been attempted in the past (this was an original intent of Fibre Channel, and more recently, Infiniband), no interface has been able to achieve this objective. Any attempt to unseat Ethernet is effectively doomed from the outset because Ethernet is so deeply entrenched in the LAN market segment. Because of this, the only practical approach to a converged network with any hope of being adopted on a widespread basis is to base the converged network on Ethernet.

One of the barriers to using Ethernet as the basis for a converged network has been the limited bandwidth that Ethernet has historically provided. However, as the bandwidth provided by Ethernet increases, it enables more traffic to be carried via fewer physical links. Particularly with the advent of 10 gigabit Ethernet (10 GBE), the available bandwidth now offers the potential to consolidate all of the traffic types over the same link.

Figure 1-2 shows this concept of Ethernet as a "fat pipe" capable of transporting multiple types of application data on the same link. As Ethernet links provide even higher bandwidth in the future (40 gigabit and 100 gigabit rates), the attractiveness of consolidation is even greater.

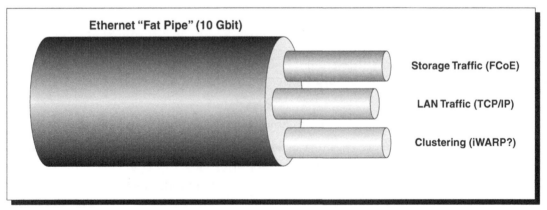

Ethernet "Fat Pipe" (10 Gbit)

Storage Traffic (FCoE)

LAN Traffic (TCP/IP)

Clustering (iWARP?)

Figure 1-2. Ethernet As A "Fat Pipe"

By adopting a converged network approach, the external connections needed by a server are greatly simplified as shown in Figure 1-3 on page 3. In this example, the server has a single Converged Network Adapter (CNA) that connects to a single converged network. The converged adapter is used to carry traditional network traffic in addition to storage (and perhaps, clustering) traffic.

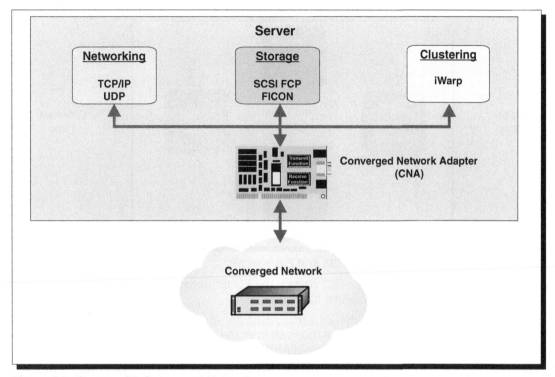

Figure 1-3. Server with Converged Network

The Converged Network Adapter may be based on a standard Ethernet NIC or an Ethernet NIC supporting enhanced functionality as may be required by the different applications.

1.2 Converged Network Adapter (CNA) Implementations

There are many approaches to implementing FCoE functionality. Whereas native Fibre Channel solutions have relied heavily on hardware functionality to maximize performance, FCoE offers a range of implementation options that can provide a wider range of cost and performance characteristics. This section examines a number of possible implementation approaches.

1.2.1 1st Generation: Hybrid Design Using "FCoE Glue" Chip

Early, first-generation CNAs, were implemented using a standard Fibre Channel HBA and Ethernet chip connected with an "FCoE glue" chip as shown in Figure 1-3 on page 3.

In this implementation, a standard Fibre Channel HBA and 10 gigabit Ethernet NIC are connected using a "FCoE glue" chip. In the transmit direction, the "glue" chip receives Fibre Channel frames from the FC HBA and encapsulates them within Ethernet frames. In the reverse

---

Converged Network Adapter (CNA) Implementations 3

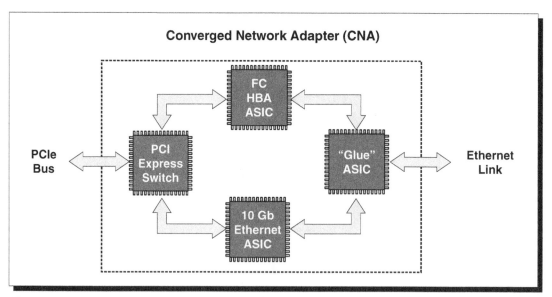

Converged Network Adapter (CNA)

PCIe Bus — PCI Express Switch — FC HBA ASIC — "Glue" ASIC — 10 Gb Ethernet ASIC — Ethernet Link

Figure 1-4. CNA Using Standard FC HBA and Ethernet NIC

direction, received Ethernet frames that contain the FCoE protocol are decapsulated and sent to the FC HBA as native Fibre Channel frames.

Ethernet frames transmitted by the Ethernet ASIC are forwarded by the "glue" chip to the Ethernet physical link. Ethernet frames received from the physical link that do not contain the FCoE protocol are forwarded to the Ethernet ASIC for processing.

The Ethernet ASIC and FC HBA are connected to the host's PCI Express bus using a PCI Express switch module. The operating system sees the CNA as two separate adapters, the Ethernet NIC and the Fibre Channel HBA. As a result, the operating system can continue to use the existing Ethernet and Fibre Channel drivers without change.

1.2.2 2nd Generation: FCoE Integrated ASIC

The 1st generation CNA implementation approach provided a straightforward method to implementing FCoE but the cost of such a solution did not realize the full benefits of a converged network. While two separate adapters were combined into one, no savings has been realized in the chip count (in fact, inclusion of the PCI Express switch and glue chips actually increased the chip count).

Second-generation CNA implementations integrate the Ethernet, Fibre Channel HBA, "FCoE glue" chip and PCI Express switch functions (that were shown as separate chips in Figure 1-3 on page 3) into a single, integrated Converged Network Adapter. This results in a single-chip solution as shown in Figure 1-4 on page 4 that offers significant cost and power saving benefits.

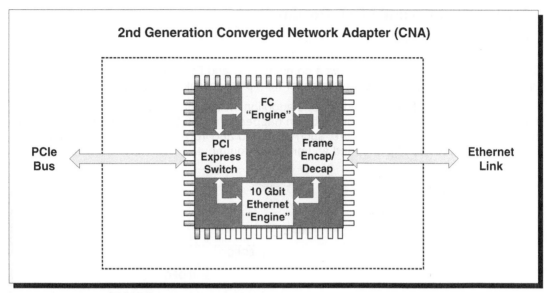

Figure 1-5. 2nd Generation Integrated CNA Solution

1.2.3 Ethernet NIC with FCoE Enhancements

Another approach to implementing FCoE is to add enhancements to an Ethernet ASIC. Many high-performance ASICs contain embedded processing capabilities and hardware assist functions. Selected FCoE functions are provided by the processor or FCoE-specific hardware (for example, the transmission or reception of a Fibre Channel Information Unit using a Sequence of frames).

Some examples of functions that may be off-loaded include Large Send Offload (LSO), Giant Send Offload (GSO), Large Receive Offload (LRO), Interrupt Coalescing and CRC generation and checking. Send and receive off-loads relieve the system processor from having to create or process multiple frames when processing a large unit of information. Interrupt coalescing allows multiple interrupt conditions to be reported in a single interrupt. CRC generation and checking is compute intensive and offloading this function can relieve system CPU overhead.

Functions that are not off-loaded to the chip could be performed with a software driver. These functions might include tasks that are not associated with the performance path such as the processing of Fabric Login (FLOGI), Name Server registrations and queries, Extended Link Services processing and similar functions.

1.2.4 Software-Only FCoE

A final approach to implementing FCoE is through the use of a software driver that provides all of the necessary FCoE processing and functions. The only hardware requirement when using this approach is that the Ethernet NIC support Ethernet pause flow control. This is the approach being taken by the open-source FCoE activity.

1.3 Fibre Channel and FCoE Roadmap

FCoE provides an alternative to using native Fibre Channel links. While the physical link is different, the protocols and functions provided by FCoE are the same as those on native Fibre Channel. Figure 1-6 on page 6 shows a combined FC and FCoE roadmap illustrating the different link rates and projected time frames for both physical link technologies.

FCoE will probably find its most widespread adoption on 10 gigabit Ethernet links in converged data center environments. This should begin happening in the 2010 time frame. As Ethernet deploys faster link rates in the future, such as 40 Gb and 100 Gb, FCoE can leverage those technologies to provide higher-speed and greater throughput.

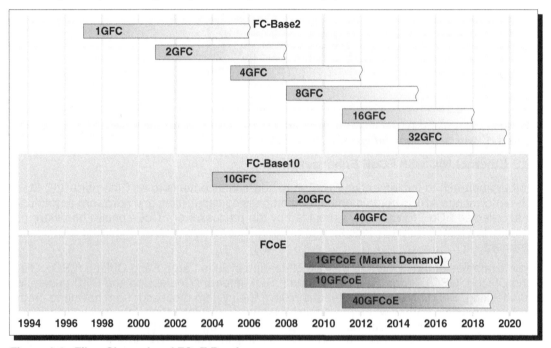

Figure 1-6. Fibre Channel and FCoE Roadmap

1.4 Benefits of a Converged Network Approach

Many of the benefits of a converged network should be immediately evident.

- A server now has a single adapter replacing multiple different types of adapters that were required when a different type of network was used for each class of application traffic.
- The datacenter has a single network Instead of two, or three, different networks. This means a single network to install, manage and maintain.
- The number of cables and connections is dramatically reduced.

The savings resulting from a converged network manifest themselves in a number of different ways that are explored further in *FCoE Benefits* on page 55. That chapter attempts to quantify the benefits of a unified, converged network for several different configurations and sets of assumptions.

1.5 What is Fibre Channel over Ethernet (FCoE)?

Fibre Channel over Ethernet (FCoE) is the transport of encapsulated Fibre Channel frames via "lossless" Ethernet. In its simplest form, there is no dependence on any native Fibre Channel devices and all of the devices in an FCoE configuration could connect to a "lossless" Ethernet network using "lossless" Ethernet NICs or Converged Network Adapters (CNAs). The "lossless" Ethernet network must contain at least one FCoE switch (functionally, a combination of an FCoE Forwarder (FCF) and an Ethernet switch) and it may contain more than one FCoE switch. An example of a pure Ethernet FCoE configuration is shown in Figure 1-7.

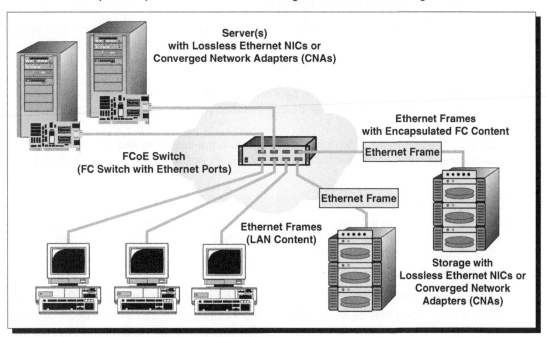

Figure 1-7. Pure Ethernet FCoE Configuration

FCoE is the marriage of two historically distinct technologies and disciplines; storage and networking. FCoE addresses the storage aspect of the converged network vision that was discussed earlier. A natural question that arises in this approach to convergence is "why use Fibre Channel and Ethernet?"

The role of Ethernet as a network was discussed earlier. Any attempt to create a converged network that has any realistic hope of widespread adoption is dependent using Ethernet.

Since its introduction as a reliable, high-performance interface for storage devices in 1994, Fibre Channel has established itself as the leading interface for Storage Area Networks. It has a proven track record and provides a robust interface for host systems, servers and storage devices in a wide variety of applications.

Fibre Channel supports the transport of multiple protocols including the Small Computer System Interface (SCSI), Fibre Connection Architecture (FICON), Serial ATA (SATA), the Internet Protocol (IP), the Virtual Interface Architecture (FC-VI) and a number of protocols used by avionics subsystems.

According to an article published by Network World in October of 2007 citing a study by IDC, Fibre Channel held a 97% share of the external disk storage systems market. Much as Ethernet has become ubiquitous in the network world, Fibre Channel has become ubiquitous in the storage world.

1.5.1 FCoE Has "Virtual" Fibre Channel Ports

An FCoE port does not meet the strict definition of a node port or fabric port as defined by the Fibre Channel standards. Rather, FCoE ports emulate the behavior of native Fibre Channel ports and are referred to a virtual ports.

An FCoE node port is referred to as a "virtual Node Port", or VN_Port. An FCoE switch port that is attached to a VN_Port is referred to as a "virtual Fabric Port", or VF_Port, and an FCoE switch port that is attached to another FCoE switch port is a "virtual Expansion Port, or VE_Port.

Other than the physical interface is provided by Ethernet, the functions and behaviors of FCoE virtual ports are identical to the functions and behaviors of the corresponding native Fibre Channel ports.

1.5.2 FCoE Objectives

One of the early activities in the development of an FCoE standard was to define a set of objectives. While there was no formal vote on the objectives, they have provided guidance for the development of the technology and may prove useful in understanding FCoE.

Key overall FCoE objectives are:

1. Seamlessly and transparently replace the Fibre Channel physical interface with Ethernet.

   By this it is intended that devices implementing FCoE can be part of the same Fabric as native Fibre Channel devices and that FCoE devices and Fibre Channel devices can communicate with one another without awareness of the underlying physical link. In effect, Ethernet simply provides an alternative data link for the transport of the Fibre Channel protocols encapsulated in Ethernet frames.

2. Make no changes to existing protocol mappings, information units, initialization steps, Fibre Channel services, etc.

   In order to provide seamless and transparent communication with existing Fibre Channel devices, there can be no changes to any of the existing protocols, information units, etc.

If any of these were to change, FCoE devices would not be able to co-exist and communicate with native Fibre Channel devices.

3. Develop a mapping that can be implemented totally in software using "lossless" Ethernet NICs (similar to what was done with the iSCSI initiator).

Because FCoE is based on Ethernet, it should be possible to implement FCoE functions totally within a software driver. This would allow the use of "lossless" Ethernet NICs for FCoE devices. Note that FCoE requires functions that may not be provided by all Ethernet adapters (An example of this type of function is Ethernet pause flow control, which is optional in the Ethernet standards).

4. Enable high-performance implementations through the use of hardware assists, much as provided by existing FC HBAs with no requirement for TCP/IP Offload Engines (TOEs).

Due to the overhead associated with software processing, a software-only implantation may not provide the same level of performance as could be realized by implementing some functions in hardware. Because FCoE does not use TCP/IP, the hardware assists may be much simpler than what is required by a TOE.

1.5.3 FCoE End Node (ENode) Objectives

Objectives for an FCoE End Node (server or device) are:

1. FCoE must not impact an endpoint's FC stack (i.e. HBA and software).

An FCoE end device (server or storage) must be able to operate with a normal Fibre Channel protocol stack. The fact that the physical link is Ethernet should not change the Fibre Channel processing.

2. A cleanly layered FC stack over Ethernet must be possible.

There must be a clean division between Fibre Channel functions and FCoE/Ethernet specific functions.

3. Endpoint Fibre Channel and Upper Level Protocols (e.g. FCP, SB-3, Fabric Login, discovery, etc....) must work as they do today, with no change required to support FC over Ethernet.

Again, this is a restatement of the requirement that FCoE does not affect existing Fibre Channel protocols. All of the existing protocols mappings and operations must function in exactly the same manner as if in a native Fibre Channel environment.

4. An FC over Ethernet mapping layer can be used to satisfy above requirement.

One possible implementation of FCoE would be to insert a "shim" or "wedge" driver between the Fibre Channel stack and the Ethernet driver. This FCoE shim would provide the functions necessary to support FCoE (e.g., encapsulation and decapsulation of Fibre Channel frames).

5. An Endpoint can have multiple network stacks mapped over Ethernet.

Consistent with the converged network and converged network adapter models, FCoE becomes one of multiple protocols that may be sent via the same adapter. One or more

---

FCoE endpoints can co-exist with one or more IP over Ethernet, or other protocols over Ethernet, on the same physical Ethernet adapter. Some examples include a single physical Ethernet port that supports:

- Virtual FC HBAs and/or,
- Virtual Ethernet NICs (with or without RDMA, iSCSI or TOE support)

6. All FC functionality must be supported, including support for max FC frame sizes (this requires support for jumbo or "baby jumbo" Ethernet frames), Zoning (access control), Virtual Fabrics, Security (FC-SP), etc.

7. Any additional attributes to existing FC Extended Link Service (ELS) payloads should be avoided (e.g., FLOGI and its ACCEPT). If it is not possible to avoid changes to an existing ELS, any changes must be standardized.

8. In-order Fibre Channel frame delivery is required.

Many existing Fibre Channel devices require in-order delivery of Fibre Channel frames. Because FCoE and Fibre Channel devices can co-exist within the same Fabric and communicate with one another, FCoE must meet the delivery needs of native Fibre Channel ports.

9. Class-3 service is required and Class-2 service should be supported (Class-1 service support is not required).

Most applications today are using Fibre Channel Class-3 service and FCoE must provide services equivalent to Class-3. Furthermore, nothing should preclude supporting Class-2 service as Class-2 is being used in some environments. To meet this objective, FCoE switches should support both Class-2 and Class-3.

10. FCoE requires a mechanism to support link down scenarios for FC over Ethernet (analogous to Fibre Channel Loss-of-Signal).

A mechanism is needed to detect a failed link. If a native Fibre Channel link fails, the port detects a loss of signal and can take the appropriate action. A similar mechanism is needed to detect a failed Ethernet link carrying FCoE traffic. An instance of a failed link needs to be reported promptly as well as interlinking of the FC Fabric reporting with the underlying Ethernet network reporting.

11. A mechanism analogous to link isolation is needed to enforce policy (e.g. Fabric binding).

If an FCoE End Node fails security, authorization or authentication policies, the link needs to be isolated to prevent potential denial-of-service attacks or unauthorized access attempts.

12. FCoE must work under benign conditions and in the presence of errors.

FCoE must not only work under normal conditions, but also in the presence of errors such a link errors, forwarding errors, lost frames or malicious behavior.

13. The differences between FC and Ethernet need to be dealt with.

Wherever differences between native Fibre Channel and Ethernet are identified, FCoE must address those differences and provide an acceptable mapping between the respective behaviors.

14. FCoE must deliver data integrity comparable to native Fibre Channel.

This objective captures the essence of what is required as far as error detection and data integrity.

1.5.4 FCoE Switch and Fabric Objectives

Specific objectives identified for an FCoE switch and Fabric are:

1. No frame drops under normal conditions or due to congestion.

   At a minimum, this requires support for a flow control mechanism such as Pause on today's Ethernet (with no frame drop in switches) or Per Priority Pause on "lossless" Ethernet switches.

2. FC Fabric timeouts (e.g. R_A_TOV) must be respected.

   An FCoE Fabric (and/or attached Fibre Channel Fabric) must reliably enforce Fibre Channel Fabric timeout requirements. Failure to enforce R_A_TOV may result in undetected data corruption if an OX_ID re-used.

3. Class-3 and Class-F are required and Class-2 should be supported.

   With the exception of Class-F, this is the switch side of the requirement to support Class-2 and Class-3. Class-F support is required in all multi-switch Fabrics.

4. Flow Control (e.g., credit recovery) must work in all cases.

   Mechanisms must exist to allow for recovery from flow control errors that may result from lost frames or signaling.

5. One or more FC over Ethernet network Controllers are required per FCoE Fabric.

   There must be at least on FCoE Fabric Controller to provide Fibre Channel services such as Fabric Login processing, Name Server, and other required Fibre Channel functions or services. If there are more than one FCoE Fabric Controllers, the protocol for coordinating them needs to function in the face of failure of one of them.

1.6 What Makes FCoE Different?

There are multiple existing mappings of storage protocols to Ethernet. They include:

- Internet SCSI (iSCSI)
- Internet FCP (iFCP)
- Fibre Channel over IP (FCIP)

All of these mappings are based on the use of TCP/IP. While TCP/IP adds several benefits, such as acknowledgement and retransmission, it also adds complexity and overhead. Addressing the complexity of TCP/IP in software results in processing overhead and adversely impacts performance. Offloading TCP/IP processing to the hardware improves performance, but adds hardware cost and complexity.

Figure 1-8 on page 12 illustrates the protocol stacks for a number of different mappings of the SCSI protocol. From this, it is clear that all of the TCP/IP based mappings have additional protocol levels and processing beyond what is required in a native Fibre Channel environment. Each of these protocol levels adds framing overhead at the data link level and processing overhead in the protocol stack.

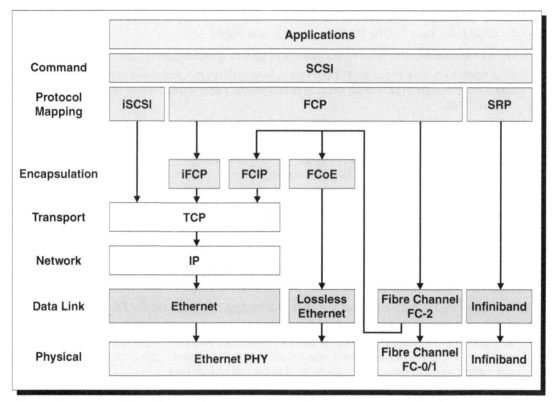

Figure 1-8. Protocol Stack Comparison

The basic assumption underlying FCoE is that TCP/IP is not required in a local datacenter network and the necessary functions can be provided by "lossless" Ethernet without the complexity and overhead associated with TCP/IP. This is based on the assumption that "lossless" Ethernet will provide reliable, lossless transport for the encapsulated Fibre Channel traffic.

FCoE uses encapsulated Fibre Channel frames, including the Fibre Channel frame header. The facilitates bridging between the two environments while taking advantage of the context information contained within the Fibre Channel frame header (e.g., protocol and operation identification and segmentation/reassembly information).

FCoE is not intended as a replacement for TCP/IP based storage protocols and TCP/IP will still be required for the Wide Area Network (WAN) or long-haul environments.

1.6.1 Fibre Channel over IP (FCIP)

Fibre Channel over IP (FCIP) is a mapping that enables the transport of encapsulated Fibre Channel frames via a TCP/IP network. FCIP was developed to provide a method of tunneling Fibre Channel traffic through an IP network in order to connect to a remote data center, branch office, disaster recovery site or off-site backup facility. Figure 1-9 shows the format of an FCIP encapsulated frame.

As mentioned previously, the use of TCP/IP introduces extra processing overhead at the TCP and IP layers. TCP/IP incurs significant processing overhead and hardware requirements. Because TCP is a "stateful" protocol, each TCP implementation must maintain state information about existing TCP connections and provide sufficient memory to accommodate reassembly of receive IP datagrams and/or retransmission of failed datagrams. This adds to the complexity of an FCIP implementation and normally limits the use of FCIP to those cases where the distance or configuration requirements preclude the use of native Fibre Channel links.

Examination of an FCIP frame encapsulation in an Ethernet frame reveals the extent of the overhead associated with the encapsulation. The Ethernet frame has the overhead associated with the Ethernet header and trailer. In addition, there is the overhead associated with the IP header (normally 20 bytes) and TCP header (also normally 20 bytes). Following this is an FCIP header and ultimately, the encapsulated Fibre Channel frame.

Not only do the headers increase the overhead associated with each frame, but processing the information in those headers adds significant processing overhead to each frame. Because TCP/IP is a stream-oriented protocol, encapsulated Fibre Channel frames may span multiple Ethernet frames. Therefore, the encapsulation and decapsulation process must locate the encapsulated frame boundaries within the TCP byte stream.

Basically, the approach taken by FCoE is to eliminate TCP/IP overhead altogether and use the smallest possible encapsulation header and package the Fibre Channel frame content directly in an Ethernet frame as shown in Figure 1-10 on page 15.

This approach translates to less framing overhead and results in greater efficiency and higher performance with simpler hardware. To further simplify the processing, FCoE maintains a one-to-one relationship between Fibre Channel frames and FCoE encapsulated frames further simplifying frame processing.

1.6.2 Internet SCSI (iSCSI)

Internet SCSI (iSCSI) is a mapping of SCSI commands for transport via a TCP/IP network. While iSCSI offers a number of desirable attributes, it has largely failed to garner significant adoption in the core data center. According to an article published by Network World in October of 2007 citing a study by IDC, Fibre Channel held a 97% share of the external disk storage systems market while iSCSI had just a 3% share. While the IDC study project a healthy growth for iSCSI, iSCSI was still projected to have only a 21% share by 2010.

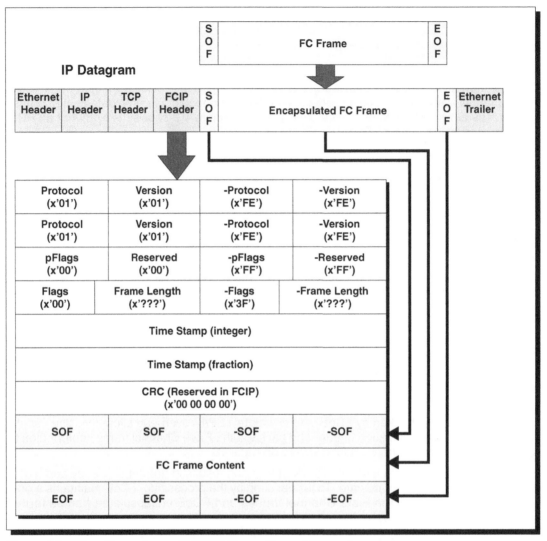

Figure 1-9. Fibre Channel over IP (FCIP) Frame Format Example

Like FCoE, iSCSI can be implemented in software or hardware. Software implementations of iSCSI can provide a low-cost solution to the transport of SCSI commands via a TCP/IP network (typically Ethernet). However, software implementations of iSCSI incur significant processing overhead and, while adequate for many small to medium business environments, may not meet the performance needs of many data center environments.

Hardware implementations of iSCSI can reduce the performance penalty associated with an all-software iSCSI implementation, but require specialized hardware such as NICs with

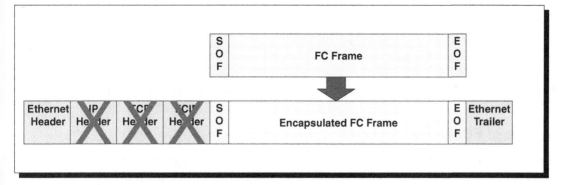

Figure 1-10. FCoE Encapsulation Concept

TCP/IP Offload Engines (TOEs) or iSCSI HBAs. Because these components are not the mainstream implementations of Ethernet NICs, they do not benefit from the high-volume economy of scale realized by many standard NICs nor the fierce price competition in the Ethernet marketplace.

Standard Ethernet (and therefore, IP and TCP/IP) does not guarantee the reliable delivery of frames or IP packets. In fact, packet drop is to be expected as a result of flow control mechanisms and congestion within an Ethernet network. Because of this, TCP must provide buffering in case retransmission of dropped packets is required.

Because iSCSI is a different mapping of SCSI commands than that done for Fibre Channel (or even Serial Attached SCSI), it is not a simple task to interconnect the two environments and requires a fairly complex gateway function. If Fibre Channel was not an already established interface in the data center, this difference might not matter. However, Fibre Channel is the established storage interface for the data center and any new, competing technology needs to offer an affordable gateway into the Fibre Channel world.

Because of these considerations, iSCSI seems to have found its market in two distinct areas. The first is the small to medium business market space where the performance provided by software iSCSI implementations meets the performance needs of the business. A second iSCSI market niche has been "greenfield" environments where Fibre Channel is not currently deployed and issues of integration with existing Fibre Channel storage networks do not arise.

1.6.3 FCoE vs. Native Fibre Channel

FCoE should not be viewed as a replacement for Fibre Channel. Most early deployments will probably incorporate FCoE into existing Fibre Channel environments. A user may deploy FCoE on new servers or systems alongside existing servers or systems using Fibre Channel. In a similar manner, an FCoE Fabric will likely become an extension of the existing Fibre Channel Fabric, just using Ethernet links instead of Fibre Channel links.

Over time, as more new equipment with FCoE interfaces is installed, the number of FCoE/Ethernet links will gradually increase. As this occurs, the percentage of native Fibre

Channel links may decline over time, but hybrid environments are likely to exist for a substantial period of time.

1.7 Benefits of FCoE

For any new technology to be successful and achieve widespread adoption, it has to offer compelling reasons to justify the change. Typically, the rationale for the adoption of new technology is either based on a clear-cut technological advantage (such as enabling new applications) or a business case based on the costs of doing business. In the case of FCoE, the principal benefits are not technological but cost-based.

1.7.1 Unified Data Center Fabric

Fibre Channel over Ethernet unifies the data center network and enables the consolidation of storage and LAN traffic over the same physical network. Having a single, consolidated network can provide significant cost benefits, both in terms of capital expenditures and ongoing operational costs.

Consolidation of the storage and LAN networks results in fewer adapters (NICs and HBAs), switches and cables to purchase, install and maintain.

On an operational basis, having a single consolidated network means that there is now one network to administer rather than two (or three if the consolidation also includes InfiniBand).

1.7.2 Common Interfaces for Storage and IP Traffic

Having common interfaces for storage and IP (LAN) traffic (and perhaps, clustering) can reduce the cost of the servers and storage devices. Instead of a server requiring separate interfaces for LAN traffic and storage traffic, the same Converged Network Adapter can serve both types of traffic.

Common interfaces reduce the support and administration costs. No longer is it necessary to support and maintain two different network technologies. The same support staff can now be trained to maintain the consolidate network and its associated interfaces. The same tools and skills used to maintain the LAN can now be used to maintain the SAN.

1.7.3 FCoE Leverages Advances in Ethernet

Because FCoE is based on using Ethernet to provide the data link, FCoE can leverage advances in the Ethernet technology.

Currently, Ethernet is on the verge of wide-scale deployment of 10 gigabit signaling technology. In fact, this is one of the reasons that there is heightened interest in the use of Ethernet as a storage interface.

1.7.4 Power and Cooling Benefits

By reducing the number of adapters in a server or storage device and the number of switches within the network, the amount of power consumed is also reduced. When factored over a large server farm or data center, the total power savings can be substantial (*FCoE Benefits* on page 55 for some hypothetical examples of potential savings).

Reducing the power consumption also results in reduced cooling and support equipment requirements. Power that is consumed by servers, switches and storage devices is dissipated as heat. The Uptime Institute approximates that as an industry average, 1.5 times as much power is consumed by support equipment (cooling, uninterruptible power supplies, power distribution, etc.) as is consumed by the IT equipment itself (i.e., 40% of the power is consumed by the IT equipment, 60% by the support equipment).

1.7.5 Floor Space

By adopting a consolidated network, the number of separate adapters in servers and storage devices is reduced. The can result in more compact packaging and enable more servers to be installed in the same amount of floor space. In addition, a consolidated network reduces the number of switches and cables required, further reducing the floor space requirements.

When the cost per square foot of data center floor space is taken into account, a converged network with its more efficient use of space may translate into a significant savings of space in the data center.

1.8 Software FCoE vs. Hardware FCoE

FCoE is a protocol transported using Ethernet frames. The required protocol functions can be implemented in software, hardware, or a combination of software and hardware. It is likely both software FCoE and hardware FCoE will be deployed alongside one another with the determination of which approach to use based on factors such as cost and performance.

1.8.1 Software FCoE

Software FCoE provides a relatively simple and low-cost entry to FCoE. With the addition of an FCoE driver to a "lossless" Ethernet NIC and the inclusion of a single FCoE switch in a "lossless" Ethernet network, FCoE can be deployed with a minimum of cost and effort.

It is likely that software FCoE will be readily available without charge (there is currently an open source FCoE driver available for Linux and it is likely that drivers will be available for other operating systems as well).

As with software iSCSI, an all software implementation of FCoE will likely incur greater overheads and provide lower overall performance that what could be achieved with a hardware implementation of FCoE. However, for many applications, the performance provided by a software FCoE implementation may be sufficient.

1.8.2 Hardware FCoE

To provide higher performance, FCoE functions may be implemented in hardware, just as Fibre Channel functions are implemented in hardware by many Fibre Channel HBAs today. Hardware implementations relieve the server or device processor of the burden of processing much of the FCoE protocol and provide more efficient use of the bandwidth of the link.

One of the strengths of Fibre Channel is the degree to which it was designed to enable performance-oriented functions to be implemented in hardware to provide maximum performance. Flow control, segmentation and reassembly, and context switching are just a few examples of where the architecture lends itself to hardware processing or assistance.

It seems likely that most companies providing Fibre Channel products will develop equivalent FCoE products. A Converged Network Adapter (CNA) is essentially a Fibre Channel HBA with an Ethernet MAC to provide the physical interface and an FCoE switch is essentially the combination of an Ethernet switch and a Fibre Channel switch (it may or may not have any native Fibre Channel ports).

1.9 Chapter Summary

Applications and Networks

- Today, each application class has its own interface
  - Networking: Ethernet
  - Storage: Fibre Channel (or SAS or SATA)
  - Clustering: Infiniband
- This results in three different networks
  - Three different adapters for each system or server
  - Three different networks, cables and switches
  - Three different skill sets and tools
  - Three different management facilities

Ethernet as a "Fat Pipe"

- One barrier to using Ethernet as the basis for a converged network has been the limited bandwidth that Ethernet has historically provided
- As Ethernet bandwidth increases, more traffic can be carried via fewer physical links
  - With the advent of 10 gigabit Ethernet (10 GBE), the available bandwidth now offers the potential to consolidate all of the traffic types over the same link

Benefits of a Converged Network

- The benefits of a converged network are:
  - A server now has a single adapter replacing multiple different types of adapters that were required when a different type of network was used for each class of application traffic.
  - The datacenter has a single network Instead of two, or three, different networks. This means a single network to install, manage and maintain.
  - The number of cables and connections is dramatically reduced.

What is FCoE?

- Fibre Channel over Ethernet (FCoE) is the transport of encapsulated Fibre Channel frames over "lossless" Ethernet
- Ethernet provides the physical interface
  - "lossless" Ethernet NICs or Converged Network Adapters (CNAs)
  - "lossless" Ethernet and/or Fibre Channel switches make up the "Fabric"
- Fibre Channel provides the transport protocol
  - Fibre Channel frame content is delivered in Ethernet frames
- Most environments will be a mixture of FCoE and FC devices.
  - FCoE end devices and switches and FC end devices and switches

FCoE Has "Virtual" Ports

- FCoE ports do not meet the strict definitions in the Fibre Channel standards
  - They do not have a Fibre Channel Physical interface
  - They emulate the behavior of a native Fibre Channel port
- Because of this, FCoE ports are referred to a "virtual" ports
  - Virtual Node Port, or VN_Port
  - Virtual Fabric Port, or VF_Port
  - Virtual Expansion Port, or VE_Port

General FCoE Objectives

- Seamlessly and transparently replace the Fibre Channel physical interface with Ethernet
  - FCoE devices and Fibre Channel devices can communicate without awareness of the underlying physical link
- No changes to protocol mappings, information units, initialization, Fibre Channel services, etc.
- Develop a mapping that can be implemented totally in software via a software driver
- Enable high-performance implementations through the use of hardware assists

End Node (ENode) Objectives (1)

- FCoE must not impact an endpoint's FC stack (i.e. HBA and software).
- A cleanly layered FC stack over Ethernet must be possible.
- There must be a clean division between Fibre Channel functions and FCoE/Ethernet specific functions.
- Endpoint Fibre Channel and Upper Level Protocols (e.g. FCP, SB-3, Fabric Login, discovery, etc....) must work as they do today, with no change required to support FC over Ethernet

End Node (ENode) Objectives (2)

- An Endpoint can have multiple network stacks mapped over Ethernet
- All FC functionality must be supported,
  - This includes support for max FC frame sizes, Zoning (access control), Virtual Fabrics, Security (FC-SP), etc.
- Any additional attributes to existing FC Extended Link Service (ELS) payloads should be avoided (e.g., FLOGI and its ACCEPT).
  - If it is not possible to avoid changes, any changes must be standardized.
- In-order Fibre Channel frame delivery is required.

End Node (ENode) Objectives (3)

- Class-3 service is required and Class-2 service should be supported
- FCoE requires a mechanism to support link down scenarios for FC over Ethernet
  - i.e., analogous to Fibre Channel Loss-of-Signal
- A mechanism analogous to link isolation is needed to enforce policy (e.g. Fabric Binding).
- If an FCoE End Node fails security, authorization or authentication policies, the link needs to be isolated to prevent potential denial-of-service attacks or unauthorized access attempts.

End Node (ENode) Objectives (4)

- FCoE must work under benign conditions and in the presence of errors.
- The differences between FC and Ethernet need to be dealt with.
  - Wherever differences between native Fibre Channel and Ethernet are identified, FCoE must address those differences and provide an acceptable mapping between the respective behaviors.
- FCoE must deliver data integrity comparable to native Fibre Channel.
  - This captures the essence of what is required as far as error detection and data integrity.

FCoE Switch Objectives

- No frame drops under normal conditions or due to congestion.
  - At a minimum, this requires support for a flow control mechanism
  - Flow Control (e.g., credit recovery) must work in all cases.
- FC timeouts (e.g. R_A_TOV) must be respected.
- Class-3 and Class-F are required and Class-2 should be supported.
- One or more FC over Ethernet network Controllers are required per FCoE Fabric.
  - Needed to provide Fibre Channel services (e.g., FLOGI processing, Name Server, etc.

What's Different About FCoE?

- There are several existing storage mappings to Ethernet
  - Internet SCSI (iSCSI)
  - Internet FCP (iFCP)
  - Fibre Channel over IP (FCIP)
- All are based on the use of TCP/IP
  - TCP/IP adds complexity and overhead
  - Argument is that TCP/IP is not required in a local network
  - TCP/IP is still required for the long-haul
- FCoE assumes a reliable, "lossless" Ethernet and bypasses TCP/IP for efficiency and simplicity

FC over IP (FCIP) Example

- FCIP has already defined an FC frame encapsulation method
  - Requires use of TCP/IP
  - This introduces extra overhead in processing at the TCP and IP layers
- For performance reasons, it would be nice to avoid TCP/IP altogether
  - TCP in software is slow
  - TCP in hardware is complicated and expensive

Why not use iSCSI?

- iSCSI needed for "lossy" or "out-of-order" networks
- • iSCSI is based on TCP/IP networks
  - TCP is a stateful, byte-oriented protocol
  - Memory is needed for reassembly, reordering, and retransmission
  - TCP processing adds considerable overhead or the complexity of TCO Offload Engines
  - Gateway between iSCSI and Fibre Channel is complex and expensive (
- TCP provides recovery and flow control
  - Not needed in a "lossless" Ethernet environment using Ethernet flow control

Why Maintain Fibre Channel Content?

- Why not get rid of Fibre Channel altogether and use something else, such as iSCSI?
  - iSCSI has made inroads into storage, but adoption has been slow
  - iSCSI is often deployed where Fibre Channel is not already in use
- Significant install base of Fibre Channel today
  - Fibre Channel is a proven technology
  - Customers don't want to "rip and replace"
  - Fibre Channel supports protocols other than SCSI (e.g., FICON, FC-SATA, etc.)
- Fibre Channel will probably continue to provide the highest performance for the data center

Rationale for FCoE

- FCoE preserves existing FC infrastructure
  - FCoE can blend seamlessly into an existing FC environment
- No need to "rip and replace" – rather an evolutionary incorporation of FCoE
  - New FCoE enabled servers can communicate with existing FC storage
- Leverages Ethernet technology
  - Ethernet is ubiquitous – its everywhere
  - Ethernet is mature and well understood
  - Ethernet should provide cost-effective transport with performance (almost?) equivalent to native Fibre Channel

2. FCoE, Fibre Channel and Ethernet Standards

Because FCoE is the merging of what had formerly been two independent technologies, standardization of the necessary functions has involved multiple standards bodies. In order to fully understand FCoE, it is necessary to understand the following standards families:

- Fibre Channel standards. These standards describe the Fibre Channel frame structure, protocols, and operations.
- Ethernet standards. Ethernet provides the physical transport for the encapsulated Fibre Channel frames.
- SCSI standards. In most environments, the Small Computer System Interface (SCSI) standards define the commands used to access storage devices.
- IETF (Internet Engineering Task Force) standards. While FCoE does not use the Internet Protocol (IP or TCP/IP), there is work taking place to define an Ethernet routing protocol in the IETF.

The Fibre Channel standard committee (iNCITS T11) has completed development of the FCoE standard. In parallel, IEEE is in the process of standardizing a number of Ethernet enhancements that provide functions desirable for the use of Ethernet as a converged data-center network (see *Data Center Bridging (DCB) Ethernet* on page 223).

2.1 FCoE and Fibre Channel Standards

The iNCITS Technical Committee T11 has developed the standards the define the Fibre Channel technology. In order to understand how FCoE works, it is necessary to understand how Fibre Channel works (with the exception of the Fibre Channel physical interface). Figure 2-1 on page 24 shows the various Fibre Channel standards and their relationships (items in the figure in red, or marked with a red "X" do not apply to FCoE).

FCoE is specified in the Fibre Channel Backbone (FC-BB-x) standard. Over the years, T11 has had a series of standards projects defining the transport of Fibre Channel traffic over non-Fibre Channel networks (e.g., IP or SONET networks). This series of standard has been collectively referred to as the Fibre Channel Backbone (FC-BB-x) standards. When the FCoE project was authorized, it was a natural fit into this set of standards that define Fibre Channel transport via non-FC networks.

Fibre Channel Framing and Signaling (FC-FS) Standard. The *Fibre Channel Framing and Signaling Standard (FC-FS-x)* specifies the functions and behavior of a Fibre Channel Node Port (generically referred to as an Nx_Port) when communicating with another Nx_Port in a point-to-point topology, or with a Fabric Port (generically referred to as an Fx_Port) in a Fabric

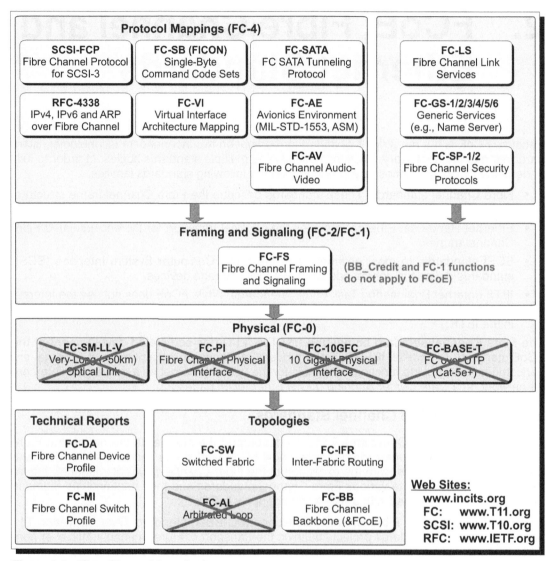

Figure 2-1. Fibre Channel Standards

environment. This standard does not define the physical interface characteristics, loop-specific behavior of an NL_Port or FL_Port used on an arbitrated loop, nor how different protocols are transported via Fibre Channel.

Fibre Channel Physical Interface Standards. The Fibre Channel physical interface standards define the speeds and characteristics of native Fibre Channel links. Because FCoE uses Ethernet as its physical interface, none of these standards apply to FCoE links.

Basic and Extended Link Services (FC-LS). The Fibre Channel Link Services standard defines the various basic and extended link service commands.

Fibre Channel Generic Services (FC-GS). Fibre Channel defines several service functions that are available to node port clients and are collectively called generic services. Examples of commonly available services are the Name Server and Management Server. The FC-GS series of standards defines the functions and commands provided by each service and the protocol used to access those services.

Fibre Channel Security Protocols (FC-SP). The Fibre Channel Security Protocols standard specifies authentication protocols, security policies and policy objects and an enhancement to zoning called SP-zoning.

Fibre Channel Protocol for SCSI-3 (SCSI-FCP). The SCSI protocol mapping was done by the SCSI standards committee (INCITS T10) as part of the SCSI standards activity and defines how various SCSI protocol objects (such as the Command Descriptor Block (CDB), Logical Unit Number (LUN), data, status, and sense information) are structured and transported via the Fibre Channel interface.

Fibre Channel Single-Byte Command Code Sets (FC-SB). The Fibre Channel Single-Byte Command Code Sets protocol mappings specify how the ESCON command protocol is transported via Fibre Channel.

Fibre Channel Avionics Environment (FC-AE). The Fibre Channel Avionics Environment project defines usage of Fibre Channel to transport information between avionics subsystems. As a part of this work, protocol mappings for the MIL-STD-1553, ASM and FC-RDMA protocols were performed.

Fibre Channel Audio-Video (FC-AV). Fibre Channel Audio Video is a project to define how high-definition and broadcast-quality audio and video information may carried via Fibre Channel. The focus of this work has been towards studio and broadcast television applications.

Fibre Channel Switched Fabric (FC-SW). The Fibre Channel Switched Fabric series of standards specifies switch behavior and inter-switch communications.

Fibre Channel Arbitrated Loop (FC-AL). The Fibre Channel Arbitrated Loop standard (FC-AL) was approved in 1996 and defined an entirely new Fibre Channel topology based upon a loop, or ring, topology. This topology was developed to provide a low-cost, shared bandwidth interconnect suitable for connecting a modest number of devices. Because of its low cost connectivity, the arbitrated loop has seen widespread adoption, particularly for attaching Fibre Channel disk drives.

Because Ethernet does not support a loop topology, there is no FCoE equivalent to the arbitrated loop.

Fibre Channel Inter-Fabric Routing (FC-IFR). The Fibre Channel Inter-Fabric Routing project was started in 2005 to provide a standard specifying how frames can be routed from one Fabric to another (and potentially travelling through intermediate Fabrics).

Fibre Channel Backbone (FC-BB). The Fibre Channel series of standards define how bridge devices can enable Fibre Channel entities to communicate through intermediate, non-Fibre Channel networks such as an IP network or a Synchronous Optical Network (SONET).

As mentioned earlier, FC-BB-5 is the standard that specifies the first generation of FCoE. Second generation FCoE will be specified in the FC-BB-6 standard.

2.2 SCSI Standards

The SCSI standards committee (INCITS Technical Committee T10) is responsible for the development of standards relating to the SCSI command protocol and the mapping of that protocol to selected physical interfaces. The SCSI standards and architecture are divided into three distinct levels:

- The architecture and command level defines the SCSI architecture and the commands that can be issued to various device types.
- The transport level defines how SCSI commands are transported via a given physical interface
- The link level defines a specific physical interface and its associated functions, behaviors and attributes.

Figure 2-2 provides an illustration of the various SCSI standards and their relationships.

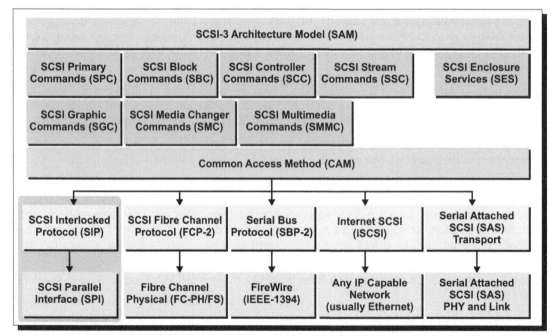

Figure 2-2. SCSI Standards Structure

2.3 Ethernet Standards

Ethernet standards are developed by IEEE. The Ethernet family of standards defines numerous aspects of local area networking, many of which are not related to FCoE. Figure 2-3 on page 27 shows the key Ethernet standards that affect FCoE or FCoE environments (Ethernet environments containing FCoE devices may also incorporate functions specified in other Ethernet standards).

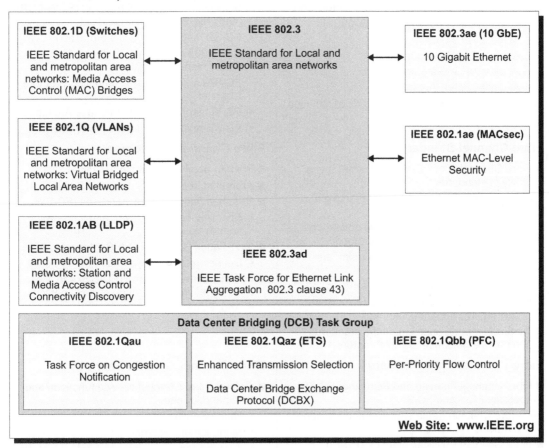

Figure 2-3. Ethernet Standards

2.4 Standards Summary

Fibre Channel over Ethernet represents the use of multiple technologies with standards defined by more than one standards body. Fully understanding the detailed workings of FCoE requires a knowledge of the Fibre Channel, SCSI and Ethernet standards.

2.5 Chapter Summary

FCoE Timeline and Roadmap

- FCoE Standard is complete
- Work is underway on Enhanced Ethernet standards
- 2nd generation products have been introduced
- Product status (as of December 2009):
  - At least two switch vendors
  - At least 3 CNA vendors
  - At least 1 FCoE storage product
  - At least 2 FCoE Analyzers
  - At least 1 complete end-to-end FCoE solution

Fibre Channel Standards

- Fibre Channel is not a single standard, but a family of standards
  - The core is the Fibre Channel Framing and Signaling standard (FC-FS)
  - Protocol mappings (FC-4s) are covered by separate standards, one per protocol
  - Topologies, except for point-to-point, are covered in separate standards
  - Link Services have their own standard
  - Generic Services (e.g., Name Server) are covered in a separate standard
- Technical reports supplement the standards and provide guidance to implementers

Fibre Channel Core Standards

- Fibre Channel Framing and Signaling (**FC-FS**) specifies FC-1 and FC-2
  - Fibre Channel frame structure and transport protocols
- Fibre Channel Physical Interface (**FC-PI**) specifies FC-0
  - Fibre Channel physical interface characteristics (not applicable to FCoE)
- Fibre Channel Link Services (**FC-LS**) defines the link services

Protocol Mappings

- Multiple upper-level protocols have been mapped to Fibre Channel
- Each protocol mapping has its own standard
  - SCSI-3 Fibre Channel Protocol (**SCSI-FCP**) maps the SCSI-3 command set
  - **FC-SB** maps the ESCON protocol (FICON)
  - **RFC-4338** maps IPv4, IPv6 and ARP over Fibre Channel (IPFC)
  - **FC-SATA** defines SATA tunneling via Fibre Channel
  - **FC-VI** maps the Virtual Interface Architecture
  - **FC-AE** maps the avionics environment

Fibre Channel Topologies

- Point-to-point is defined in FC-PH/**FC-FS**
- Arbitrated Loop has its own standard (**FC-AL**)
- Switched Fabric has its standards (**FC-SW**)
  - Specifies Fabric behavior and inter-switch communication
- Inter-Fabric Routing (**FC-IFR**) started in 2005
  - Defines routing between separate Fabrics
- Fibre Channel Backbone (**FC-BB**) specifies sending FC frames through non-FC network
  - And, FCoE

Fibre Channel Generic Services

- Defines Fibre Channel service functions and command for each
  - Name Server
  - Management Server
  - Time Server
- Defines the protocol used to communicate with these servers:
  - Fibre Channel Common Transport (**FC-CT**)

T11 FCoE Standard (FC-BB-5)

- FCoE Standard (FC-BB-5) was developed by the INCITS T11 (Fibre Channel) committee
  - Draft has completed committee approval and is in the process of adoption as an ANSI standard
- Work has begun on the 2nd generation FCoE
  - Incorporate expanded functionality
  - Specified in FC-BB-6 draft standard

SCSI-3 Architecture & Standards

- SCSI-3 is a multi-level architecture
  - Upper level defines the command architecture and command sets
  - Middle level defines the protocol used to send SCSI commands across the lower level
  - Lower level defines the physical interface
- Many different physical interfaces and associated transport protocols are supported
  - SCSI bus and the SCSI Interlocked Protocol
  - Fibre Channel and the SCSI Fibre Channel Protocol (FCP)
  - Internet and iSCSI protocol

SCSI Layered Architecture Benefits

- Multi-level approach allows SCSI commands to be sent over a variety of interfaces
  - Each with its own unique characteristics; speed, distance, number of devices
- Command sets and command behavior remains the same
  - Same device class driver (tape and disk), regardless of interface
  - This helps preserve the existing investment in software

Ethernet Standards

- To support Ethernet for data storage some features are required
- Pause is required for reliable delivery
  - Already in IEEE 802.3 Annex 31B (optional)
  - May desire an extension called Per Priority Flow Control" to manage individual flows
- VLANs (802.1Q) to provide priority (or flow identification)
- While not absolutely necessary, other enhancements are desirable

Approved Ethernet Standards

- The following Ethernet standards are applicable to FCoE:
  - 802.3: Ethernet core standard
  - 802.1AB: Station and Media Access Control Connectivity Discovery (LLDP)
  - 802.1AE: Media Access Control (MAC) Security
  - 802.1D: Media Access Control (MAC) Bridges
  - 802.1P: Quality of Service considerations
  - 802.1Q: Virtual Bridged Local Area Networks (VLANs)

Data Center Bridging (DCB) Ethernet

- FCoE leverages several Ethernet standards that are under development
  - Provide enhancements to satisfy the requirements of protocols and applications in the data center
- DCB Ethernet Standards
  - IEEE 802.1Qbb: Priority Flow Control (PFC)
  - IEEE 802.1Qau: Congestion Notification
  - IEEE 802.1Qaz: Enhanced Transmission Selection (and Data Center Bridge Capability Exchange protocol – DCBX)
- See www.IEEE.org for the current status

3. FCoE Configurations

Many different FCoE configurations are possible, but they can all be reduced to a few basic variations. This chapter shows a number of different configurations to illustrate some of the potential variations.

3.1 Point-to-Point: All Ethernet

The simplest FCoE configuration is an all Ethernet point-to-point configuration having an FCoE host directly connected to an FCoE storage device (using an Ethernet crossover cable) as shown in Figure 3-1.

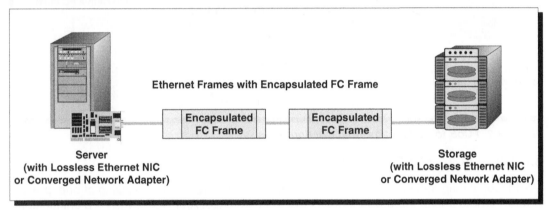

Figure 3-1. FCoE Point-to-Point Configuration

In this configuration, no Fibre Channel services (e.g., Name Server) are required and the Fibre Channel initialization can use the protocols already defined for a point-to-point Fibre Channel configuration. While this may seem like a trivial configuration, it does provide a dedicated path between the host and storage with guaranteed bandwidth and latency. Point-to-point configurations are not common in Fibre Channel, but are used in environments where a dedicated physical path is desired.

> NOTE – This configuration is not supported by the first generation of the FCoE standard because the FCoE-specific protocols necessary to support point-to-point operation were not included in that standard (this was one of the work items deferred to the second-generation FCoE standard)

3.2 Point-to-Point: FCoE to Native Fibre Channel

An FCoE configuration can have both FCoE devices and native Fibre Channel devices. In an extension of the point-to-point configuration shown previously, either of the two devices could be FCoE attached while the other is a native Fibre Channel device.

When bridging between the two environments, an encapsulation/decapsulation function is required in addition to an Ethernet and Fibre Channel port. The encapsulation/decapsulation is provided by a function called the FCoE Link End Point (FCoE_LEP). Normally, the FCoE_LEP function would be provided by an FCoE switch but it could also be implemented as a separate entity as shown in Figure 3-2 on page 32. This figure shows an FCoE host connected to a native Fibre Channel storage device through an FCoE_LEP.

NOTE – This configuration is also not supported by the first generation of the FCoE standard because the FCoE-specific protocols necessary to support point-to-point operation were not included in that standard (this was one of the work items deferred to the second-generation FCoE standard).

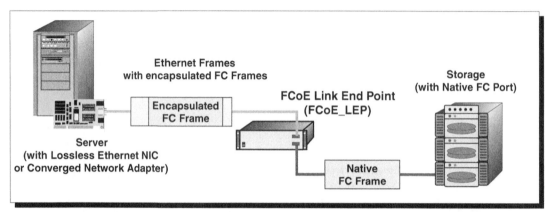

Figure 3-2. FCoE to FC Point-to-Point Configuration

3.3 What is an FCoE Switch?

Most FCoE configurations will be based on a switched environment consisting of one or more FCoE switches and/or Fibre Channel and Ethernet switches. An FCoE switch is a unique combination of both a "lossless" Ethernet switch and a Fibre Channel switching function (called an FCoE Forwarder, or FCF) as shown in Figure 3-3 on page 33.

When an Ethernet frame is received on one of the lossless Ethernet links, the Ethernet bridge forwards the received frame based on its Ethernet destination address. If the Ethernet destination address is a MAC address associated with the FCoE Forwarder (FCF) function, the frame is forwarded to the corresponding FCF MAC where the encapsulated Fibre Channel frame is decapsulated by the FCoE Link End Point (as shown by 1 in Figure 3-3 on page 33). The decapsulated FC frame is then forwarded by the FC switching element based in its Fibre Channel Destination_ID. If the frame is forwarded out a native Fibre Channel port, the frame is transmitted as a native Fibre Channel frame on the associated FC link. If the frame is forwarded out an Ethernet port, the Fibre Channel frame is encapsulated within an Ethernet frame with the Ethernet source address set to the associated FCF MAC address and the Ethernet destination address set to the appropriate destination MAC address.

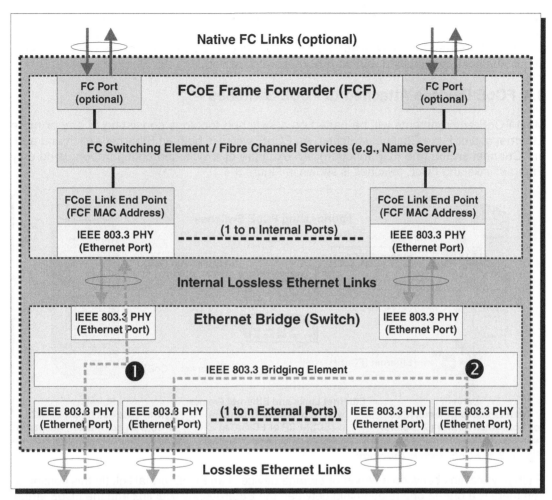

Figure 3-3. FCoE Switch

If the received Ethernet frame is not addressed to a MAC address associated with the FCoE Forwarder (FCF) function, the Ethernet bridge simply forwards the frame in the normal manner based on its Ethernet destination address (see 2 in Figure 3-3 on page 33).

The FCF function is basically a Fibre Channel switch with one or more Ethernet ports. It may or may not have any native Fibre Channel ports. The FCF is an Ethernet destination with its own Ethernet MAC address (or addresses). The FCF does not forward Ethernet frames. It does forward decapsulated Fibre Channel frames based on their Fibre Channel Destination ID, not the Ethernet destination address. From an FCoE perspective, Ethernet addresses simply serve to identify the two ends of an FCoE virtual link (or tunnel) through the Ethernet environment.

While this discussion shows the FCF and Ethernet bridge functions integrated into a single product, there is no reason that these functions could not be provided by separate entities (in fact, the FCoE standard only describes the function of the FCF and makes no assumption about whether it is combined with an Ethernet switch or not).

3.4 FCoE Devices Attached to FCoE Switches

Most FCoE environments will be based on a switched topology consisting of one or more Ethernet and/or Fibre Channel switches. An FCoE switch is both an Ethernet switch and a Fibre Channel switch (the FCF function). An example of a switched configuration using only Ethernet links and FCoE switches is shown in Figure 3-4.

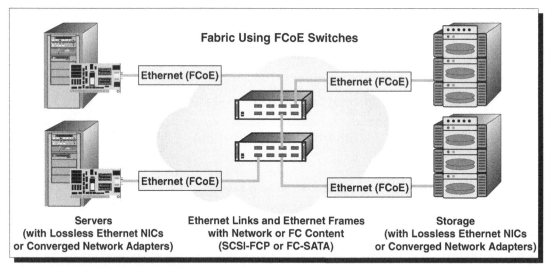

Figure 3-4. FCoE Switch Topology

Each physical link between a server or storage device is an FCoE virtual link (in this configuration there is a one-to-one relationship between the Ethernet physical link and the FCoE virtual link. The Ethernet physical link between the two FCoE switches is an FCoE virtual inter-switch link. At the end of each FCoE virtual link is an FCoE Link End Point (FCoE_LEP) that performs the encapsulation and decapsulation function.

The FCF functions in the FCoE switches provide the usual Fibre Channel services (for example, FLOGI processing, address assignment, Name Server, etc.). The two FCoE switches utilize the virtual inter-switch link to perform normal Fibre Channel inter-switch link initialization using Switch Internal Link Services (SW_ILS). As with native Fibre Channel switches, path information is communicated between the FCF functions using the Fibre Channel FSPF protocol. When an FCoE switch receives an Ethernet frame, it decapsulates the embedded Fibre Channel frame and forwards it based on the Fibre Channel Destination_ID (if the FC frame is being sent out on an Ethernet link, the frame is encapsulated before it is sent).

Each FCoE switch also functions as a normal Ethernet switch and forwards non-FCoE frames based on their Ethernet Destination addresses. The path between the Ethernet switching functions is established using the normal Ethernet Spanning Tree Protocol.

Observe that in this example FCoE configuration, there are no native Fibre Channel links or switches, only Ethernet links and FCoE switches.

3.5 FCoE Device to FCoE Switch via an Intervening Ethernet Network

There is no requirement for FCoE devices to attach directly to an FCoE switch. FCoE devices may attach to a "lossless" Ethernet network that provides access to an FCoE switch as shown in Figure 3-5. Again, in this configuration, observe that there are no native Fibre Channel devices, links or switches.

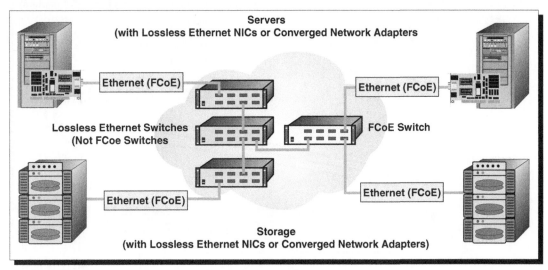

Figure 3-5. Intervening "Lossless" Ethernet Network

The FCF function within the FCoE switch provides the usual Fibre Channel services such as FLOGI processing, Fibre Channel address assignment, Name Server, etc. Ethernet frames containing FCoE encapsulated Fibre Channel frames are decapsulated by the FCF function in the FCoE switch and forwarded based on the Fibre Channel Destination_ID field (in this example, the Fibre Channel frame will be re-encapsulated before forwarding on an Ethernet link).

In this configuration, the FCoE devices need a way to discover the Ethernet MAC address associated with the FCF function in the FCoE switch. This MAC address will be used as the destination address for FCoE Ethernet frames sent by the end devices to the FCF function (while the Fibre Channel addresses used for services such as FLOGI or the Name Server are known, it is not possible to reach the FCoE switch without first knowing the FCF's MAC address). Discovery of the FCF's MAC address is discussed in *FCoE Discovery and Virtual Link Initialization* on page 121.

Paths between Ethernet switches are identified and managed using the standard Ethernet Spanning Tree Protocol (or one of the Ethernet variations of the Spanning Tree Protocol). The Ethernet switch function within the FCoE switch functions as a normal Ethernet switch and participates in the Spanning Tree Protocol along with the other Ethernet switches.

3.6 Hybrid Ethernet and FCoE Fabrics

Many FCoE configurations will be mixed configurations consisting of both FCoE attached devices and native Fibre Channel attached devices as shown in Figure 3-6. In this example, FCoE devices are attached directly to one or more FCoE switches. In turn, the FCoE switches connect to a Fibre Channel fabric (using a standard Fibre Channel inter-switch link) and the existing LAN (using an Ethernet inter-switch link).

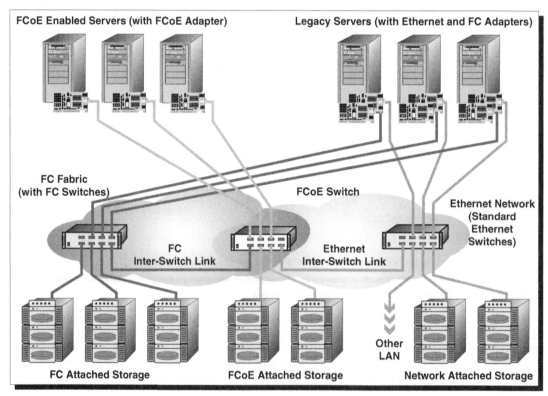

Figure 3-6. Hybrid FCoE Configuration

This example serves to illustrate the dual nature of an FCoE switch. For non-FCoE traffic, the FCoE switch behaves as a normal Ethernet switch, forwarding the Ethernet frames based on the Ethernet destination address. For FCoE traffic, the FCoE switch decapsulates the embedded Fibre Channel frame and forwards that frame based on its Fibre Channel address (either as a native Fibre Channel frame, or by re-encapsulating the frame for transmission over an Ethernet link.

3.7 Hybrid Configuration with Intervening "Lossless" Ethernet Switches

FCoE devices may be attached to a "lossless" Ethernet network made up of switches that provide the functions required by FCoE, but otherwise have no awareness or special processing of the FCoE protocol. The "lossless" Ethernet network may connect to an FCoE switch having both "lossless" Ethernet ports (for FCoE devices) and native Fibre Channel ports (for Fibre Channel connectivity) as shown in Figure 3-7.

In this example, the FCoE switch connects to a Fibre Channel Fabric using a standard Fibre Channel Interswitch Link (ISL) and to the existing LAN through the lossless Ethernet network.

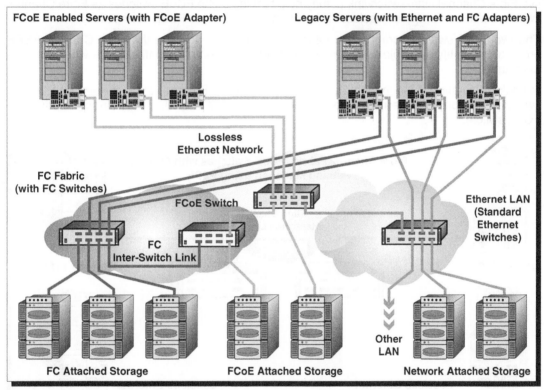

Figure 3-7. Hybrid FCoE Configuration with Intervening Ethernet Switches

While this configuration is just a combination of configurations shown in earlier examples, it does serve to illustrate the kind of configuration flexibility that FCoE can enable.

3.8 Fibre Channel and Ethernet Forwarding Protocols

Fibre Channel and Ethernet switches use different pathing protocols. Fibre Channel switches use the Fabric Shortest Path First (FSPF) protocol while Ethernet switches use the Spanning Tree Protocol (STP), Rapid Spanning Tree Protocol (RSTP), Per VLAN Spanning Tree protocol (PVST), or some other Ethernet defined protocol. But what happens when a Fibre Channel Fabric and Ethernet network overlap as can happen with FCoE?

3.8.1 Forwarding Example: No Ethernet Switching

Assume a configuration consisting of two FCoE switches as shown in Figure 3-8 on page 38. Each FCoE switch has both native Fibre Channel ports (shown on the top row) and "lossless" Ethernet ports (shown on the bottom row). The two FCoE switches are connected using a native Fibre Channel inter-switch link (it may help to think of the FCoE switches as Fibre Channel switches with one or more "lossless" Ethernet ports to provide FCoE connectivity).

The two FCoE switches comprise a Fibre Channel Fabric and use the Fibre Channel FSPF protocol to identify available paths and subsequently compute the paths to use when forwarding frames.

In this configuration, even though the FCoE switches have Ethernet ports, there is no Ethernet switched network or Ethernet forwarding (or if there is, it is confined within each individual FCoE switch).

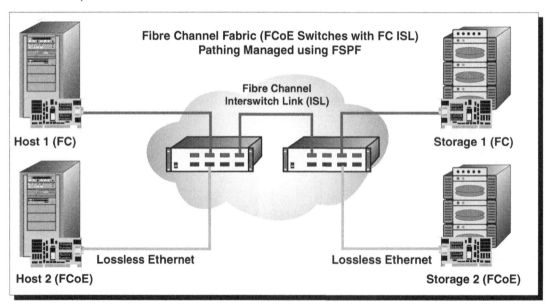

Figure 3-8. FCoE Forwarding: No Ethernet Switching

3.8.2 Forwarding Example: Non-Overlapping Ethernet Network(s)

As was shown earlier, a "lossless" Ethernet network may be present between an FCoE end device and an FCoE switch as shown in Figure 3-9 on page 39.

In this example, each of the FCoE end devices is connected to a "lossless" Ethernet network consisting of one or more "lossless" Ethernet switches. As shown, the two FCoE devices connect to two independent Ethernet networks. Within each Ethernet network, the Ethernet switches use the STP (or equivalent) protocol to manage Ethernet frame forwarding.

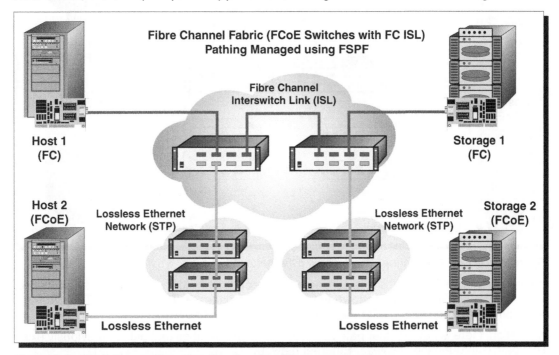

Figure 3-9. FCoE Forwarding: Non-Overlapping Ethernet networks

The two FCoE switches that make up the Fibre Channel Fabric continue to use the normal Fibre Channel Fabric Shortest Path First (FSPF) protocol to manage pathing information for the forwarding of Fibre Channel frames.

Because there is no overlap between the Fibre Channel and Ethernet networks, the switches in each network continue to use their normal forwarding protocols.

3.8.3 Forwarding Example: Overlapping Fabrics

So far, each switch has continued to use its normal forwarding protocol because there was no overlap between the Fibre Channel and Ethernet networks. However, FCoE allows configurations to be created where links between switches appear as interswitch links in both networks

---

and may participate in both forwarding protocols. An example of this type of configuration is shown in Figure 3-10 on page 40.

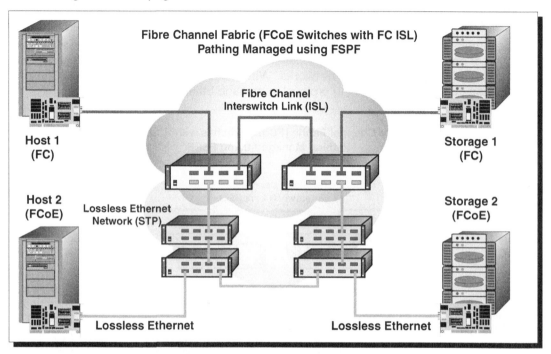

Figure 3-10. FCoE Forwarding: Overlapping Ethernet networks

In this example, an Ethernet link is connected between the two formerly independent Ethernet networks that were previously shown in Figure 3-9 on page 39. The Spanning Tree Protocol recomputes the spanning tree for the newly created Ethernet network.

In addition, there is now another path between the FCoE switches that did not previously exist. That path is through the "lossless" Ethernet network.

The FCF function within the FCoE switches will discover the path through the Ethernet network using the Discovery protocol described in *FCoE Discovery and Virtual Link Initialization* on page 121. Upon discovery of the path to the other FCoE switch, the switches may perform an Exchange Link Parameters (ELP) Switch Internal Link Service. If the ELP is successful, the FCoE switches instantiate an instance of a VE_Port for the newly discovered interswitch link.

The Fibre Channel FSPF protocol will add the new ISL into the topology database so that it can be used for forwarding frames between the FCF functions in the two FCoE switches (if the newly created ISL path is the least-cost path between the FCoE switches).

> NOTE – The FCoE standards do not define a method to assign a Link Cost to an ISL through an Ethernet network. The path between FCoE switches may traverse multiple Ethernet switches and links. The FCoE switches have no visibility to the nature of the Ethernet links between Ethernet switches, and therefore, no straightforward method of assigning a rational link cost to the Ethernet path.

If the Fibre Channel ISL between the two FCoE switches fails, the FCF function in each FCoE switch updates its topology database and recomputes available paths. Each will find an available path through the Ethernet network and can continue forwarding frames using the Ethernet path. If the Ethernet link between the Ethernet switches fails, or any of the Ethernet links in the path between switches fail, the switches remove the failed ISL path from their topology databases and can continue forwarding frames via the Fibre Channel ISL.

3.8.4 Forwarding Example: Ethernet Link Aggregation

If multiple links exist between Ethernet switches, the Spanning Tree Protocol blocks one or more switch ports to prevent loops within an Ethernet network. This prevents the use of redundant paths to provide more bandwidth or facilitate load balancing. To overcome this limitation, Ethernet switches may use a technique called Link Aggregation to allow multiple links to be aggregated to provide higher bandwidth as shown in Figure 3-11 on page 41.

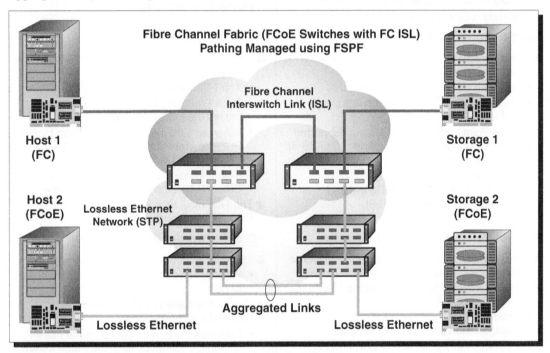

Figure 3-11. FCoE Forwarding: Ethernet Link Aggregation

When link aggregation is used, the aggregated links functionally appear as if they were a single logical link having higher bandwidth. This prevents the Spanning Tree Protocol from disabling the redundant ports. If one of the aggregated links fails, frames can still be forwarded via the remaining links (although with reduced bandwidth and throughput).

> NOTE – As mentioned earlier, the FCoE switch has no visibility to the links between Ethernet switches and no straightforward method to assign a link cost to ISLs through an Ethernet network.

3.9 Chapter Summary

FCoE Configurations

- There are many potential FCoE configurations:
  - Point-to-Point Ethernet
  - Point-to-Point Ethernet to Fibre Channel
  - FCoE devices directly connected to FCoE switch
  - FCoE devices connected to FCoE switch via intervening "lossless" Ethernet switches
  - Hybrid configurations consisting of:
  - FCoE devices and switches
  - Fibre Channel devices and switches
  - Standard Ethernet devices and switches

Point-to-Point: All Ethernet

- In this configuration, an FCoE host is directly connected to an FCoE storage device
  - e.g., with an Ethernet crossover cable
  - No Fibre Channel services are required (e.g., Name Server)
- Point-to-Point configurations are not supported by the 1st generation FCoE standard (FC-BB-5)
  - There was not enough market interest to justify the initial effort
  - Point-to-Point was deferred to the 2nd generation of FCoE (FC-BB-6)

Point-to-Point: Ethernet to FC Bridge

- In this configuration, an FCoE host is connected to a native FC storage device (or vice-versa)
- Requires a bridge function called the FCoE Link End Point (FCoE_LEP)
  - The FCoE_LEP performs the encapsulation/decapsulation function
  - Forwards frames between FCoE and FC environments
  - Normally provided by an FCoE switch
- No Fibre Channel services are required (e.g., Name Server)
- Point-to-Point configurations are not supported by the 1st generation FCoE standard (FC-BB-5)
  - This was deferred to 2nd generation FCoE

What is an FCoE Switch?

- An FCoE (or Converged Network) switch is a unique combination of both an Ethernet switch and a Fibre Channel switch
- When an Ethernet frame is received, it is forwarded by the Ethernet switch based on the Ethernet Destination Address
  - Destination could be an Ethernet device, or
  - Destination could be the Fibre Channel switch function (called the FCoE Forwarder, or FCF)
- The Ethernet switch function behaves as a normal Ethernet switch

FCoE Forwarder (FCF) - part 1

- The FCF is the Fibre Channel frame forwarding component of an FCoE switch
  - The FCF has one or more Ethernet MACs
  - Each Ethernet MAC has a MAC address (called the FCF-MAC address)
  - When an Ethernet frame is received by the FCF, the embedded Fibre Channel frame is decapsulated before processing
  - Before sending a Fibre Channel frame on an Ethernet link, the frame is encapsulated
- The FCF may, or may not, have any native Fibre Channel ports

FCoE Forwarder (FCF) - part 2

- The FCF function is a Fibre Channel switch
  - Whether it has any native Fibre Channel ports or not
- The FCF provides all of the normal Fibre Channel switch functions:
  - Forwards FC frames based on the Fibre Channel Destination ID in the frame header
  - Processes FLOGI and FDISC and assigns Fibre Channel addresses
  - Provides the Name Server and Fabric Controller functions
  - Provides normal Fibre Channel Zoning
  - Participates in Fabric protocols with other FCFs and Fibre Channel switches

FCoE Devices Direct to FCoE Switch

- FCoE end devices may be connected directly to an FCoE switch
  - This mimics a native Fibre Channel environment where FC devices connect directly to an FC switch
  - The FC Fabric may have both FCoE switches and native Fibre Channel switches
  - Interswitch links may be either Ethernet or Fibre Channel (or both)
- FCoE switches provide Fibre Channel services, the same as native Fibre Channel switches
  - e.g., Name Server and Fibre Channel address assignment (FLOGI)
- *Reference: Figure 3-4 on page 34*

FCoE via an Intervening Ethernet LAN

- FCoE end devices may be connected to FCoE switches via an intervening "lossless" Ethernet network
  - Lossless Ethernet switches forward Ethernet frames based on the MAC address
  - To another Ethernet device or to the FCF function in an FCoE switch
- An FCoE switch is required to provide services such as the Name Server and Fibre Channel address assignment (FLOGI)

Mixed FC and FCoE Configurations

- FCoE supports mixed configurations consisting of both:
  - FCoE end devices and switches, and
  - Native FC end devices and switches
- The two environments need to work together seamlessly
  - Requires a "bridge" function at the boundary
  - Normally, this is provided by the FCoE Forwarder function within an FCoE switch
  - Decapsulates Fibre Channel frames received via an Ethernet link
  - Encapsulates Fibre Channel frames before transmission on an Ethernet link

Hybrid Configuration: Example 1

- Initially, most FCoE products will be deployed into existing environments that already have:
  - FC hosts, switches and storage
  - Ethernet NICs, network and Network Attached Storage
- New FCoE hosts and switches can co-exist with existing devices
  - New FCoE enabled servers can access legacy storage
  - Legacy FC servers can access new FCoE enabled storage
- *Reference: Figure 3-6 on page 36*

Hybrid Configuration: Example 2

- FCoE Devices may connect to "lossless" Ethernet switches
- "Lossless" Ethernet switches may connect to:
  - FCoE switches,
  - Standard Ethernet switches, or
  - FCoE end devices
- FCoE switches may connect to other FCoE switches, FCoE devices, or Fibre Channel devices
- *Reference: Figure 3-7 on page 37*

Forwarding Protocols

- Fibre Channel and Ethernet switches use different forwarding protocols to identify inter-switch links and determine paths used for frame forwarding
- Fibre Channel switches use:
  - Fabric Shortest Path First (FSPF) protocol
- Ethernet Switches use:
  - Spanning Tree Protocol (STP), or
  - Rapid Spanning Tree Protocol (RSTP), or
  - Per VLAN Spanning Tree protocol (PVST), or
  - Some other Ethernet defined protocol
- What happens when a Fibre Channel Fabric and Ethernet network overlap as can happen with FCoE?

Forwarding: No Ethernet Switching

- One or more FCoE devices may be directly connected to an FCoE switch
  - The FCoE switch provides Fibre Channel services such as the Name Server and FC address assignment (FLOGI)
  - An FCoE switch may have both "lossless" Ethernet and Fibre Channel links
  - FCoE switch may connect to other FCoE switches and/or Fibre Channel switches using FC inter-switch links
  - The Fibre Channel Fabric uses its normal path selection mechanism (FSPF)
- *Reference: Figure 3-8 on page 38*

Forwarding: Non-Overlapping Fabrics

- FCoE devices may connect to an FCoE switch via a "lossless" Ethernet network
  - "lossless" Ethernet switches forward frames between the FCoE devices and the FCoE switches
  - Fibre Channel services are provided by the FCoE switches (e.g., Name Server and FC address assignment (FLOGI))
  - Each uses its normal path selection mechanisms (FSPF or STP)
- *Reference: Figure 3-9 on page 39*

Forwarding: Overlapping Fabrics

- If we add a link between the two Ethernet switches:
- The Ethernet networks are joined
  - STP resolves this to a single Ethernet spanning tree
- The FCoE switches discover each other using the Discovery process (described later)
  - FSPF sees a new inter-switch link (ISL) and adds it to the topology database
  - Based on link metrics, FSPF may use this ISL for forwarding frames
- *Reference: Figure 3-10 on page 40*

Forwarding: Link Aggregation

- With Link Aggregation, multiple Ethernet links are seen as one
  - STP allows both aggregated Ethernet ports to remain enabled
- FSPF continues to see two paths
  - One path via the FC link, the other path via the aggregated links in the Ethernet network
- *Reference: Figure 3-11 on page 41*

4. Deployment Scenarios

There are many different scenarios surrounding how FCoE might be deployed in a user's environment. Some of the scenarios in this chapter represent evaluation of test configurations while others are representative of data center environments. The objective of this chapter is to examine and discuss some of these scenarios.

4.1 FCoE Point-to-Point Evaluation Scenario

In this scenario, a user deploys the simple point-to-point implementation of FCoE shown in Figure 4-1 in order to become familiar with, or evaluate, the FCoE technology. While this configuration is probably not applicable to production environments, it does offer an environment to develop and test FCoE implementations.

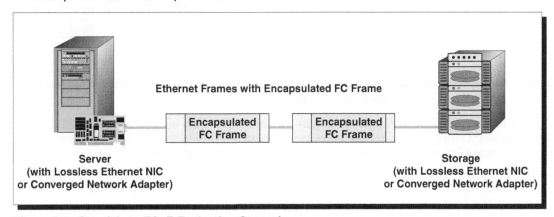

Figure 4-1. Standalone FCoE Evaluation Scenario

This configuration can be created using open source FCoE software drivers (see www.Open-FCoE.org for availability of open source FCoE software) or as a platform for testing or evaluation of FCoE hardware or software during development. Open source software is being developed for both the SCSI initiator and target functions.

The configuration shown in Figure 4-1 does not rely on FCoE-specific hardware and can be implemented using currently available Ethernet adapters that support full-duplex operation and Ethernet pause flow control.

Because a switched environment requires an FCoE Forwarder to provide Fibre Channel services (such as Fabric Login (FLOGI) processing and the Fibre Channel Name Server), this type of configuration (no FCoE or Ethernet switches) is most likely limited to a point-to-point configuration as shown.

4.2 FCoE Gateway Evaluation Scenario

The deployment scenario shown in Figure 4-2 is another example of a configuration that can be created without the need for FCoE-specific hardware. While the previous example was limited to a point-to-point configuration, this scenario supports the connection of an FCoE host to an existing Fibre Channel Fabric and devices using a "gateway" function.

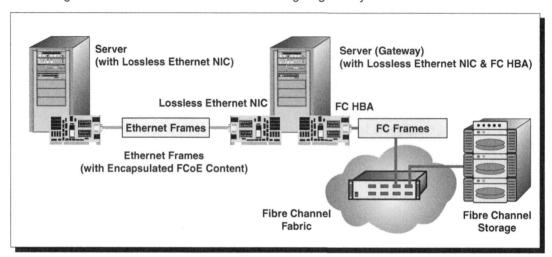

Figure 4-2. FCoE Evaluation Gateway Scenario

The gateway (or soft-server) function can be implemented using either software or FCoE-specific hardware. Again, open source software is being developed to provide the gateway function (see www.Open-FCoE.org for information about the fcgw program).

An advantage of this configuration is that it enables an FCoE server to communicate with multiple native Fibre Channel devices and uses the facilities within the Fibre Channel Fabric to provide FLOGI processing and Name Server functions.

While primarily intended for evaluation and testing, this configuration may be suitable for some production environments. When the gateway function is implemented in software, the software overhead may limit the performance and potential applications.

4.3 Standalone FCoE Evaluation Scenario

In this example, a user deploys a standalone evaluation configuration as shown in Figure 4-3 on page 47. This configuration uses an FCoE Fabric to provide connectivity and enables FCoE device and applications to be evaluated and tested without the risk of affecting the production environment.

The servers and storage devices shown in Figure 4-3 on page 47 may implement the FCoE functionality in software (via software drivers as discussed previously) or by using Converged Network Adapters (CNAs).

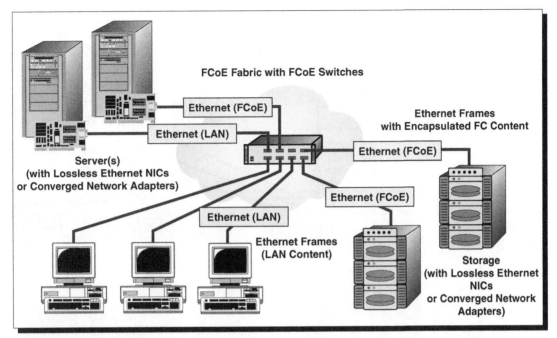

FCoE Fabric with FCoE Switches

Ethernet (FCoE)

Ethernet (LAN)

**Ethernet Frames
with Encapsulated FC Content**

Ethernet (FCoE)

**Server(s)
(with Lossless Ethernet NICs
or Converged Network Adapters)**

Ethernet (FCoE)

Ethernet (LAN)

**Ethernet Frames
(LAN Content)**

**Storage
(with Lossless Ethernet
NICs
or Converged Network
Adapters)**

Figure 4-3. FCoE Switch Evaluation Scenario

The FCoE Fabric shown in Figure 4-3 must contain at least one FCoE switch to provide Fibre Channel services such as the Name Server and processing of Fabric Login (FLOGI). The FCoE Fabric may also contain one or more "lossless" Ethernet switches.

4.4 FCoE Blade Server Deployment

FCoE may find its initial market application in blade servers. The limited space available for adapters and cables, along with the desire to reduce power and cooling requirements makes this a natural environment for the deployment of converged networks. An example of a blade server configuration is shown in Figure 4-4 on page 48.

In this example, redundant converged networks are contained within the blade server enclosure and largely hidden from the user. Each enclosure contains redundant embedded FCoE switches (shown at the ends of the enclosures in the example). Each blade contains redundant "lossless" Ethernet NICs or Converged Network Adapters (CNAs). Connections between the blade servers and embedded FCoE switches are provided by enclosure backplane wiring.

Using FCoE in this environment reduces the number of adapters needed on each of the blade servers, reduces the backplane wiring, eliminates the need for separate Ethernet and Fibre Channel switches within the enclosure and reduces the enclosure power and cooling requirements. These benefits may significantly reduce the cost of the blade server enclosure.

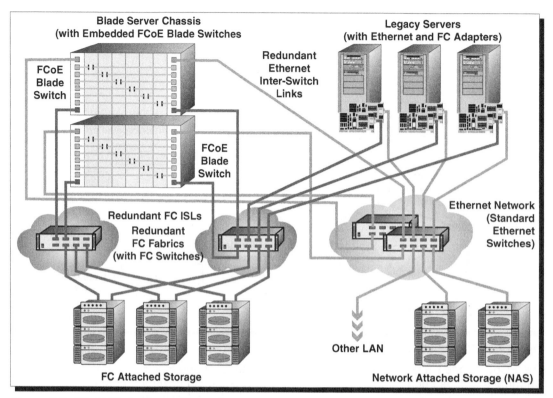

Figure 4-4. FCoE Blade Server Scenario

Frames carrying the FCoE protocol are received and decapsulated by the FCoE switches and sent via normal Fibre Channel inter-switch links to the attached Fibre Channel Fabric. The embedded blade switches appear as normal Fibre Channel switches to the rest of the Fibre Channel Fabric and observe all of the normal Fibre Channel switch behaviors.

Frames that not carrying the FCoE protocol (e.g., TCP/IP or other network traffic) are either forwarded to another blade server within the enclosure or to the attached Ethernet network depending upon the destination MAC address. The FCoE switches appear as normal Ethernet switches to the attached Ethernet network and participate in the normal Ethernet protocols, such as the Spanning Tree Protocol (STP).

Because the converged network is confined within the blade enclosure, problems of traffic management and administration are more contained than might be the case with a larger external converged network and may help alleviate management concerns.

4.5 FCoE Rack Server Deployment

Another area where FCoE may find initial market applications is in rack-mounted servers. As with blade servers, there is limited space available for adapters and cables and a strong desire to reduce power and cooling requirements making this a natural environment for the deployment of converged networks. An illustration of a rack mounted server configuration is shown in Figure 4-5.

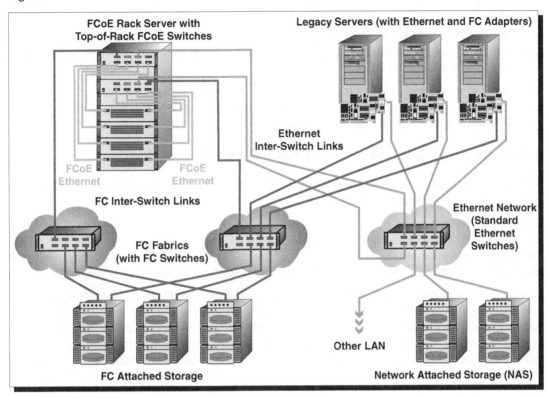

Figure 4-5. FCoE Rack Server Scenario

In this example, redundant converged networks are configured within the rack and largely hidden from the user. Each rack contains redundant FCoE switches. Each server contains redundant "lossless" Ethernet NICs or Converged Network Adapters (CNAs). Connections between the servers and FCoE switches are provided by either optical or electrical cables.

As with blade servers, using FCoE in this environment reduces the number of adapters needed for each of the servers, reduces the amount of cabling, eliminates the need for separate Ethernet and Fibre Channel switches within the rack and reduces the overall power and cooling requirements. Compare the number of adapters and cables by the FCoE servers with those required by the legacy servers to see the reduction. These benefits may result in a significant cost savings, both in terms of capital expenses and ongoing operational expenses.

Frames carrying the FCoE protocol are received and decapsulated by the FCoE switches and sent via normal Fibre Channel inter-switch links to the attached Fibre Channel Fabric. The

---

FCoE switches appear as normal Fibre Channel switches to the rest of the Fibre Channel Fabric and observe all of the normal Fibre Channel switch behaviors.

Frames not carrying the FCoE protocol (e.g., TCP/IP or other network traffic) are either forwarded to another server within the enclosure or to the attached Ethernet network depending upon the destination MAC address. The FCoE switches appear as normal Ethernet switches to the attached Ethernet network and participate in the normal Ethernet protocols, such as the Spanning Tree Protocol (STP).

Because the converged network is confined within the rack, problems of traffic management and administration are more contained than might be the case with a larger external converged network and may help alleviate management concerns.

4.6 Deploying FCoE via a Fibre Channel Switch Line Card

As FCoE is deployed into production environments, it will probably co-exist with existing Fibre Channel attached servers and hosts.

One potential approach to FCoE deployment is to use an FCoE line card (port card) installed into an existing Fibre Channel switch chassis as shown in Figure 4-6 on page 51. The FCoE line card provides Ethernet connectivity for attached FCoE (and Ethernet) devices while the existing Fibre Channel line cards provide connectivity for native Fibre Channel devices.

The advantage of this approach is that it leverages the existing Fibre Channel infrastructure and can be potentially implemented through a straightforward upgrade to existing Fibre Channel switches. The Fibre Channel switch provides all of the necessary services such as Fabric Login processing, address assignment, Name Server functions and zoning enforcement. For those switches that support hot-swapping a line card and concurrent firmware updates, adding an FCoE line card may not even require taking the switch down or creating a service interruption.

Frames that carry the FCoE protocol are received by the FCoE line card, decapsulated and processed by the switch as if they were normal Fibre Channel frames. The frames may be re-encapsulated and forwarded to other FCoE devices, forwarded to native Fibre Channel devices using normal Fibre Channel frames, or forwarded to internal services such as the Name Server.

Frames that are not carrying the FCoE protocol are forwarded based on their Ethernet destination MAC address and may be sent to non-FCoE devices connected to the FCoE line card or to attached Ethernet switches. This allows FCoE enabled servers to use the FCoE protocol to communicate with existing Fibre Channel storage devices while still using the normal network protocols (e.g., TCP/IP) for other communications.

If the FCoE line card connects to other Ethernet switches (as would normally be the case), it participates in the normal Ethernet switch protocols such as the Spanning Tree Protocol (STP).

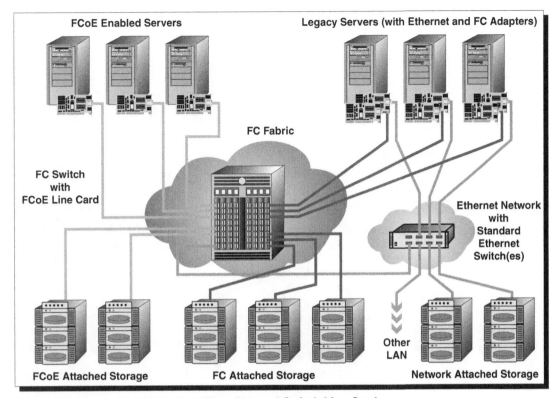

FCoE Enabled Servers   Legacy Servers (with Ethernet and FC Adapters)

FC Fabric

FC Switch
with
FCoE Line Card

Ethernet Network
with
Standard
Ethernet
Switch(es)

Other
LAN

FCoE Attached Storage   FC Attached Storage   Network Attached Storage

Figure 4-6. Deploying FCoE via a Fibre Channel Switch Line Card

4.7 Deploying FCoE via an FCoE Switch

Another alternative for FCoE deployment is to add an FCoE switch to an existing Fibre Channel Fabric as shown in Figure 4-7 on page 52. Functionally, this configuration is identical to the one shown in Figure 4-6 except that the FCoE attachment is via a separate switch instead of a line card in a Fibre Channel switch.

While the FCoE switch is a distinct entity, it functions as both an Ethernet switch and a Fibre Channel switch and provides all of the normal Fibre Channel services such as FLOGI processing, Fibre Channel address assignment and the Name Server. An FCoE switch may contain only Ethernet ports or a mixture of Ethernet and native Fibre Channel ports.

The FCoE network shown in Figure 4-7 on page 52 may consist of a single FCoE switch, or multiple interconnected FCoE switches. While this figure makes a distinction between the FCoE network and Fibre Channel fabrics, they are really one and the same (an FCoE switch connected to a Fibre Channel fabric becomes another switch in that fabric). The only difference in the figure is that the FCoE portion uses Ethernet links and ports while the Fibre Channel portion uses Fibre Channel links and ports.

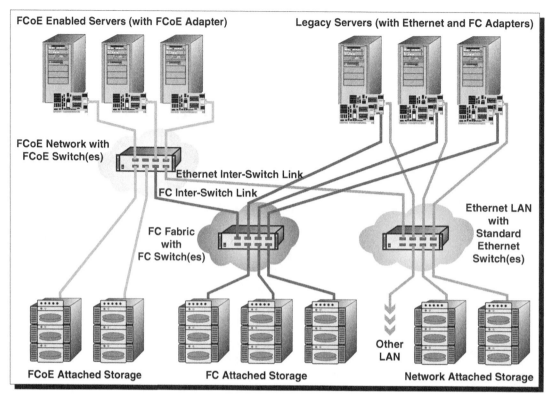

Figure 4-7. FCoE via FCoE Switch

Frames carrying the FCoE protocol are received, decapsulated and processed by the FCoE switch as if they were normal Fibre Channel frames. The Fibre Channel frames may be re-encapsulated and forwarded to other FCoE devices, forwarded to native Fibre Channel devices, forwarded to internal services such as the Name Server, or forwarded via Fibre Channel interswitch links to native Fibre Channel switches.

Frames that do not carry the FCoE protocol are forwarded based on their Ethernet destination address and may be sent to non-FCoE devices connected to the FCoE switch or to attached Ethernet switches. This allows FCoE enabled servers to use the FCoE protocol to communicating with storage devices and to use other protocols for other communications.

4.8 FCoE via "Lossless" Ethernet Switches

The scenario shown in Figure 4-7 on page 52 can be expanded to include one or more lossless Ethernet switches between and FCoE end device and an FCoE switch or line card in a Fibre Channel switch.While Figure 4-8 on page 53 shows a configuration with a lossless Ethernet switch between the FCoE end devices and the FCoE switch, it is equally applicable when an FCoE line card is used in a Fibre Channel switch.

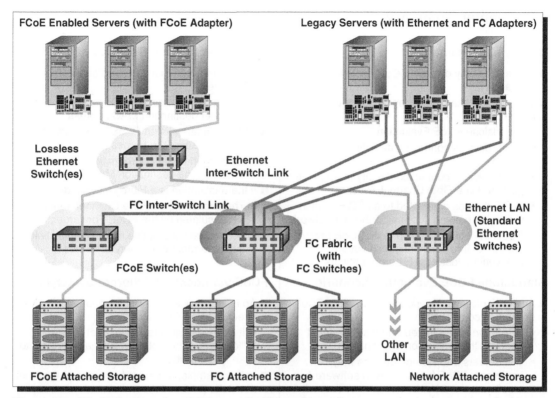

FCoE Enabled Servers (with FCoE Adapter)   Legacy Servers (with Ethernet and FC Adapters)

Lossless
Ethernet
Switch(es)

Ethernet
Inter-Switch Link

FC Inter-Switch Link

Ethernet LAN
(Standard
Ethernet
Switches)

FCoE Switch(es)

FC Fabric
(with
FC Switches)

Other
LAN

FCoE Attached Storage   FC Attached Storage   Network Attached Storage

Figure 4-8. FCoE via "Lossless" Ethernet Switches Scenario

In this example, there are two types of Ethernet networks (and switches). Lossless Ethernet switches (sometimes referred to as Data Center Bridging switches - see *Data Center Bridging (DCB) Ethernet* on page 223) are required to support FCoE traffic while standard Ethernet switches can be used where there is no FCoE traffic (it is not necessary to use "lossless" Ethernet throughout an entire configuration).

The FCoE requirements placed on a lossless switch are that it provides full-duplex operation and lossless frame delivery. These requirements may already be provided by many data center Ethernet switches that are currently deployed making them suitable for FCoE traffic.

When a lossless Ethernet switch receives an Ethernet frame, it forwards the frame based on the Ethernet destination MAC address. The frame may be forwarded to another lossless Ethernet switch, an FCoE switch, an FCoE line card in a Fibre Channel switch, or a normal Ethernet switch not associated with FCoE operations.

There may be FCoE-specific Ethernet switches deployed that provide functions specific to the FCoE environment such as FCoE protocol snooping and the automatic creation of static forwarding table entries and access control lists (ACLs). These enhancements are not required for FCoE to function but can add to the robustness of an FCoE environment.

4.9 Chapter Summary

Deployment Scenarios

- There are many different FCoE deployment scenarios
- This chapter examines a few of the potential cases:
  - Standalone FCoE Evaluation
  - FCoE devices connected directly to an FCoE switch
  - FCoE devices connected directly to an FCoE port card in a Fibre Channel switch
  - FCoE devices connected to an FCoE switch via an intervening "lossless" Ethernet network
  - FCoE devices connected to an FCoE port card in a Fibre Channel switch via an intervening "lossless" Ethernet network

Standalone FCoE Evaluation Scenario

- A user deploys an independent, separate FCoE evaluation configuration
  - FCoE can be evaluated and tested without affecting the production environment
  - The servers and storage devices may implement FCoE functionality in software (via a software driver) or by using a specialized FCoE host bus adapter (HBA) or hardware
- The FCoE Fabric must contain at least one FCoE switch
  - FCoE switch provides Fibre Channel services such as FLOGI processing and the Name Server

FCoE Direct Attach Scenario

- FCoE devices connect directly to an FCoE switch or an FCoE port card in a Fibre Channel switch
- The FCoE Fabric processes Ethernet frames containing the FCoE protocol in addition to Ethernet frames containing normal LAN traffic such as TCP/IP
  - The FCoE Fabric is an extension of the existing Fibre Channel Fabric
  - The FCoE fabric may also be an extension of the existing Ethernet network

FCoE Direct Attach Scenario

- Ethernet frames that carry protocols other than FCoE are:
  - Forwarded to their destination based on the Ethernet destination MAC address
- If the destination is an FCoE device attached to the FCoE Fabric, the frames are:
  - Forwarded to the appropriate destination based on the destination MAC address
- If the destination is a Fibre Channel device:
  - The encapsulated Fibre Channel frame is decapsulated by the FCoE Forwarder, and
  - Forwarded via a native Fibre Channel link using normal Fibre Channel frames

FCoE via Lossless Ethernet Switches

- An FCoE device does not have to be connected directly to an FCoE switch
  - It may be connected to an intervening "lossless" Ethernet network that connects to an FCoE switch
- In the example, there are two types of Ethernet networks (and switches):
  - "lossless" Ethernet switches are required to support FCoE traffic
  - Standard Ethernet switches can be used where there is no FCoE traffic
- It is not necessary to use "lossless" Ethernet throughout the entire configuration

5. FCoE Benefits

Earlier discussions have mentioned the benefits of a converged network in general terms. This chapter examines each of those benefits in greater detail and provides example case studies to quantify the benefits for different configurations.

5.1 Benefits of a Converged Network

The are numerous benefits to a converged network. These benefits accrue at the server, network, storage device and in the installation, administration and maintenance of each. Cost savings result from the following:

- Reduced bill-of-materials costs
- Reduced power
- Reduced cooling
- Reduced floor space
- Reduced spares and inventory
- Improved reliability
- Improved serviceability
- Improved manageability

5.1.1 Benefits at the Server

A traditional server has separate adapters for LAN and storage traffic (it may also have another, separate adapter for a clustering interface such as InfiniBand). A server using a Converged Network Adapter has a single adapter that carries LAN and storage traffic (and, perhaps clustering traffic).

The benefit of this is obvious - a single adapter has replaced multiple separate adapters. This provides the following immediate benefits at the server:

1. A single converged adapter should be less expensive than multiple separate adapters. A single Converged Network Adapter can replace an Ethernet NIC, a Fibre Channel HBA and (potentially) an InfiniBand Host Channel Adapter (HCA).

2. A single converged adapter should consume less power than multiple separate adapters and may reduce the server's power supply cost due to the lower power consumption.

3. If the total adapter power consumption is reduced, the amount of electricity consumed by the server is also reduced.

4. If the power consumption is reduced, the cooling load is also reduced and should result in a lower cost of cooling for the server and data center.

5. A single converged adapter requires less physical space than multiple separate adapters and may reduce packaging costs of the server and result in a more compact package.

6. With a single converged adapter, there is a single cable to connect the server. With multiple adapter types, there are multiple, often different, cables to connect to the server. In the case of a blade server, there are fewer connections to the server and fewer traces to layout and run on the enclosure backplane.

7. With a single converged adapter, there is one adapter to fail. With multiple, different adapters there are multiple adapters that may fail. Associated with each adapter are the motherboard connections and external cable connections, both of which represent additional potential failure points.

8. When the server has multiple instances of an adapter type to provide redundancy or higher performance, convergence multiplies the benefits by the number of instances of adapters installed.

5.1.2 Benefits at the Network

If the server has separate adapters for LAN and storage traffic (and, perhaps another, separate adapter for a clustering interface such as InfiniBand) three different networks are required. A server using a converged network has a single network that carries both LAN and storage traffic (and, perhaps clustering traffic).

Again, the immediate benefit of convergence is obvious - a single network has replaced multiple separate networks. This provides the following immediate benefits:

1. A single converged network should be less expensive than multiple separate networks. A single converged network switch can replace separate Ethernet, Fibre Channel, and (potentially) InfiniBand switches.

2. A single converged network should consume less power than multiple, independent networks and reduce the cost of electricity consumed by the switches within the data center.

3. If the power consumption is reduced, the cooling load is also reduced and should result in a lower cost of cooling for the server and data center.

4. A single converged network requires less physical space than multiple separate networks because multiple different switches are being replaced with a single switch. This should reduce the amount of floor space required in the data center.

5. With a single converged network, the number of cables and cable types are reduced and the cable costs are reduced. With multiple network types, there are multiple, often different, cables to connect to the devices in the different networks.

6. With a single converged network, there is one switch to fail versus multiple, different switches (one FCoE switch versus an Ethernet switch, a Fibre Channel switch and an InfiniBand switch).

7. When multiple networks are used to provide redundancy or higher performance, convergence multiplies the benefits by the number of instances of networks that are used.

5.1.3 Reliability and Maintainability Benefits

1. With a single converged adapter and network, the service technician only has to learn a single physical network and needs only a single set of tools and test equipment. This can reduce the training and service costs. With multiple adapter and network types, the service technician needs to be able to maintain three different types of adapters and networks using three different sets of tools and test equipment.

2. In a converged network, it is only necessary to track and manage firmware updates for a single adapter type. With separate networks, it may be necessary to track and manage firmware updates for three different types of adapters.

3. In a converged network, it is only necessary to track and manage firmware updates for a single switch type. With separate networks, it may be necessary to track and manage firmware updates for three different types of switches.

4. With a single converged network, there are fewer adapters and switches. Due to the reduced number of adapters and switches, the overall failure rate should be reduced and result in fewer service calls.

5. With a single converged network, there are fewer cables to install and maintain. By reducing the number of cables, the likelihood of mis-plugging a cable is reduced and should result in fewer service calls.

5.1.4 Administration Benefits

1. With a single converged network, the administrator only has to configure and manage a single network type. With multiple network types, the administrator may have to configure and manage three different types of networks.

2. With a single converged adapter, the administrator only has to configure and manage a single adapter type. With multiple adapter types, the administrator may have to configure and manage three different types of adapters.

3. With multiple separate networks, each switch type is a different Field Replaceable Unit (FRU) or set of FRUs. A single converged network has a single Field Replaceable Unit or set of FRUs for the switches resulting in a reduced number of part numbers that need to be stocked as spares.

4. With multiple separate adapters, each adapter type is a different Field Replaceable Unit (FRU). A single converged adapter represents a single Field Replaceable Unit resulting in a reduced number of part numbers that have to be stocked as spares.

5. With multiple separate networks, each network may use a different type of cable. Each cable type is a different Field Replaceable Unit (FRU) or set of FRUs. A single converged network has a single Field Replaceable Unit or set of FRUs for the cables resulting in a reduced number of part numbers that have to be stocked as spares.

5.1.5 Design, Test and Qualification Benefits

1. With a single converged network, there is a single Converged Network Adapter to design, procure, qualify or test.

2. With a single converged network, there is a single switch type to design, procure, qualify or test.

3. With a single converged network, there is a single set of verification tools and tests rather than a different set for Ethernet and Fibre Channel.

5.2 Blade Server Example Case Study

In order to quantify the potential cost savings resulting from a converged network and FCoE, let's examine the 40-server blade server configuration shown in Figure 5-1 and compare the cost of a traditional approach versus the cost of a converged network. In this example, each chassis has twelve slots. Both configurations connect to redundant Ethernet networks with dual, redundant links and both connect to redundant Fibre Channel Fabrics, as shown.

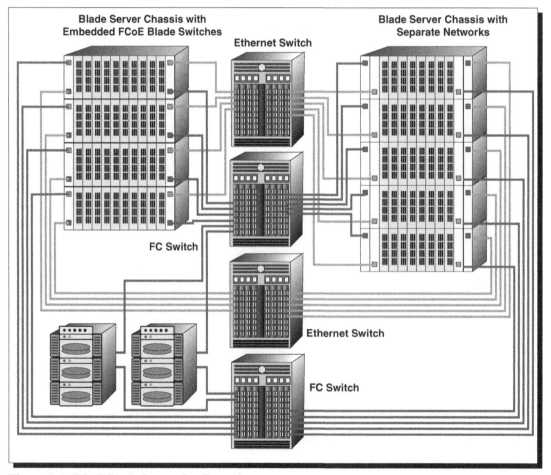

Figure 5-1. FCoE Blade Server Configuration

Separate Network Configuration. The blade server enclosures shown on the right of Figure 5-1 have eight server blades each, two Ethernet switch blades and two Fibre Channel switch blades (note that there are twelve slots total but four slots are taken by the switches leaving eight slots for the servers). This configuration requires five chassis to provide 40 servers. Each server blade has two redundant Ethernet NICs and two redundant Fibre Channel HBAs.

One of the Ethernet NICs in each server blade connects to the leftmost Ethernet switch blade and the other Ethernet NIC connects to the rightmost Ethernet switch blade. Each Ethernet switch blade has eight internal ports that connect to the eight server blades via backplane wiring. Each Ethernet blade switch also has one external port that connects to the Ethernet network.

In a similar manner, one of the Fibre Channel HBAs in each server blade connects to the leftmost Fibre Channel switch blade and the other Fibre Channel HBA connects to the rightmost Fibre Channel switch blade. Each Fibre Channel switch blade has eight internal ports that connect to the eight server blades via backplane wiring and one external port that connects to one of the Fibre Channel Fabrics.

Blade Server Configuration Cost Analysis. The separate network configuration shown on the right in Figure 5-1 has the components listed in Table 5-1. Assigning some (very) hypothetical costs to each of the components results in a total cost for 40 servers as shown on the bottom line of Table 5-1.

Capital Expense Item	Qty	Cost (ea)	Total
Blade Servers	40	$1,500.00	$60,000.00
Blade Server Enclosures (12 slots)	5	$1,500.00	$7,500.00
Dual 10 Gb Ethernet NICs (assumed on blade)	80	-	-
Dual-Port 8 Gb Fibre Channel HBAs (Mezzanine card)	40	$750.00	$30,000.00
Ethernet Cables (enclosure to core switch)	10	$50.00	$500.00
Fibre Channel Cables (enclosure to core switch)	10	$50.00	$500.00
10-Port Ethernet Blade Switches (10 Gb)	10	$10,000.00	$100,000.00
10-Port Fibre Channel Blades Switches (8 Gb)	10	$5,000.00	$50,000.00
Ethernet Ports and Transceivers on Core Switch (10Gb)	10	$200.00	$2,000.00
Fibre Channel Ports and Transceivers on Core Switch	10	$500.00	$5,000.00
Total			$255,500.00

Table 5-1. 40 Server Cost Estimate (Legacy Blade Server)

Converged Network Configuration. The blade server chassis on the left in Figure 5-1 contains ten server blades and two embedded FCoE switch blades. Four chassis are required to provide the desired 40 servers. Each server blade has two redundant Converged Network Adapters (either "lossless" Ethernet adapters with software FCoE or CNAs). One of the Converged Network Adapters in each server blade connects to the leftmost switch and the other adapter connects to the rightmost switch.

Each FCoE switch blade has ten internal ports that connect to the ten server blades via backplane wiring. Each FCoE blade switch also has two external ports, one connecting to the Ethernet network and the other connecting to the Fibre Channel Fabric.

FCoE Blade Server Configuration Cost Analysis. The converged network configuration shown on the left in Figure 5-1 on page 58 has the components listed in Table 5-2. Again, assigning some (very) hypothetical costs to each of the components results in a total cost for 40 servers as shown on the bottom line of Table 5-2. While the cost numbers used in these examples are hypothetical, it does show that using a converged network with FCoE can result in a significant capital expenditure savings.

Capital Expense Item	Qty	Cost (ea)	Total
Blade Servers	40	$1,500.00	$60,000.00
Blade Server Enclosures (12 slots)	4	$1,500.00	$6,000.00
10 Gb Converged Network Adapter (assumed on blade)	80	-	-
Dual-Port 8 Gb Fibre Channel HBAs (Mezzanine card)	0	-	-
Ethernet Cables (enclosure to core switch)	8	$50.00	$400.00
Fibre Channel Cables (enclosure to core switch)	0	-	-
12-Port Ethernet Blade Switches (10 Gb)	0	-	-
12-Port Fibre Channel Blades Switches (8 Gb)	0	-	-
12-Port FCoE Converged Blades Switches (10 Gb)	8	$12,000.00	$96,000.00
Ethernet Ports and Transceivers on Core Switch (10Gb)	8	$1,500.00	$12,000.00
Fibre Channel and Transceivers Ports on Core Switch	8	$500.00	$4,000.00
Total			**$178,400.00**

Table 5-2. 40 Server Cost Estimate (FCoE Blade Server)

A more thorough cost analysis would also include the cost of electricity, cooling, data center floor space, service costs and administrative costs. Assessing these costs is beyond the scope of this book.

5.3 Chapter Summary

Benefits of a Converged Network

- The are many to a converged network
- Cost savings result from the following:
  - Reduced bill-of-materials costs
  - Reduced power
  - Reduced cooling
  - Reduced floor space
  - Reduced spares and inventory
  - Improved reliability
  - Improved serviceability
  - Improved manageability

Server Benefits: Bill of Material Costs

- A single Converged Network Adapter can replace:
  - An Ethernet NIC,
  - A Fibre Channel HBA, and potentially, and
  - An InfiniBand Host Channel Adapter (HCA)
- A single converged adapter should be less expensive than multiple separate adapters
  - Fewer adapters = less cost

Server Benefits: Power & Cooling

- A single converged adapter should consume less power than multiple separate adapters
- This may reduce the cost of a server's power supply due to the lower power consumption
- If the power consumption is reduced
  - Electricity consumption is reduced
  - The cooling load is also reduced and should result in lower costs of cooling the server and data center

Server Benefits: Physical Packaging

- A single converged adapter should require less physical space than multiple separate adapters
  - This can reduce the packaging costs of the server and result in a more compact package
  - A smaller package should save materials cost
  - A smaller package should allow more servers in the same amount of floor space

Server Benefits: Cabling

- With multiple adapter types, there are multiple cables to connect to the server
  - The cables are often different
- With a single converged adapter, there is a single cable to connect
  - Fewer cables = less cost
  - Fewer cables = smaller physical package
  - Fewer cables = lower failure rates
  - Fewer cables = less opportunity for cabling errors

Server Benefits: Reliability

- With a single converged adapter, there are fewer adapter to fail
  - One adapter versus multiple adapters
  - Fewer failures = fewer customer outages and fewer service calls
  - Fewer failures = reduced warranty costs
- Associated with each adapter are secondary potential failure points:
  - Motherboard connections
  - External cable connections

Network Benefits: Bill of Material Costs

- A single converged network should be less expensive than multiple separate networks
- A single converged network switch can replace
  - An Ethernet switch,
  - A Fibre Channel switch, and potentially,
  - An InfiniBand switch

Network Benefits: Power and Cooling

- A single converged network should consume less power than multiple separate networks
- This should reduce the cost of electricity consumed by the switches within the data center
- If the power consumption is reduced, the cooling load is also reduced and should result in a lower cost of cooling for the server and data center
-

Network Benefits: Floor Space

- A single converged network requires less physical space than multiple separate networks
  - Multiple different switches are being replaced with a single switch
  - This should reduce the amount of floor space required in the data center
- Multiple patch panels are replaced with a single patch panel
  - Results in a further space savings

Network Benefits: Cables

- With multiple network types, there are multiple cables to connect to the devices in the different networks
  - The cables may be different for each network
- With a single converged network, the number of cables and cable types are reduced and the cable costs are reduced
  - There are fewer cables to connect
  - Fewer cables = less cost
  - Fewer cables = smaller physical package
  - Fewer cables = lower failure rates
  - Fewer cables = less opportunity for cabling errors

Network Benefits: Reliability

- With multiple network types, there are multiple switches
- With a single converged network, there is one switch to fail versus multiple, different switches
- One FCoE switch versus
  - An Ethernet switch,
  - A Fibre Channel switch, and potentially,
  - An InfiniBand switch

Maintainability Benefits: Skills and Tools

- With multiple network types,
  - The service technician needs to be able to maintain multiple different types of adapters and networks
  - The service technician needs test equipment for each network
- With a single converged adapter and network,
  - The service technician only has to learn a single physical network and needs only a single set of tools and test equipment
  - This can reduce the training and service costs associated with supporting the server

Maintainability Benefits: Firmware

- In a converged network, it is only necessary to track and manage firmware updates for a single adapter type
- With separate networks, it may be necessary to track and manage firmware updates for three different types of adapters
- In a converged network, it is only necessary to track and manage firmware updates for a single switch type
- With separate networks, it may be necessary to track and manage firmware updates for three different types of switches

Reliability and Maintainability Benefits

- With a single converged network, there are fewer adapters and switches
- Fewer adapters and switches should result in fewer outages and fewer service calls
- With a single converged network, there are fewer cables to install and maintain
- By reducing the number of cables, the likelihood of mis-plugging a cable is reduced and should result in fewer service calls.

Administration Benefits

- With a single converged network
  - The administrator only has to configure and manage a single network type
  - With multiple network types, the administrator may have to configure and manage three different types of networks
- With a single converged adapter
  - The administrator only has to configure and manage a single adapter type
  - With multiple adapter types, the administrator may have to configure and manage three different types of adapters.

Serviceability: Replaceable Units

- With multiple networks, each switch type is a Field Replaceable Unit (FRU) or set of FRUs
  - A converged network has a single FRU or set of FRUs for each switch
- With multiple different adapters, each adapter type is a different Field Replaceable Unit (FRU)
  - A single converged adapter is a single Field Replaceable Unit resulting in fewer part numbers that have to be stocked as spares
- With multiple separate networks, each network type may use a different type of cable
  - Each cable type is a different Field Replaceable Unit (FRU) or set of FRUs
  - A converged network has a single Field Replaceable Unit or set of FRUs for the cables resulting in a reduced number of FRUs

Development Benefits: Design & Test

- A manufacturer supporting a converged network only has a reduced development workload
  - A single Converged Network Adapter to design, procure, qualify or test
  - A single converged switch to design, procure, qualify or test
  - A single set of verification tools and tests rather than one for each interface

Summary of Benefits

- A converged network offers the potential for significant benefits
  - Lower cost
  - Fewer adapters and fewer switches
  - Fewer cables
  - Fewer spares (or at least fewer part numbers)
  - Fewer skill sets and types of test equipment
  - Less power, less cooling
  - Less floor space
- Consolidate management and administration of converged network requires a paradigm shift in that networking and storage cannot be treated as separate entities
  - Need to understand, and plan for, the needs of both types of traffic

6.   FCoE Technology

This chapter, and the subsequent chapters in this section, examine the technical details of FCoE. The technical aspects involve both Ethernet and Fibre Channel functions as well as functions and operations unique to FCoE. This chapter provides a brief introduction to the technical elements which are covered in more detail in the subsequent chapters.

6.1 FCoE and "Lossless" Ethernet

FCoE is the transport of encapsulated Fibre Channel frames over "lossless" Ethernet. The term "lossless" Ethernet is used to distinguish Ethernet implementations supporting functions required by FCoE from implementations that do not support these functions. The terms "Data Center Ethernet (DCE)" and "Converged "lossless" Ethernet (CEE)" have also been used to identify these functions, but this book avoids the use of those terms in order to avoid any associations with functions that are not specifically required by FCoE. What is required by FCoE is:

> "A lossless, full-duplex Ethernet environment providing in-order frame delivery."

These capabilities may be provided by default in an existing Ethernet NIC or switch. Many existing implementations already support the necessary capabilities even though they are not required by the Ethernet standards.

More information about Ethernet and the enhancements required for FCoE can be found in *Ethernet Essentials* on page 69.

6.2 FCoE Frame Encapsulation

A key aspect of FCoE is the encapsulation of Fibre Channel frames within "lossless" Ethernet. The technical details of the encapsulation are covered in *FCoE Encapsulation* on page 173.

6.3 Architectural Models and Configurations

The FCoE standard defines several architectural models that identify the various FCoE entities and their relationships, functions and attributes. The models are described in *Architecture Models* on page 97.

6.4 MAC Addressing

Because FCoE has both a Fibre Channel component and an Ethernet component, it has to deal with both types of addresses (the Fibre Channel addresses in the encapsulated Fibre Channel frame header and the Ethernet MAC addresses in the Ethernet frame header). *FCoE Addressing* on page 117 describes the relationship between the two address spaces and how MAC addresses are used in an FCoE environment.

6.5 Discovery and Virtual Link Initialization

In a native Fibre Channel environment, a node port is directly connected to a fabric port and a switch port is connected directly to another switch port by a physical link.

As a result, a node port can simply login with the Fabric by sending the FLOGI request down the physical link connected to the Fabric. In FCoE, a node port may not connect directly to an FCoE Fabric port (it may be connected via one or more "lossless" Ethernet switches). Because of this, an FCoE node port needs a discovery protocol that enables the node port to discover available Fabric ports before it can perform Fabric Login.

In a similar manner, switch E_Ports may not be directly connected to other switch E_Ports as they are in native Fibre Channel and also require a discovery protocol that enables a switch port to discover other available switch ports in order to initialize the inter-switch link.

The discovery protocols used by both node ports and switch ports is described in *FCoE Discovery and Virtual Link Initialization* on page 121.

6.6 Access Control

Fibre Channel provides access controls through the use of Fibre Channel zoning and access control lists. Access controls prevent devices from accessing resources that they are not authorized to access. FCoE needs to provide the same level of access control in and FCoE environment to prevent access to unauthorized resources. FCoE access control methods are described in *Ethernet Access Control* on page 211.

6.7 Error Scenarios and Handling

FCoE must provide a level of error detection and handling that is at least as robust as that provided within a native Fibre Channel environment. The use of Ethernet as a data link introduces a number of unique considerations that are discussed in *FCoE Error Conditions* on page 189.

6.8 Chapter Summary

What is FCoE?

- FCoE is the transport of encapsulated Fibre Channel frames over "lossless" Ethernet
  - Lossless Ethernet distinguishes implementations supporting functions required by FCoE from those that do not support these functions
  - The terms "Data Center Ethernet (DCE)" and "Converged Enhanced Ethernet (CEE)" have also been used to identify these functions
- FCoE requires:
  - "A lossless, full-duplex Ethernet providing in-order frame delivery."

FCoE Frame Encapsulation

- FCoE Encapsulates Fibre Channel frame content in Ethernet frames
  - There is a one-to-one relationship between the frames
  - 1 Fibre Channel frame = 1 Ethernet frame
- Fibre Channel frame content is unchanged
  - Exactly the same content as on a native Fibre Channel Link
  - Including the fields in the Fibre Channel frame header

Architectural Models

- FCoE standard defines architectural models that identify the FCoE entities and their relationships, functions and attributes
- There are models for an FCoE:
  - Node Port (VN_Port)
  - Fabric Port (VF_Port)
  - Expansion Port (VE_Port)
- FCoE uses the concept of a "virtual link"
  - A logical link connecting two FCoE entities
  - Identified by the local MAC address and a remote MAC address
- At each end of a virtual link is an FCoE Link End Point that performs the encapsulation and decapsulation of frames

MAC Addressing

- FCoE has both a Fibre Channel component and an Ethernet component
- It must deal with both types of addresses
  - The Fibre Channel addresses in the encapsulated Fibre Channel frame header, and
  - Ethernet MAC addresses in the Ethernet frame header

Discovery & Virtual Link Initialization

- In a native Fibre Channel environment a node port is directly connected to a Fabric port
  - The node port simply sends FLOGI on the physical link connected to the Fabric
- In FCoE, a node port is not necessarily connected directly to an FCoE Fabric port
  - It may be connected via one or more "lossless" Ethernet switches
  - Because of this, an FCoE node port needs a discovery protocol that enables a node port to discover available Fabric ports
- Switch port also require a discovery protocol to discover other available switch ports

Access Control

- Fibre Channel provides access controls
  - Through the use of Fibre Channel zoning and access control lists
  - Access controls prevent devices from accessing resources that they are not authorized to access
- FCoE needs to provide the same level of access control in an FCoE environment to prevent access to unauthorized resources
  - Ethernet only provides Access Control Lists

7. Ethernet Essentials

Ethernet is the dominant local area network (LAN) technology and has enjoyed a huge success in all segments of the LAN marketplace. There are numerous reasons for this success:

- Ethernet is inexpensive
- Ethernet uses simple hardware
- Ethernet uses low-cost electrical cables or optical cables for higher speeds and longer distances
- Ethernet has a simple frame structure and link-level protocols
- Ethernet can transport information associated with a wide variety of protocols. TCP/IP is one of the most common protocols.

In the Open Systems Interconnect (OSI) reference model, Ethernet is a Layer-2 network that provides a data link for transporting higher-level information (such as TCP/IP). While not usually described as such, Fibre Channel is also essentially a Layer-2 network. The OSI reference model is shown in Figure 7-1 on page 69.

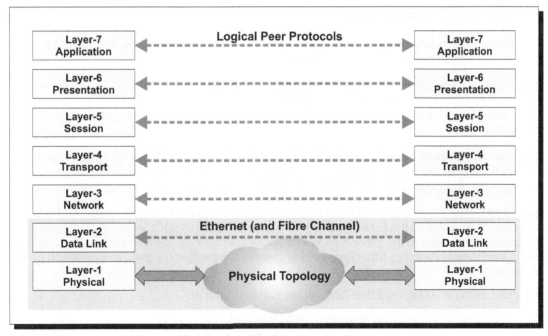

Figure 7-1. Ethernet and the OSI Reference Model

Fibre Channel over Ethernet is based on the availability of certain optional Ethernet characteristics that are not part of the behavior required by Ethernet standards. Because of this, this book uses the term "lossless" Ethernet" to distinguish an Ethernet environment having those characteristics from a standard Ethernet environment. In some publications, you may see the terms "Data Center Ethernet (DCE)" or "Converged Enhanced Ethernet (CEE)" also used. Details of enhancements being discussed for Data Center Ethernet are described in *Data Center Bridging (DCB) Ethernet* on page 223.

The "lossless" Ethernet attributes required by FCoE are:

- Lossless frame delivery (see *Making Ethernet "Lossless"* on page 85)
- In-order frame delivery (provided by the *Spanning Tree Protocol (STP)* on page 76
- Full-duplex operation, and
- In order to encapsulate full-sized Fibre Channel frames, Ethernet support for jumbo frames of at least 2.5 KB is required (see *Ethernet Jumbo Frames* on page 73)

None of these requires new functions beyond what already exists within the Ethernet standards or is commonly implemented in products. FCoE does require functions that are optional in the Ethernet standards and FCoE may benefit from functions beyond those that are currently specified in the Ethernet standards (such as an enhanced flow control method or congestion management). For performance reasons, it is also desirable to have high-speed adapters and switches with low-latency characteristics.

7.1 Ethernet Frame Format

To minimize hardware complexity and cost while providing the utmost in flexibility, Ethernet uses a very simple frame format as shown in Figure 7-2.

Preamble. An Ethernet frame begins with a Preamble followed by the Start-of-Frame delimiter and ends with an End-of-Frame delimiter. The preamble and delimiters are not considered to be part of the frame and the nature of these delimiters depends on the physical link that is being used.

Destination Address and Source Address. The Destination Address (DA) field specifies the destination of the frame and the Source Address (SA) field the source of the frame. The format of the addresses is described in *MAC Address Format* on page 71.

EtherType. The EtherType field has two different interpretations (largely based on historical reasons). If the value in the EtherType field is less than 1500 (0x5DC), it specifies the length of the frame. If the value in the EtherType field is more than 1536, it identifies the protocol carried within the frame. Using the EtherType field to identify the protocol is the more common usage of the field.

A current listing of assigned EtherType values can be found at:

> http://standards.ieee.org/regauth/ethertype/eth.txt

The EtherType value is 8906h for FCoE and 8914h for the FCoE Initialization Protocol.

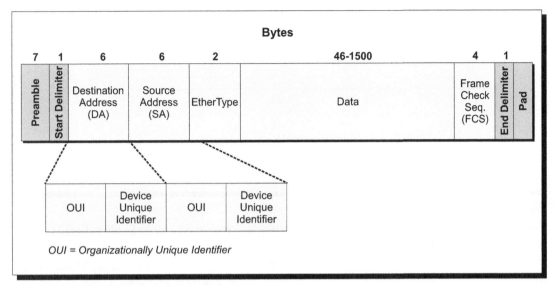

Figure 7-2. Ethernet Frame Format

Data. The Data portion of the frame contains the information being transported from the Source address to the Destination address. The size of the data portion of a standard Ethernet frame is limited to a maximum of 1500 bytes.

Frame Check Sequence (FCS). The Frame Check Sequence (FCS) is a 32-bit cyclic redundancy check (CRC) computed on the frame content beginning with the Destination Address. The algorithm is based on the same polynomial as used by Fibre Channel and is computed using the following 32-bit polynomial:

$$X^{32}+X^{26}+X^{23}+X^{22}+X^{16}+X^{12}+X^{11}+X^{10}+X^{8}+X^{7}+X^{5}+X^{4}+X^{2}+X+1$$

7.1.1 MAC Address Format

Each Ethernet adapter has an Ethernet address that is commonly referred to as the Media Access Control, or MAC address. The MAC address is usually personalized at the time of manufacture and often called the "burned-in" MAC address. An Ethernet MAC address is 48 bits long and has the format shown in Figure 7-3.

The first 24 bits are the Organizationally Unique Identifier (OUI). Normally, the OUI is a value assigned to an organization by IEEE to ensure uniqueness among different organizations. This is referred to as a Universally Administered OUI and is indicated by setting bit 41 to a zero. A list of assigned OUI values is available at:

http://standards.ieee.org/regauth/oui/oui.txt.

An OUI may also be locally administered. This is indicated by setting bit 41 to a one. A locally administered OUI must be unique within a given Ethernet network, but may not be globally unique.

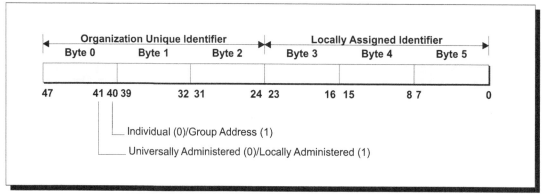

Figure 7-3. Ethernet MAC Address Format

The remaining 24 bits of the 48-bit MAC address are the device unique identifier. This is a unique value assigned within an organization.

The combination of the Universally Administered 24-bit Organizationally Unique Identifier and the 24-bit device unique identifier result in a 48-bit globally unique identifier.

7.1.2 Reserved Ethernet Group MAC Addresses

The Ethernet standards reserve a set of group addresses that are used for various link-level protocols and are not forwarded by an Ethernet switch. A listing of these Group MAC Addresses is provided in Table 7-1.

Assignment	MAC Address
Bridge Group Address	01-80-C2-00-00-00
IEEE Std 802.3x Full Duplex PAUSE operation	01-80-C2-00-00-01
IEEE Std 802.3ad Slow_Protocols_Multicast address (See *Link Aggregation (NIC Teaming)* on page 88 for an example of the usage of this address)	01-80-C2-00-00-02
IEEE P802.1X PAE address	01-80-C2-00-00-03
IEEE MAC-specific control protocols	01-80-C2-00-00-04
Reserved for future standardization	01-80-C2-00-00-05
Reserved for future standardization	01-80-C2-00-00-06
Reserved for future standardization	01-80-C2-00-00-07
Provider Bridge group address	01-80-C2-00-00-08
Reserved for future standardization	01-80-C2-00-00-09
Reserved for future standardization	01-80-C2-00-00-0A

Table 7-1. Ethernet Group MAC Addresses (Part 1 of 2)

Assignment	MAC Address
Reserved for future standardization	01-80-C2-00-00-0B
Reserved for future standardization	01-80-C2-00-00-0C
Provider Bridge MVRP address	01-80-C2-00-00-0D
IEEE Std 802.1ab Link Layer Discovery Protocol (LLDP)	01-80-C2-00-00-0E
Reserved for future standardization	01-80-C2-00-00-0F

Table 7-1. Ethernet Group MAC Addresses (Part 2 of 2)

7.1.3 FCoE Ethernet Group (Multicast) MAC Addresses

FCoE has reserved three Ethernet group addresses for multicast operations. These addresses are listed in Table 7-2 on page 73.

Assignment	MAC Address
ALL_FCoE_MACS	01-10-18-01-00-00
ALL_ENODE_MACS	01-10-18-01-00-01
ALL_FCF_MACS	01-10-18-01-00-02

Table 7-2. FCoE Group (Multicast) MAC Addresses

7.1.4 Ethernet Jumbo Frames

In an Ethernet environment where each frame interrupts the software, minimizing the number of interrupts, and associated software processing, can improve the overall efficiency. To provide better performance, some Ethernet devices support (non-standard) larger frame sizes referred to as "jumbo" frames that may be up to 9 KB in size. Because a 9 KB jumbo frame carries as much data as six standard-size Ethernet frames, the number of interrupts is reduced by a factor of six with the resulting improvement in performance.

While jumbo frames are not part of the Ethernet standard, they are widely supported by many Ethernet implementations, especially at one gigabit and faster.

Jumbo frames also provide a solution to the problem of how to transport a full-size Fibre Channel frame in FCoE. While a standard 1500-byte Ethernet frame cannot contain a full-sized Fibre Channel frame, an Ethernet jumbo frame of approximately 2.5 KB can.

7.2 Ethernet Topologies

Ethernet supports multiple topology configurations and medium types. Supported topology configurations include, multi-tap cable, hubs, and switched networks.

7.2.1 Shared-Medium Topology

Ethernet devices can connect to a shared "bus" consisting of a single coaxial cable as shown in Figure 7-4. By using a hub, this topology can also use unshielded twisted pair cabling.

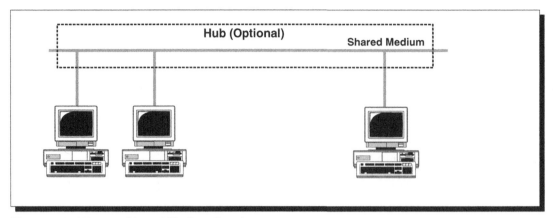

Figure 7-4. Ethernet Shared Medium Topology

Devices in this topology use the Carrier Sense Multiple Access/Collision Detect (CSMA/CD) access protocol. When a device need to transmit a frame, it:

1. Listens for traffic (Carrier Sense)

2. If none, it transmits the frame and listens to the bus at the same time

3. If another device also transmits at the same time (Multiple Access), there is a "collision"

4. The collision is detected because the transmitted frame is corrupted (Collision Detect)

5. If a collision occurs, the device backs off and tries again later

The shared medium topology using CSMA/CD is a common configuration for 10 and 100 megabit Ethernet (although most 100 megabit Ethernet is now based on the switched topology configuration).

While initially inexpensive, the shared-medium topology has been largely replaced by the switched topology. This is due to a number of limitations inherent in this type of topology:

• Because transmission and reception take place on the same coaxial cable or unshielded twisted pair, this topology only supports half-duplex behavior. That is, a device can transmit or receive a frame at any point in time but cannot do both at the same time (other than receiving the frame it is currently sending).

• When a collision occurs, no useful information is transferred. This represents wasted bandwidth on the link. As the level of activity increases, the number of collisions increase and the throughput is severely impacted.

• Only one device can be transmitting at a time. This limits the overall throughput that a shared medium topology can provide.

7.2.2 Ethernet Switched Topology

The switched topology is based on the use of one or more Ethernet switches. An illustration of a switched topology is shown in Figure 7-5. In this topology, each device connects to a port on an Ethernet switch (note that a shared-medium topology can also connect to a switch port).

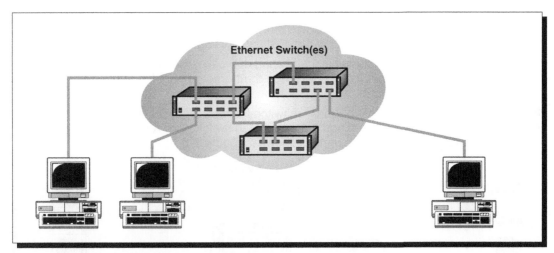

Ethernet Switch(es)

Figure 7-5. Ethernet Switched Topology

Devices that are connected to a switch may still implement the CSMA/CD access protocol to determine when a frame can be sent, but each link is in effect a separate collision domain. As a result, collisions caused by other devices are eliminated along with the wasted bandwidth and the need to retransmit frames as the result of a collision.

Finally, the links between devices and switch ports are usually full-duplex links that enable simultaneous frame transmission and reception. Full-duplex operation potentially doubles the available bandwidth when compared to half-duplex operation.

All one-gigabit and ten-gigabit Ethernet use the switched topology, effectively removing collisions and the need for the CSMA/CD protocol.

Ethernet networks may consist of multiple switches interconnected to create an Ethernet switched topology. Using multiple switches enables larger configurations to be created (more ports and physically distributed) than would be possible by using a single switch.

7.2.3 Ethernet Switch Learning

Ethernet switches have no control over the MAC addresses of attached devices. MAC addresses are normally assigned to an Ethernet NIC and the time of manufacture and an Ethernet switch has no control over which NIC is connected to which switch port. Instead of controlling addressing as is done in Fibre Channel, Ethernet switches learn the addresses of attached devices. Each Ethernet switch has a filtering database that associates MAC addresses with switch ports.

When a switch receives a unicast frame, it looks at the Source Address (SA) in the received frame. If the Source Address it is not in the filtering database, the switch associates that switch port with the MAC address and enters it into the filtering database.

The switch also looks in its filtering database to see if it already has an entry matching the Destination Address.

- If the Destination Address (DA) is in the filtering database, the switch forwards the frame out the associated switch port. Because it had previously received a frame from that address in on that switch port, it know the destination is reachable via that port.

- If the Destination Address is not in the filtering database, the switch has no knowledge of the location of the destination and forwards the frame out all of its other ports. This ensures that the frame will reach the destination, if it exists.

Using this learning approach, each Ethernet switch learns the MAC addresses off all devices sending frames through that switch and the associated switch port. An example of the association of MAC addresses with switch ports is shown in Figure 7-6.

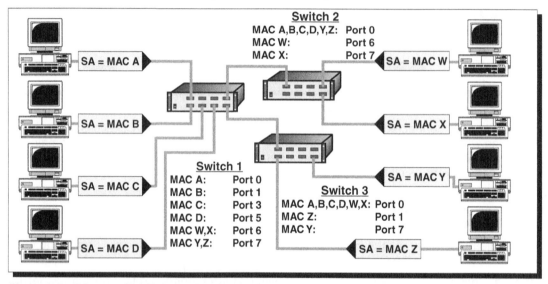

Figure 7-6. Ethernet Switch Learning Database

Because a device may be removed from the network after its MAC address has been learned by one or more switches, a method is required to remove its address. Removal is accomplished through an aging process. If there has been no activity for a given MAC address and the aging time expires (the recommended default value is 300 seconds), the entry is removed from a switch's forwarding table. An address may also be removed from a switch's forwarding table in order to make room for a newly-learned MAC address.

7.2.4 Spanning Tree Protocol (STP)

When an Ethernet network consists of multiple switches, the Ethernet switches use a Spanning Tree Protocol to identify links to other switches, prevent loops within the network and re-route traffic around failed inter-switch links, if possible.

The Spanning Tree Protocol creates a tree structure within the switched network by identifying a root switch and disabling redundant links that might result in loops within the network. An illustration of a network with disabled links is shown in Figure 7-7 on page 77. This example assumes that Switch B becomes the root switch (disabled links are marked with an X in the figure).

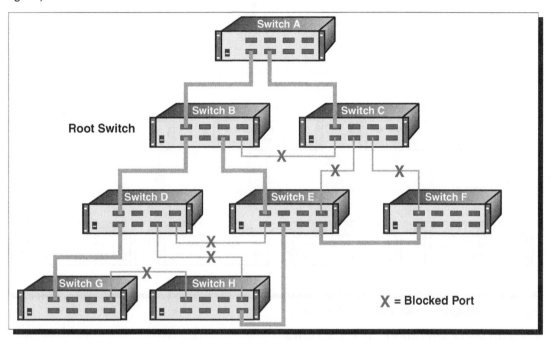

Figure 7-7. Ethernet Spanning Tree

While the tree structure created by the Spanning Tree Protocol is not immediately evident from Figure 7-7, it becomes clear when the same network is redrawn as shown in Figure 7-8. As can be seen, the result is a tree structure with each switch (and attached devices) having one, and only one, path to every other switch and device.

While a spanning tree eliminates loops within the network and ensures that frames are delivered in order, it does not allow redundant links or paths. Disabled links carry no traffic and the active links are the only links allowed to carry frames. This has the potential to create excessive congestion on the active links and the subsequent poor performance.

7.2.5 Per-VLAN Spanning Tree Protocol (PVST)

The basic Spanning Tree Protocol creates a single spanning tree for the entire Ethernet network. When VLANs are being used, it may be more efficient to create separate spanning trees for each VLAN. This may reduce the congestion on inter-switch links and provide better performance.

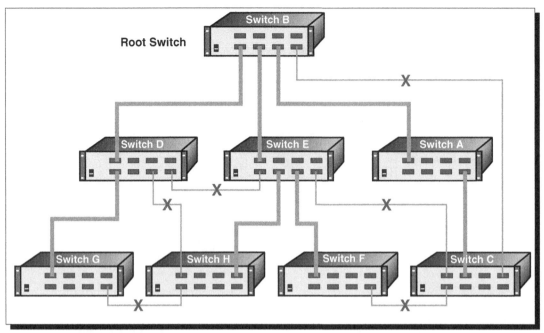

Figure 7-8. Ethernet Spanning Tree (Redrawn)

7.3 Ethernet Physical Link Variants

Like Fibre Channel, Ethernet supports multiple speeds and transmission mediums. Each variant is identified using a nomenclature consisting of the speed, signaling type and cable type. For example,100BASE-T is 100 megabit baseband signaling over unshielded twisted pair cabling. 1000BASE-T is 1,000 megabit (1 gigabit) baseband signaling over unshielded twisted pair cabling.

Table 7-3 on page 79 summarizes some of the different physical link variants that have been defined for 100 megabit, 1 gigabit and 10 gigabit Ethernet (Note that many of the defined physical variants have not been widely used and are not listed in the table). It is also interesting to note that there are 10 gigabit variants that use multiple lanes to provide the required bandwidth (e.g., 10 GBASE-LX4 and 10 GBASE-CX4).

7.3.1 Ethernet Transceivers

The majority of 100 megabit Ethernet devices use unshielded twisted pair (UTP) cabling and fixed transceivers. At the higher data rates, Ethernet devices may use pluggable transceiver modules. Pluggable transceivers are not specified by the Ethernet standards, but rather as Multi-Source Agreements (MSAs) developed by industry alliances.

Name	Standard	Description
100BASE-T		A term for any of the three standards for 100 Mbit/s Ethernet over twisted pair cable up to 100 meters long. Includes 100BASE-TX, 100BASE-T4 and 100BASE-T2. All of which use a star topology.
100BASE-TX	802.3 (24)	4B5B MLT-3 coded signaling, CAT5 unshielded twisted pair (UTP) copper cabling with two twisted pairs.
100BASE-FX	802.3 (24)	4B5B NRZI coded signaling, two strands of multi-mode optical fiber. Maximum length is 400 meters for half-duplex connections (to ensure collisions are detected) or 2 kilometers for full-duplex.
100BASE-SX	TIA	100 Mbit/s Ethernet over multi-mode optical fiber. Maximum length is 300 meters. Unlike 100BASE-FX that uses a laser as the light source, 100BASE-SX uses LEDs and is less expensive.
100BASE-BX10	802.3	100 Mbit/s Ethernet bidirectionally over a single strand of single-mode optical fiber. A multiplexer is used to split transmit and receive signals into different wavelengths allowing them to share the same fiber. Supports up to 10 km.
100BASE-LX10	802.3	100 Mbit/s Ethernet up to 10 km over a pair of single mode fibers.
1 Gigabit Ethernet		
1000BASE-T	802.3 (40)	PAM-5 coded signaling using CAT5/CAT5e/CAT6 unshielded twisted pair (UTP) copper cables with four bi-directional twisted pairs.
1000BASE-SX	802.3	8B10B NRZ coded signaling, multi-mode fiber (up to 550 m).
1000BASE-LX	802.3	8B10B NRZ coded signaling, multi-mode fiber (up to 550 m) or single-mode fiber (up to 2 km; can be optimized for longer distances, up to 10 km).
1000BASE-LH	multi-vendor	A long-haul solution using 8B10B NRZ coded signaling over single-mode fiber (up to 100 km).
1000BASE-CX	802.3	8B10B NRZ coded signaling, balanced shielded twisted pair (up to 25 m) over special copper cable. Predates 1000BASE-T and rarely used.
1000BASE-BX10	802.3	Up to 10km. Bidirectional over single strand of single-mode fiber.
1000BASE-LX10	802.3	Up to 10 km over a pair of single-mode fibers.
1000BASE-PX10-D	802.3	Downstream (from head-end to tail-ends) over single-mode fiber using point-to-multipoint topology (supports at least 10 km).
1000BASE-PX10-U	802.3	Upstream (from a tail-end to the head-end) over single-mode fiber using point-to-multipoint topology (supports at least 10 km).
1000BASE-PX20-D	802.3	Downstream (from head-end to tail-ends) over single-mode fiber using point-to-multipoint topology (supports at least 20 km).
1000BASE-PX20-U	802.3	Upstream (from a tail-end to the head-end) over single-mode fiber using point-to-multipoint topology (supports at least 20 km).

Table 7-3. Ethernet Physical Link Variants (Part 1 of 2)

Name	Standard	Description
1000BASE-ZX	Unknown	Up to 100 km over single-mode fiber.[1]
10 Gigabit Ethernet		
10GBASE-SR	802.3ae	Designed to support short distances over deployed multi-mode fiber cabling, it has a range of between 26 m and 82 m depending on cable type. It also supports 300 m operation over a new 2000 MHz.km multi-mode fiber.
10GBASE-LX4	802.3ae	Uses wavelength division multiplexing to support ranges of between 240 m and 300 m over deployed multi-mode cabling. Also supports 10 km over single-mode fiber.
10GBASE-LR	802.3ae	Supports 10 km over single-mode fiber
10GBASE-ER	802.3ae	Supports 40 km over single-mode fiber
10GBASE-SW	802.3ae	A variation of 10 GBASE-SR using the WAN PHY, designed to interoperate with OC-192 / STM-64 SONET/SDH equipment
10GBASE-LW	802.3ae	A variation of 10 GBASE-LR using the WAN PHY, designed to interoperate with OC-192 / STM-64 SONET/SDH equipment
10GBASE-EW	802.3ae	A variation of 10 GBASE-ER using the WAN PHY, designed to interoperate with OC-192 / STM-64 SONET/SDH equipment
10GBASE-CX4	802.3ak	Designed to support short distances over copper cabling, it uses InfiniBand 4x connectors and CX4 cabling and allows a cable length of up to 15 m.
10GSFP+CU 10GBASE-CU		Non-standard designations for the Direct Attach Cable (see *Ethernet Direct Attach Cable* on page 83). Distance anticipated to be up to 10 meters.
10GBASE-T	802.3an	Uses unshielded twisted-pair wiring.
10GBASE-LRM	draft 802.3aq	Extend to 220 meters over deployed 500 MHz.km multimode fiber
40GBASE-?	tbd	40 Gigabit Ethernet (to be defined)
100GBASE-?	tbd	100 Gigabit Ethernet (to be defined)

Table 7-3. Ethernet Physical Link Variants (Part 2 of 2)

XENPAK. XENPAK is a 10 Gbps Ethernet (10GbE) transceiver that incorporates the complete transmit and receive physical layer functionality from the 10.3 Gbps optical interface to the XAUI (4 lanes at 3.125 Gbps) electrical interface, including 8B/10B and 64B/66B coding.

An illustration of the XENPAK module is shown in Figure 7-9.

XPAK. XPAK is a second generation, hot pluggable, 10 Gbps optical module designed for Enterprise and SAN applications. It addresses need for smaller footprint, top side pluggable module using the industry standard, proven XAUI interface. The electrical interface is identical to 70 pin XENPAK 2.1 interface.

Figure 7-9. XENPAK Transceiver Module

An illustration of the XPAK module is shown in Figure 7-10.

XPAK features a bezel opening of1.54" by 0.506" and extends 2.685" behind the bezel. Unlike the XENPAK, which requires a cutout in the PC board, XPAK features single side mounting and allows 10 units across on a line card or can be stacked for 20 on a line card.

XPAK features 4 watts power dissipation with internal SERDES, supports uncooled laser applications up to 10 km today. It supports serial 850 nm (multi-mode) and 1310nm (single-mode) fiber with plans to include 1550nm in the future.

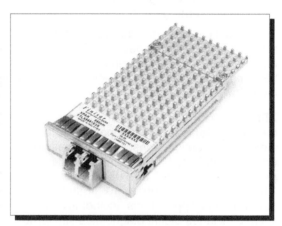

Figure 7-10. XPAK Transceiver Module

X2. "X2" is a multi-source agreement (MSA) supported by leading networking component suppliers. X2 defines a smaller form-factor 10 Gbps pluggable fiber optic transceiver optimized for 802.3ae Ethernet, ANSI/ITUT OC192/STM- 64 SONET/SDH interfaces, ITUT G.709, OIF OC192 VSR, INCITS/ANSI 10GFC (10 Gigabit Fibre Channel) and other 10 Gigabit applications. An illustration of the X2 module is shown in Figure 7-11.

X2 is initially focused on optical links to 10 kilometers and is ideally suited for Ethernet, Fibre Channel and telecommunication switches and standard PCI (peripheral component interconnect) based server and storage connections, where a "half size" XENPAK optical transceiver is desired.

X2 is physically smaller than XENPAK but maintains the mature electrical I/O specification defined by the XENPAK MSA and continues to provide robust thermal performance and electromagnetic shielding. Electrically, X2 is compatible with the XENPAK MSA. X2 uses the same Tyco Electronics-designed, 70-pin electrical connector as XENPAK supporting four wire XAUI (10-gigabit attachment unit interface). X2 also will support the OIF SFI4_P2 interfaces and serial electrical interfaces as they emerge.

Figure 7-11. X2 Transceiver Module

The X2 optical platform has been designed so that the heat sink and front bezel can be easily adapted to the different needs of the key 10 Gb markets. X2 can be mounted on the front panel, mid board, or in a conventional PCI card. X2's flexibility to address a wide range of high-bandwidth applications is expected to drive higher volumes on this one platform, thereby leading to lower optics costs.

XFP. The XFP (10 Gigabit Small Form Factor Pluggable) is a hot-swappable, protocol-independent optical transceiver, typically operating at 850nm, 1310nm or 1550nm, for 10 gigabit per second SONET/SDH, Fibre Channel, gigabit Ethernet, 10 gigabit Ethernet and other applications, including DWDM links. It includes digital diagnostics similar to SFF-8472, but more extensive, that provide a robust management tool. An illustration of the XFP module is shown in Figure 7-12.

The XFI electrical interface specification is a portion of the XFP Multi Source Agreement specification and uses a single lane operating at 10.3125 Gbps when using 64B/66B encoding.

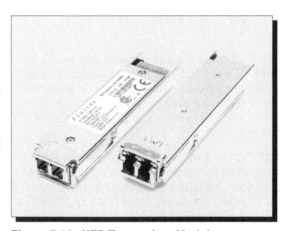

Figure 7-12. XFP Transceiver Module

SFP+ Module. The SFP+ is an enhanced version of the familiar SFP package that is used by gigabit Ethernet and 1, 2, and 4 gigabit Fibre Channel products. An illustration of the SFP+ module is shown in Figure 7-13.

The SFP+ module is 30% smaller than the XFP transceiver. This is achieved by moving the signal conditioning function from the module to the host card along with the serializer/deserializer (SerDes), clock and data recovery (CDR), electronic dispersion correction (EDC) and MAC functions. Benefits of the SFP+ include higher port density, lower power modules, and lower system costs through better integration of IC functions at the host card level.

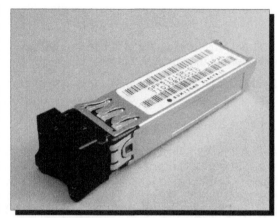

Figure 7-13. SFP+ Transceiver Module

Currently available SFP+ modules support the 10GBASE-SR, 10GBASE-LR, and 10GBASE-LRM physical link variants.

Ethernet Direct Attach Cable. The Ethernet Direct Attach Cable is an electrical cable with integrated SFP+ form factor connectors. This variant is referred to as 10GSFP+CU or 10GBASE-CU. An illustration of the Direct Attach Cable is shown in Figure 7-14.

Direct Attach Cables are available in lengths from one meter to ten meters.

7.3.2 Ethernet Link Initialization

Ethernet devices exchange capability information following power-on, reset or renegotiation. This enables the devices to identify a common set of operational parameters based on the devices' capabilities. The manner in which this information is exchange depends on the physical link technology (i.e, optical links signal capabilities in a different manner than do copper links).

Figure 7-14. Direct Attach Cable

7.4 Virtual LANs (VLANs)

A Virtual LAN (VLAN) is a way to provide segmentation of an Ethernet network. A VLAN consists of a set of stations that communicate as if they were attached to the same wire even though the stations may be connected to different switches or segments of the network. Devices within a VLAN can only communicate with other devices in the same VLAN. This constraint is enforced by the Ethernet switches.

A VLAN limits the scope of broadcast traffic. Frames are forwarded and flooded only to other members of the same VLAN.

Each VLAN may run a separate instance of the Spanning Tree Protocol by using the Per VLAN Spanning Tree (PVST) protocol (see *Per-VLAN Spanning Tree Protocol (PVST)* on page 77).

7.4.1 VLAN Tagging

A VLAN is identified using the VLAN Tag specified by Ethernet standard 802.1Q (see reference 32 in the Bibliography on page 290) that defines an optional 4-byte tag for Ethernet frames. The VLAN tag has a 3-bit field to specify a priority (or, traffic class) and a 12-bit field to identify a VLAN. These two fields can be used independently of one another (e.g., you can have priority without using VLANs or vice-versa).

When present, the 802.1Q tag follows the source MAC address as shown in Figure 7-15.

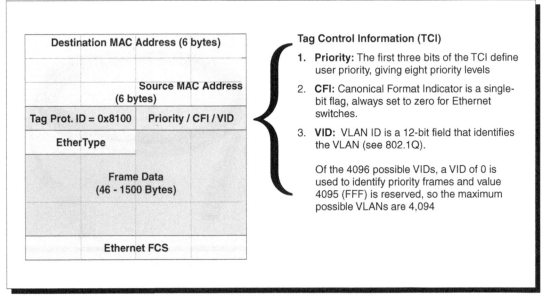

Figure 7-15. Ethernet Frame with 802.1Q VLAN Tag

7.4.2 Static and Dynamic VLANs

Static VLANs are created by assigning switch ports to a VLAN. When a device is connected to the switch port it becomes part of the associated VLAN. If the device is moved to a different switch port, it may become part of a different VLAN. The device itself probably has no awareness of the VLAN assignment and the Ethernet switch will insert or remove the VLAN Tag as appropriate.

Chapter 7. Ethernet Essentials

Dynamic VLANs are created by assigning devices to a VLAN based on their MAC address or a username entered during a login. As the device enters the network, it queries a database for VLAN membership using the VLAN Query Protocol (VQP). The query goes to the VLAN Membership Policy Server (VMPS) that informs the device of its VLAN membership. If the device is moved to a different switch port, it retains its VLAN membership.

7.5 Making Ethernet "Lossless"

Storage requires "reliable" information delivery. Reliable delivery consists of two aspects, the transmission Bit Error Rate (BER) and frame loss.

7.5.1 Transmission Reliability (Bit Error Rate)

Many Ethernet physical links provide bit error rates comparable to Fibre Channel. The Bit Error Rate (BER) objective for both 1 Gb and 10 Gb Ethernet is the same objective as for Fibre Channel (10^{-12}).

Some Ethernet links may have higher bit error rates and they are not be suitable for FCoE traffic. This may occur because the Ethernet cable plant may be more variable than a Fibre Channel cable plant or Ethernet frames may be sent vial links that inherently have a higher bit error rate (such a wireless links).

The bit error rate of the links need to be taken into consideration for FCoE planning to ensure that the required level of transmission reliability is provided.

7.5.2 Fibre Channel Flow Control

Fibre Channel uses a "credit-based" flow control method. Credit is permission given by a receiver to a sender giving the sender permission to send a specified number of frames. The amount of credit given is a reflection of the buffers that are available to receive frames.

When a frame is sent, the available credit is decremented (a receiver's buffer has been used). When the frame has been processed, and the recipient is ready for another frame, a credit reply is sent to replenish the credit. As long as a sender has credit available, it may send another frame (which of course causes the available credit to be decremented). A model of Fibre Channel's credit-based flow control is shown in Figure 7-16.

Fibre Channel provides two levels of flow control, a link-level mechanism called Buffer-to-Buffer flow control and a source to destination mechanism called End-to-End flow control. Both are based on a credit mechanism. The scope of each method is shown in Figure 7-17 on page 86.

Buffer-to-Buffer flow control controls the flow of frames on an individual link. Every Fibre Channel link is subject to link-level flow control. Buffer-to-Buffer credit is established using login parameters during Fabric Login (FLOGI) in a Fabric environment and N_Port Login (PLOGI) is a point-to-point environment. The response that replenishes Buffer-to-Buffer credit is the Receiver Ready (R_RDY) Ordered Set.

End-to-End credit manages the flow of frames between a given source and destination port pair and is only used by some Fibre Channel classes of service (consequently, it may not be

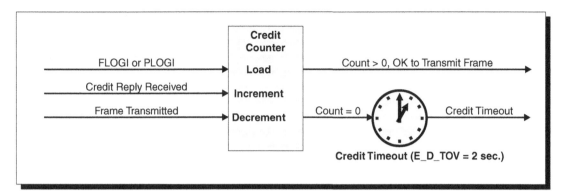

Figure 7-16. Credit-Based Flow Control

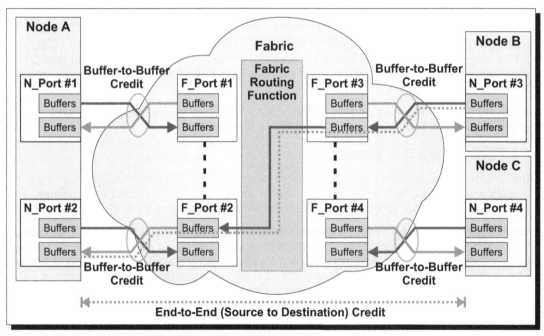

Figure 7-17. Fibre Channel Flow Control Models

used in all application environments). End-to-End credit is replenished by Fibre Channel Link Control frames such as ACK and BSY.

7.5.3 Frame Loss and Ethernet Flow Control

Ethernet defines an optional "pause" based flow control described in IEEE 802.3 Annex 31B. In the pause flow control, the receiver tells the sender when to pause or resume frame transmission (done in hardware, not software). The receiver must send the pause while there is

---

enough buffer space to accommodate frames in transit plus the time for the pause frame to be received and processed. An example of this method is shown in Figure 7-18 on page 87

While pause is part of the Ethernet standard, it is an optional feature and may not be implemented by all devices. This function, or an equivalent or enhanced flow control function is required by FCoE to prevent frame loss due to buffer overrun conditions.

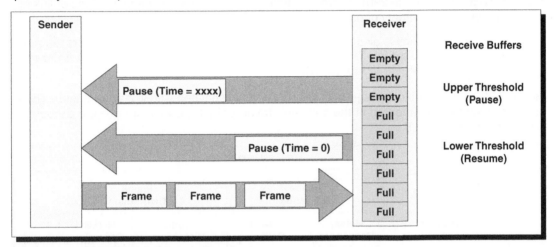

Figure 7-18. Ethernet Pause Flow Control

7.5.4 Pause Frame Format

Pause is a MAC Control frame that is created and processed by the Ethernet MAC layer, and not the software driver. MAC Control frames are identified by an EtherType value of 8808h. The format of the pause frame is shown in Figure 7-19.

The Pause frame uses a MAC Control Op-Code of 0001h to identify this as a Pause.

The Destination Address (DA) is set to a specified group address to prevent the frame from being forwarded beyond this physical link.

The Source Address is set to the NIC card's unicast address.

Destination MAC Address (01:80:C2:00:00:01)	
Source MAC Address	
EtherType = 0x8808	OpCode = 0x0001
Pause_time	Pad = 0x0000
Pad = 42 bytes of 0x00	
Ethernet FCS	

Figure 7-19. Pause Frame Format

The Pause function has a single parameter, the pause_time. The Pause_time is specified as 512-bit increments on the associated physical link. This provides a Pause_time range of 0 to 33.6 msec. on a 1 gigabit link. A Pause_time value of zero means resume transmission.

7.6 Link Aggregation (NIC Teaming)

Link aggregation is an optional capability that enables multiple Ethernet ports (MACs) to be "aggregated" and treated as if they were a single, higher-speed port. Link aggregation was defined by the 802.3ad task force and standardized in clause 43 of IEEE 802.3 (see reference 33 in the Bibliography on page 290). There are also many proprietary implementations of link aggregation that go by a variety of names.

> NOTE – Link aggregation is also known as: NIC Teaming, Ethernet trunking, port teaming, "EtherChannel", "Multi-Link Trunking (MLT)", "NIC bonding", "Network Fault Tolerance (NFT)" and "link aggregate group" (LAG).

Figure 7-20 contains a block diagram of the functions associated with link aggregation. These functions may be implemented in the software driver, or by hardware or firmware associated with an adapter or switch.

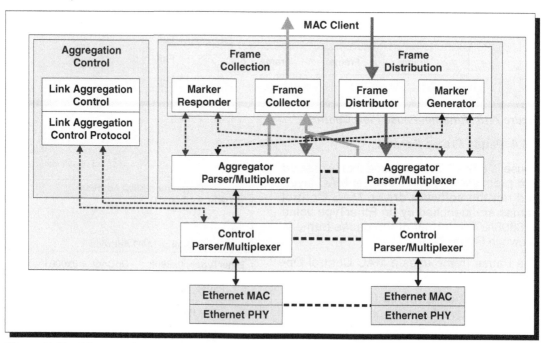

Figure 7-20. Ethernet Link Aggregation

Link aggregation is transparent to the MAC client and appears as a normal MAC function to the client. Each Ethernet MAC has a normal MAC address that is used as the source address for transmitted unicast frames and the destination address of received unicast frames. The Aggregation function is also assigned an Ethernet MAC address which is the address seen by the MAC client (this MAC address may be a unique MAC address, or the address of one of the aggregated MACs). The MAC client does not directly see the MAC addresses of the individual

---

Ethernet MACs. MACs that are to be aggregated must operate at the same speed and need to support full-duplex operation.

Frames to be transmitted are sent by the MAC client to the frame distribution function. The frame distribution function distributes frames to the appropriate Ethernet MAC. To provide in-order frame delivery, frames associated with a given "conversation" are distributed to a specific Ethernet MAC. Frames associated with other conversations may be distributed to other MACs associated with the aggregation function. The standard does not define the algorithm to be used by the distributor, it only requires that the distributor operate in a manner to provide in-order frame delivery and prevent frame duplication. With proper attention to the in-order delivery requirements, conversations may be moved from one MAC to another within the aggregation group to provide load balancing or rerouting of traffic around failed links or MACs.

NOTE – If dissimilar NICs are aggregated (e.g., one provides TCP off load and another doesn't) performance may vary depending on which NIC is being used for a particular conversation.

NOTE – Link aggregation may apply to LAN traffic on a Converged Network Adapter, but may not apply to storage traffic using the FCoE protocol. This is due to the fact that most CNAs provide separate driver interfaces for LAN traffic and FCoE traffic.

When a frame is received by one of the MACs, it is forwarded to the frame collector for delivery to the MAC client. While frames from different conversations may be interleaved by the collector, frames within a conversation are delivered to the MAC client in order.

7.6.1 Link Aggregation Control Protocol (LACP)

In 802.3ad, the Link Aggregation Control Protocol is used to automatically inform the switch of the ports that are to be aggregated. This is done between an end device and a switch, or between two switches using Link Aggregation Protocol Data Units sent to MAC address 01-80-C2-00-00-02, one of the addresses not forwarded by a switch (see Table 7-1 on page 72). The Link Aggregation Protocol can alleviate the need for manual configuration of the devices.

7.7 Chapter Summary

Why Ethernet?

- Ethernet is the dominant local area network (LAN) technology and has enjoyed a huge success in all segments of the LAN marketplace
  - There are multiple reasons for this success:
  - Ethernet is inexpensive
  - Ethernet uses simple hardware
  - Ethernet uses low-cost electrical cables, or, optical cables for high-speed and longer distances
  - Ethernet has a simple frame structure and link-level protocols
  - Ethernet can transport information associated with a wide variety of protocols. TCP/IP is one of the most common protocols.

Open Systems Interconnect (OSI) Model

- OSI defines a seven-layer model for networking
- Ethernet is a Layer-2 (data link) network
- Fibre Channel is also basically a Layer-2 network
  - Although it incorporates some functions usually associated with Layer-4

"Lossless" Ethernet

- The converged network is based on an enhanced version of Ethernet
  - Designed to provide attributes required in a data center environment
- "Lossless" Ethernet provides:
  - Reliable, "loss-less" frame delivery
  - Full-duplex operation
  - In-order frame delivery
- For performance reasons,
  - High bandwidth, and
  - Low-latency frame delivery are desirable

Ethernet Frame Format

- Ethernet uses a very simple frame format
  - Minimizes the hardware complexity and cost while providing the utmost in flexibility
- An Ethernet frame begins with a Start-of-Frame (SOF) and ends with an End-of-Frame (EOF)
  - The delimiters are not considered to be part of the frame
  - The composition of the delimiters depends on the physical link that is being used.
- An Ethernet frame contains two address fields:
  - The Destination Address (DA) specifies the destination of the frame
  - The Source Address (SA) identifies the source of the frame

EtherType

- EtherType field has two different interpretations
  - If the value in the EtherType field is less than 1500, it specifies the length of the frame
  - If the EtherType field is more than 1536, it identifies the protocol carried within the frame
  - Using the EtherType field to identify the protocol is the more common usage of the field.
- For FCoE:
  - FCoE Encapsulation Protocol is 8906h
  - FCoE Initialization Protocol is 8914h

Frame Check Sequence (FCS)

- The Frame Check Sequence (FCS) is a 32-bit cyclic redundancy check (CRC) computed on the frame content
  - Computation begins with the Destination Address
- The algorithm is based on the same polynomial as used by Fibre Channel

MAC Address Format

- Each Ethernet adapter has an Ethernet address
  - Commonly referred to as the Media Access Control, or MAC address
- The MAC address is usually personalized at the time of manufacture
  - Often called the "burned-in" MAC address
- An Ethernet MAC address is 48 bits long
- *See: Figure 7-3 on page 72*

Organization Unique Identifier (OUI)

- An Organizationally Unique Identifier (OUI) is a 24-bit identifier
- Normally, an OUI is a value assigned to an organization by IEEE
  - IEEE registration ensures uniqueness among different organizations
  - An IEEE assigned OUI is referred to as a Universally Administered OUI
  - A list of IEEE assigned OUI values is available at:

    http://standards.ieee.org/regauth/oui/oui.txt

Organization Unique Identifier (OUI)

- An OUI may also be locally administered
  - This is indicated by setting bit 41 to a one
  - A locally administered OUI must be unique within a given Ethernet network, but may not be globally unique
- The combination of:
  - A Universally Administered 24-bit Organizationally Unique Identifier, and
  - The 24-bit device unique identifier results in a 48-bit globally unique identifier

Ethernet Jumbo Frames

- In many Ethernet implementations, each frame interrupts the driver
  - Reducing the number of interrupts can improve performance
- Some Ethernet devices support (non-standard) larger frame sizes referred to as "jumbo" frames
  - Jumbo frame may be up to 9 KB in size
- A 9 KB jumbo frame carries as much data as six standard-size Ethernet frames
  - The number of interrupts may be reduced by a factor of six with the resulting improvement in performance.
- While jumbo frames are not part of the Ethernet standard, they are widely supported by many Ethernet implementations

FCoE and "Baby" Jumbo Frames

- Jumbo frames also provide a solution to the transport of encapsulated Fibre Channel frames by FCoE
  - A standard Ethernet frame cannot contain a full-sized Fibre Channel frame
  - A "baby" jumbo frame of approximately 2.5 KB can
- Alternatively, FCoE can use normal Fibre Channel methods to establish a smaller frame size
  - Done during FLOGI and PLOGI with the "Receive Data Field size" parameter
  - This would enable encapsulated FC frames to fit within a standard Ethernet frame

Ethernet Configurations (Topologies)

- Ethernet supports multiple topology configurations and medium types
- Supported topology configurations include:
  - Shared-Medium multi-tap cable,
  - Hubs (also a Shared-Medium Topology),
  - Switched networks, and
  - Combinations of the above

Shared-Medium Topology

- Ethernet devices can connect to a shared "bus" consisting of a single coaxial cable
  - Devices tap into the cable or connect with a T
- By using a hub, this topology can also use unshielded twisted pair cabling
  - Unshielded twisted pair (UTP) is the most common electrical cable
- Devices in a shared-medium topology use the Carrier Sense Multiple Access/Collision Detect (CSMA/CD) access protocol

CSMA/CD Access Protocol

- When a device need to transmit a frame, it:
  - Listens for traffic (Carrier Sense)
  - If none, it transmits the frame and listens to the bus at the same time
  - If another device also transmits at the same time (Multiple Access), there is a "collision"
  - The collision is detected because the transmitted frame is corrupted (Collision Detect)
  - If a collision occurs, the device backs off and tries again later

CSMA/CD Protocol Limitations

- The shared-medium topology has been largely replaced by the switched topology
- Due to limitations inherent in this topology:
  - Transmission and reception use the same coaxial cable or unshielded twisted pair and only supports half-duplex operation
  - When a collision occurs, no useful information is transferred. This represents wasted bandwidth on the link.
  - As the level of activity increases, the number of collisions increase and throughput may be severely impacted.
  - Only one device can be transmitting at a time. This limits the overall throughput that a shared medium topology can provide

Ethernet Switched Topology

- The switched topology is based on the use of one or more Ethernet switches
  - In this topology, each device connects to a port on an Ethernet switch
  - Note that a shared-medium topology can also connect to a switch port
- Paths are established and loops prevented using a "Spanning Tree Protocol (STP)"
- See: Figure 7-5 on page 75

Ethernet Switched Topology

- Devices connected to a switch may still use the CSMA/CD access protocol
  - Each link is a separate collision domain
  - Collisions are eliminated along with the wasted bandwidth and the need to retransmit frames as the result of a collision.
- The links between devices and switch ports are usually full-duplex links
  - Full-duplex enables simultaneous frame transmission and reception
  - Full-duplex operation potentially doubles the available bandwidth compared to half-duplex
- All 1Gb and 10 Gb Ethernet are switched
  - Removes collisions and the need for the CSMA/CD protocol

Ethernet Switch Learning

- Ethernet switches have no control over the MAC addresses of attached devices
  - MAC addresses are normally assigned to an Ethernet NIC at the time of manufacture
  - An Ethernet switch has no control over which NIC is connected to which switch port
- Instead of controlling addressing, Ethernet switches learn the addresses of attached devices
- Each Ethernet switch has a filtering database that associates MAC addresses with switch ports

Ethernet Switch Learning

- When a switch receives a unicast frame, it looks at the Source Address (SA) in the received frame
- If the Source Address is not in its filtering database
- The switch associates the ingress port with the MAC address and enters the association into its filtering database
- *See: Figure 7-6 on page 76*

Ethernet Switch Forwarding Behavior

- When a switch receives a frame, it looks in its filtering database to see if it has an entry matching the Destination Address (DA)
- If the DA is in the filtering database:
  - The switch forwards the frame out the associated switch port
  - Because it had previously received a frame from that address on the switch port, it knows that address is reachable via that port
- If the DA is not in the filtering database:
  - the switch has no knowledge of the location of the destination
  - It forwards the frame out all of its other ports
  - This ensures that the frame will reach the destination, if it exists

Spanning Tree Protocol (STP)

- When a network has multiple switches, a protocol is needed to allow the switches to determine which path to use when forwarding a frame
- Ethernet switches use a Spanning Tree Protocol to:
  - Identify links to other switches
  - Prevent loops within the network and
  - Reroute traffic around failed inter-switch links, if possible
- When VLANs are used a separate spanning tree may be created for each VLAN
  - Using the Per-VLAN Spanning Tree (PVST) protocol
- PVST may help alleviate congestion and poor link utilization

Spanning Tree Limitations

- A spanning tree eliminates loops within the network and ensures that frames are delivered in order
- However, it may not make good use of redundant links
  - Disabled links carry no traffic and the active links are the only links allowed to carry frames
  - This may result in excessive congestion on the active links and poor performance.

Virtual LANs (VLANs)

- A Virtual LAN (VLAN) is a way to provide segmentation of an Ethernet network
  - A VLAN consists of a set of stations that communicate as if they were attached to the same wire
  - Even though the stations may be connected to different switches or segments of the network
- Devices within a VLAN can only communicate with other devices in the same VLAN
  - This is enforced by the Ethernet switches
- A VLAN limits the scope of broadcast traffic
  - Frames are forwarded and flooded only to other members of the same VLAN

VLAN Tagging

- A VLAN is identified using the VLAN Tag
  - Specified by Ethernet standard 802.1Q
  - VLAN tag is an optional 4-byte tag for Ethernet frames
- The VLAN tag has:
  - A 3-bit field to specify a priority (or, traffic class)
  - A 12-bit field to identify a VLAN
  - These two fields can be used independently of one another (e.g., you can have priority without using VLANs or vice-versa)
- When present, the 802.1Q tag follows the source MAC address
- *See: Figure 7-15 on page 84*

Static VLANs

- Static VLANs are created by assigning switch ports to a VLAN
  - When a device is connected to the switch port it becomes part of the associated VLAN
  - If the device is moved to a different switch port, it may become part of a different VLAN
  - The device itself probably has no awareness of the VLAN assignment
  - The Ethernet switch will insert or remove the VLAN Tag as appropriate

Dynamic VLANs

- Dynamic VLANs are created by assigning devices to a VLAN based on MAC address or a username entered during a login
  - As the device enters the network, it queries a database for VLAN membership using the VLAN Query Protocol (VQP)
  - The query goes to the VLAN Membership Policy Server (VMPS) that informs the device of its VLAN membership
- If the device is moved to a different switch port, it retains its VLAN membership.

Making Ethernet "Lossless"

- Storage requires "reliable" delivery
- Reliable delivery consists of two aspects:
- Bit Error Rate (BER)
  - Transmission errors can corrupt frames
  - Must provide an acceptable bit error rate to prevent frame corruption
  - Fibre Channel requires 10^{-12} minimum
- Frame Loss
  - Switches and devices must not discard frames
  - Flow control is necessary to prevent frame drop due to buffer conditions
- Note that this use of the term "reliable" is different from TCP. TCP uses the term reliable to mean "acknowledged"

Bit Error Rate Considerations

- Many Ethernet physical link bit error rates are comparable to Fibre Channel
  - Bit Error Rate (BER) objective for 1 Gb and 10 Gb Ethernet is the same as for Fibre Channel (10^{-12})
- Some Ethernet links may have higher rates
  - They are not suitable for FCoE traffic
  - Ethernet cable plant may be more variable
  - This needs to be taken into consideration for FCoE planning

Fibre Channel Flow Control

- On a Fibre Channel link, the receiving port gives the sending port permission to send a specified number of frames
- That permission is called credit
  - When a frame is sent, the available credit is decremented (consumed)
  - When a reply is received, the available credit is incremented (replenished)
  - As long as a port has available credit, it may send additional frames
  - If the credit is exhausted, frame transmission is suspended until the credit is replenished
- *See: Figure 7-16 on page 86 and Figure 7-17 on page 86*

Ethernet "Pause" Flow Control

- Ethernet defines an optional "pause" based flow control
  - Described in IEEE 802.3 Annex 31B
  - Receiver tells the sender when to pause or resume frame transmission (done in hardware, not software)
  - Receiver must send pause while there is enough buffer space to accommodate any frames in transit plus the time for the pause frame to be received and processed
- *See: Figure 7-18 on page 87 and*

Pause Frame Format

- Pause is a MAC Control frame
  - Created and processed by the Ethernet MAC layer
  - EtherType = 0x8808
  - MAC Control OpCode = 0x0001
- Sent to a specified group address
- Source address is the source's unicast address
- Pause has a single parameter, the pause_time
  - Time is specified as 512-bit increments
  - Provides a range of 0 to 33.6 msec. on a 1 gigabit link
  - Value of zero means resume transmission
- *See: Figure 7-19 on page 87*

Link Aggregation

- Link aggregation is an optional capability that enables multiple Ethernet ports (MACs) to be "aggregated" and treated as if they were a single, higher-speed port
  - Link aggregation was defined by the 802.3ad task force and standardized in clause 43 of IEEE 802.3
- There are many proprietary implementations of link aggregation that go by a variety of names

Link Aggregation

- Link aggregation is transparent to the client and appears as a normal MAC to the client
- Each Ethernet MAC has a normal MAC address
  - Used as the source address for transmitted unicast frames and the destination address of received unicast frames
- The Aggregation function is also assigned an Ethernet MAC address
  - This is the address seen by the MAC client
  - This MAC address may be a unique MAC address, or the address of one of the aggregated MACs
- The MAC client does not directly see the MAC addresses of the individual Ethernet MACs
- MACs that are to be aggregated must operate at the same speed and support full-duplex operation

Frame Distribution Function

- Frames to be transmitted are sent by the MAC client to the frame distribution function
- The frame distribution function distributes frames to the appropriate Ethernet MAC
  - To provide in order frame delivery, frames associated with a given "conversation" are distributed to a specific Ethernet MAC
  - Frames associated with other conversations may be distributed to other MACs associated with the aggregation function
  - The standard does not define the algorithm to be used by the distributor
  - Conversations may be moved from one MAC to another within the aggregation group with attention to in-order delivery requirements

Frame Reception

- When a frame is received by one of the MACs:
  - It is forwarded to the frame collector for delivery to the MAC client
  - Frames from different conversations may be interleaved by the collector
  - Frames within a conversation are delivered to the MAC client in order

Link Aggregation Protocol

- In 802.3ad, the Link Aggregation Protocol is used to automatically inform the switch of the ports that are to be aggregated.
  - This is done between an end device and a switch, or between two switches
- Uses the Link Aggregation Protocol Data Units sent to MAC address 01-80-C2-00-00-02
  - One of the addresses not forwarded by a switch
- The Link Aggregation Protocol can alleviate the need for manual configuration of the devices

8. Architecture Models

The FCoE standard uses architecture models to identify the various FCoE entities, their functions and attributes. While the architecture models do not necessarily represent an implementation, the provide a basis for ensuring that an implementation is consistent with the standard. The architecture models also define the terminology associated with the various entities.

8.1 FC Physical Links vs. FCoE Virtual Links

In a native Fibre Channel environment, a node port connects directly to another node port (point-to-point) or switch port (fabric) via a physical link as shown in Figure 8-1. The physical link can be either optical or electrical and operate at any of the link rates defined by the Fibre Channel standards. When a port transmits a frame, the frame travels down the link and is received by the port at the other end of that physical link (assuming there are no transmission errors). When a node port logs-in with the fabric, it can simply send the FLOGI request on the link and it will arrive at the attached switch port regardless of the addresses within the frame.

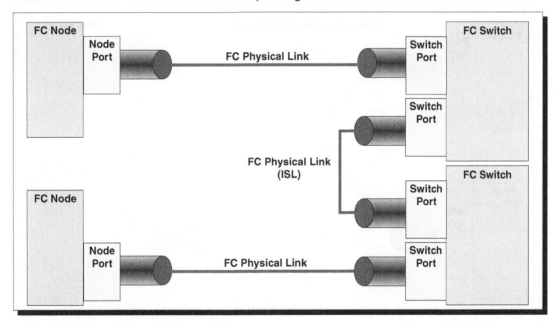

Figure 8-1. Fibre Channel Physical Links

Because the ports are directly attached via the link, each port is directly aware of the state of the link. If the link fails, or is disconnected, both ports detect the link failure and can take the appropriate actions. For example, if the link between a node port and switch port fails, the fab-

---

ric implicitly logs-out the node port and removes any associated entries from the Name Server database.

8.1.1 FCoE Virtual Links

In an FCoE environment, an FCoE node port may connect to another FCoE node port or FCoE switch port through an intervening "lossless" Ethernet network as shown in Figure 8-2 on page 98. This results in a fundamental difference between a native Fibre Channel environment and an FCoE environment.

In a native Fibre Channel environment all links are direct physical point-to-point links; in an FCoE environment the path between a node port and switch port (or two switch ports) might consist of multiple Ethernet physical links and intervening Ethernet switches. In order to map this fundamental difference into the Fibre Channel architecture, FCoE defines the concept of a "virtual link" that represents the path between a node port and switch port (or two switch ports). An FCoE virtual link might correspond to a single Ethernet physical link that connects a node port MAC directly to an FCoE switch port MAC or to a logical path between a pair of Ethernet MACs communicating via a "lossless" Ethernet network.

NOTE – A virtual link can be viewed as a "tunnel" through the Lossless Ethernet Network that is used to carry encapsulated Fibre Channel frames from the source MAC to the destination MAC.

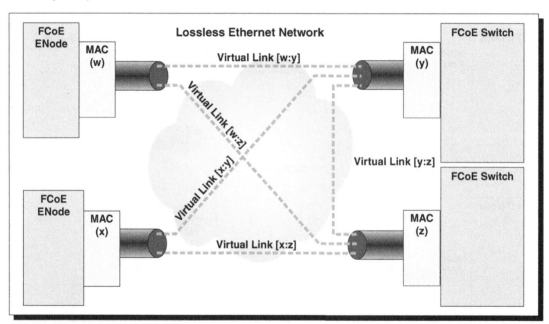

Figure 8-2. FCoE Virtual Links

Fibre Channel physical links always provide a one-to-one relationship between the ports. One node port connects to one switch port (or one switch port connects to one other switch port). In FCoE, Ethernet introduces the potential for one-to-many relationships between the physical ports. One Ethernet MAC might communicate with many other Ethernet MACs. Each of these relationships represents a separate virtual link (through the same Ethernet MAC).

The virtual link is identified by the combination of the local MAC address and a remote MAC address. In the example shown in Figure 8-2 on page 98, five virtual links are shown: [w:y], [w:z], [x:y], [x:z] and [y:z].

8.2 FCoE Link Endpoint (FCoE_LEP)

At each end of an FCoE virtual link is an FCoE Link Endpoint (FCoE_LEP) as shown in Figure 8-3 on page 99. The FCoE Link Endpoint is the entity that performs encapsulation and decapsulation of Fibre Channel frames and sends or receives the resulting Ethernet frames over a single virtual link.

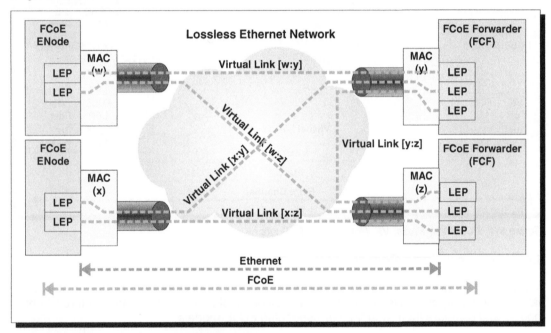

Figure 8-3. FCoE Link End Point (FCoE_LEP)

The FCoE_LEP exists at the boundary between the Fibre Channel environment and the encapsulated FCoE Ethernet environment. Between the two Link Endpoints associated with a virtual link, Fibre Channel frames are encapsulated and transported within Ethernet frames. Outside of this boundary, processing is based on the decapsulated Fibre Channel frames and follows the normal behaviors defined by the Fibre Channel standards, both for node ports and switch ports.

8.3 FCoE VN_Ports, VF_Ports and VE_Ports

A VN_Port, VF_Port or VE_Port can be associated with each FCoE Link Endpoint (FCoE_LEP). FCoE_LEPs in an ENode only support VN_Ports, FCoE_LEPs in an FCF can support VF_Ports and/or VE_Ports as shown in Figure 8-4 on page 100.

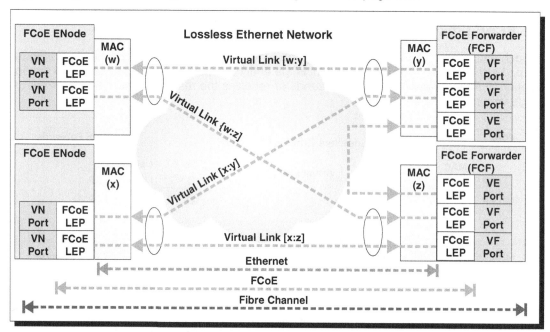

Figure 8-4. FCoE VN_Ports, VF_Ports and VE_Ports

8.4 Node and Node Port Models

To provide a foundation for defining the behavior of node ports and switch ports, the standards have defined a set of architectural models. It may be helpful to review the native Fibre Channel models and compare them with the corresponding FCoE models.

8.4.1 Fibre Channel N_Port Model

Figure 8-5 on page 101 shows the structure of the architectural model for a native Fibre Channel node and node port. Observe that this model separates the node port into two parts, the physical node port (PN_Port) and a virtual node port (VN_Port) instantiated upon the physical port (this change in the node port structure was incorporated into FC-FS-3 and related standards, partly to provide a model for N_Port_ID Virtualization, NPIV).

The basic structure of Fibre Channel is based on the following architecture levels:

- **Node:** A Node is an entity that controls one or more Node Ports. Commonly, the node corresponds to the driver or software that controls a node port (or ports).

Chapter 8. Architecture Models

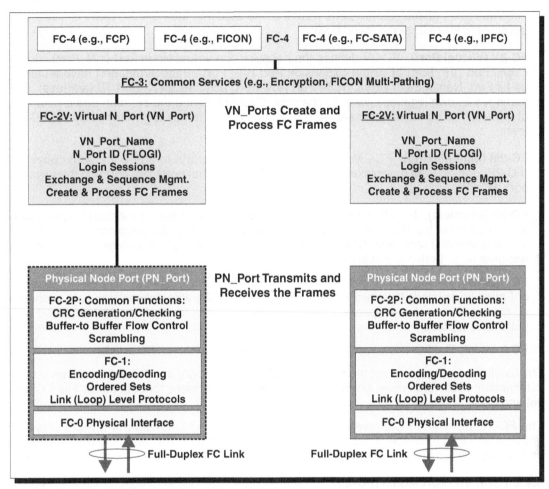

Figure 8-5. Fibre Channel Node and Node Port Model

- **FC-4 Level:** The FC-4 protocol mapping level in the Fibre Channel structure defines how various protocols are mapped to Fibre Channel. The FC-4 defines the content and structure of the information units (IUs) and how that particular protocol uses the various capabilities and functions of the Fibre Channel interface.

- **FC-3 Level:** The FC-3 level provides a level for the implementation of (optional) common functions, that is functions the might span multiple node ports or protocols, or perform some kind of transformation of information units before transmission or upon receptions.

- **FC-2 Level:** The FC-2 level manages the delivery of the information units defined by an FC-4 protocol mapping or Fibre Channel defined protocol. The FC-2 functionality is divided into three sublevels (these sub-divisions were incorporated into the FC-FS-3 and FC-SW-5 versions of the Fibre Channel standards):

FC-2V (Virtual Port). FC-2V defines the behavior of a virtual Node Port (VN_Port), virtual Fabric Port (VF_Port) or virtual Expansion Port (VE_Port). Each virtual port have a unique 64-bit Port_Name. Each virtual Node Port (VN_Port) acquires an N_Port_ID (address), and manages its own login sessions, Exchanges, Sequences and the creation and processing of frames. The actual transmission and reception of the frames is performed by the FC-2P level.

FC-2M (Multiplexing). FC-2M enables multiple virtual ports to share the same physical (FC-2P) port. FC-2M multiplexes frames between the virtual ports (FC-2V) and the physical port (FC-2P)

FC-2P (Physical). FC-2P defines the functions associated with the actual transmission and reception of frames on the underlying physical link. It includes functions such as frame transmission and reception, CRC generation and checking, optional frame scrambling and link-level (e.g., Buffer-to-Buffer) flow control.

- **FC-1 Level:** The FC-1 level defines the Ordered Sets that identify the Start-of-Frame, End-of-Frame and provide link-level signaling and control. FC-1 also defines how data is encoded for transmission via a specific physical link and the link-level protocols associated with that link or topology.

- **FC-0 Level:** The FC-0 level specifies the characteristics of the physical link.

The functions and behaviors of the Node, the FC-4, FC-3, FC-2V and FC-2M levels are largely independent of the underlying physical interface and are the same for both native Fibre Channel and FCoE.

The FC-2P, FC-1 and FC-0 levels specify the functions and behaviors of a Fibre Channel physical port and interface. These functions are replaced by FCoE and Ethernet behaviors and functions in an FCoE environment.

8.4.2 FCoE VN_Port Model (FC-2V)

Figure 8-6 on page 103 shows the architectural model for an FCoE Node with two FCoE_LEPs and two VN_Ports. While both FCoE_LEPs and VN_Ports are associated with the same physical Ethernet MAC, they appear as two separate VN_Ports connected to two separate ("virtual") links. This is somewhat analogous to a dual-ported HBA in native Fibre Channel, but of course with a single physical Ethernet MAC and cable in FCoE.

Each VN_Port has a 24-bit Fibre Channel address and a unique 64-bit VN_Port_Name, just as each Fibre Channel VN_Port has a 24-bit address and a unique 64-bit Port_Name. Each VN_Port conforms to all of the behaviors associated with a standard VN_Port as specified in the Fibre Channel Framing and Signaling (FC-FS-3) standard.

Each VN_Port is associated with an FCoE Link Endpoint (FCoE_LEP). That is, the VN_Port exists at the end of an FCoE virtual link (just as a Fibre Channel PN_Port exists at the end of a

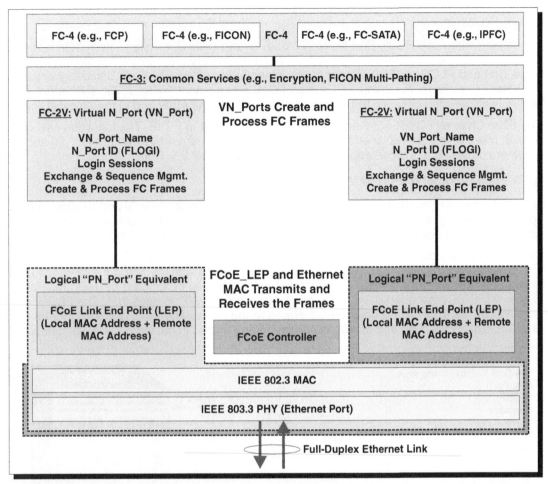

Figure 8-6. FCoE Node with Two FCoE_LEPs and VN_Ports

Fibre Channel physical link). An FCoE_LEP may be associated with multiple VN_Ports as will be seen shortly.

A VN_Port is dynamically created upon successful completion of a Fabric Login (FLOGI) or Fabric Discover (FDISC) Extended Link Service. This is somewhat different than native Fibre Channel where the PN_Port exists as a physical entity whether or not FLOGI or FDISC has been performed.

NOTE – In fact, the Fibre Channel standards define N_Port behavior and service parameters for an N_Port that has not completed FLOGI or FDISC, but no behavior is defined for an FCoE node port before it has completed FLOGI or FDISC (the port simply does not exist under these conditions).

NOTE – At the time of writing, the FCoE draft did not fully address the possibility of a point-to-point FCoE link. Whether this will be included in the final version of the standard remains to be seen.

Associated with each FCoE End Node (ENode) is an FCoE Controller. The function of the FCoE Controller is to perform Discovery (see *FCoE Discovery and Virtual Link Initialization* on page 121) and FLOGI or FDISC prior to the instantiation of the VN_Port. Discovery enables the ENode to discover reachable FCFs in an FCoE environment (in native Fibre Channel, discovery is not needed because the switch port is located at the other end of the physical link).

The Fibre Channel FC-2P, FC-1 and FC-0 levels do not exist in FCoE. The functions associated with these levels are replaced by the FCoE_LEP and Ethernet MAC and PHY (in a sense, these are providing a "logical" equivalent to the Fibre Channel PN_Port).

8.4.3 Fibre Channel N_Port ID Virtualization (NPIV)

N_Port ID virtualization is a Fibre Channel feature that enables a physical port to support multiple virtual node ports (VN_Ports). Each VN_Port is associated with a unique N_Port context and has all the appearances of being a separate N_Port to other ports in the fabric.

When N_Port ID virtualization is used, the node port performs a normal Fabric Login (FLOGI) to create the first VN_Port and exchange service parameters with the fabric. Once Fabric Login has been successfully completed, additional VN_Ports may be created by using the Fabric Discover (FDISC) extended link service as shown in Figure 8-7 on page 104. The FLOGI and each FDISC must provide a unique Port_Name to the fabric. The fabric will assign a unique address to each VN_Port and make the corresponding entries in the Name Server's database.

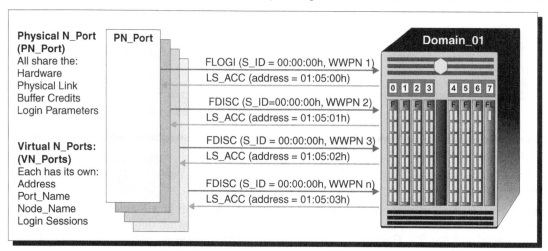

Figure 8-7. N_Port ID Virtualization (NPIV)

Because each VN_Port has its own unique address and Port_Name, each can is subject to its own access controls, zoning and security considerations.

A VN_Port may relinquish its address by performing a Logout (LOGO) with the fabric (the destination address is FF:FF:FEh. The logout specifies the address and Port_Name of the

VN_Port that is being removed. If all VN_Ports are removed, it is necessary for the node port to perform another FLOGI to create a new VN_Port and exchange service parameters with the fabric.

Because all of the virtual N_Ports share the same physical link and PN_Port hardware, link events can affect multiple VN_Ports.

- All of the VN_Ports on a link share the same buffer-to-buffer credit (BB_Credit). When one VN_Port sends a frame, the available BB_Credit for that link is decremented. When R_RDY is received, the available BB_Credit for that link is incremented. If the available BB_Credit is zero no frames can be sent by any VN_Port on that link.

- If a Link Reset occurs (LR/LRR), the available BB_Credit for that link is restored to the FLOGI values. In addition, frames may be discarded for any VN_Port associated with that link.

- If a Link Failure (NOS) or Link Initialization (OLS) occurs all VN_Ports associated with that link are implicitly logged-out from the fabric and it is necessary to re-login using FLO-GI and reestablish any VN_Ports using FDISC in order to continue.

8.4.4 Fibre Channel N_Port Model with NPIV

Fibre Channel defines a function called N_Port_ID Virtualization (NPIV). With NPIV, a single physical node port (PN_Port) can be associated with multiple VN_Ports.

The first VN_Port is created using the Fabric Login (FLOGI) Extended Link Service request. Additional VN_Ports may be created using the Fabric Discover (FDISC) Extended Link Service request. When an additional VN_Port is created using FDISC, a separate 64-bit unique Port_Name is provided in the request. When the Fabric accepts the FDISC request, it assigns an address to the newly created VN_Port and makes the appropriate entries in Name Server database associating the assigned address with the supplied Port_Name.

An illustration of a Fibre Channel physical node port with NPIV is shown in Figure 8-8 on page 106. While there is a single physical node port (the PN_Port), multiple virtual node ports (VN_Ports) are sharing use of the underlying PN_Port (each VN_Port has its own unique address, 64-bit Port_Name and its own login sessions and independent operations).

A VN_Port is created using FLOGI or NPIV FDISC and can be removed using the Logout (LOGO) Extended Link Service. If the physical link fails, or is reset or re-initialized, all VN_Ports associated with the PN_Port are implicitly logged-out from the fabric.

8.4.5 FCoE Virtual N_Port Model with NPIV

As in native Fibre Channel, NPIV can be used to create additional VN_Ports. Each physical Ethernet MAC can have more than one FCoE_LEP because it may be associated with more than one virtual link (each FCoE_LEP is associated with a separate VN_Port). While there is no direct equivalent to the virtual links and the FCoE_LEPs in native Fibre Channel, the behavior of each VN_Port is still consistent with the behavior of a normal Fibre Channel node port. This is shown in Figure 8-9 on page 107.

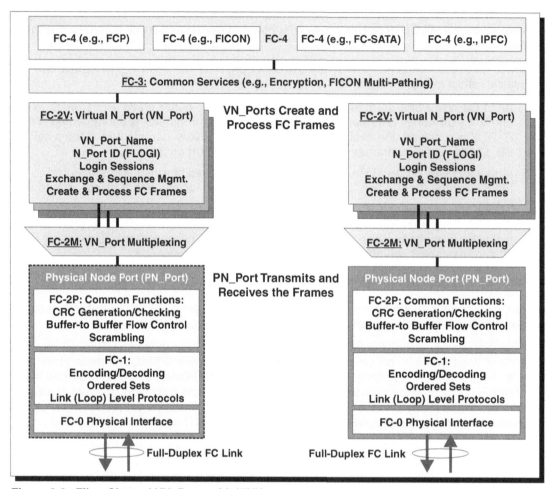

Figure 8-8. Fibre Channel VN_Ports with NPIV

8.5 Fabric and Fabric Port Models

A Fibre Channel Fabric consists of one, or more, interconnected Fibre Channel switches. The Fibre Channel standards do not dictate the number of switches within a Fabric, nor the number and type of interconnections between those switches (Due to addressing limitations, however, the standards do limit the maximum number of switches in a single Fabric to 239 maximum).

Within each Fabric, a switch is selected to manage the assignment of addresses to the other switches. This switch is referred to as the principal switch and the principal switch's name is used as the 64-bit name of the Fabric.

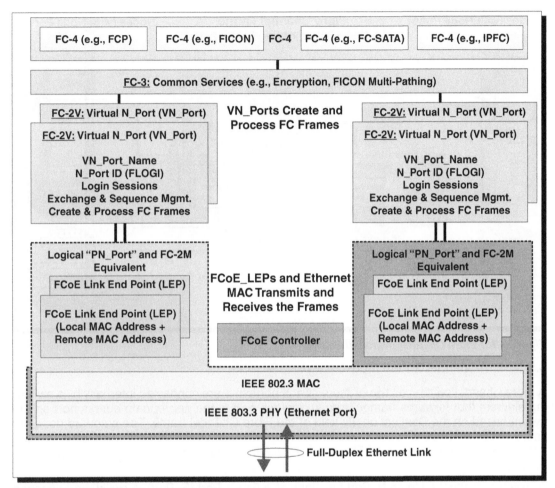

Figure 8-9. FCoE VN_Ports with NPIV

Nodes, with their node ports, connect to the Fabric (with its fabric ports) as shown in Figure 8-10 on page 108. Node ports login with the Fabric using the Fabric Login (FLOGI) Extended Link Service to establish a session with the Fabric and acquire an address from the Fabric.

The standards specify communications among the switches using a protocol called the Switch Internal Link Services (SW_ILS). Switch Internal Link services enable switches within a Fabric to perform link and Fabric initialization, select a principal switch, distribute path information, distribute zoning information and other operations needed within the Fabric.

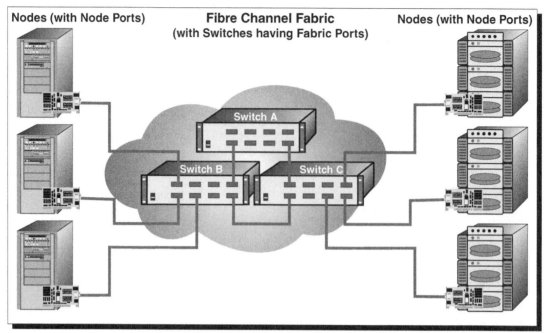

Nodes (with Node Ports)   **Fibre Channel Fabric**   Nodes (with Node Ports)
(with Switches having Fabric Ports)

Switch A

Switch B   Switch C

Figure 8-10. Fibre Channel Switched Fabric

8.5.1 Fibre Channel Switch Model

A Fibre Channel switch has two or more switch ports that are connected internally by a switching element that forwards frames from an ingress port to the appropriate egress port on the switch based on the Destination_ID field of the Fibre Channel frame. The standard does not limit the number of switch ports that a switch may have, although addressing limitations do limit the maximum to 65,636 ports. The model for a Fibre Channel switch is shown in Figure 8-11 on page 109.

A switch port attached to an N_Port functions as a Fabric Port (F_Port). A switch port attached to one or more NL_Ports on an arbitrated loop functions as a Fabric Loop Port (FL_Port). A switch port attached to another switch functions as an Expansion Port (E_Port). In many implementations, the same physical port may function as an F_Port, FL_Port or E_Port depending upon the device to which it is attached.

A switch port consists of a physical entity and one or more virtual entities.

- For an F_Port, the physical entity is referred to as the Physical F_Port (PF_Port) and the virtual entity as a Virtual F_Port (VF_Port).

- For an E_Port, the physical entity is referred to as the Physical E_Port (PE_Port) and the virtual entity as a Virtual E_Port (VE_Port).

Each VF_Port or VE_Port has a unique 64-bit Port_Name. VE_Ports and VF_Ports do not have Fibre Channel addresses.

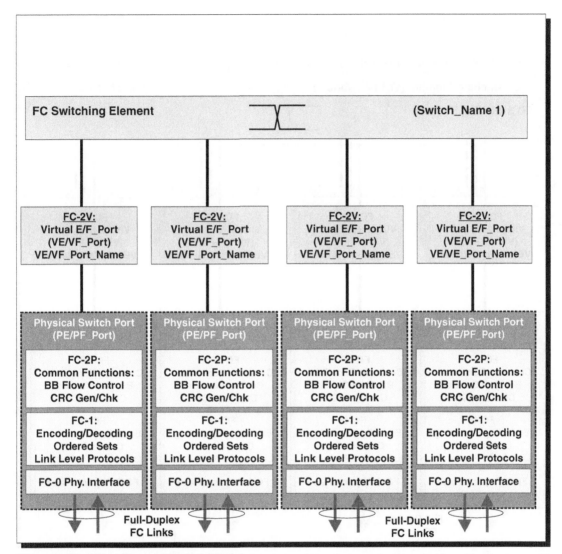

Figure 8-11. Fibre Channel Switch Model

VE_Ports and VF_Ports are interconnected by a Fibre Channel Switching Element that forwards received frames from an ingress port to the egress port. Each Fibre Channel Switching Element has a unique 64-bit Switch_Name.

When virtual fabrics are used, there may be multiple virtual fabric switching elements, each with its own unique Switch_Name. A Core Switch Name is associated with the collection of VE_Ports, VF_Ports and Switching Elements. An illustration of the model for a Fibre Channel switch with Virtual Fabrics is shown in Figure 8-12 on page 110.

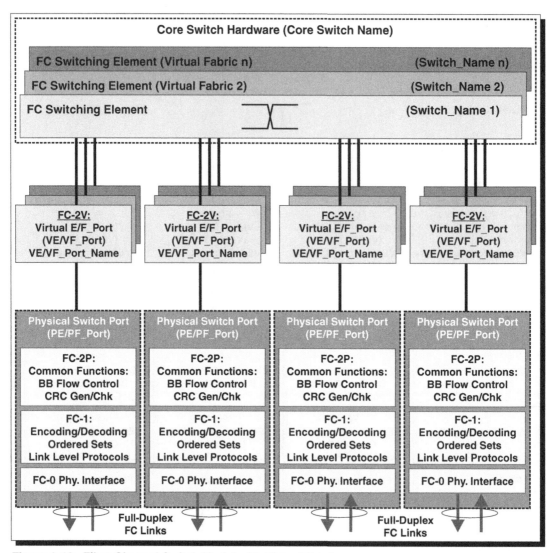

Figure 8-12. Fibre Channel Switch Model with Virtual Fabrics

8.5.2 FCoE Forwarder (FCF) Model

While an FCoE switch, with its FCoE Forwarder function, processes encapsulated Fibre Channel frames and protocols like a normal Fibre Channel switch, it does not meet the strict definition of a switch as defined in the Fibre Channel standards. Because of this, it is referred to as an FCoE Forwarder (FCF). An FCF may contain both "lossless" Ethernet ports and native Fibre Channel ports as shown in Figure 8-13 on page 111.

Behavior of the native Fibre Channel switch ports (F_Ports, FL_Ports, and/or E_Ports) is as defined by the existing Fibre Channel standards. The FCF contains a Fibre Channel switching element whose behavior is also defined by the Fibre Channel standards (or multiple switching elements in the case of Virtual Fabrics).

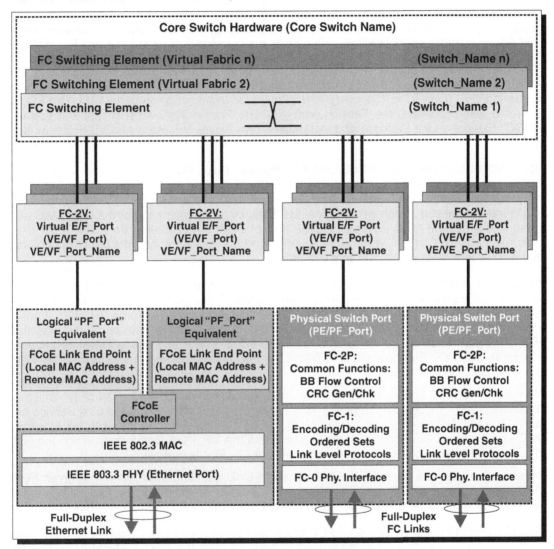

Figure 8-13. FCoE Forwarder (FCF) Model (with Virtual Fabrics)

FCF Ethernet MACs. By definition, an FCF must contain at least one, and may contain more than one, "lossless" Ethernet MACs. Each Ethernet MAC has an associated MAC address that is referred to as the FCF-MAC address. The FCF MAC is the destination of, or the source of, FCoE frames received from or being sent to ENodes. Because there can be more than one MAC associated with an FCF, the FCF may have more than one FCF-MAC address.

FCoE ports on end devices may connect directly to an FCF MAC, or to an integrated "lossless" Ethernet Bridge (an embedded Ethernet switching function as was shown earlier in Figure 3-3 on page 33). When the external ports are connected to an FCF MAC via an integrated "lossless" Ethernet Bridge multiple FCoE switch ports may provide access to the same FCF MAC.

FCoE Controller. Associated with each FCF MAC is an FCoE Controller. The function of the FCoE Controller is to perform the Discovery and virtual link initialization functions that are unique to FCoE (see *FCoE Discovery and Virtual Link Initialization* on page 121). The FCoE controller also processes the Fabric Login (FLOGI), Fabric Discover (FDISC) and Logout (LOGO) Extended Link Services and instantiates or removes VF_Ports and VE_Ports as appropriate.

FCF MAC, Virtual Links and FCoE Link End Points. Each FCF MAC may be associated with one or more virtual links. As was seen earlier with an End Node, a single Ethernet MAC can potentially communicate with multiple, other Ethernet MACs through an intervening "lossless" Ethernet network. Each virtual link is identified by the combination of the local MAC address and a remote MAC address. At the end of each virtual link is an FCoE_LEP that performs the Fibre Channel frame encapsulation and decapsulation and the transmission and reception of Ethernet frames over that virtual link.

Virtual F_Port (VF_Port). While an FCF fabric port processes Fibre Channel protocols and functions in the same manner as a native Fibre Channel F_Port, it does not meet the strict definition of an F_Port as defined by the Fibre Channel standards (as with the VN_Port, it does not implement the FC-1 and FC-0 levels defined by Fibre Channel standards). Rather, the FCF fabric port emulates the behavior of an F_Port and is referred to as a Virtual Fabric port (VF_Port). Each VF_Port has a unique 64-bit VF_Port Name, just as a Fibre Channel F_Port has a unique 64-bit Port_Name.

Whereas a native F_Port exists by virtue of the physical hardware, a VF_Port is dynamically instantiated upon successful completion of a Fabric Login (FLOGI) Extended Link Service request. The FLOGI request is processed by the FCoE Controller associated with the Ethernet MAC and it is the FCoE Controller that instantiates the VF_Port. Conversely, when the last VN_Port on a virtual link logs out or is removed, the VF_Port is removed.

Because there can be multiple virtual links and FCoE_LEPs associated with a given FCF MAC, it is possible to have multiple VF_Ports instantiated for the same FCF MAC (each VF_Port associated with a virtual link to a different VN_Port MAC.

Virtual E_Port (VE_Port). While an FCF fabric port processes Fibre Channel protocols and functions in the same manner as an E_Port, it does not meet the strict definition of an E_Port as defined by the Fibre Channel standards (as with the VN_Port and VF_Port, it does not implement the FC-1 and FC-0 levels as defined by Fibre Channel standards). Rather, the FCF fabric port emulates the behavior of an E_Port and is referred to as a Virtual Expansion port (VE_Port).

Each VF_Port has a unique 64-bit VE_Port Name, just as an E_Port has a unique 64-bit Port_Name.

Whereas a native E_Port exists by virtue of the physical hardware, a VE_Port is dynamically instantiated upon successful completion of the Exchange Link Parameters (ELP) Switch Internal Link Service request. The ELP request is processed by the FCoE Controller associated with the Ethernet MAC and it is the FCoE Controller that instantiates the VE_Port.

Because there might be multiple virtual links and FCoE_LEPs associated with a given FCF MAC, it is possible to have multiple VE_Ports instantiated for the same FCF MAC (each VF_Port associated with a virtual link to a different VE_Port MAC. In fact, a single FCF MAC might have one or more VF_Ports and/or one or more VE_Ports instantiated at the same time; a situation that has no equivalent in native Fibre Channel.

Optional Embedded Ethernet Bridge(s). An FCF may contain an embedded Ethernet bridge (switch) between an FCF-MAC and its external connections. When this is the case, multiple external FCoE switch ports may be associated with the same FCF-MAC address. The FCoE standard neither requires nor precludes this configuration. When an embedded Ethernet switch is present, it behaves as defined by the Ethernet standards and may be part of an Ethernet network that includes other Ethernet switches. Frames addressed to the FCF-MAC address are forwarded to the corresponding FCF MAC for decapsulation and processing and frames addressed to other Ethernet destinations are forwarded as appropriate.

8.6 Architecture Models Conclusion

While the intent of FCoE is the "transparently and seamlessly replace the Fibre Channel physical interface with Ethernet," it is not possible to ignore the fundamental differences at the physical link level. Fibre Channel is logically and physically point-to-point. While Ethernet may physically point-to-point, the introduction of "lossless" Ethernet switches between FCoE entities means that a single ENode MAC can potentially communicate with multiple FCF MACs.

From the FCF's perspective, a single FCF MAC can potentially communicate with multiple ENode MACS and/or multiple FCF MACs.

In order to map this very different fundamental behavior into the Fibre Channel architecture, FCoE created the concept of the virtual link to logically emulate the behavior of native Fibre Channel's physical link.

Because a MAC can have one or more virtual links (and in the case of an FCF, it is not know what is at the other end of the virtual link), port are dynamically instantiated as a part of the virtual link initialization.

8.7 Chapter Summary

Ethernet LANs

- In FCoE, one or more Ethernet switches can be between an end device and the FCoE switch
- Intervening Ethernet switches provide a "multiple access" capability
  - A single ENode MAC may be able access more than one FCoE switch port MAC
  - More than one ENode may be able to access the same switch port
  - A switch MAC may be accessed by more than one ENode
  - This has no equivalent in native Fibre Channel with its direct physical connections

FCoE Virtual Links

- In native FC, every link is a direct physical connection between devices
  - Path between the node port and Fabric is a dedicated physical link
  - In FCoE, the path between devices may consist of multiple physical links if there are one or more Ethernet switches in the path
- Because of this, the path between devices is called a "Virtual Link"
  - Virtual link is like a "tunnel" through the Ethernet environment
  - Virtual link is identified by the local and remote MAC addresses
  - Fibre Channel frames are encapsulated for transmission through the virtual link

FCoE Link End Point (FCoE_LEP)

- At each end of a virtual link is an FCoE Link End Point (FCoE_LEP)
  - MAC can have more than one FCoE_LEP
  - At an ENode, each FCoE LEP is associated with one VN_Port
  - At an FCF, each FCoE LEP is associated with one VF_Port or VE_Port
- The FCoE Link End Point performs the:
  - FC frame encapsulation and decapsulation
  - Transmission and reception of encapsulated frames through a single virtual link

Fibre Channel Node and Node Port

- **Node:** Controls one or more Node Ports
- **FC-4:** Maps various protocols to Fibre Channel
- **FC-3:** Provides common services
- **FC-2V:** (virtual port): Provides WWPN, acquires N_Port_ID, manages Exchanges, Sequences and Frames
- **FC-2P:** (physical port): Transmits and receives frames, provides link-level flow control, does optional frame scrambling
- **FC-1:** Defines encoding, Ordered Sets, implements link-level protocols
- **FC-0:** Defines the physical interface

FCoE Virtual N_Port (VN_Port)

- FCoE node port has both Ethernet and FC parts
  - IEEE 802.3 Ethernet PHY and MAC
  - Fibre Channel FC-2V, FC-3 and FC-4
- Virtual N_Port (VN_Port):
  - Identical behavior between FC and FCoE
  - Implements the FC-2V functions
  - Has a unique VN_Port_Name
  - Acquires N_Port_ID using FLOGI or FDISC
  - Creates and processes frames (but does not physically transmit or receive them)
- The Fibre Channel PN_Port is replaced by the FCoE_LEP and Ethernet MAC and PHY
  - Performs the frame transmission and reception on the virtual link

FC N_Port_ID Virtualization (NPIV)

- With NPIV, a single physical port can support multiple VN_Ports
- Each VN_Port has:
  - A unique Port_Name
  - A unique N_Port_ID
  - Its own Login Sessions
  - Its own Exchanges, Sequences and Frames
- The VN_Ports share use the physical port's resources
  - e.g., buffers and use of the physical link

FCoE VN_Port Model with NPIV

- FCoE can use NPIV just like a normal FC node port
  - FLOGI is used to create the 1st VN_Port
  - FDISC is used to create each additional VN_Ports
- All of the VN_Ports share use of the same Ethernet MAC and PHY
  - The Ethernet MAC can have multiple LEPs, each associated with a different VN_Port

FCoE Forwarder (FCF) Port Model

- FCF Port has both Ethernet and FC parts
  - Ethernet MAC & PHY
- FCoE Link End Point identifies a path between a local and remote MAC address
  - Can be multiple LEPs per physical FCoE port
  - Each LEP is associated with one or more Virtual F_Ports or Virtual E_Ports
- Virtual F_Port (VF_Port) has a VF_Port_Name
  - Is created at successful completion of FLOGI
- Virtual E_Port (VE_Port) has a VE_Port_Name
  - Is created upon successful completion of ELP

Optional Embedded Ethernet Switch

- FCoE switch may optionally contain one or more embedded Ethernet switches
  - Multiple external ports may access the same FCoE Forwarder MAC
- When present, an embedded Ethernet switch behaves as defined by the Ethernet standards
  - Forwards frames to the FCF MAC
  - Forwards frames to other Ethernet destinations as appropriate
  - Participates in the Spanning Tree Protocol (STP) with other Ethernet switches

FCoE Virtual F_Port (VF_Port)

- FCF port has both Ethernet and FC parts
  - IEEE 802.3 Ethernet PHY and MAC
  - Fibre Channel FC-2V, FC-3 and FC-4
- Virtual F_Port (VF_Port):
  - Identical behavior between FC and FCoE
  - Implements the FC-2V functions for a switch port
  - Has a unique VF_Port_Name
  - Processes Fibre Channel frames (but does not physically transmit or receive them)
- The Fibre Channel PF_Port is replaced by the FCoE_LEP and Ethernet MAC and PHY
  - Performs the frame transmission and reception on the virtual link

FCoE Virtual E_Port (VE_Port)

- FCF port has both Ethernet and FC parts
  - IEEE 802.3 Ethernet PHY and MAC
  - Fibre Channel FC-2V, FC-3 and FC-4
- Virtual E_Port (VE_Port):
  - Identical behavior between FC and FCoE
  - Implements the FC-2V functions for a switch port on an inter-switch link
  - Has a unique VE_Port_Name
  - Processes Fibre Channel frames (but does not physically transmit or receive them)
- The Fibre Channel PE_Port is replaced by the FCoE_LEP and Ethernet MAC and PHY

Virtual Fabrics

- With Virtual Fabrics, a single physical switch port can support multiple virtual ports (VF_Ports or VE_Ports)
  - Each VF_Port or VE_Port is associated with a different virtual fabric
  - All of the VF_Ports or VE_Ports share the underlying Ethernet MAC and PHY
- Internally, the VF_Ports and VE_Ports are interconnected by a virtual fabric switching element
  - Forwards frames from an ingress port to the egress port

Some FCoE Terminology

- "Lossless" Ethernet MAC definition:
  - A full duplex Ethernet MAC implementing extensions to avoid Ethernet frame loss due to congestion (e.g., the Pause mechanism)
- "Lossless" Ethernet Bridging Element definition:
  - An Ethernet bridging function supporting the minimum required capabilities of "lossless" Ethernet MACs.
- "Lossless" Ethernet network definition:
  - An Ethernet network composed only of full duplex links, "lossless" Ethernet MACs, and "lossless" Ethernet Bridging Elements.

More FCoE Terminology (continued)

- FC Entity definition:
  - The interface between an FC Switching Element or an FC stack and the FCoE Entity
  - Each FC Entity contains a single instance of either a VE_Port, a VF_Port, or a VN_Port
- FCoE Entity definition:
  - The interface between the FC Entity and a "lossless" Ethernet MAC
  - Each FCoE Entity contains one or more FCoE_LEPs

More FCoE Terminology (continued)

- FCoE Node (ENode) definition:
  - A Fibre Channel Node (see FC-FS) with one or more "lossless" Ethernet MACs, each coupled with an FCoE Controller
- FCoE Controller definition:
  - A functional entity, coupled with a "lossless" Ethernet MAC, instantiating new VE_Ports, VF_Ports, and VN_Ports, and/or creating new FCoE_LEPs
- FCF (FCoE Forwarder) definition:
  - A Fibre Channel Switching Element (see FC-SW) with one or more "lossless" Ethernet MACs, each coupled with an FCoE Controller
  - FCF forwards FCoE frames based on the D_ID of the encapsulated FC frames

9. FCoE Addressing

FCoE introduces some rather interesting addressing challenges and possibilities. FCoE may share the same "lossless" Ethernet NIC along with other protocols and their associated protocol stacks. Figure 9-1 shows an example of a "lossless" Ethernet NIC having an FCoE stack and a TCP/IP stack along with stacks for other protocols that are also using the NIC.

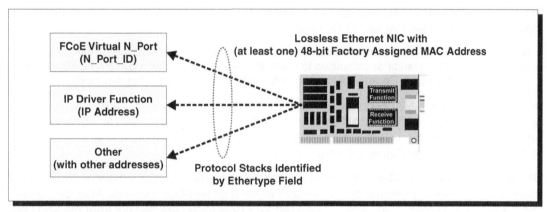

Figure 9-1. Multiple Protocols Sharing the Same NIC

9.1 Fibre Channel and Ethernet Addresses

Every Ethernet adapter has at least one unique 48-bit address called the Media Access Control (MAC) address. At least one MAC address is normally assigned at the time of manufacture, is globally unique and is often referred to as the "burned-in" MAC address. MAC addresses can also be created dynamically (such as in a virtual machine environment, or by FCoE). When MAC addresses are created dynamically, they must be unique within the local network but are not necessarily globally unique. For a description of the MAC address format, see *MAC Address Format* on page 71.

Each Fibre Channel node port (or virtual node port) has a 24-bit address called the N_Port Identifier, or N_Port_ID (sometimes also referred to as the Fibre Channel ID or FC_ID). N_Port_IDs are only unique within a given Fibre Channel topology and are not necessarily globally unique. N_Port_IDs are dynamically assigned by the Fibre Channel Fabric during Fabric Login (FLOGI) in a Fabric topology, by one of the node ports during N_Port Login (PLOGI) in a Point-to-Point topology, or during Loop Initialization on an Arbitrated Loop.

9.2 Fabric Provided MAC Addresses (FPMA)

Because an FCoE physical port is an Ethernet port, each FCoE physical port has an Ethernet MAC address. This is true whether the port is a VN_Port in an ENode or a VE_Port or VF_Port in an FCoE Forwarder (FCF). One of the more hotly-debated topics during FCoE development was the relationship between Ethernet MAC addresses and Fibre Channel N_Port_IDs. Two addressing methods were proposed (and incorporated into the first generation FCoE standard). They were called Server Provided MAC Addressing (SPMA) and Fabric Provided MAC Addressing (FPMA).

In the Server Provided MAC Address method (SPMA), the end device (server or storage) provided the MAC address that was to be used for each VN_Port.

> NOTE – While the FC-BB-5 standard describes Server Provided MAC Addressing (SPMA), it is the expressed intent of the standards committee to obsolete this addressing method in the FC-BB-6 version of the standard (FCoE-2). Because of this, the SPMA addressing method is not described in this book.

In the Fabric Provided MAC Address method (FPMA), a VN_Port's MAC addresses is created by concatenating a 24-bit FC-MAP value provided by the Fabric and the VN_Port's 24-bit Fibre Channel N_Port_ID. This results in a 48-bit MAC address having the format of (FC-MAP ∥ N_Port_ID) as shown in Figure 9-2 on page 118.

Because FCoE VN_Port MAC addresses are created dynamically in this manner, they are not assumed to be globally unique, but are unique within a given FCoE network. Also, because of this addressing method, MAC addresses used for FCoE traffic are distinct from the MAC addresses that are used for LAN traffic.

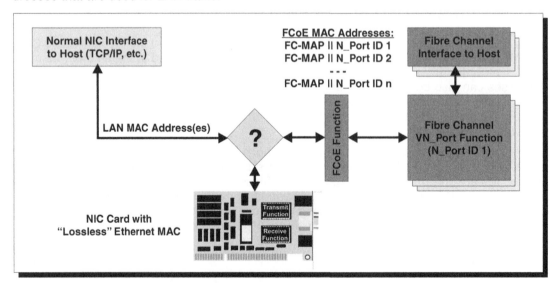

Figure 9-2. Fabric Provided MAC Addresses (FPMA)

The 24-bit FC-MAP value is provided by an FCF when it sends a Discovery Advertisement to an ENode during the discovery process (see *FCoE Discovery and Virtual Link Initialization* on page 121). This enables the ENode to construct the appropriate MAC address for the VN_Port upon successful completion of FLOGI or NPIV FDISC.

Because the FC-MAP value is used to construct the VN_Port's MAC address and is the same for all FCoE devices on a given Fabric, an address lookup table is not required when the FCF encapsulates a Fibre Channel frame for transmission on an Ethernet link. This is shown in Figure 9-3 on page 119.

NOTE – The default FC-MAP value is 0E:FC:00h but may be configurable by an administrator. One common thought is that the FC-MAP value would be used as a Fabric identifier in a multi-fabric FCoE environment. Using a different FC-MAP value in each Fabric provides an additional level of identification associated with each Ethernet frame.

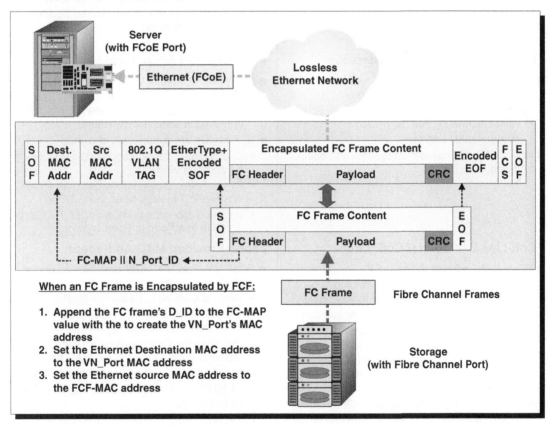

Figure 9-3. Fabric Provided MAC Addresses

9.3 Chapter Summary

FCoE and Ethernet MAC Addresses

- FCoE introduces interesting addressing challenges and possibilities
- Each VN_Port has an N_Port_ID
  - When using N_Port ID Virtualization (NPIV), there may be multiple VN_Ports associated with the same Ethernet MAC
- Strictly speaking, VF_Ports and VE_Ports do not have Fibre Channel addresses.
  - VF_Ports and VE_Ports do have MAC addresses
- Each Ethernet port has one or more MAC addresses

FCoE and Ethernet MAC Addresses

- An FCoE port has both a Fibre Channel address component and an Ethernet address component
  - Fibre Channel N_Port_ID (FCID)
  - Ethernet MAC address
- How do FC addresses map to MAC addresses and vice versa?

FCoE Link End Point (FCoE_LEP)

- FCoE Link Endpoint (FCoE_LEP):
  - An FCoE_LEP is the data forwarding component of an FCoE Entity that handles:
  - FC frame encapsulation and decapsulation
  - Transmission and reception of encapsulated frames through a single Virtual Link
  - Link end point is defined by the local MAC address and remote MAC address
- Virtual Link:
  - The logical link connecting two FCoE_LEPs over a "lossless" Ethernet network and is identified by the pair of MAC addresses of the two link end-points.
  - An FCoE node port can have more than one LEP, even if it only has a single MAC address

Ethernet MAC Addresses

- Every Ethernet adapter has at least one unique 48-bit address
  - Called the Media Access Control (MAC) address
  - Can be globally unique, or
  - Locally assigned (must be unique within the network)
- MAC addresses are normally assigned at the time of manufacture and globally unique
  - Referred to as the "burned-in" address in some presentations

Fibre Channel Addresses

- Every Fibre Channel VN_Port has a 24-bit address
  - The N_Port_ID (Fibre Channel ID, FCID) is only unique within a given fabric
- N_Port_IDs are dynamically assigned
  - By the Fabric during Fabric Login (FLOGI) in a Fabric Topology
  - By the Fabric during Fabric Discover (FDISC) in a Fabric Topology when using NPIV
  - By one of the node ports during N_Port Login (PLOGI) in a Point-to-Point Topology

Fabric Provided MAC Addresses

- FCoE VN_Port MAC addresses are based on a 24-bit fabric-supplied value
  - Value is referred to as the FC-MAP
  - The 24-bit FC-MAP value is provided by an FCF during the discovery process
  - Occupies the Organizationally Unique Identifier (OUI) portion of the MAC address
- MAC address is created by concatenating the:
  - 24-bit FC-MAP value and the VN_Port's 24-bit N_Port_ID

10. FCoE Discovery and Virtual Link Initialization

Because of the "virtual" links between FCoE entities, rather than point-to-point physical links as in native Fibre Channel, additional processing is needed before normal Fibre Channel operations can begin. There are three distinct initialization and operational phases performed using two different FCoE-related protocols; the FCoE Initialization Protocol (FIP) and the FCoE Encapsulation Protocol. The relationship of these protocols is illustrated by Figure 10-1.

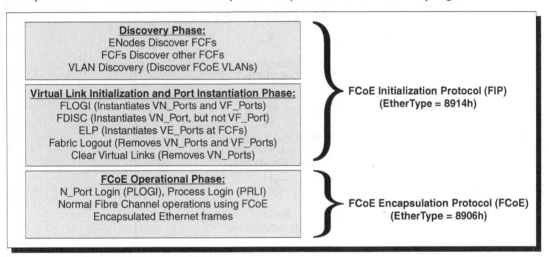

Figure 10-1. FCoE Operational Phases

10.1 FIP VLAN Discovery Protocol

FCoE environments may include both FCoE devices and non-FCoE devices and traffic. To provide enhanced security and traffic isolation, FCoE traffic may be assigned to one or more dedicated Ethernet VLANs. When this is done, the administrator may configure the ENodes or FCFs with the appropriate VLAN information. Alternatively, ENodes or FCFs may use the optional FIP VLAN Discovery protocol to determine which VLAN or VLANs are associated with FCoE traffic.

When the VLAN Discovery protocol is used, the protocol is performed prior to ENode-to-FCF or FCF-to-FCF discovery. This ensures that the ENode and FCF discovery protocols (see *FCoE FIP Discovery* on page 123) are performed using the correct VLAN.

The FIP VLAN Discovery protocol uses the FIP VLAN Request (see *FIP VLAN Request* on page 164) and the FIP VLAN Notification (see *FIP VLAN Notification* on page 165) operations. The FIP VLAN Discovery protocol is shown in Figure 10-2 on page 122.

The ENode MAC or FCF-MAC initiating the discovery protocol transmits a FIP VLAN Request using any available (or, a default) VLAN. The destination MAC address is the "ALL-FCF-MACs" address and the source MAC address is the sender's ENode MAC or FCF-MAC address. FCFs that support the VLAN Discovery protocol listen for the FIP VLAN Request on all VLANs.

The FIP VLAN Notification returns a list of VLANs available to the requestor for FCoE operations. The FCF sending the FIP VLAN Notification may return a different list of VLANs to different requestors.

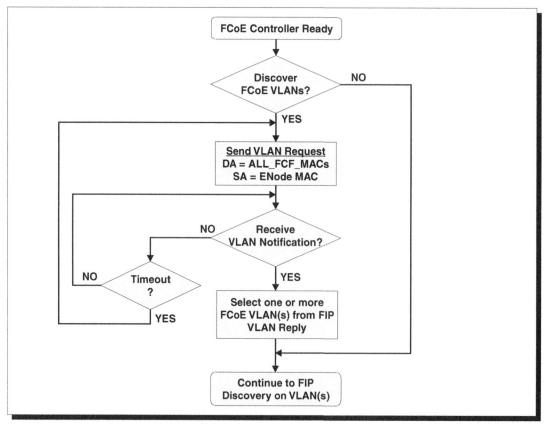

Figure 10-2. FIP VLAN Discovery

If the VLAN(s) available for FCoE traffic on a given FCF-MAC changes, the FCF-MAC should send a unicast FIP VLAN Notification message to each ENode MAC or FCF-MAC with which it has established virtual links. The unicast FIP VLAN Notification message carries an updated list of VLANs over which the FCF-MAC now supports FCoE operations.

10.2 FCoE FIP Discovery

In a native Fibre Channel environment, the F_Port or E_Port is located at the other end of the physical link and no discovery phase is needed. In FCoE, an ENode needs to discover reachable FCFs (the FCFs may not be located at the other end of a direct physical link but may be connected via a "lossless" Ethernet network). The discovery phase provides a method for FCoE entities to discover other reachable entities in order to begin the necessary virtual link initialization.

As per the architecture models described earlier in *Architecture Models* on page 97, each FCoE ENode is assumed to have a "lossless" Ethernet MAC with a universal "burned-in" MAC address (the ENode MAC address), an FCoE Controller to perform the discovery process, and recognizes the "All-FCoE-ENodes" group address.

Each FCoE Forwarder (FCF) is assumed to have a "lossless" Ethernet MAC with a universal "burned-in" MAC address (the FCF-MAC address), an FCoE Controller to perform the discovery process, and recognizes the "All-FCoE-Forwarders" group address.

With these assumptions, let's examine how Discovery and Virtual Link Initialization works.

10.2.1 ENode-to-FCF Discovery

ENode-to-FCF discovery uses two FCoE Initialization Protocol (FIP) operations, the Discovery Solicitation and Discovery Advertisement as shown in the simplified process in Figure 10-3.

Multicast Discovery Solicitation. When an ENode MAC initializes, its FCoE Controller transmits a multicast FIP Discovery Solicitation to announce its presence and solicit responses from reachable FCFs (see *FIP Discovery Solicitation From an ENode* on page 147 for the format of the Discovery Solicitation). While not recommended, an ENode may simply wait to receive a multicast Discovery Advertisement from one or more FCFs. In a multicast Discovery Solicitation, the Ethernet Destination Address (DA) is set to the "All-FCF-MACs" group address and the Ethernet Source Address (SA) is set to the ENode's "burned-in" MAC address.

The Discovery Solicitation contains the Max_FCoE_Size parameter that indicates if the ENode MAC supports jumbo frames, and if so, the size supported for FCoE content.

If the ENode is connected to an intervening "lossless" Ethernet network (as is shown in Figure 10-3), the multicast Discovery Solicitation request is forwarded to all reachable FCFs by the Ethernet switches. If the ENode is connected directly to an FCF, the multicast Discovery Solicitation is received only by the attached FCF.

Multicast Discovery Advertisement. Each FCF transmits multicast Discovery Advertisement to the "All-FCoE-ENodes" multicast address on a periodic basis. The source address is the FCF-MAC address and the Solicited bit in the FIP flags is set to zero (see *Solicited Flag (S)* on page 138). If the FCF is available for accepting logins, it sets the "A" bit in the FIP flags.

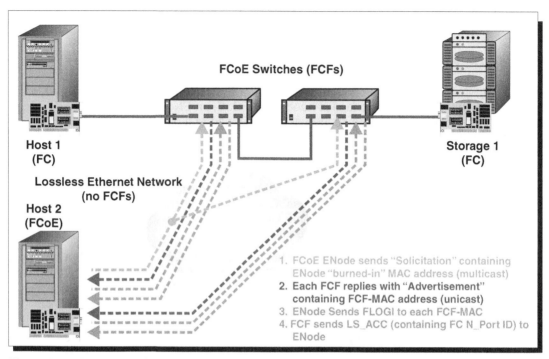

Figure 10-3. ENode-to-FCF Discovery

The period for the multicast Discovery Advertisements is determined by the FKA_ADV_Period (see *FIP FKA_ADV_Period Descriptor* on page 144). The multicast Discovery Advertisement enables an ENode to discover reachable FCFs, even if the ENode does not transmit a multicast Discovery Solicitation or its Discovery Solicitation is lost or corrupted. The format of the Discovery Advertisement is shown in *FIP Discovery Advertisement* on page 148.

When an ENode receives a multicast Discovery Advertisement, it adds the FCF to its FCF Login set, but sets the Max_FCoE_Size Verified indication to zero. When the Max_FCoE_Size Verified indication is set to zero, the ENode is not permitted to originate a FLOGI with the FCF.

The absence of periodic multicast Discovery Advertisements enables an ENode to detect if the virtual link to an FCF fails, or if the FCF itself fails or is removed.

Unicast Discovery Solicitation. Once an ENode has detected a reachable FCF, it may send a unicast Discovery Solicitation to the FCF-MAC address of that FCF. The unicast Discovery Solicitation contains the Max_FCoE_Size parameter indicating if the ENode MAC supports jumbo frames, and if so, the size supported for FCoE content.

Solicited Unicast Discovery Advertisement. When an FCF receives a Discovery Solicitation from an ENode, it transmits a solicited unicast Discovery Advertisement to the ENode's FCoE controller (the format of the Discovery Advertisement is shown in *FIP Discovery Advertisement* on page 148).

In a solicited unicast Discovery Advertisement, the destination MAC address is set to the ENode's MAC Address, the source MAC address is set to the FCF-MAC address, the Solicited (S) bit is set to one and the Ethernet frame is padded to the Max_FCoE_Size value from the received Discovery Solicitation. Padding the Discovery Advertisement provides a method to determine that the path between the requestor and the FCF is capable of passing a frame of the Max_FCoE_Size. If the Discovery Advertisement is not being sent in response to a Discovery Solicitation, this padding is not present.

NOTE – This does not ensure that Max_FCoE_Size frames will be supported if the path through an intervening Ethernet network changes and a switch in the new path does not support frames of this size.

When an ENode receives a solicited unicast Discovery Advertisement, it sets its Max_FC0E_Size Verified indication and may initiate a Fabric Login (FLOGI) with that FCF if the "A" bit in the FIP flags is set.

ENode-to-FCF Discovery Flow. Figure 10-4 on page 126 provides a flow diagram illustrating the ENode to FCF discovery protocol.

10.3 ENode Virtual Link Initialization

Once an ENode has discovered reachable FCFs, it performs Fabric Login (FLOGI) to establish a virtual link with the FCF and acquire a Fibre Channel N_Port_ID (see *FIP FLOGI Request and Reply* on page 151 for the format of the FLOGI request and reply). The ENode may perform FLOGI with one, some, or all of the discovered FCFs. It may use the Priority Field from the Discovery Advertisement (or other Discovery Advertisement parameters) to decide to which FCF, or FCFs, to send FLOGI.

10.3.1 FCF Virtual Link Initialization

Upon successful completion of FLOGI, the FCF instantiates an instance of a VF_Port for this virtual link and the ENode instantiates an instance of a VN_Port. Subsequent operations (with the exception of FLOGI, NPIV FDISC, Fabric LOGO and FIP Keep Alive) use the FCoE protocol and normal encapsulated Fibre Channel frames.

The VF_Port uses the VF_Port Name and Fabric_Name that were sent in the LS_ACC to the FLOGI and the FCF makes the appropriate entries in the Fibre Channel Name Server database for the associated VN_Port.

10.3.2 Fabric Provided MAC Addressing (FPMA)

When the Enode and FCF are using Fabric Provided MAC addressing (FPMA), the Discovery protocol is the same as was shown earlier, but the VN_Port MAC addresses are based on a parameter provided by the Fabric (the FC-MAP). With the exception of the setting of the FPMA Capability bit, the Discovery and Virtual Link Initialization steps are the same as those shown in Figure 10-5 on page 127.

If the ENode sets the FPMA Capability bit and the FCF does not support Fabric Provided MAC Addressing, the FCF will not send a Discovery Advertisement and will not be discovered by the ENode.

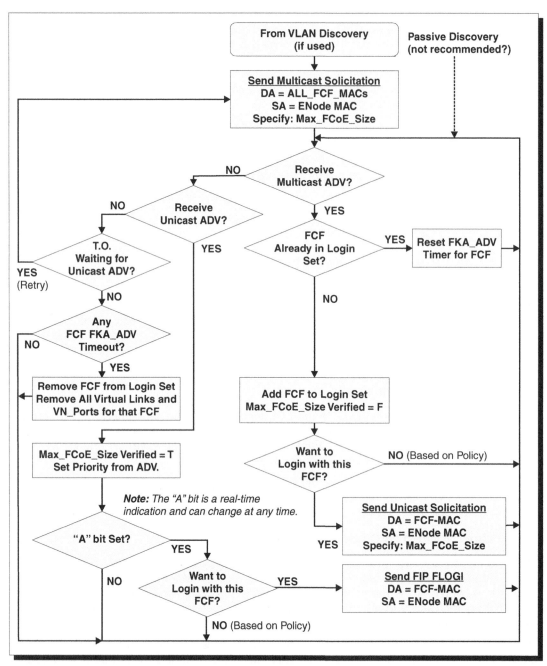

Figure 10-4. ENode-to-FCF Discovery Flow Diagram

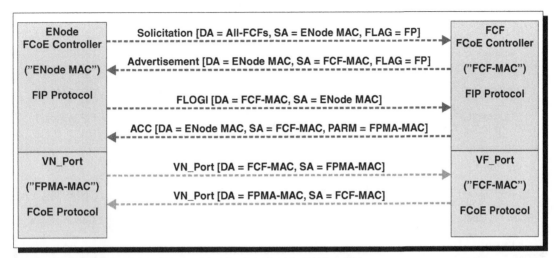

Figure 10-5. Enode Discovery and Virtual Link Initialization Steps

FPMA Fabric Login (FLOGI). Based on Discovery Advertisements received, the ENode sends FLOGI to establish the virtual link and acquire a VN_Port_ID. When the FCF sends an Accept to the FLOGI, it returns the FPMA MAC address to be used by the VN_Port.

Upon successful completion of the FLOGI, the FCF instantiates a VF_Port, the ENode instantiates a VN_Port associated with the Fabric Provided MAC Address, and normal operation using the FCoE protocol can begin.

FPMA N_Port ID Virtualization (NPIV). .When an ENode sends an FDISC request to acquire another N_Port_ID, it uses the "burned-in" ENode MAC address as the Ethernet Source Address and the FCF_MAC address as the Destination Address (it learned the FCF-MAC address from the previous Discovery Advertisement). An example is shown in Figure 10-6 on page 128.

When the FCF sends an Accept to the FDISC, it returns the assigned FPMA MAC address.

Upon successful completion of the FDISC, the ENode instantiates a VN_Port associated with the Fabric Provided MAC Address, and normal operation using the FCoE protocol can begin. The FCF does not instantiate a new instance of a VF_Port.

If the ENode wishes to relinquish a VN_Port_ID, it can use the Logout FIP function as described in *Relinquishing a VN_Port_ID (LOGO)* on page 128. It can use this function to relinquish an address acquired using FDISC, or even the address initially acquired using FLOGI.

10.3.3 Unreachable VN_Port Discovery

An FCF may have no direct visibility to the state of ENode links because ENodes may be connected via one or more "lossless" Ethernet switches. In order to detect a failed link or removed VN_Port, the FCF may send a "Discovery Advertisement" periodically to the "All-FCoE-ENodes" group address.

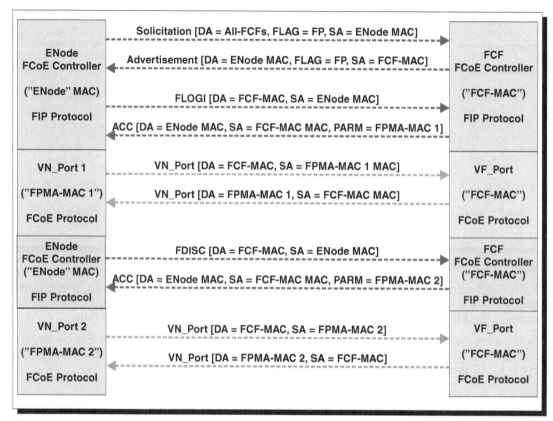

Figure 10-6. Enode Discovery and Virtual Link Initialization Steps (with NPIV)

This periodic polling by an FCF facilitates discovery of newly connected ENode and detection of ENodes that are no longer reachable due to a failed link or as a result of the ENode being removed from the Fabric.

Because a multicast Discovery Advertisement, and the associated responses, may create an unacceptable amount of traffic, an FCF may choose to selectively poll only those ENodes that have not sent or received frames within an FCF-dependent time period.

10.3.4 Relinquishing a VN_Port_ID (LOGO)

An ENode can relinquish a VN_Port address (and remove the VN_Port and virtual link) using the Logout (LOGO) FCoE Initialization Protocol function (the format of the Logout is shown in *FIP Fabric LOGO Request and Reply* on page 155). An example of relinquishing an address is shown in Figure 10-7 on page 129.

Relinquishing a VN_Port address does not remove the VF_Port unless all addresses associated with the VF_Port have been relinquished. This behavior is consistent with N_Port ID virtualization behavior as defined by the Fibre Channel standards.

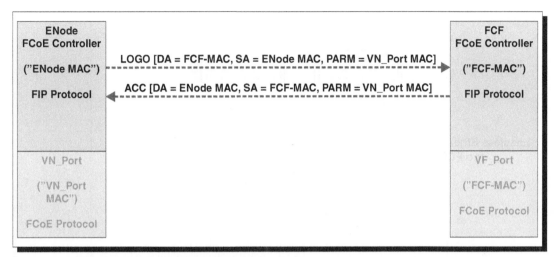

Figure 10-7. Relinquishing a VN_Port_ID with LOGO

As long as any VN_Port associated with the VF_Port has an active login session with the FCF, additional VN_Port_IDs are acquired using FDISC. If there are no active login sessions with the FCF, the ENode must perform FLOGI in order to acquire a VN_Port_ID (subsequent VN_Port_IDs can then be acquired using FDISC, if desired).

10.4 FCF Interswitch Link (ISL) Discovery and Initialization

The same basic discovery method used by an ENode is also used by an FCF to discover other reachable FCFs. When connected, each FCF sends a FIP "Discovery Solicitation" to the "All-FCoE-Forwarders" group address (the format of the Discovery Solicitation is shown in *FIP Discovery Solicitation From FCF* on page 148). The Discovery Solicitation contains the sender's FCF-MAC address and has the FCF flag bit (F) set to one to indicate that the sender is an FCF rather than an ENode (the Discovery Solicitation may contain other discovery parameters as well).

10.4.1 FCF-to-FCF Discovery

The FCF-to-FCF discovery protocol is similar to the ENode-to-FCF discovery with minor differences. One of the key differences is that, unlike an ENode, an FCF may both send and receive Discovery Solicitations and Discovery Advertisements. An ENode only sends Discovery Solicitations and receives Discovery Advertisements.

When an FCF receives a "Discovery Solicitation" from another FCF, it replies with an FIP "Discovery Advertisement" sent to the FCF-MAC address received in the "Discovery Solicitation". Based on Discovery Advertisements received, the FCF builds a list of other reachable FCFs and can proceed to the ISL Initialization. The FCF Discovery Solicitation and Discovery Advertisement protocol is shown in Figure 10-8 on page 130.

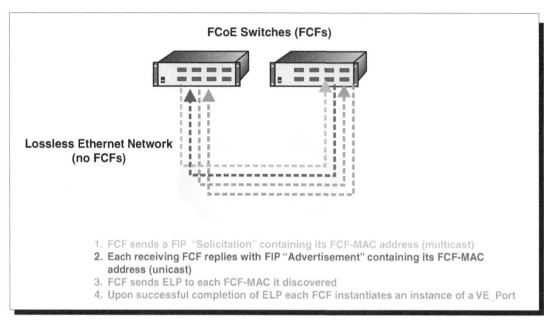

FCoE Switches (FCFs)

Lossless Ethernet Network (no FCFs)

1. FCF sends a FIP "Solicitation" containing its FCF-MAC address (multicast)
2. Each receiving FCF replies with FIP "Advertisement" containing its FCF-MAC address (unicast)
3. FCF sends ELP to each FCF-MAC it discovered
4. Upon successful completion of ELP each FCF instantiates an instance of a VE_Port

Figure 10-8. FCoE FCF Interswitch Link (ISL) Discovery

If an FCF receives a Discovery Solicitation containing its own Switch_Name, it does not respond to the Discovery Solicitation.

Figure 10-9 on page 131 provides a flow diagram illustrating the FCF-to-FCF discovery protocol.

10.4.2 ISL Initialization

The FCF sends an Exchange Link Parameters (ELP) Switch Internal Link service to the FCF-MAC address of other FCF (see *FIP ELP Request and Reply* on page 158 for the format of the ELP). Upon successful completion of the ELP, both FCFs instantiate an instance of a FCoE_LEP and VE_Port. Once this is complete, subsequent operations use the FCoE protocol and encapsulated Fibre Channel frames. An example of the Discovery and Virtual Link Initialization is shown in Figure 10-10 on page 132.

As with ENode Discovery, the Discovery Solicitation and Discovery Advertisement are sent using the FIP protocol. However, unlike ENode Discovery, the FCFs use an Exchange Link Parameters operation to setup the virtual link parameters. Upon successful completion the ELP, each FCF instantiates an instance of a VE_Port for the virtual link.

Periodically, FCFs may send a FIP "Discovery Advertisement" to the "All-FCoE-Forwarders" group address to facilitate discovery of a newly available FCF or a no-longer reachable FCF.

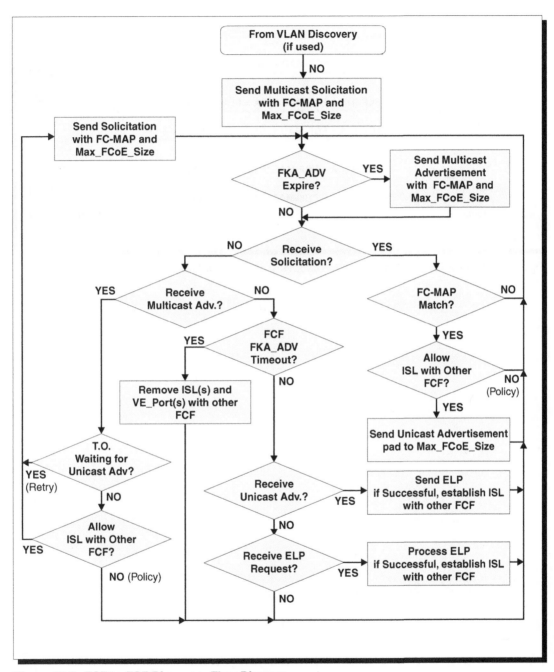

Figure 10-9. FCF-to-FCF Discovery Flow Diagram

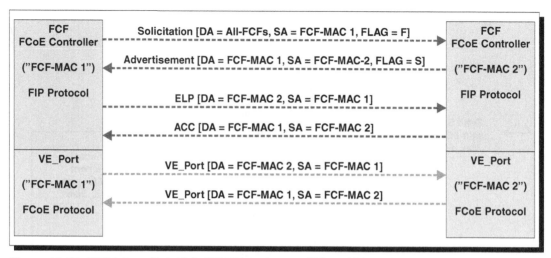

Figure 10-10. FCF Interswitch Link (ISL) Discovery and Virtual Link Initialization

10.5 Chapter Summary

Discovery and Virtual Link Initialization

- FCoE entities communicate via "virtual" links
  - Rather than point-to-point physical links as in native Fibre Channel
  - Additional processing is required before normal Fibre Channel operations can begin
- There are three distinct initialization and operational phases along with two different FCoE-related protocols

What Needs Discovering?

- ENodes need to discover reachable FCFs
  - This is where FLOGI(s) will be sent
- FCFs need to discover other FCFs
  - In order to discover potential inter-switch (inter-FCF?) links
- FCFs need to discover a newly connected FCF
  - If an FCF is added, other FCFs need to be able to discover that
- FCFs need to discover an FCF that is no longer available
  - If an FCF fails or is removed, other FCFs need to be able to discover that fact
- FCFs need to discover if an FCoE VN_Port is no longer available

Discovery Assumptions

- Each FCoE ENode has:
  - A "lossless" Ethernet MAC with a "burned-in" MAC address
  - An FCoE Controller to perform discovery
  - Recognition of an "All-FCoE-ENodes" group address
- Each FCoE Forwarder (FCF) has:
  - A "lossless" Ethernet MAC with a "burned-in" MAC address (the FCF-MAC address)
  - An FCoE Controller to perform discovery
  - Recognition of the "All-FCoE-Forwarders" group address

ENode to FCF Discovery: Solicitation

- When the ENode MAC initializes, its FCoE Controller transmits a FIP "Solicitation" request
  - The Discovery Solicitation uses the FCoE Initialization Protocol (FIP) as its EtherType
  - The Destination Address (DA) is set to the "All-FCoE Forwarders" group address
  - The Ethernet Source Address (SA) is set to its "burned-in" ENode MAC address
- If the ENode is connected to an intervening "lossless" Ethernet network the Solicitation request is multicast to all reachable FCFs.

FIP Discovery Solicitation

- The Discovery Solicitation contains a Descriptor List with the following parameters:
  - The ENode MAC Address
  - The Node_Name
  - The Ethernet frame Max_FCoE_Size
- The Max_FCoE_Size parameter is used to determine support for jumbo frames
  - Indicates the maximum quantity of FCoE information that can be contained in an Ethernet frame

ENode Discovery: Advertisement

- Each FCF that receives a Solicitation from an ENode responds with an "Advertisement"
- The Discovery Advertisement contains
  - The FCF-MAC address of the FCF
  - Name of the FCF and the name of the Fabric
  - The FC-MAP value
  - A Priority parameter that can be used by the Enode when selecting an FCF
  - Timeout Parameter called FKA_ADV_Period
- Based on Advertisements received, the Enode:
  - Builds a list of reachable FCFs and
  - Proceeds to Enode Virtual Link Initialization

ENode Virtual Link Establishment

- Once an ENode has discovered reachable FCFs, it:
  - Performs Fabric Login (FLOGI) to establish a link with the FCF and acquire an N_Port_ID.
  - The ENode may perform FLOGI with one, some, or all of the discovered FCFs.
  - It may use the Priority Field, or other parameters, from the Advertisements to decide which FCFs to send FLOGI to
- FLOGI request is sent using the FIP protocol
  - FLOGI Descriptor has the FLOGI frame content
  - MAC Address Descriptor (unused in request, contains assigned MAC address in LS_ACC)

FLOGI LS_ACC: FCF Actions

- Upon successful completion of the FLOGI the FCF:
  - Sends an LS_ACC (using the FIP protocol)
  - Instantiates an instance of a VF_Port for this virtual link
  - The VF_Port uses the VF_Port Name and Fabric_Name sent in the LS_ACC reply
  - The FCF makes the appropriate entries in the Fibre Channel Name Server database for the VN_Port

FLOGI LS_ACC: Enode Actions

- Upon completion of FLOGI, the Enode:
  - Instantiates an instance of a VN_Port for this virtual link
  - VN_Port uses the N_Port_ID assigned by the FCF in the LS_ACC reply to the FLOGI request and the Node_Name and Port_Name provided when it sent the FLOGI request
- The VN_Port MAC address used depends on the addressing method
- Subsequent operations (with the exception of FLOGI, NPIV FDISC and Fabric LOGO) use the FCoE protocol and normal encapsulated Fibre Channel frames.

FIP NPIV FDISC Request

- An ENode may issue an FDISC to acquire an additional N_Port_ID
  - The FC Destination ID = FF:FF:FEh
  - The FC Source ID = 00:00:00h
  - A unique Port_Name is provided
  - If the FDISC is successful, a Fibre Channel address is allocated and a new VN_Port instantiated
- NPIV FDISC is performed using the FIP protocol
  - The format is similar to a FIP FLOGI request

FCF Discovery and Virtual ISL Init.

- The same basic discovery method is used by an FCF to discover other reachable FCFs.
- Each FCF sends a FIP "Discovery Solicitation" to the "All-FCoE-Forwarders" group address.
- The Discovery Solicitation contains:
  - The sender's FCF-MAC address
  - The FCF flag bit (F) indicates that the sender is an FCF rather than an ENode
- Each receiving FCF sends an "Advertisement" to the FCF-MAC address in the "Solicitation"
  - Based on Advertisements received, the FCF builds a list of other reachable FCFs and can proceed to ISL virtual link initialization

FIP Exchange Link Parameters (ELP)

- Fibre Channel switches and FCFs establish link parameters using the ELP Switch Internal Link Service
  - Because this creates a virtual link, it is mapped to a FIP operation in FCoE
  - This enables intervening Ethernet switches to snoop the FIP protocol and setup or remove access control lists

---

11. FCoE Initialization Protocol (FIP)

Because of the "virtual" links between FCoE entities, rather than point-to-point physical links in native Fibre Channel, additional processing is required before normal Fibre Channel operations can begin. There are three distinct initialization and operational phases performed using two different FCoE-related protocols; the FCoE Initialization Protocol (FIP) and the FCoE Encapsulation Protocols. The relationship of these protocols is illustrated by Figure 11-1.

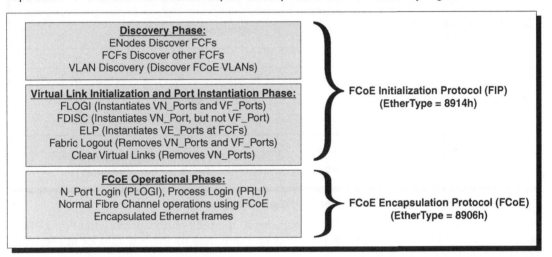

Figure 11-1. FCoE Operational Phases

11.1 FCoE Initialization Protocol (FIP)

During the Discovery and Virtual Link Initialization phases, FCoE devices use the FCoE Initialization Protocol (FIP). The FIP protocol is identified by the EtherType field of the Ethernet frame header (8914h) and uses the general frame format shown in Figure 11-2 on page 136.

An Ethernet frame containing a FIP operation is also referred to as a FIP message. The MAC Client Data field contains a FIP Header and one or more FIP Descriptors that provide parameters associated with the FIP operation (the combination of the FIP Header and FIP Descriptors is also referred to as a FIP Frame). The maximum size of a FIP frame is specified by the Max_FCoE_Size parameter (see *FIP Max FCoE Size Descriptor* on page 141).

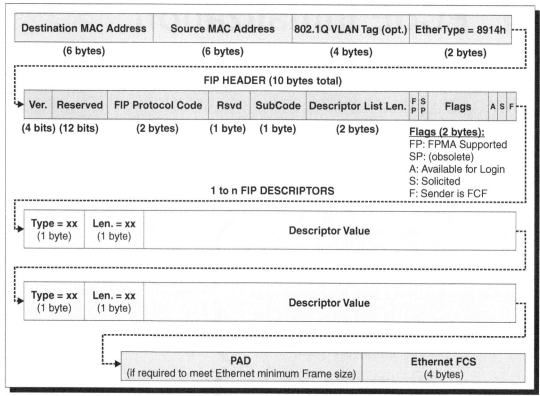

Figure 11-2. FCoE Initialization Protocol (FIP) General Frame Format

From a Fibre Channel perspective, FIP is "classless". It does not encapsulate the Fibre Channel SOF, EOF or CRC. Because FIP is classless, there may be implications for applications that perform FLOGI using Class-2.

By having a distinct protocol for Discovery and Virtual Link Initialization, operations that are associated with the establishment and removal of virtual links and ports can be readily distinguished from normal FCoE operations. Frames associated with these operations can be directed to the FCoE controller in an ENode or FCF (or the control plane of an FCoE aware "lossless" Ethernet switch) based on the EtherType field without having to examine the frame content.

Some FCoE-aware "lossless" Ethernet switches may snoop the FIP protocol as it is being used to initialize virtual links and their associated ports in order to automatically configure access control lists. Again, having a readily identifiable initialization protocol simplifies this type of snooping by switches. Frames with the FIP EtherType can be directed to an Ethernet switch's control plane or processor for processing or inspection. Frames with the FCoE EtherType field can simply be forwarded by the data plane.

11.1.1 Ethernet Frames, FIP Frames, FIP Messages and FIP Operations

FCoE uses several terms to reference FIP-related items as shown by Figure 11-3 on page 137. Note that an Ethernet MAC may be capable of sending or receiving a larger quantity of data in non-FCoE frames than the value specified by the MAX_FCoE_Size. A solicited unicast Discovery Advertisement is padded to the Max_FCoE_Size. Some FIP frames require Ethernet padding to meet the Ethernet minimum frame size requirement.

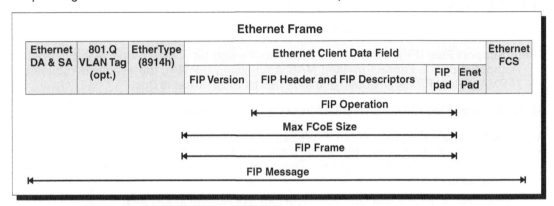

Figure 11-3. FIP Frame and FIP Message Format

11.1.2 FIP Protocol Code Field

The FIP operation is identified by the 16-bit FIP Protocol Code and 8-bit SubCode fields as listed in Table 11-1 on page 137. Currently there are four categories of operations defined that correspond to the Discovery and Virtual Link Initialization phases. The specific operation within each phase is identified using the SubCode field.

FIP Protocol Code	FIP SubCode	Operation
0001h	01h	Discovery Solicitation
	02h	Discovery Advertisement
0002h	01h	FLOGI/FDISC/LOGO/ELP Request
	02h	FLOGI/FDISC/LOGO/ELP Reply
0003h	01h	FIP Keep Alive (FKA)
	02h	FIP Clear Virtual Link
0004h	01h	FIP VLAN Discovery Request
	02h	FIP VLAN Discovery Notification
FFF8h - FFFEh	00h - FFh	Vendor Specific
All others	All others	Reserved

Table 11-1. FIP Protocol Codes and SubCodes

11.1.3 FIP Descriptor List Length Field

The FIP Descriptor List Length field specifies the number of 4-byte words in the Descriptor List contained within this FIP operation. While each Descriptor contains its own length field, the FIP Descriptor List Length field is necessary because the FIP frame may contain PAD bytes following the last Descriptor.

11.1.4 FIP Flags

The FIP Flags provide specific indications associated with FIP operations.

FPMA Support Flag (FP). When the FP Capability flag bit is set to one, it indicates the sender supports Fabric Provided MAC Addressing (FPMA), the sender is requesting FPMA, or that FPMA has been granted. This bit must be set to one.

SPMA Support Flag (SP). Obsolete addressing method. Must be set to zero.

Available for Login Flag (A). When the A flag bit is set to one, it indicates that the sending FCF is available for accepting Fabric Login (FLOGI), NPIV Fabric Discover (FDISC), or Exchange Link Parameters (ELP). This bit is only set by an FCF in a FIP Discovery Advertisement.

Note: The "A" bit is a real-time indication and can change at any time.

Solicited Flag (S). When the S flag bit is set to one, it indicates that this FIP operation (Discovery Advertisement) was sent in response to a Discovery Solicitation request.

FCF Flag (F). When the F flag bit is set to one, it indicates that this FIP operation was sent by an FCF. When set to zero, the FIP operation was sent by an ENode.

11.2 FIP Descriptors

FIP descriptors provide parameters associated with FIP operations. Descriptors use a "Type, Length, Value (TLV)" format so that each descriptor is self-describing and new descriptors can be added as necessary without changing the format of existing descriptors. A listing of the descriptors is provided in Table 11-2 on page 139.

If an FCoE device receives a FIP operation containing a descriptor categorized as "critical" and it does not recognize that descriptor, or the descriptor is improperly formed, the entire FIP operation is ignored.

If an FCoE device receives a FIP operation containing a descriptor categorized as "non-critical" and it does not recognize that particular descriptor, or the descriptor is improperly formed, that descriptor is ignored, but other FIP descriptors in the FIP operation are still processed.

11.2.1 FIP Priority Descriptor

The FIP Priority Descriptor is used in the FIP Discovery Advertisement. The ENode may use the Priority Field value to determine to which FCFs is should send Fabric Login (FLOGI) and establish virtual links. The Priority descriptor format is shown in Table 11-3 on page 139.

Descriptor Type Value	Description	See Page	Category
1	Priority Descriptor	138	
2	MAC Address Descriptor	139	
3	FC-MAP Descriptor	140	
4	Name_Identifier Descriptor	140	
5	Fabric Descriptor	140	
6	Max FCoE Size Descriptor	141	
7	FLOGI Descriptor	142	
8	NPIV_FDISC Descriptor	142	Critical
9	LOGO Descriptor	143	
10	ELP Descriptor	143	
11	Vx_Port Identification Descriptor	144	
12	FKA_ADV_Period	144	
13	FIP Vendor_ID Descriptor	145	
14	FCoE VLAN Descriptor	145	
15 - 127	Reserved		
128 - 240	Reserved		
241 - 254	Vendor Specific Descriptor		Non-Critical
255	Reserved		

Table 11-2. FIP Descriptors

	Byte 0	Byte 1	Byte 2	Byte 3
Word 0	Type = 1	Len = 1 (word)	Reserved	Priority

Table 11-3. FIP Priority Descriptor Format

A Priority value of 0 indicates highest priority and a value of 255 (FFh) indicates lowest priority. The default Priority Descriptor value is 128 (80h).

The FCoE standard does not specify how an FCF determines the value for the Priority descriptor. It could be used to indicate the relative availability of login-related resources at an FCF. For example, as the number of attached VN_Ports increases, the Priority value could be lowered in order to "encourage" ENodes to login with other FCFs (if they discover multiple FCFs during the Discovery process).

11.2.2 FIP MAC Address Descriptor

The MAC Address Descriptor is used to communicate an Ethernet MAC address. The format of the descriptor is shown in Table 11-4 on page 140.

	Byte 0	Byte 1	Byte 2	Byte 3
Word 0	Type = 2	Len = 2 (words)	MAC Address	
Word 1	MAC Address (continued)			

Table 11-4. FIP MAC Address Descriptor Format

11.2.3 FIP FC-MAP Descriptor

The FC-MAP Descriptor is used to transfer an FC-MAP value from an FCF to an ENode. The format of the FC-MAP descriptor is shown in Table 11-5.

	Byte 0	Byte 1	Byte 2	Byte 3
Word 0	Type = 3	Len = 3 (words)	Reserved	
Word 1	Reserved	FC-MAP (3 bytes) - default value = 0E:FC:00h		

Table 11-5. FIP FC-MAP Descriptor Format

It is anticipated that the FC-MAP value will be used to identify a given FCoE fabric in a multi-fabric installation. By having a different FC-MAP value for each, it is possible to determine if a frame is associated with a given fabric. This may provide an additional level of error detection in the event that an Ethernet frame is somehow delivered to an FCoE destination in another fabric.

11.2.4 FIP Name_Identifier Descriptor

The Name_Identifier Descriptor is used to communicate a 64-bit Fibre Channel name (Port_Name, Node_Name or Switch_Name). The format of the descriptor is shown in Table 11-6.

	Byte 0	Byte 1	Byte 2	Byte 3
Word 0	Type = 4	Len = 3 (words)	Reserved	
Word 1	Name_Identifier			
Word 2	Name_Identifier (continued)			

Table 11-6. FIP Name_Identifier Descriptor Format

11.2.5 FIP Fabric Descriptor

The Fabric Descriptor is used to communicate Fabric-related parameters, including a Virtual Fabric ID, the FC-MAP and 64-bit Fibre Channel Fabric_Name of the Fabric to which the sending FCF belongs. The format of the Fabric descriptor is shown in Table 11-7.

	Byte 0	**Byte 1**	**Byte 2**	**Byte 3**
Word 0	Type = 5	Len = 4 (words)	Virtual Fabric ID	
Word 1	Reserved	FC-MAP		
Word 2	Fabric_Name			
Word 3	Fabric_Name (continued)			

Table 11-7. FIP Fabric_Name Descriptor Format

NOTE – The format of the Fabric descriptor was modified by the T11 working group during the standard development process to include the Virtual Fabric ID and FC-MAP values. Some early documentation and products may reflect the earlier definition.

FIP Max FCoE Size Descriptor. The ENode sets the Max FCoE Size Descriptor value to specify the size to which a solicited Advertisement is to be padded by an FCF. The Max FCoE Size Descriptor provides a method to determine whether a specified frame size is able to propagate successfully from an FCF to the ENode. The format of the descriptor is shown in Table 11-8.

	Byte 0	**Byte 1**	**Byte 2**	**Byte 3**
Word 0	Type = 6	Len = 1 (word)	Max_FCoE_Size (number of bytes)	

Table 11-8. FIP Max FCoE Size Descriptor Format

In order to encapsulate a maximum size FCoE frame, the Max_FCoE_Size value is computed as shown in Figure 11-4 on page 141 (note that the presence of FC Extended Headers increases the Max_FCoE_Size value).

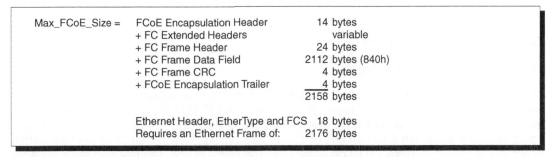

Figure 11-4. Max_FCoE_Size Value for Maximum-Size Fibre Channel Frame

An Ethernet MAC may be capable of receiving a non-FCoE Ethernet frame with a MAC Client Data Field size larger than the Max_FCoE_Size value.

If an Ethernet MAC only supports a MAC Client Data Field size of 1500 bytes, the Fibre Channel Receive Data Field Size value must be reduced to limit the size of encapsulated Fibre

Channel frames. Figure 11-5 on page 142 (note that the presence of FC Extended Headers increases the Max_FCoE_Size value).

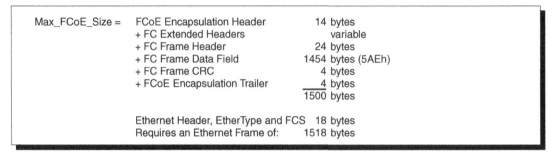

Figure 11-5. Max_FCoE_Size Value for Standard Ethernet Frame Size

11.2.6 FIP FLOGI Descriptor

The FLOGI Descriptor is used to transport a Fabric Login Request (FLOGI) and its associated LS_ACC or LS_RJT reply. The FLOGI request and reply consists of the FC Frame Header and Data Field (note that the Fibre Channel SOF, EOF and FC Frame CRC are not included). The format of the FLOGI descriptor is shown in Table 11-9.

The Length field is set to 36 (words) for a FLOGI request or LS_ACC reply and 9 (words) for an LS_RJT reply.

	Byte 0	**Byte 1**	**Byte 2**	**Byte 3**
Word 0	Type = 7	Len = 36 or 9 (words)	Reserved	
Word 1:6	Encapsulated Fibre Channel Frame Header (6 words)			
Word 7:n	FLOGI Request or LS_ACC Reply Payload (29 words), or LS_RJT Reply Payload (2 words)			

Table 11-9. FIP FLOGI Descriptor Format

11.2.7 FIP NPIV_FDISC Descriptor

The NPIV_FDISC Descriptor is used to transport an NPIV Fabric Discover Request (FDISC) with a S_ID = 00:00:00h and its associated LS_ACC or LS_RJT reply. A Fabric Discover request having a non-zero S_ID field is transported using the FCoE protocol, not the FIP protocol (it does not establish a virtual link or instantiate ports). The format of the FDISC_NPIV descriptor is shown in Table 11-10 on page 143. The NPIV FDISC request and reply consists of the FC Frame Header and Data Field (SOF, EOF and FC Frame CRC are not included).

The Length field is set to 36 (words) for a NPIV_FDISC request or LS_ACC reply and 9 (words) for an LS_RJT reply.

	Byte 0	Byte 1	Byte 2	Byte 3
Word 0	Type = 8	Len = 36 or 9 (words)	Reserved	
Word 1:6	Encapsulated Fibre Channel Frame Header (6 words)			
Word 7:n	NPIV_FDISC Request (S_ID = 00:00:00h) or LS_ACC Reply Payload (29 words), or LS_RJT Reply Payload (2 words)			

Table 11-10. FIP NPIV_FDISC Descriptor Format

11.2.8 FIP LOGO Descriptor

The LOGO Descriptor is used to transport a Fabric Logout Request (LOGO) with a D_ID of FF:FF:FEh and its associated LS_ACC or LS_RJT reply. A LOGO with a Fibre Channel Destination_ID other than FF:FF:FEh is communicated using the FCoE protocol, not the FIP protocol (it does not remove a virtual link or ports).

The format of the LOGO descriptor is shown in Table 11-11. The LOGO request and reply consists of the FC Frame Header and Data Field (note that the Fibre Channel SOF, EOF and FC Frame CRC are not included)

The length of the descriptor is set to 11 (words) for a LOGO request, 8 (words) for a LS_ACC reply and 9 (words) for an LS_RJT reply.

	Byte 0	Byte 1	Byte 2	Byte 3
Word 0	Type = 9	Len = 11, 8 or 9 (words)	Reserved	
Word 1:6	Encapsulated Fibre Channel Frame Header (6 words)			
Word 7:n	Fabric LOGO Request (D_ID = FF:FF:FEh) (4 words), or LS_ACC Reply Payload (1 word), or LS_RJT Reply Payload (2 words)			

Table 11-11. FIP LOGO Descriptor Format

11.2.9 FIP ELP Descriptor

The ELP Descriptor is used by an FCF to Exchange Link Parameters with another FCF. The format of the ELP descriptor is shown in Table 11-12 on page 144. The ELP request and reply consists of the FC Frame Header and Data Field (note that the Fibre Channel SOF, EOF and FC Frame CRC are not included).

The length of the descriptor is set to 33 (words) for an ELP request or SW_ACC reply and 9 (words) for an SW_RJT reply.

	Byte 0	Byte 1	Byte 2	Byte 3
Word 0	Type = 10	Len = 33 or 9 (words)	Reserved	
Word 1:6	Encapsulated Fibre Channel Frame Header (6 words)			
Word 7:n	Exchange Link Parameters (ELP) Request or LS_ACC Reply (26 words), or LS_RJT Reply Payload (2 words)			

Table 11-12. FIP Exchange Link Parameters (ELP) Descriptor Format

11.2.10 FIP Vx_Port Identification Descriptor

The Vx_Port Identification Descriptor is used by a Vx_Port in the FIP Keep Alive message to notify an FCF that the VN_Port is functional (see *ENode FCoE Controller Behavior* on page 196). The format of the Vx_Port Identification Descriptor is shown in Table 11-13.

	Byte 0	Byte 1	Byte 2	Byte 3
Word 0	Type = 11	Len = 5 (words)	VN_Port MAC Address	
Word 1	VN_Port MAC Address (continued)			
Word 2	Reserved	VN_Port N_Port_ID (3 bytes)		
Word 3	VN_Port_Name			
Word 4	VN_Port_Name (continued)			

Table 11-13. FIP Vx_Port Identifier Descriptor Format

11.2.11 FIP FKA_ADV_Period Descriptor

The FKA_ADV_Period Descriptor is sent by an FCF in a Discovery Advertisement and specifies the time between periodic Discovery Advertisements or FIP Keep Alive messages (see *FIP Keep Alive (FKA)* on page 162). The value of the FKA_ADV_Period should be the same in all FCFs within a Fabric. The value is specified in milliseconds with a recommended default value of 8 seconds (8000 msec.). A value of zero, or absence of the FKA_ADV_Period descriptor in a Discovery Advertisement, means that no Keep Alive messages are requested.

The format of the FKA_ADV_Period Descriptor is shown in Table 11-14 on page 144.

	Byte 0	Byte 1	Byte 2	Byte 3	
Word 0	Type = 12	Len = 2 (words)	Reserved		D
Word 1	FKA_ADV_Period (in milliseconds: default value = 8000)				

Table 11-14. FIP FKA_ADV_Period Descriptor Format

D (Disabled) bit. The D bit may be configured by an administrator at an FCF.

When set to one, the receiving ENode MAC may optionally verify periodic reception of Discovery Advertisements and should not transmit periodic FIP Keep Alive frames. A VF_Port capable FCF-MAC does not verify periodic reception of FIP Keep Alive frames and may discard any received FIP Keep Alive frames.

When set to zero, the receiving ENode MAC does verify periodic reception of Discovery Advertisements and does transmit periodic ENode FIP Keep Alive and VN_Port FIP Keep Alive frames. A VF_Port capable FCF-MAC does verify periodic reception of ENode FIP Keep Alive and VN_Port FIP Keep Alive frames.

FKA_ADV_Period. An administrator may change the FKA_ADV_Period. If this occurs, the FCF begins using the new value in subsequent unsolicited Discovery Advertisements.

If the new FKA_ADV_Period is shorter than the previous FKA_ADV_Period, the FCF will transmit subsequent unsolicited Discovery Advertisements based on the new value. The FCF will not use the updated value for detecting missing FIP Keep Alives until five times the old value has elapsed since transmission of the first unsolicited Discovery Advertisement using the updated value.

If the new FKA_ADV_Period is greater than the previous FKA_ADV_Period, the FCF continues to transmit unsolicited Discovery Advertisements based on the old value until five times the updated value has elapsed since transmission of the first unsolicited Discovery Advertisement using the new value. The FCF will use the updated value for detection of missing FIP Keep Alive messages.

Upon detection of an updated FKA_ADV_Period value, an ENode will transmit FIP Keep Alive messages based on the updated value and use that updated value for detection of missing unsolicited Discovery Advertisements.

11.2.12 FIP Vendor_ID Descriptor

The FIP Vendor_ID Descriptor identifies the vendor associated with a vendor-specific FIP operation. The format of the FIP Vendor_ID descriptor is shown in Table 11-15 on page 145.

	Byte 0	**Byte 1**	**Byte 2**	**Byte 3**
Word 0	Type = 13	Len = 3 (words)	Reserved	
Word 1	Vendor_ID			
Word 2	Vendor_ID (continued)			

Table 11-15. FIP Vendor_ID Descriptor Format

11.2.13 FIP FCoE VLAN Descriptor

The FCoE VLAN descriptor is used to identify an Ethernet VLAN associated with FCoE traffic. The FCoE VLAN descriptor contains a single parameter, the VLAN Identifier as shown in Table 11-16 on page 146.

	Byte 0	Byte 1	Byte 2	Byte 3
Word 0	Type = 14	Len = 1 (word)	FCoE VLAN Identifier	

Table 11-16. FIP VLAN Descriptor Format

NOTE – The VLAN Identifier is consists of the 10 least significant bits of bytes 2 and 3. The 6 most significant bits of byte 2 are reserved.

11.2.14 FIP Vendor-Specific Descriptor

A vendor-specific descriptor uses a Type value within the range of 241 to 254 and has the format shown in Table 11-17 on page 146.

	Byte 0	Byte 1	Byte 2	Byte 3
Word 0	Type = (241:254)	Len = 3+ (words)	Reserved	
Word 1	Vendor_ID			
Word 2	Vendor_ID (continued)			
Word 3:n	Vendor-Specific Information (variable)			

Table 11-17. FIP Vendor-Specific Descriptor Format

11.3 FIP Messages

A FIP message consists of an Ethernet frame containing a FIP operation. Each FIP operation contains one or more FIP descriptors. The formats of the various FIP messages are shown on the following pages.

11.3.1 FIP Discovery Solicitation From an ENode

The format of the ENode FIP Discovery Solicitation is shown in Figure 11-6. The Discovery Solicitation Descriptor List contains two parameters, the ENode MAC address and the Node_Name Descriptor (it may contain other Discovery parameters in the future). While including the ENode MAC address as a parameter may seem redundant (it is already in the Ethernet frame header Source Address field), the Ethernet header may not be available to the level that is processing the FIP protocol.

The Destination MAC Address is set to the 'ALL_FCF_MACS' group address and the Source MAC Address is set to the ENode's MAC address.

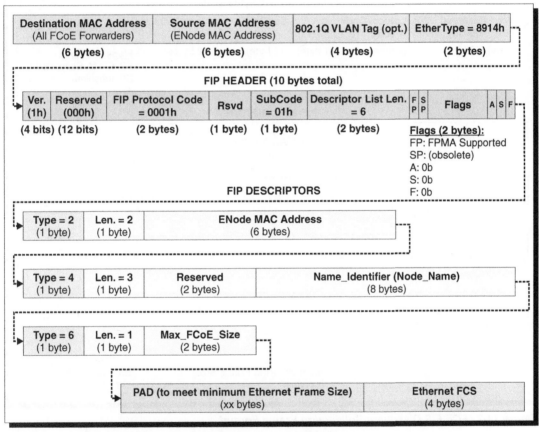

Figure 11-6. ENode FIP Discovery Solicitation Frame Format

NOTE – Padding is required to meet the minimum Ethernet frame size requirement.

11.3.2 FIP Discovery Solicitation From FCF

The format of an FCF FIP Discovery Solicitation is shown in Figure 11-7 on page 148. The Discovery Solicitation Descriptor List contains the FCF-MAC address, the FC-MAP value, the Switch_Name and the Max FCoE Size Descriptors.

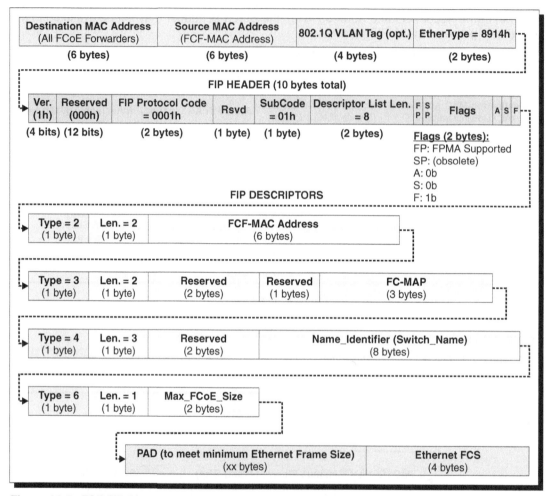

Figure 11-7. FCF FIP Discovery Solicitation Frame Format

NOTE – Padding is required to meet the minimum Ethernet frame size requirement.

11.3.3 FIP Discovery Advertisement

The FCF transmits a Discovery Advertisement to an ENode FCoE controller in response to a Discovery Solicitation. In this case, the Destination MAC Address is set to the ENode's MAC

Address, the Solicited (S) bit is set to one and the frame is padded to the Max_FCoE_Size value from the received Discovery Solicitation. This provides a method to determine that the path between the requestor and the FCF is capable of passing a frame with the Max_FCoE_Size. If the Discovery Advertisement is not being sent in response to a Discovery Solicitation, padding is not required.

> NOTE – This method does not ensure that Max_FCoE_Size frames will be supported if the path through an intervening Ethernet network is reconfigured and a switch in the new path does not support frames of this size.

The format of the FIP Discovery Advertisement is shown in Figure 11-8 on page 150.

In addition, an FCF transmits Discovery Advertisements on a periodic basis. This provides a method for ENodes to detect an FCF without sending a Discovery Solicitation, or if the Discovery Solicitation failed due to a transmission error. When a periodic Discovery Advertisement is sent, the destination MAC address is set to the "ALL ENodes" group address (see Table 7-2 on page 73) and the source MAC address is set to the FCF-MAC address. The Solicited bit (S) is set to zero to indicate that the Discovery Advertisement is not being sent in response to a Discovery Solicitation.

The default time between periodic Discovery Advertisements is specified by D_A_TOV and is five seconds, although this time may be configurable by an administrator to a value between one second and 60 seconds.

Periodic Discovery Advertisements also provide a way for ENodes or intermediate Ethernet switches to detect a no-longer available FCF. If a Discovery Advertisement is not received from an FCF within three times FKA_ADV_Period, the ENode Controller may assume that the FCF is no-longer reachable and terminate any login sessions associated with that VF_Port. In a similar manner, intermediate Ethernet switches my remove any automatically created access control lists or static forwarding table entries if they fail to detect a Discovery Advertisement from the VF_Port within three times FKA_ADV_Period.

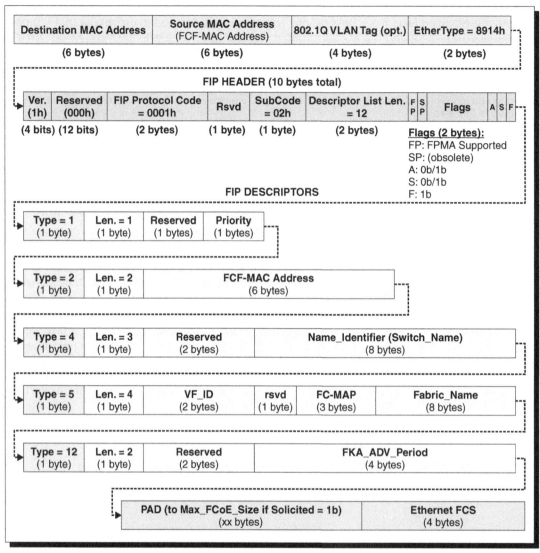

Figure 11-8. FIP Discovery Advertisement Frame Format

11.3.4 FIP FLOGI Request and Reply

A Fabric Login (FLOGI) request is sent by an ENode to an FCF to establish a session with the Fabric and exchange service parameters with the Fabric. The FCF responds with either LS_ACC or LS_RJT to indicate whether the FLOGI request was successful or failed.

FLOGI Request. The format of the FLOGI request is shown in Figure 11-9 on page 151. The SubCode field in the FIP Header is set to 01h in the FLOGI request and 02h in the reply. The FIP Descriptors must be in the specified order.

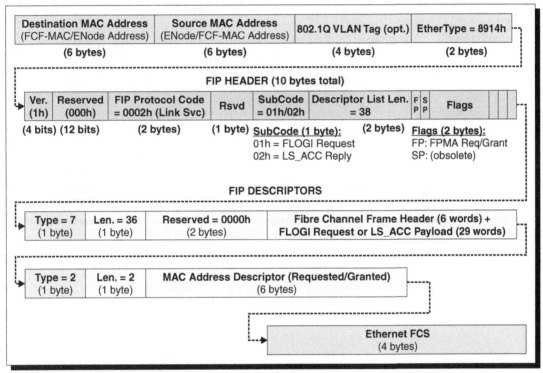

Figure 11-9. FIP FLOGI Request and LS_ACC Frame Format

In an FLOGI request, the MAC address descriptor contains the previously assigned MAC address (in the case of a relogin) or to zeros.

FLOGI LS_ACC Reply. If a FLOGI request is successful, the FCF sends an LS_ACC reply to the ENode. The format of the LS_ACC is the same as the FLOGI request shown in Figure 11-9 on page 151. The LS_ACC descriptor contains the FLOGI parameters of the FCF (and associated Fabric). The MAC address descriptor contains the MAC address associated with this login session (i.e., the MAC address being assigned by the FCF). The FIP Descriptors must be in the specified order.

FLOGI LS_RJT Reply. If a FLOGI request is not accepted by the FCF, an LS_RJT reply is sent to the ENode. The format of the LS_RJT is shown in Figure 11-10 on page 152. The FIP Descriptors must be in the specified order.

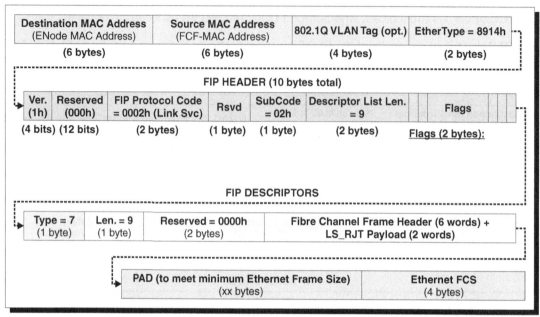

Figure 11-10. FIP FLOGI LS_RJT Frame Format

11.3.5 FIP NPIV FDISC Request and Reply

An ENode sends an NPIV FDISC request to an FCF to request the assignment of an additional address and instantiation of an additional VN_Port. The NPIV FDISC request and associated LS_ACC or LS_RJT reply are sent in FIP frames. An NPIV FDISC request has the Fibre Channel Destination ID set to FF:FF:FEh and the Source ID set to 00:00:00h (if the S_ID is not 00:00:00h, this is not an NPIV FDISC request and is encapsulated as an FCoE frame). The LS_ACC or LS_RJT reply is sent by an FCF to an ENode.

NPIV FDISC Request and LS_ACC Reply. The NPIV FDISC request and its LS_ACC reply have the format shown in Figure 11-11 on page 153. The SubCode field is set to 01h in the request and 02h in the reply. The FIP Descriptors must be in the specified order.

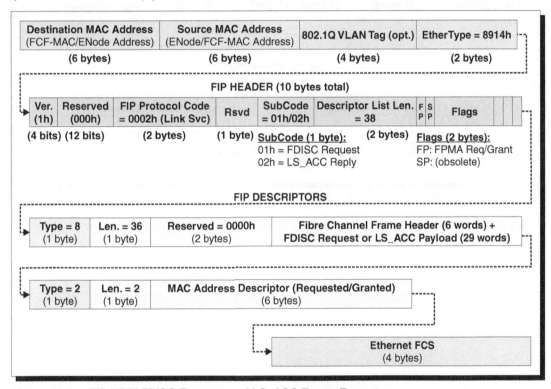

Figure 11-11. FIP NPIV FDISC Request and LS_ACC Frame Format

In an NPIV FDISC request, the MAC address descriptor field is set to zeros.

NPIV FDISC LS_ACC Reply. In an LS_ACC reply to a NPIV FDISC, the LS_ACC descriptor contains the service parameters of the FCF (and associated Fabric). The MAC address descriptor contains the MAC address associated with this login session (the MAC address being assigned by the FCF).

NPIV FDISC LS_RJT Reply. If the NPIV FDISC is not accepted, an LS_RJT reply is returned by the FCF. The format of the LS_RJT frame is shown in Figure 11-12 on page 154. The FIP Descriptors must be in the specified order.

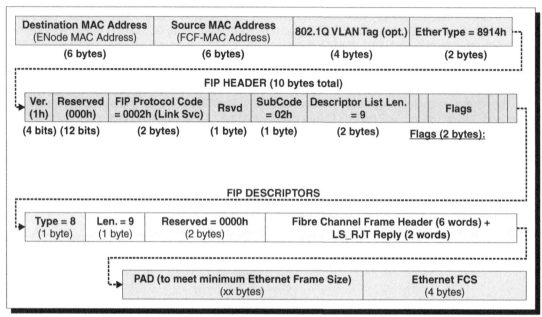

Figure 11-12. FIP NPIV FDISC LS_RJT Frame Format

11.3.6 FIP Fabric LOGO Request and Reply

A Fabric Logout requests removal of the session between a VN_Port and the Fabric. A Fabric Logout can be sent from an ENode to an FCF or from and FCF to an ENode.

When an ENode sends a Fabric Logout request, the Fibre Channel Destination_ID field is set to FF:FF:FEh and the Source_ID is set to the VN_Port's N_Port_ID.

When an FCF initiates a Fabric Logout, the Fibre Channel Destination_ID is set to the VN_Port's N_Port_ID and the Source_ID is set to FF:FF:FEh.

FIP Fabric LOGO Request. A FIP Fabric LOGO request has the format shown in Figure 11-13 on page 155. The FIP Descriptors must be in the specified order.

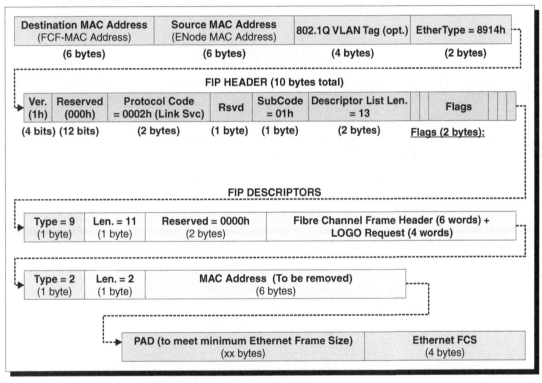

Figure 11-13. FIP Fabric LOGO Request Frame Format

FIP Fabric LOGO LS_ACC Reply. A FIP Fabric LOGO LS_ACC reply has the format shown in Figure 11-14 on page 156. The FIP Descriptors must be in the specified order.

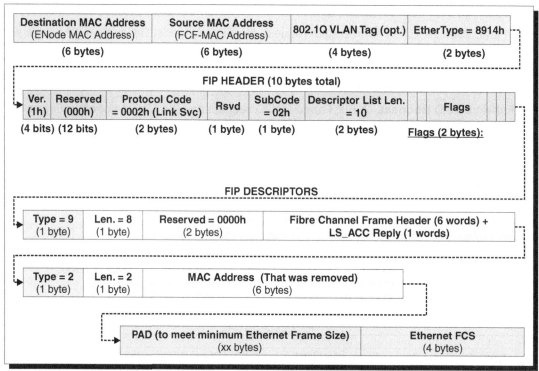

Figure 11-14. FIP Fabric LOGO LS_ACC Reply Frame Format

FIP Fabric LOGO LS_RJT Reply. If a LOGO request is not accepted, an LS_RJT reply is returned. The format of the LS_RJT is shown in Figure 11-14 on page 156. The FIP Descriptors must be in the specified order.

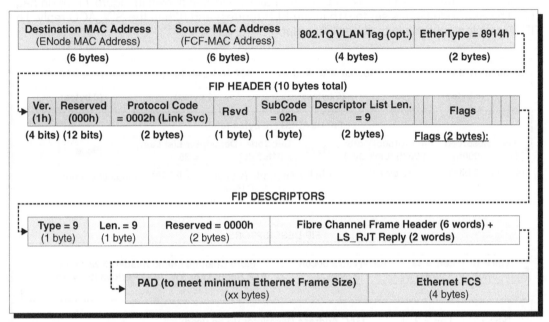

Figure 11-15. FIP Fabric LOGO LS_RJT Reply Frame Format

11.3.7 FIP ELP Request and Reply

The ELP request and associated SW_ACC or SW_RJT reply are sent in FIP frames. The format of the ELP request and its SW_ACC reply have the format shown in Figure 11-16 on page 158. The SubCode field is set to 01h in the ELP request and 02h in the SW_ACC reply. The FIP Descriptors must be in the specified order.

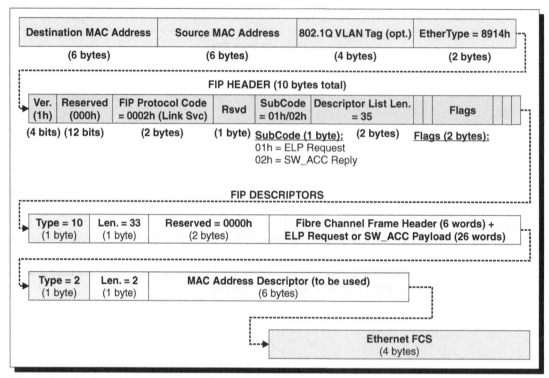

Figure 11-16. FIP ELP Request and SW_ACC Frame Format

FIP ELP SW_RJT Reply. If the ELP is not accepted, an SW_RJT reply is returned by the FCF. The format of the SW_RJT is shown in Figure 11-17 on page 159. The FIP Descriptors must be in the specified order.

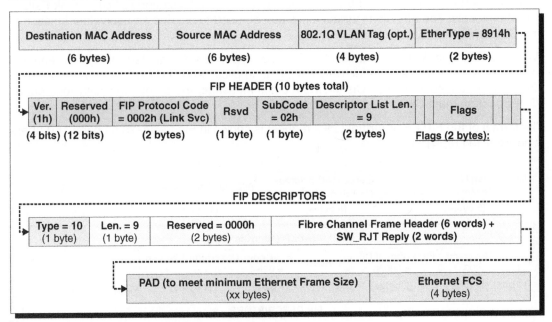

Figure 11-17. FIP ELP SW_RJT Reply Frame Format

11.3.8 FIP Clear Virtual Links

In a native Fibre Channel environment, certain link-related state information, such as login states and virtual N_Ports can be cleared using the Link Initialization (OLS) or Link Failure (NOS) protocols. The FIP Clear Virtual Links can be used to provide an equivalent function in an FCoE environment.

When the FIP Clear Virtual Links function is used, it removes designated VN_Port(s) and any associated state information (effectively forcing an implicit Fabric Logout). If no VN_Port Identifiers are contained in the FIP Clear Virtual Links message, the ENode implicitly logs out all VN_Ports from that FCF.

The format of the FIP Clear Virtual Links request is shown in Figure 11-18 on page 160 (there is no expected reply).

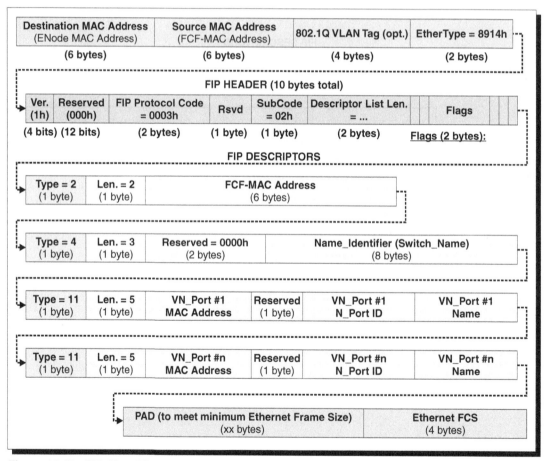

Figure 11-18. FIP Clear Virtual Links Frame Format

If an FCF receives a FIP Keep Alive from a VN_Port that it is not logged in with, it transmits a Clear Virtual Links message to logout the VN_Port. This provides a method to recover if a FIP Clear Virtual Links message is lost or corrupted due to a transmission error.

To protect against errant or malicious devices, only FCFs are allowed to issue the FIP Clear Virtual Links function. The FCF-MAC Address descriptor in the FIP Clear Virtual Links message may be different than the FCF-MAC address of the sender. In the case of a link failure, this capability enables an FCF to logout ports associated with a different physical link.

11.3.9 FIP Keep Alive (FKA)

Unlike native Fibre Channel, it is not possible for the VN_Port or VF_Port to determine when an intermediate Ethernet link fails and the VN_Port or VF_Port is no longer reachable. Periodic Advertisements and FIP Keep Alive messages provide a method to determine if an ENode, VN_Port or VF_Port is still accessible.

Two different FIP Keep Alive messages are defined:

- ENode FIP Keep Alive messages are transmitted at a more frequent rate (as defined by the FKA_ADV_Period) to enable timely detection of a failed ENode or virtual link.
- VN_Port FIP Keep Alive messages are transmitted less frequently (once every 90 seconds) to indicate that a specific VN_Port is functional.

By having two different FIP Keep Alive messages (sent a different rates), timely detection of a failed link can be accomplished without creating an excessive amount of traffic.

11.3.10 ENode FIP Keep Alive

An ENode transmits FIP Keep Alive to signal that the ENode and virtual link are functional. ENode FIP Keep Alive is transmitted every FKA_ADV_Period (see *FIP FKA_ADV_Period Descriptor* on page 144). When an ENode FIP Keep Alive is sent, the Destination MAC Address is set to the 'ALL_FCF_MACS' group address and the Source MAC Address is set to the ENode's MAC address. The format of an ENode FIP Keep Alive is shown in Figure 11-19 on page 162.

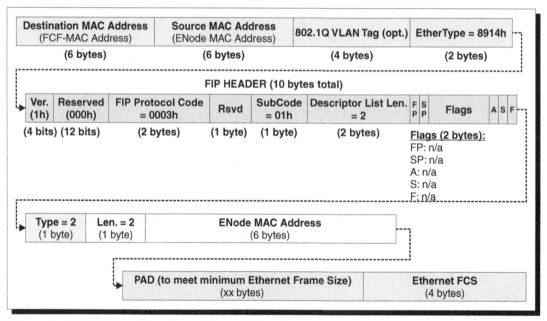

Figure 11-19. FIP Keep Alive Frame Format (ENode)

11.3.11 VN_Port FIP Keep Alive

An ENode transmits a VN_Port FIP Keep Alive every 90 seconds to signal that the designated VN_Port is functional. A VN_Port FIP Keep Alive contains both the ENode's MAC address descriptor and a VN_Port Identification descriptor containing the VN_Port's MAC Address, N_Port_ID and VN_Port_Name.

Absence of an expected VN_Port FIP Keep Alive enables detection of a no-longer functional ENode or VN_Port and may by used by intervening Ethernet switches to automatically delete access control list entries associated with a no-longer functional VN_Port.

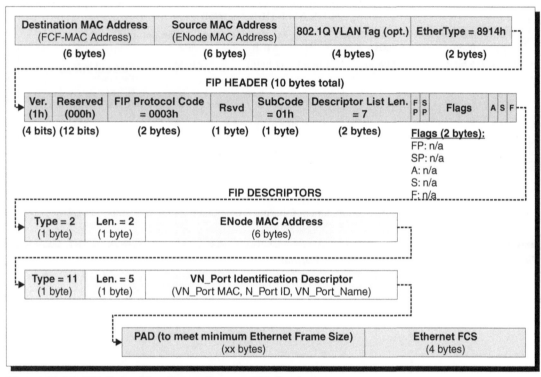

Figure 11-20. FIP Keep Alive Frame Format (VN_Port)

11.3.12 FIP VLAN Request

The FIP VLAN Request provides a means for an ENode to discover VLANs that are associated with FCoE traffic. The destination MAC address in the FIP VLAN Request is set to the "All-FCFs" group address and the source MAC address is set to the ENode's MAC address.

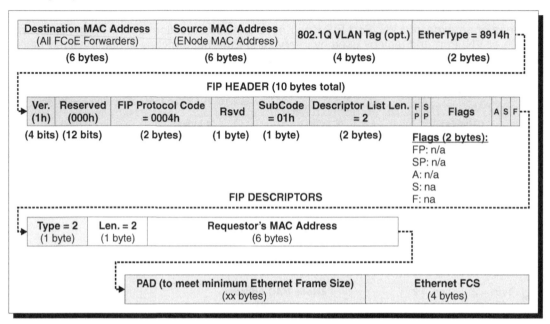

Figure 11-21. FIP VLAN Request Frame Format

11.3.13 FIP VLAN Notification

The FIP VLAN Notification specifies VLANs that are associated with FCoE traffic. The FIP VLAN Notification would normally be sent in response to a FIP VLAN Request received from an ENode. The destination MAC address is set to the requesting ENode's MAC address and the source MAC address is set to the FCF-MAC address of the sending FCF.

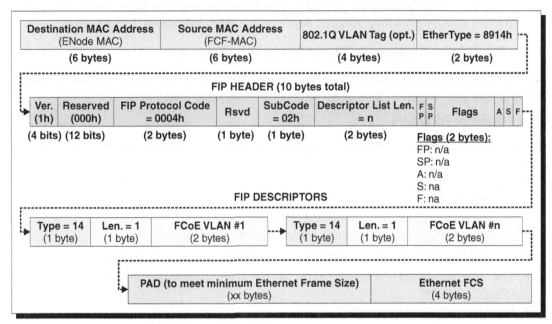

Figure 11-22. FIP VLAN Notification Frame Format

11.4 FIP Protocol Timers

There is no specified time relationship between when a Discovery Solicitation is sent and a Discovery Advertisement is received. If no reply is received within an implementation-specific time, the FCoE Controller may simply retry the Discovery Solicitation or wait for a periodic Discovery Advertisement.

FIP operations associated with encapsulated Fibre Channel Link Services (FLOGI, NPIV FDISC, ELP, LOGO) are timed by the corresponding Fibre Channel timer value (2 * R_A_TOV). If an expected reply is not received within this time the operation may be aborted using ABTS.

Two FCoE Initialization Protocol-related timers have been defined: the FKA_ADV_Period and MAX_RANDOM_DELAY.

FKA_ADV_Period. The value of the FKA_ADV_Period is recommended as 30 seconds (30,000 milliseconds) and is used to specify the time between periodic Discovery Advertisements and FIP Keep Alive messages. A value of zero means that FIP Keep Alive messages are not requested.

MAX_RANDOM_DELAY. The MAX_RANDOM_DELAY is used to randomize the time between multicast messages and their associated responses. The helps protect against inadvertent synchronizations between multicast senders and responders. The recommended default value for MAX_RANDOM_DELAY is 1,000 milliseconds with multicast transmissions or responses delayed uniformly between zero and the MAX_RANDOM_DELAY value.

11.5 FCoE Initialization Protocol Error Processing

For the purposes of error handling and recovery, FIP operations can be divided into two categories, those that transport Fibre Channel Link Services and those that do not.

11.5.1 General FIP Errors

There are several error conditions that may occur in one, or more, FIP operations. They include:

- There does not appear to be any upper bound on the size of an FCoE frame (i.e., it could theoretically be 9k bytes, or more)
- A FIP frame is larger than the MAX_FCoE_Size parameter
- An operation required to use FIP is done in the FCoE protocol
- The FIP message length does not match the Descriptor List Length field value
- The value appearing in a length field is large enough to cause unintended treatment as a negative number
- Pad fields are used as a covert channel
- Illegal settings of SP and FP flags in a FIP Operation header are not detected because descriptors later in the operation payload are wrong
- Certain messages are received by an FCoE_Port type that should not receive them (e.g., an ENode MAC should not process FIP messages from other ENodes)
- Embedded FC operations within FIP operations are malformed and passed to an FC element that does not check carefully
- A multicast address appears within a FIP payload in a way that causes it to destructively replace a unicast address
- A pathologically large or small value is sent as FKA_ADV_PERIOD
- Illegal values of VLAN ID appear in a FIP VLAN descriptor

11.5.2 Solicitation/Advertisement Errors

The following errors are specific to the Solicitation and Advertisement operations:

- No response to Solicitation (transmission error on Solicitation)
- No response to Solicitation (transmission error on solicited Advertisement)

- No response to Solicitation (padded Advertisement dropped by intervening Ethernet switch)
- Advertisement is not padded to MAX_FCoE_Size received in a Solicitation (e.g., what if the FCF does not support MAX_FCoE_Size?)

11.5.3 FIP FLOGI/FDISC Errors

- FPMA is specified and the LS_ACC returns a MAC address with the FC-MAP different than the one in the Advertisement.

11.5.4 Clear Virtual Link

- The Clear Virtual Links is corrupted and not recognized by the intended ENode. (if the FCF receives a FIP Keep Alive from a VN_Port after issuing a Clear Virtual Link, it sends a FIP Clear Virtual Links to the VN_Port.
- The list of ports in the Clear Virtual Links is larger than the MAX_FCoE_Size

11.5.5 FIP Encapsulated Link Service Operations

For FIP operations that transport Fibre Channel Link Services (FLOGI, NPIV FDISC, Fabric LOGO and ELP) errors are handled using normal Fibre Channel protocols.

If a FIP Link Service request does not receive a reply within 2 times R_A_TOV, the Fibre Channel process uses ABTS to abort the associated Fibre Channel Exchange. The ABTS request and associated reply are encapsulated as FCoE (EtherType 8906h) and not FIP. After R_A_TOV has elapsed, a Reinstate Recovery Qualifier (RRQ) Extended Link Service request is sent. The RRQ and its reply are also encapsulated as FCoE protocol and not FIP. This processing ensures proper termination and cleanup of Fibre Channel Exchange resources.

Note that this processing may leave Ethernet switches that snoop the FIP protocol in order to setup access control lists and static forwarding table entries in an incorrect state. This may occur because the ABTS and RRQ operations are not encapsulated as the FIP protocol and may not be inspected by the switch in order to detect the creation or removal of virtual links. An illustration of how this can occur is shown in Figure 11-23 on page 168.

In this example, the VN_Port transmits a Fabric LOGO to relinquish a Fibre Channel address. The FCF sends an LS_ACC reply (encapsulated as a FIP operation because it is removing the VN_Port and path. The Fabric LOGO is received by Ethernet switch 2 which removes any associated ACL and static forwarding entries. However, due to a transmission error, the LS_ACC is not received by Ethernet switch 1. When the subsequent ABTS is used to abort the failed exchange, it is encapsulated and an FCoE frame, not a FIP frame, and is not directed to the control plane in either Ethernet switch.

11.5.6 FIP Non-Link Service Operations

FIP operations that do not correspond to Fibre Channel Link Services (Discovery Solicitation, Discovery Advertisement, FIP Keep Alive, and FIP Clear Virtual Link) do not have an associated direct reply. The protocols associated with these operations are based on either periodic

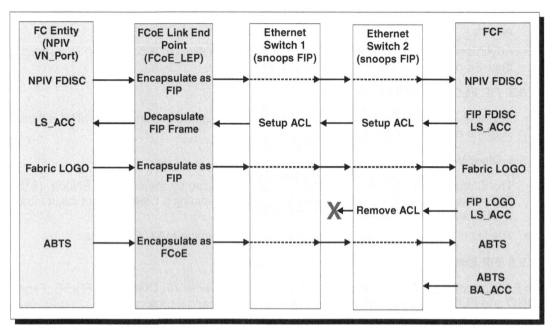

Figure 11-23. FIP Error and Ethernet Switches

transmissions or lack of an anticipated FIP operation (e.g., the sender of a Discovery Solicitation may reasonably expect to receive one or more Discovery Advertisements).

If any of these FIP operations are unsuccessful due to an error, no explicit error recovery action is required.

11.6 Chapter Summary

Discovery and Virtual Link Initialization

- FCoE entities communicate via "virtual" links
  - Rather than point-to-point physical links as in native Fibre Channel
  - Additional processing is required before normal Fibre Channel operations can begin
- There are three distinct initialization and operational phases along with two different FCoE-related protocols

FCoE Initialization Protocol (FIP)

- During Discovery and Virtual Link Initialization, devices use the FCoE Initialization Protocol (FIP)
  - The FIP protocol is identified using the Ether-Type field in the Ethernet frame header
- By having a distinct protocol for Discovery and Virtual Link Initialization, operations associated with the establishment and removal of virtual links and ports can be readily distinguished from normal FCoE operations
- Based on the EtherType, Discovery and Virtual Link initialization frames can be directed to:
  - The FCoE controller in an ENode or FCF, or
  - The control plane (supervisor) in an FCoE-aware "lossless" Ethernet switch

FIP Protocol Code Field

- The FIP operation is identified by
  - A 16-bit FIP Protocol Code, and
  - An 8-bit SubCode
- Currently there are two categories of operations defined that correspond to the Discovery and Virtual Link Initialization phases

FIP Flags

- FIP Flags provide specific indications associated with the FIP operation.
  - FPMA Support Flag (FP): When the FP Capability flag bit is set to one, it indicates the sender supports Fabric Provided MAC Addressing (FPMA).
  - Solicited Flag (S): When the S flag bit is set to one, it indicates that this FIP operation was sent in response to a Solicitation request.
  - FCF Flag (F): When the F flag bit is set to one, it indicates that this FIP operation was sent by an FCF.

FIP Descriptors

- A FIP operation transfers one or more FIP Descriptors
  - FIP Descriptors are parameters associated with the operation
- Each Descriptor consists of:
  - Type: identifies the type of Descriptor
  - Length: specifies the size of the Descriptor
  - Value: contains the parameter value
- FIP Descriptor List Length
  - The FIP Descriptor List Length field specifies the size of the Descriptor List contained within this FIP operation
  - Each Descriptor contains its own length field
  - This field is necessary because the FIP frame may contain PAD bytes following the last Descriptor

FIP Descriptors: Priority

- The FIP Priority Descriptor is used in the FIP Discovery Advertisement.
- An ENode may use the Priority Field value to determine to which FCFs it should send Fabric Login (FLOGI) and establish virtual links.

FIP Descriptors (continued)

- The FIP MAC Address Descriptor is used to communicate an address parameter
- The FIP FC-MAP Descriptor is used to communicate an FC-MAP parameter
  - The FC-MAP may be used to construct a MAC address of the form: (FC-MAP || VN_Port_ID)
- The FIP Switch_Name Descriptor is used to communicate an FCF's 64-bit Switch_Name
- The FIP Fabric Descriptor communicates FCF's 64-bit Fabric_Name and Fabric parameters
- The FIP Port_Name Descriptor is used to communicate a 64-bit Port_Name

FLOGI/FDISC/LOGO Descriptors

- The FIP FLOGI/FDISC/LOGO Descriptor is used to communicate
  - An FLOGI request or its LS_ACC response
  - An FDISC request or its LS_ACC response
  - A LOGO request or its LS_ACC response

FIP ENode Discovery Solicitation

- When the ENode MAC initializes, its FCoE Controller transmits a FIP "Discovery Solicitation" request to announce its presence
- The Solicitation Descriptor List contains:
  - The ENode MAC Address parameter
  - Flags indicating the address method(s) supported
  - Fabric Provided MAC Addresses (FPMA)
- It may contain other Discovery parameters in the future
- *See Figure 11-6 on page 147*

FIP Discovery Advertisement

- Each FCF that receives a Solicitation from an ENode responds with an "Advertisement"
- The Advertisement contains
  - The FCF-MAC address of the FCF
  - The name of the FCF, the name of the Fabric
  - Optionally, an FC-MAP value that can be used to construct a Fabric Provided MAC Address (FPMA).
- Based on Advertisements received, the Enode:
  - Builds a list of reachable FCFs and
  - Proceeds to Enode Virtual Link Initialization
- *See Figure 11-8 on page 150*

FIP Fabric Login (FLOGI)

- Once an ENode has discovered FCFs, it:
  - Performs Fabric Login (FLOGI) to establish a link with the FCF and acquire an N_Port_ID.
  - The ENode may perform FLOGI with one, some, or all of the discovered FCFs.
  - It may use the Priority field, or other parameters, from the Advertisements to decide which FCFs to send FLOGI to.
- The FLOGI request is sent in a FIP frame:
  - FLOGI Descriptor contains Fibre Channel FLOGI parameters
- *See Figure 11-9 on page 151*

FIP FLOGI LS_ACC: FCF Actions

- Upon successful completion of the FLOGI the FCF:
  - Instantiates an instance of a VF_Port for the virtual link
  - The VF_Port uses the VF_Port Name and Fabric_Name sent in the LS_ACC reply
  - The FCF makes the appropriate entries in the Fibre Channel Name Server database for the VN_Port
- *See Figure 11-9 on page 151*

FIP FLOGI LS_ACC: ENode Actions

- Upon successful completion of FLOGI, the Enode:
  - Instantiates an instance of a VN_Port for this virtual link.
  - The VN_Port uses the N_Port_ID assigned by the FCF in the LS_ACC reply to the FLOGI request and the Node_Name and Port_Name provided when it sent the FLOGI request.
- The VN_Port MAC address used depends on the addressing method
- Subsequent operations (with the exception of FLOGI, NPIV FDISC and Fabric LOGO) use the FCoE protocol and normal encapsulated Fibre Channel frames

FIP NPIV FDISC Request and Reply

- An NPIV FDISC request and its LS_ACC or LS_RJT reply are sent using the FIP protocol
  - An NPIV FDISC request has the Fibre Channel Destination ID set to FF:FF:FEh and the Source ID set to 00:00:00h
  - if the S_ID is not 00:00:00h, this is not an NPIV FDISC request
- See *Figure 11-11 on page 153*

FIP Fabric Logout Request

- A Fabric Logout request and associated reply are sent using the FIP protocol
  - i.e., a LOGO sent to Fibre Channel Destination_ID FF:FF:FEh
- See *Figure 11-13 on page 155*

FIP Exchange Link Parameters (ELP)

- ELP is used to exchange parameters between E_Ports (or virtual E_Ports)
- A VE_Port sends and ELP using the FIP protocol
  - Destination Address is the FCF-MAC of the other FCF
  - Source Address is the FCF-MAC of this FCF
  - Fibre Channel S_ID and D_ID are both FF:FF:FDh'
- See *Figure 11-16 on page 158*

FIP Clear Virtual Link

- In Fibre Channel, link-related state information can be cleared using the Link Initialization (OLS) or Link Failure (NOS) protocols
  - e.g., login states and virtual N_Ports created using NPIV
- FIP Clear Virtual Links can be used to provide an equivalent function in an FCoE environment
- When the FIP Clear Virtual Links function is used, it removes:
  - Designated VN_Port(s)
  - Associated state information (effectively forcing an implicit Fabric Logout)
- Only FCFs are allowed to issue the FIP Clear Virtual Links function
- See *Figure 11-18 on page 160*

FIP Protocol Errors

- For the purposes of error handling and recovery, FIP operations can be divided into two categories
- Operations that transport Fibre Channel Link Services
  - FLOGI, NPIV FDISC, Fabric LOGO, etc.
- Operations that are not associated with Fibre Channel Link Services
  - Discovery Solicitation, FIP Keep Alive, Clear Virtual Link, etc.

Non-Link Service Operation Errors

- FIP operations that do not correspond to Fibre Channel Link Services do not have an associated direct reply
  - e.g., Discovery Solicitation, Discovery Advertisement, FIP Keep Alive, and FIP Clear Virtual Link
- The protocols associated with these operations are based on either periodic transmissions or lack of an anticipated FIP operation
  - Solicitation sender may reasonably expect to receive one or more Discovery Advertisements.
- If any of these FIP operations are unsuccessful due to an error, no explicit error recovery action is required.

FIP Link Service Operation Errors

- For operations that transport Fibre Channel Link Services errors are handled using normal Fibre Channel protocols
  - Originator times for a response within using 2 * R_A_TOV
- If an expected response is not received, Originator aborts the associated Exchange using ABTS
  - ABTS is encapsulated as FCoE, not FIP
- Operation is retried in a new Exchange

FIP Errors and Snooping Switches

- Ethernet switches that snoop the FIP protocol may be left in an incorrect state after an error
- For example:
  - a VN_Port logs out from the Fabric
  - LS_ACC is corrupted between Ethernet switches
  - Exchange is aborted with ABTS, but this is not FIP protocol and not snooped
  - One or more switches may remove ACLs and static forwarding table entries, one or more may not
- Condition is remedied as a result of no FIP Keep Alive messages

12. FCoE Encapsulation

The basic concept of FCoE is the simple encapsulation of one Fibre Channel frame into one Ethernet frame. The entire Fibre Channel frame is encapsulated within a single Ethernet frame. Multiple Fibre Channel frames are not combined into the same Ethernet frame and a Fibre Channel frame is never split across multiple Ethernet frames. The format of an FCoE encapsulated frame is shown in Figure 12-1 on page 173.

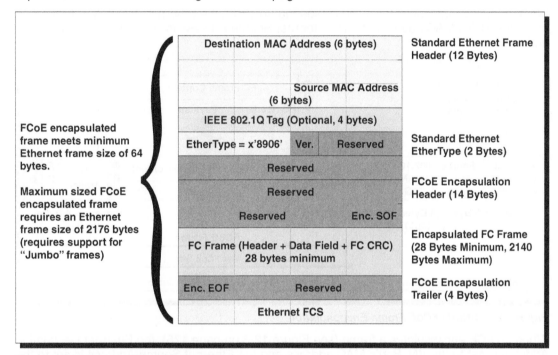

Figure 12-1. Encapsulated Frame Format

By maintaining a one-to-one relationship between the encapsulated Fibre Channel frames and Ethernet frames, it is not necessary to maintain state or context information associated with the encapsulation or decapsulation process. This minimizes the complexity and cost of encapsulation when compared to alternative technologies based on TCP/IP.

> NOTE – The FCoE Link End Point does need to maintain information associated with the virtual link including the local and remote MAC addresses.

Because FCoE encapsulates the entire Fibre Channel frame, including the Fibre Channel frame header, all of the Fibre Channel functions, operations and protocols can map directly to

FCoE. This means that an existing Fibre Channel protocol stack can operate over FCoE without change.

An FCoE frame contains an FCoE Encapsulation Header containing a representation of the SOF and FCoE Encapsulation Trailer containing a representation of the EOF. This is necessary because both the Fibre Channel SOF and EOF communicate information beyond simply indicating when the frame begins and ends (e.g., Fibre Channel's Class-of-Service is indicated by the particular SOF used). The Encapsulation Header and Trailer also ensure that a minimum size Fibre Channel frame always results in a valid minimum size Ethernet frame.

12.1 Ethernet Source and Destination Addresses

When an ENode encapsulates a frame (see Figure 12-2), the Ethernet Destination Address is set to the FCF's MAC address and the Ethernet Source Address is set to the VN_Port's MAC address.

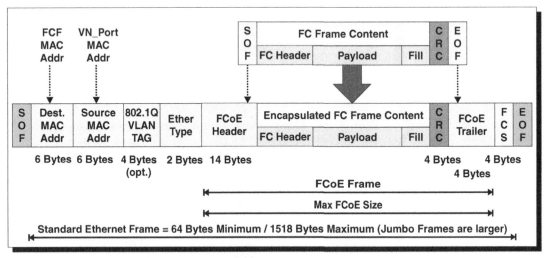

Figure 12-2. ENode FCoE Frame Encapsulation

When an FCF encapsulates a frame (see Figure 12-3 on page 175), the Ethernet Destination Address is set to the VN_Port's MAC address and the Ethernet Source Address is set to the FCF's MAC address.

- When using Fabric Provided MAC Addresses (see *Fabric Provided MAC Addresses (FP-MA)* on page 118), the VN_Port's MAC address is constructed by appending the VN_Port's FC N_Port_ID to the FC-MAP value (i.e., FC-MAPI II FCID).

12.2 Start-of-Frame and End-of-Frame

The Fibre Channel Start-of-Frame (SOF) and End-of-Frame (EOF) Ordered Set delimiters contain the characters created by the encoding. These characters cannot be represented as a normal 8-bit byte value, and therefore, cannot be placed inside an Ethernet frame. Because of

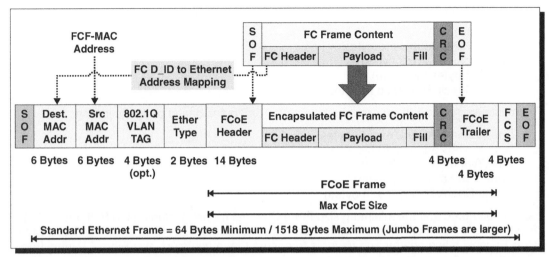

Figure 12-3. FCF FCoE Frame Encapsulation

this, an encoded value is used to specify the Fibre Channel SOF and EOF. This same situation arose for the encapsulation of Fibre Channel over IP and iFCP and FCoE uses the same values as previously defined in RFC3643 for those protocols. Table 12-1 on page 175 shows the values used to represent each of the frame delimiters supported by FCoE.

Fibre Channel Delimiter	Code in Encapsulated Frame	Class-of-Service
SOFf	0x28	F
SOFi2	0x2D	2
SOFn2	0x35	2
SOFi3	0x2E	3
SOFn3	0x36	3
EOFn	0x41	2,3,F
EOFt	0x42	2,3,F
EOFni	0x49	2,3,F
EOFa	0x50	2,3,F

Table 12-1. SOF and EOF Representation in Encapsulated Frame

12.3 Fibre Channel and Ethernet Frame Sizes

The minimum valid Ethernet frame size is 64 bytes. This size is based on the need to transmit a minimum number of bytes to ensure that a collision will be reliably detected when using the Carrier Sense Multiple Access/Collision Detect (CSMA/CD) access protocol.

A minimum frame size of 64 bytes corresponds to the following:

> Destination MAC address (6 bytes) +
> Source MAC address (6 bytes) +
> EtherType/Length (2 bytes) +
> Data (46 bytes minimum) +
> Frame Check Sequence (4 bytes)

The maximum (standard) Ethernet frame size is 1518 bytes based on the following:

> Destination MAC address (6 bytes) +
> Source MAC address (6 bytes) +
> EtherType/Length (2 bytes) +
> Data (1500 bytes maximum) +
> Frame Check Sequence (4 bytes)

It should be noted that the minimum size Fibre Channel frame (excluding the SOF and EOF) is 28 bytes (which is smaller than the minimum Ethernet frame size). One of the functions of the FCoE Encapsulation header and trailer is to ensure that a minimum-size Fibre Channel frame will always result in a valid Ethernet frame.

Also, the maximum size Fibre Channel frame (excluding SOF and EOF) is 2140 bytes (which is larger than the maximum Ethernet frame size. To accommodate a maximum-size Fibre Channel frame, FCoE requires the use of "baby" jumbo Ethernet frames of at least 2.5 kilobytes (see *Ethernet Jumbo Frames* on page 73).

12.4 Ethernet and Fibre Channel Comparison

When one compares the Ethernet and Fibre Channel technologies, it becomes evident that there are very few fundamental differences between the two technologies. Both are essentially Layer-2 networks that provide a data link for the transport of higher-level information.

12.4.1 Signaling Rate Comparison

Ethernet and Fibre Channel both support a variety of signaling rates. Because of the overhead associated with encoding the data prior to transmission, the actual character rate is less than the signaling rate. Table 12-2 on page 177 summarizes the signaling rates of interest from an FCoE perspective. From this table, it can be seen that at the 1 Gbps and 10 Gbps signaling rates there is very little difference between the two technologies. Note that Fibre Channel has link signaling rates of 2.125 Gbps, 4.250 Gbps and 8.500 Gbps for which there are no Ethernet equivalents.

> NOTE – The character rate differs from the signaling rate due to transmission encoding overhead.

12.4.2 Framing Efficiency Comparisons

Ethernet and Fibre Channel both use frames to transport information and have overhead associated with transporting the data in frames. The overhead consists of the start-of-frame (SOF), end-of-frame (EOF), frame header, frame check characters (FCS or CRC) and any required inter-frame gap (IFG).

Ethernet		Fibre Channel	
Signaling Rate	Character Rate	Signaling Rate	Character Rate
125 Mbit/s	12.5 MB/s	-	-
1.25 Gbit/s	125 MB/s	1.0625 Gbit/s	106.25 MB/s
-	-	2.125 Gbit/s	212.5 MB/s
-	-	4.250 Gbit/s	425.0 MB/s
-	-	8.500 Gbit/s	850.0 MB/s
10.2 Gbit/s	1250 MB/s	10.5 Gbit/s	1275 MB/s

Table 12-2. Ethernet and Fibre Channel Signaling Rate Comparison

The maximum theoretical link throughput can be computed by multiplying the character rate from Table 12-2 by the framing efficiency of the protocol. Keep in mind that other overheads such as software processing or device activities will further reduce the actual throughput to a value that is less than the theoretical maximum.

Ethernet Framing Efficiency. Standard Ethernet frames can transport a maximum of 1500 bytes of data per frame. In order to do so requires that a total of 1538 bytes be sent as shown in Figure 12-4 on page 177. This results in a framing efficiency of 97.53%, or a framing overhead of 2.47%. Note that this framing efficiency computation does not include the overhead associated with the optional 802.1Q VLAN tag or TCP/IP protocols (which are not used by FCoE).

$$\text{Ethernet Framing Efficiency} = \frac{\text{Number of Data Bytes}}{\text{Total Bytes Sent}}$$

$$= \frac{\text{Data}}{\text{Start + Header + Data + FCS + End +IFG}}$$

$$= \frac{1500}{4 + 14 + 1500 + 4 + 4 +12}$$

$$= \frac{1500}{1538} = 97.53\%$$

Figure 12-4. Ethernet Framing Efficiency

Fibre Channel Framing Efficiency. Fibre Channel has a frame structure similar to that of Ethernet and the framing efficiency can be computed using the same method.

A Fibre Channel frame can transport a maximum of 2112 bytes of data. In order to do so requires a total of 2172 bytes be sent as shown in Figure 12-5 on page 178. This results in a framing efficiency of 97.24% and a framing overhead of 2.76%.

Note that the Fibre Channel framing efficiency is slightly less than the Ethernet framing efficiency due to the larger Fibre Channel frame header (although the difference of approximately 0.29% is insignificant from a practical standpoint). From this it can be seen that Fibre Channel and Ethernet have almost identical framing overhead when sending a maximum-sized frame.

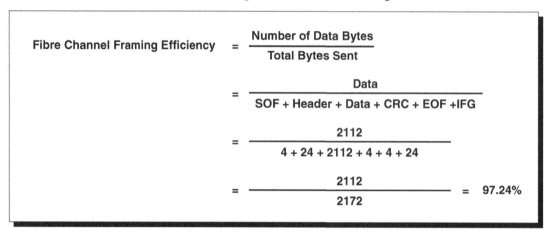

Figure 12-5. Fibre Channel Framing Efficiency

FCoE Framing Efficiency. Fibre Channel over Ethernet incurs both the Ethernet framing overhead and the encapsulated Fibre Channel frame overhead. In addition, each FCoE frame includes an encapsulation header and trailer that further add to the total framing overhead as shown in Figure 12-6 on page 179.

When standard size Ethernet frames are used, the amount of data per frame is reduced to 1454 bytes due to the inclusion of the encapsulation header and trailer and the overhead of the encapsulated Fibre Channel frame. This results in a framing efficiency of 94.54% or a framing overhead of 5.46%.

Because a maximum size Ethernet frame is not large enough to contain a maximum size Fibre Channel frame, FCoE requires the use of "baby jumbo" frames in order to transport a maximum size Fibre Channel frame. The term "baby jumbo" frame is used to differentiate the approximately 2.5 kilobyte frame size needed from the more common 9 kilobyte size that is commonly associated with the term "jumbo" frame.

Using "baby jumbo" frames also has the effect of improving the framing efficiency because each FCoE frame can now transport more data while incurring the same overhead as when using a standard Ethernet frame. The framing efficiency of FCoE when using "baby jumbo" Ethernet frames is 96.17% and is just 1.07% less than the framing efficiency on a native Fibre Channel link.

Chapter 12. FCoE Encapsulation

$$\text{FCoE Framing Efficiency} = \frac{\text{Number of Data Bytes}}{\text{Total Bytes Sent}}$$

$$= \frac{\text{Data}}{\text{Start + Header + (Enc. Hdr + FC Hdr + Data + FC CRC + Enc. Tlr) + FCS + End + IFG}}$$

$$= \frac{1454}{4 + 14 + (14 + 24 + 1454 + 4 + 4) + 4 + 4 + 12}$$

$$= \frac{1454}{1538} = 94.54\%$$

Figure 12-6. FCoE Framing Efficiency (Standard Ethernet Frame)

$$\text{FCoE Framing Efficiency} = \frac{\text{Number of Data Bytes}}{\text{Total Bytes Sent}}$$

$$= \frac{\text{Data}}{\text{Start + Header + (Enc. Hdr + FC Hdr + Data + FC CRC + Enc. Tlr) + FCS + End + IFG}}$$

$$= \frac{2112}{4 + 14 + (14 + 24 + 2112 + 4 + 4) + 4 + 4 + 12}$$

$$= \frac{2112}{2196} = 96.17\%$$

Figure 12-7. FCoE Framing Efficiency ("Baby Jumbo" Ethernet Frame)

12.5 Encapsulation/Decapsulation Flow

As defined in the architecture model, the FCoE Link End Point (FCoE_LEP) performs the encapsulation and decapsulation of Fibre Channel frames. While the architecture does not specify how the FCoE_LEP functions are performed, they could be done within an FCoE port implementation, through an intermediary driver ("wedge" or "shim" driver), or by an external gateway function. The description in this section approaches the FCoE_LEP as if it were an intermediary function between a standard FC driver or port and an Ethernet link as shown in Figure 12-8.

Selected frames are encapsulated and processed using the FCoE Initialization Protocol (FIP) while others are simply encapsulated and processed as FCoE. This section examines how an

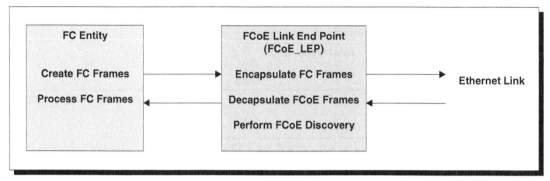

Figure 12-8. FCoE Link End Point (FCoE_LEP)

implementation might determine which frames to encapsulate as FIP and which to encapsulate as FCoE.

12.5.1 ENode FCoE_LEP Frame Encapsulation

Figure 12-9 on page 181 illustrates a process by which the ENode encapsulation function could determine how to handle encapsulation of frames. This diagram is intended as an example and is not necessarily representative of how the encapsulation function should be implemented.

The flow diagram shown in Figure 12-9 on page 181 assumes that the processing shown is performed between a standard FC driver or device and an FCoE link. This example also assumes that the encapsulation function uses the FLOGI request as the stimulus to initiate the discovery process and select an FCF. Using FLOGI to initiate the discovery process ensures that the encapsulation function will discover available FCFs whenever the Fibre Channel source attempts to establish, or reestablish, a login session with the Fabric.

> NOTE – An alternative implementation would be to perform the discovery process at startup of the encapsulation function. In this case, when the FLOGI was received, discovery would have already been performed and the FLOGI request could simply be encapsulated and forwarded. One potential disadvantage of this approach is that if the FCF becomes unreachable or a new FCF becomes reachable, there is no mechanism to stimulate the encapsulation function to re-perform discovery.

When a Fibre Channel frame is received by the encapsulation function, various tests are performed to determine if this is a virtual link establishment or removal frame that should be directed to the FCF. If so, the frame content (along with FIP defined parameters) are encapsulated as a FIP frame and sent to the FCF-MAC address.

FLOGI Processing. If a FLOGI request is received, it is encapsulated as a FIP frame and sent to the FCF selected during the discovery process. Before the encapsulated frame is transmitted, the encapsulation function may perform the discovery process to identify available FCFs.

The Fibre Channel frame content is encapsulated as a FIP request with the encapsulation function adding the necessary FIP descriptors to the FLOGI payload (see *FIP FLOGI Request*

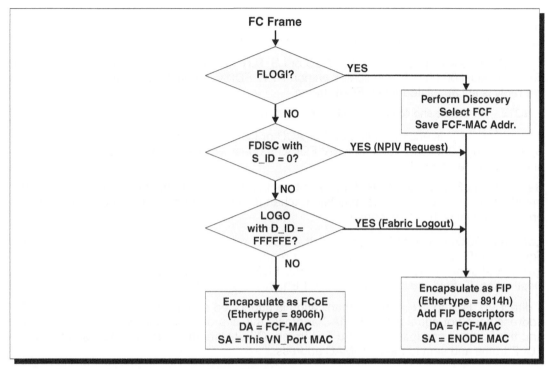

Figure 12-9. ENode Frame Encapsulation Flow

and Reply on page 151). In an FLOGI request, the MAC address descriptor value is set to zeros.

> NOTE – The MAC address descriptor in the FLOGI request is an artifact of the SPMA addressing method. For compatibility reasons, it has been left in the operation.

LS_ACC or LS_RJT to FLOGI. If an ENode is encapsulating an LS_ACC or LS_RJT in response to a received FLOGI, it means that the ENode is connected in a point-to-point topology and has received a FLOGI request from the attached ENode.

> NOTE – Currently, this configuration is not supported by FCoE and should not occur.

If the FCoE_LEP is encapsulating an LS_ACC or LS_RJT in response to a FLOGI request received by a switch, the LS_ACC or LS_RJT is encapsulated as a FIP frame. Because the LS_ACC or LS_RJT does not contain information identifying the original command, the FCoE_LEP needs to maintain Exchange state information in order to associate the original request with this response.

FDISC Request Processing. If an FDISC request is received and the Source_ID field is equal to 00:00:00h, this is an NPIV request and is encapsulated as a FIP frame. If the Source_ID field is not equal to 00:00:00h, the request is not an NPIV request and the frame is encapsulated as an FCoE frame and sent to the FCF-MAC address.

LS_ACC or LS_RJT to FDISC. If an ENode is encapsulating an LS_ACC or LS_RJT in response to a received FDISC having a S_ID of 00:00:00h, it indicates an NPIV FDISC request was sent to the ENode and the reply is encapsulated as a FIP frame.

If the ENode is encapsulating an LS_ACC or LS_RJT to a received FDISC having a S_ID that does not equal 00:00:00h, it indicates an non-NPIV FDISC request was sent to the ENode and the reply is encapsulated as an FCoE frame.

NOTE – An ENode should never receive an FDISC request.

If the FCoE_LEP is encapsulating an LS_ACC or LS_RJT in response to an FDISC having a S_ID of 00:00:00h, it indicates an NPIV FDISC request was sent to the switch and the reply is encapsulated as a FIP frame.

Because an LS_ACC or LS_RJT does not contain information identifying the original command, the FCoE_LEP needs to maintain Exchange state information in order to associate the original request with this response.

Logout (LOGO) Request Processing. If a LOGO request is received and the D_ID field is equal to FF:FF:FEh, this is a Fabric Logout request and the frame is encapsulated as a FIP frame and sent to the MAC address of the FCF. If a LOGO request is received and the Destination_ID field is not equal to FF:FF:FEh, this is an N_Port logout request.

If direct VN_Port to VN_Port communication is supported and the Ethernet Destination MAC address does not equal the FCF-MAC address, this is a direct LOGO with another VN_Port and the frame is encapsulated as a FIP frame. Otherwise, the frame is encapsulated as an FCoE frame and sent to the FCF-MAC address.

12.5.2 ENode FCoE_LEP Frame Decapsulation

When the ENode decapsulation function receives an FCoE or FIP frame, it decapsulates the embedded Fibre Channel frame content. Figure 12-9 on page 181 illustrates a process by which the decapsulation function can determine how to handle decapsulation of each frame. This diagram is intended as an example and is not necessarily representative of how the decapsulation function should be implemented.

LS_ACC to FLOGI. If the received frame is a FIP frame containing the LS_ACC to a Fabric Login (FLOGI), the decapsulation function decapsulates the FC frame header and payload and passes it to the Fibre Channel process.

The FCoE_LEP instantiates the VN_Port, saves the MAC address and uses that address as the Ethernet source address for subsequent VN_Port operations. The MAC address is not passed to the FC function.

LS_ACC to NPIV FDISC. If the received frame is a FIP frame containing the LS_ACC to a Fabric Discover (FDISC), the decapsulation function decapsulates the FC frame header and payload and passes it to the Fibre Channel process.

The FCoE_LEP instantiates the VN_Port, saves the MAC address and uses that address as the Ethernet source address for subsequent VN_Port operations. The MAC address is not passed to the FC function.

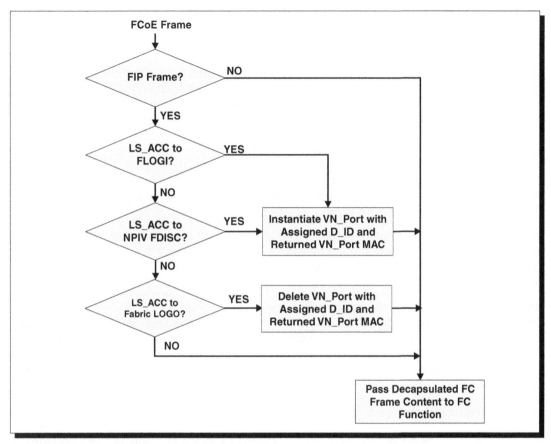

Figure 12-10. ENode Frame Decapsulation Flow

LS_ACC to Fabric LOGO. If the received frame is a FIP frame containing the LS_ACC to a Fabric Logout (LOGO), the decapsulation function decapsulates the FC frame header and payload and passes it to the Fibre Channel process.

The FCoE_LEP deletes the VN_Port, if it exists, and any associated context information such as the VN_Port_ID and VN_Port MAC address.

LOGO Received from FCF. In a native Fibre Channel environment, a Fibre Channel switch can implicitly logout an attached node port by disabling or reinitializing the link. In an FCoE environment, reinitializing the physical link may not affect the VN_Port (which may be on a different physical link). If an FCF wishes to logout a VN_Port, it requires a different mechanism.

Theoretically, a Fibre Channel switch can explicitly logout a VN_Port using the LOGO Extended Link Service sent to the VN_Port. While supported by the standard, it is not clear how many VN_Ports implement this function making it potentially unreliable.

The FIP Clear Virtual Links function (see *FIP Clear Virtual Links* on page 160) provides a way for an FCF to logout one or more VN_Ports and is the preferred method in an FCoE environment.

LS_RJT to FIP Request. If the received frame is a FIP frame containing an LS_RJT, the decapsulation function decapsulates the FC frame header and payload and passes it to the Fibre Channel process. This action is not explicitly shown in the flow diagram, but results from the failure to match any of the tested conditions.

12.6 FCoE and FC Class-2 Considerations

Because Ethernet provides frame delivery options similar to Fibre Channel's Class-3, mapping of Class-3 behavior to FCoE is relatively straightforward. However, mapping Fibre Channel's Class-2 service to FCoE raises a number of interesting issues.

In Class-2, when the destination receives a valid frame, and that frame can be processed, it responds with ACK to indicate the frame was received successfully. If a destination is unable to process an otherwise valid Class-2 frame it responds with P_RJT or P_BSY. Because these behaviors are associated with the destination, they are not affected by the presence of FCoE.

However, if the Fabric is unable to deliver a frame, it responds with F_RJT or F_BSY. Fibre Channel switches that support Class-2 understand and implement this requirement. Because Ethernet switches do not generate Fibre Channel F_RJT or F_BSY, failed Ethernet links or paths do not provide the same behavior as native Fibre Channel links. Figure 12-11 on page 185 illustrates the difference between a native Fibre Channel environment and an FCoE environment.

12.6.1 Failed Interswitch Link (Class-2)

In a native Fibre Channel environment, if Link B in Figure 12-11 on page 185 fails and the FC Fabric is unable to reroute traffic around the failure, Switch 1 returns an F_RJT response to the FC Node Port. Depending upon the implementation of Switch 1 and amount of congestion present, the F_RJT may be returned immediately, or with a delay of up to 500 milliseconds. F_RJT notifies the Node Port that the destination has become unreachable.

In an FCoE environment, if Link B in Figure 12-11 on page 185 fails and the Ethernet network is unable to reroute traffic around the failure, Switch 1 either discards the frame or floods it on all of its ports (except the one the frame was received on). In either case, the FCoE Node Port does not receive an immediate indication that the destination is unreachable. When the FCoE Node Port fails to receive the periodic Advertisements from the FCF, it will eventually time out and detect the failed virtual link. Depending on the rate of periodic Advertisements, detection of a failed interswitch link may take several seconds (or, even minutes).

NOTE – Failure to deliver a Class-2 Data Frame or Link Control Frame response is also detected directly as a result of an E_D_TOV timeout waiting for the expected Link Control Frame (see *Class-2 and E_D_TOV* on page 186).

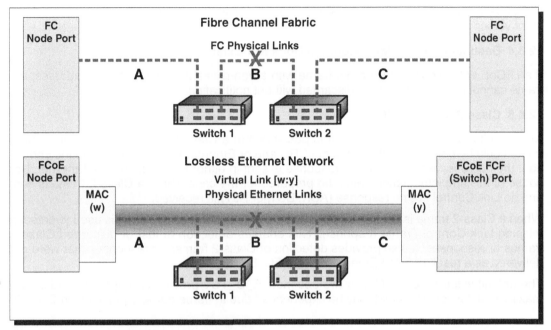

Figure 12-11. FC vs. FCoE Class-2 Virtual Link

12.6.2 Failed Destination Link (Class-2)

In a native Fibre Channel environment, if Link C in Figure 12-11 on page 185 fails, Switch 2 returns an F_RJT response to the FC Node Port. Depending upon the implementation of Switch 2 and amount of congestion present, the F_RJT may be returned immediately, or with a delay of up to 1,000 milliseconds. F_RJT notifies the Node Port that the destination has become unreachable.

In an FCoE environment, if Link C in Figure 12-11 on page 185 fails, Switch 2 discards the frame or floods it on all of its ports (except the port the frame was received on). In either case, the FCoE node port does not receive an immediate indication that the destination is unreachable. When the FCoE node port fails to receive the periodic Advertisements from the FCF, it will eventually time out and detect the failed virtual link. Depending on the rate of periodic Advertisements, detection of a failed link may take several seconds (or, even minutes).

12.6.3 Destination FC N_Port_ID Does Not Exist

If a frame is sent that has a non-existent Fibre Channel Destination_ID, the Fibre Channel switch sends F_RJT indicating that the frame cannot be delivered.

In an FCoE environment, if a frame has a non-existent Fibre Channel Destination_ID, the FCoE Forwarder (in reality a Fibre Channel switch with one or more Ethernet ports) sends F_RJT indicating that the frame cannot be delivered.

In this case, there is no difference between the behavior in a native Fibre Channel environment versus an FCoE environment.

12.6.4 Destination FCoE MAC Address Does Not Exist

If an FCoE entity sends an Ethernet frame with a non-existent destination MAC address, the frame cannot be delivered and is discarded without notification.

12.6.5 Class-2 and E_D_TOV

As a result of a transmission error, it is possible that a Class-2 Data frame or Link Control frame could be corrupted (Fibre Channel CRC and/or Ethernet FCS error). Due to the corruption, the frame is discarded and no response is sent in either Fibre Channel or Ethernet. Because of this, implementations must be prepared for the case where a Class-2 frame is sent and no Link Control Frame response (ACK, BSY, or RJT) is received.

When a Class-2 frame is sent, the Error Detect TimeOut Value (E_D_TOV) is used to detect a missing Link Control Frame response. This enables detection of lost or discarded Class-2 frames or responses. It also provides detection of Class-2 frames or responses that were not delivered as a result of failed Ethernet links in FCoE.

The default value for E_D_TOV is two seconds. E_D_TOV provides an upper bound on the maximum detection delay that may be experienced due to frame delivery problems in Class-2.

12.7 Chapter Summary

FCoE Encapsulation

- FCoE is a simple one-to-one encapsulation of a Fibre Channel frame into an Ethernet frame
  - Multiple Fibre Channel frames are not combined into the same Ethernet frame
  - a Fibre Channel frame is never split across multiple Ethernet frames
- It is not necessary to maintain state or context information associated with encapsulation or decapsulation
  - This minimizes the complexity and cost of encapsulation when compared to alternative technologies based on TCP/IP

FCoE Encapsulation

- FCoE encapsulates the entire Fibre Channel frame including:
  - Fibre Channel frame header,
  - Any Extended headers,
  - Any Optional headers,
  - The Payload, and
  - The Fibre Channel CRC
- All Fibre Channel functions, operations and protocols can map directly to FCoE
  - Selected operations map to the FIP protocol but still encapsulate the FC frame content
  - An existing Fibre Channel protocol stack can operate over FCoE without change

Encapsulation Header and Trailer

- FCoE frames (not FIP) contain an FCoE Encapsulation Header and Trailer
  - Header contains a representation of the SOF
  - Trailer contains a representation of the EOF
  - Necessary because the K28.5 in the Ordered Set cannot be put in an Ethernet frame
- Fibre Channel SOF and EOF communicate more than just when a frame begins and ends
  - Fibre Channel's Class-of-Service is indicated by the particular SOF used
- Header and Trailer also ensure that a minimum size Fibre Channel frame always results in a valid minimum size Ethernet frame

FCoE Encapsulation and Frame Sizes

- FC and Ethernet have different minimum frame sizes
  - Minimum Ethernet frame size is 64 bytes
  - The minimum actual Fibre Channel frame size is 28 bytes (excluding the SOF and EOF)
- Need to ensure that a minimum-size FC frame will result in a valid Ethernet frame
  - FCoE Header and FCoE Trailer ensure a minimum size FC frame results in a valid Ethernet frame

Minimum Ethernet Frame Size

- The minimum Ethernet frame size of 64 bytes corresponds to the following:
  - Destination MAC address (6 bytes) +
  - Source MAC address (6 bytes) +
  - EtherType/Length (2 bytes) +
  - Data (46 bytes minimum) +
  - Frame Check Sequence (4 bytes)

Maximum Ethernet Frame Size

- The maximum (standard) Ethernet frame size is 1518 bytes based on the following:
  - Destination MAC address (6 bytes) +
  - Source MAC address (6 bytes) +
  - EtherType/Length (2 bytes) +
  - Data (1500 bytes maximum) +
  - Frame Check Sequence (4 bytes)

FCoE Frame Considerations

- FC frame content is delivered in Ethernet frame
  - Maintain a 1:1 correspondence between FC frames and Ethernet frames
  - Each FC frame = 1 Ethernet frame
  - Multiple short FC frames are not put into the same Ethernet frame
  - No fragmentation of Ethernet frames
- FC frames are larger than Ethernet frames
  - FC data field maximum is 2112 bytes (+ 24 byte header + CRC)
  - Standard Ethernet frame data field is 1500 bytes maximum
- Options: Use larger Ethernet frames ("jumbo" frames) – probable solution or limit FC frame data field size during login

Framing Efficiency Comparisons

- Ethernet and Fibre Channel both use frames to transport information
  - Both have overhead associated with transporting the data in frames
  - The overhead consists of the start-of-frame (SOF), end-of-frame (EOF), frame header, frame check characters (FCS or CRC) and any required inter-frame gap (IFG).
- The maximum theoretical link throughput can be computed by multiplying the character rate by the framing efficiency of the protocol
  - Other overheads such as software processing or device activities will further reduce the actual throughput to a value that is less than the theoretical maximum

Standard Ethernet Framing Efficiency

- Standard Ethernet frames can transport a maximum of 1500 bytes of data per frame
  - In order to do so requires that a total of 1538 bytes be sent
  - This results in a framing efficiency of 97.53%, or a framing overhead of 2.47%
  - Note: this framing computation does not include overhead associated with the optional 802.1Q VLAN tag or TCP/IP protocols
- *See: Figure 12-4 on page 177*

Fibre Channel Framing Efficiency

- Fibre frames can transport a maximum of 2112 bytes of data per frame
  - In order to do so requires a total of 2172 bytes be sent
  - This results in a framing efficiency of 97.24% and a framing overhead of 2.76%
  - Note the Fibre Channel framing efficiency is slightly less than the Ethernet framing efficiency due to the larger Fibre Channel frame header (although the difference of approximately 0.29% is insignificant from a practical standpoint).
- *See: Figure 12-5 on page 178*

FCoE Framing Efficiency (Standard)

- FCoE incurs both Ethernet framing overhead and the encapsulated Fibre Channel frame overhead
  - In addition, each FCoE frame includes an encapsulation header and trailer that further add to the total framing overhead
  - When standard size Ethernet frames are used, the amount of data per frame is reduced to 1454 bytes due to the inclusion of the encapsulation header and trailer and the overhead of the encapsulated Fibre Channel frame
  - This results in a framing efficiency of 94.54% or a framing overhead of 5.46%
- *See: Figure 12-6 on page 179*

FCoE Framing Efficiency (Jumbo)

- Using "baby jumbo" frames improves the FCoE framing efficiency
  - Each FCoE frame can now transport more data while incurring the same overhead as when using a standard Ethernet frame.
  - The framing efficiency of FCoE when using "baby jumbo" Ethernet frames is 96.17%
  - This is just 1.07% less than the framing efficiency on a native Fibre Channel link
- *See: Figure 12-7 on page 179*

---

13. FCoE Error Conditions

FCoE introduces the potential for additional FCoE and Ethernet-specific errors along with errors associated with normal Fibre Channel protocols and operations.

Three different categories of Ethernet-specific errors have been identified, cross connect errors (traffic swap between two VN_Port/VF_Port sessions), association errors (a VN Port logs into the wrong VF_Port), and forwarding loop errors where a frame loops forever. This chapter examines some of these potential error conditions and their detection or prevention.

13.1 Ethernet and Fibre Channel's R_A_TOV

In order to detect missing events such as lost frames or lost ACKs, Fibre Channel defines a general purpose timer called the Error Detect Timeout Value (E_D_TOV). The default value for E_D_TOV is 2 seconds (this value can be changed by an administrator).

Fibre Channel also specifies a Resource Allocation Timeout Value (R_A_TOV) that is used to determine when a frame either has been delivered or it is guaranteed by the Fabric that the frame never will be delivered. The default value for R_A_TOV is 10 seconds (again, the value can be changed by an administrator).

The minimum value for R_A_TOV is based on the following relationship:

$$R\_A\_TOV \geq E\_D\_TOV + (2 * Maximum\ Fabric\ Transit\ Time)$$

Rearranging this a bit, one can calculate the maximum allowed fabric transit time as:

$$Maximum\ Fabric\ Transit\ Time = (R\_A\_TOV - E\_D\_TOV) / 2$$

Using the default values for R_A_TOV and E_D_TOV, the Maximum Fabric Transit Time equals 4 seconds as shown in Figure 13-1.

13.1.1 R_A_TOV Induced Errors

After R_A_TOV elapses following an error, it is assumed that it is safe to reuse the Sequence and Exchange identifiers (SEQ_ID and OX_ID) associated with the failed operation. By this time all of the frames associated with the failed operation will be gone and there is no possibility of ambiguity or aliasing.

If a frame were to be delivered after R_A_TOV has elapsed, the frame may appear to be part of a new Exchange or Sequence that reuses the same OX_ID or SEQ_ID. This can potentially result in undetectable data integrity errors.

An illustration of how such an error can occur as the result of a late frame is shown in Figure 13-2 on page 190. In this example, Data and Status frames for OX_ID 1234 are delayed due to congestion within the Fabric. Upon detecting a command timeout, the Initiator aborts the Exchange using the ABTS function. To ensure that all frames associated with the aborted Ex-

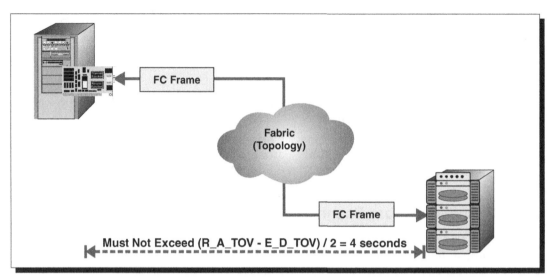

Figure 13-1. R_A_TOV and Maximum Fabric Transit Time

change have flushed out of the Fabric, the Initiator waits a minimum or R_A_TOV before reusing the Exchange ID. After R_A_TOV has elapsed, Exchange ID value is released and the Initiator reuses the same OX_ID for a new command with the same target. The Fabric (in violation of the R_A_TOV requirement) now delivers the frames for the original command. The initiator interprets the frames as belonging to the new command resulting in a data integrity error.

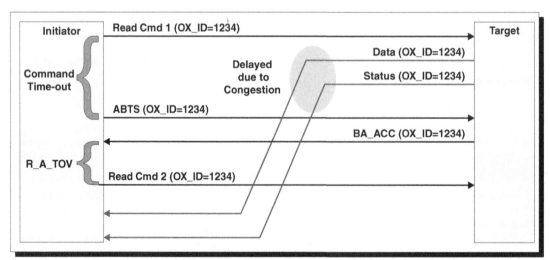

Figure 13-2. Read Data Corruption Due to Late Frames

Another example of a data integrity error due to frames being delivered after R_A_TOV is shown in Figure 13-2 on page 190.

In this example, the Status frame for OX_ID 1234 is delayed due to congestion. Upon detecting a command timeout, the initiator aborts the Exchange using ABTS. After R_A_TOV has elapsed, the initiator reuses OX_ID 1234 for a new write command to the same target.

The new write command encounters a write error on the media. Before the Check Condition status is returned, the Fabric (in violation of the R_A_TOV requirement) delivers the Good status for the first command. The initiator concludes that the second command completed successfully. When the status with the Check Condition arrives, the Exchange has already completed at the initiator and no recovery for the write error occurs.

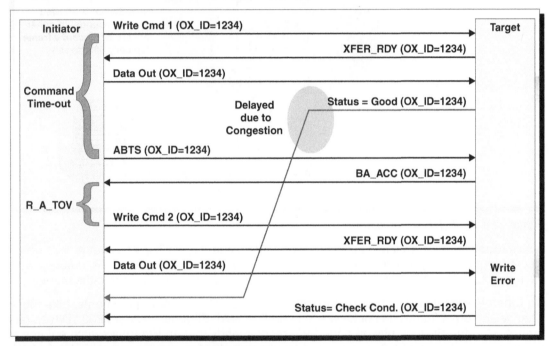

Figure 13-3. Write Error Due to Late Frames

While these examples may seem contrived and unlikely to occur in real-world environments, undetected data integrity problems have been observed in cases where the Fabric fails to observe the R_A_TOV requirement and delivers frames late as shown in these examples.

13.1.2 R_A_TOV Enforcement

The Fibre Channel standards do not specify how R_A_TOV is enforced and a frame may go through multiple switches on its way from the source to destination. There are no mechanisms defined in the standards to enable switches to communicate how much of allowed time has been used (there is no "time-to-live" field in the Fibre Channel frame header).

Implementations today enforce R_A_TOV by limiting the number of switches in the path and allocating an equal portion of R_A_TOV to each switch as shown in Figure 13-4.

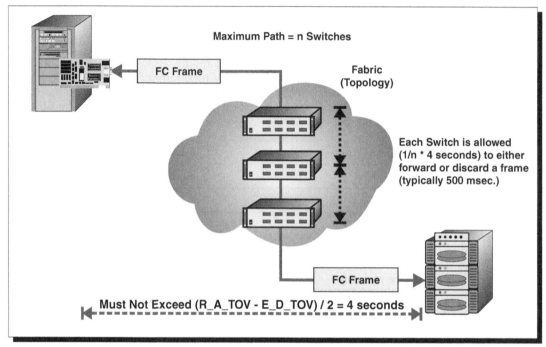

Maximum Path = n Switches

FC Frame

Fabric (Topology)

Each Switch is allowed (1/n * 4 seconds) to either forward or discard a frame (typically 500 msec.)

FC Frame

Must Not Exceed (R_A_TOV - E_D_TOV) / 2 = 4 seconds

Figure 13-4. R_A_TOV Enforcement

In this example, each switch is allocated 1/n of "Maximum Fabric Transit Time" to forward or discard frame. In a typical implementation, the path would be limited to eight switches with each switch allocated 500 msec. (1/8 of 4 seconds) to either forward or discard the frame.

No Ethernet mechanism is provided to enforce FCoE's R_A_TOV requirements. Like Fibre Channel, Ethernet frames do not have a "time-to-live" field. Ethernet standard 802.1D (see reference 31 in the Bibliography on page 290) recommends that an Ethernet switch enforce a maximum transit delay of 1.0 seconds and requires an absolute maximum transit delay of 4.0 seconds.

In a mixed environment, Fibre Channel switches have no visibility to the Ethernet switches' behavior. There is no way to for a Fibre Channel switch to determine how long a frame has existed within an Ethernet network. This raises the concern about how can FCoE enforce R_A_TOV?

Figure 13-4 shows a configuration consisting of "lossless" Ethernet switches connected to a Fibre Channel Fabric. While the Fibre Channel switches can ensure frame delivery within the allowed time as discussed above, the Fibre Channel switches have no way of knowing how long a frame has been in transit through the Ethernet network.

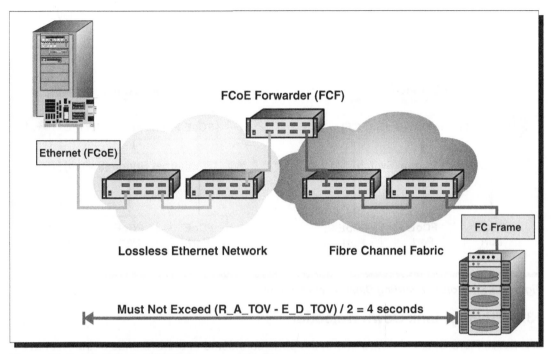

Figure 13-5. FCoE R_A_TOV Enforcement Problem

The solution is to characterize Ethernet switches based on their frame forwarding behavior.

- If a switch behaves in a manner similar to a Fibre Channel switch and either forwards of discards a frame within 500 milliseconds, one can construct a Fabric with a maximum of eight hops and be assured that the Maximum Fabric Transit time and R_A_TOV are not violated.

- If an Ethernet switch either forwards or discards a frame with the Ethernet recommended maximum transit delay of 1.0 seconds, the switch can still be used for FCoE traffic, but the number of hops may need to be reduced to ensure that the Maximum Fabric Transit time and R_A_TOV are not violated.

- If an Ethernet switch either forwards or discards a frame within the require absolute maximum transit delay of 4.0 seconds (or perhaps, not at all) the switch may simply not be suitable for FCoE applications because R_A_TOV enforcement (and therefore data integrity) cannot be guaranteed.

With these constraints, it is possible to design a Fabric that meets Fibre Channel's requirements. Care must be taken regarding the accumulation of delays that might occur under worst-case conditions resulting in the maximum delay at each switch. In Figure 13-6 on page 194, if each Ethernet switch has a maximum forwarding delay of 1 second and each FC switch has a maximum forwarding delay of 500 milliseconds and each switch experiences its maximum delay due to congestion, the total path delay is 5 seconds and exceeds the delay allowed by the default R_A_TOV value.

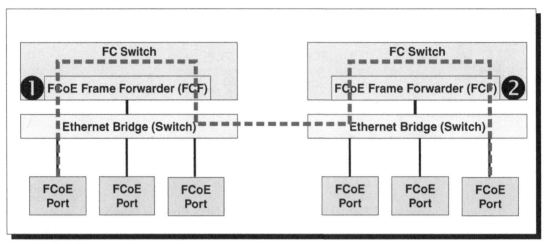

Figure 13-6. FCoE Forwarding Delay Accumulation

13.2 Ethernet Link Down Detection

In a native Fibre Channel environment, the ports connected at the two ends of the link have a direct awareness of the state of the link. If the link fails, it readily apparent to the two ports. In an FCoE environment, the two ports communicate via a virtual link that may consist of multiple physical Ethernet links. If an intermediate Ethernet link fails, the FCoE ports may have no direct awareness of the failed link. An example this is shown in the bottom half of Figure 13-7 on page 195.

Unlike a native Fibre Channel environment, neither MAC or FCoE port is directly aware of the failed link between the Ethernet switches. The FCoE Forwarder has no direct indication that the device is no longer reachable and that it needs to implicitly logout the node port and generate a Registered State Change Notification (RSCN).

Detection of failed FCoE paths is provided through the use of periodic Advertisements (see *FIP Discovery Advertisement* on page 148) sent by the FCF and periodic FIP Keep Alives (see *FIP Keep Alive (FKA)* on page 162) sent by the ENode FCoE Controller. An example of this signaling is shown in Figure 13-8 on page 195.

13.2.1 FCF FCoE Controller Behavior

The FCoE controller associated with each VF_Port capable FCF MAC periodically transmits Discovery Advertisements. When a periodic Discovery Advertisement is sent by the VF_Port capable FCF MAC, the destination MAC address is set to the "ALL ENodes" group address (01-10-18-01-00-01, see Table 7-2 on page 73) and the source MAC address is set to the FCF's MAC address. The Solicited bit (S) is set to zero to indicate that the Discovery Advertisement is not being sent in response to a Discovery Solicitation.

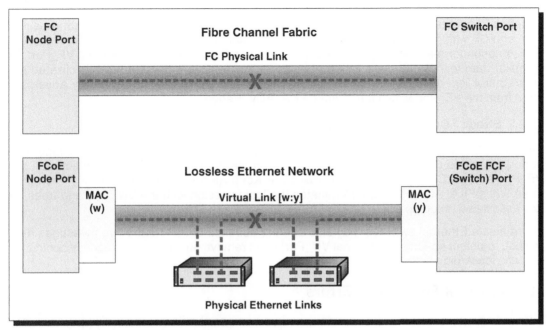

Figure 13-7. Ethernet Link Down Condition

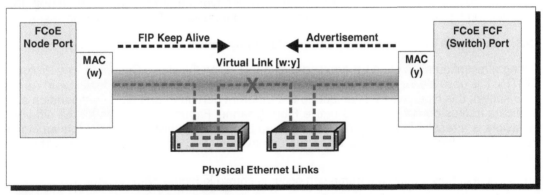

Figure 13-8. Ethernet Link Down Signaling

The FCoE controller associated with each VE_Port capable FCF MAC periodically transmits Discovery Advertisements. When a periodic Discovery Advertisement is sent by the VE_Port capable FCF MAC, the destination MAC address is set to the 'ALL_FCF_MACS' group address (01-10-18-01-00-02, see Table 7-2 on page 73) and the source MAC address is set to the FCF's MAC address. The Solicited bit (S) is set to zero to indicate that the Discovery Advertisement is not being sent in response to a Discovery Solicitation and the Available (A) bit is set to one indicating that the FCF is available for an ELP.

Periodic Discovery Advertisements also provide a way for ENodes or intermediate Ethernet switches to detect a no-longer available FCF. If a Discovery Advertisement is not received from an FCF within three times FKA_ADV_Period, the ENode Controller may assume that the FCF is no-longer reachable and terminate any login sessions associated with that VF_Port. In a similar manner, intermediate Ethernet switches my remove any automatically created access control lists or static forwarding table entries if they fail to detect a Discovery Advertisement from the VF_Port within three times FKA_ADV_Period.

13.2.2 ENode FCoE Controller Behavior

The FCoE Controller associated with each VN_Port transmits a FIP Keep Alive message on a periodic basis to notify the VF_Port's FCoE Controller that the VN_Port is functional. If the VF_Port's FCoE Controller fails to receive a FIP Keep Alive message from a VN_Port within three times FKA_ADV_Period, it terminates the login session with the VN_Port and frees up any associated resources.

Intermediate Ethernet switches may also use the absence of FIP Keep Alive messages as a method to detect no-longer functional VN_Ports and remove any associated access control list or static forwarding table entries.

13.3 Ethernet Forwarding Errors

Forwarding errors may manifest themselves in a number of different ways. Among them are dropped frames, misrouted frames delivered to the wrong destination, duplicate frames received by the recipient and misordered frames. These types of errors can occur in both the Ethernet and Fibre Channel networks. This section addresses the Ethernet specific cases.

13.3.1 Duplicate Ethernet Frames During Reconfiguration

During a reconfiguration of an Ethernet spanning tree using the Rapid Spanning Tree Protocol (RSTP), it is possible for duplicate copies of a frame to be delivered to the destination. As far as is known, this type of error is unique to the Ethernet portion of an FCoE configuration and duplicate frames do not occur in a native Fibre Channel Fabric. The reason for the different behaviors is a result of the learning method used by Ethernet switches and the forwarding of frames out multiple egress ports when the destination MAC address is not in an Ethernet switch's filtering database.

An example of how a duplicate frame can occur is shown in Figure 13-9 on page 197.

In this example, assume that A1 is the root of the Ethernet spanning tree, B1 is the root at switch B, C1 the root at switch C. B3 is an alternate port for switch B and discards received frames to prevent a spanning tree loop.

Under static conditions, frames are not duplicated, even if switch A forwards a frame out of both of its designated ports (A2 and A3). However, during a spanning tree reconfiguration, the following may occur:

1. Switch A receives a frame at port A1 with an unknown destination MAC address and transmits it out ports A2 and A3 (this is normal forwarding behavior when the destination

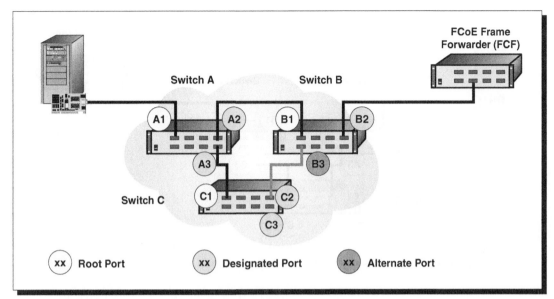

Figure 13-9. Duplicate Ethernet Frame During Reconfiguration

address is unknown). An unknown MAC address can occur when a VN_Port makes its initial unicast transmission to the FCF.

2. Switches B and C each receive a copy of the frame and queue it for transmission via output ports B2, C2 and C3.

3. Port B2 transmits its copy of the frame to the FCF.

4. Switch B detects that the link between ports A2 and B1 has failed and makes port B3 its new root port.

5. Port C2 transmits its copy of the frame with the result that switch B receives and forwards a second copy to the frame to the FCF.

In this example, the FCF receives the same frame twice as a result of the reconfiguration of the Ethernet spanning tree. Once the FCF transmits a frame, the switches learn the path to the FCF and duplicate frames would not occur.

13.3.2 Mis-Ordered Ethernet Frames During Reconfiguration

During a reconfiguration of an Ethernet spanning tree using the Rapid Spanning Tree Protocol (RSTP), it is possible for frames to be delivered out-of-order at the destination. Assume the configuration shown in Figure 13-10 on page 198 with port A3 a designated port at switch A and port A2 an alternate port.

Now, assume that the following occurs:

1. Frame F1 is received via input port A1, forwarded via output port A3, received at port C1 and queued for transmission at port C2.

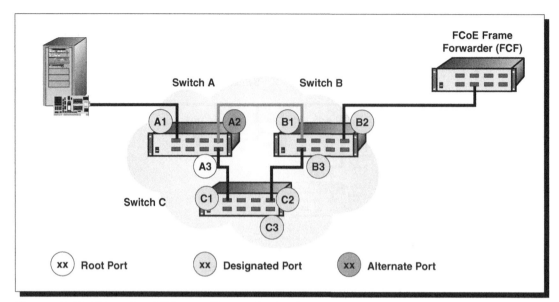

Switch A Switch B

FCoE Frame
Forwarder (FCF)

A1 A2 B1 B2

A3 B3

Switch C C1 C2

C3

(xx) Root Port   (xx) Designated Port   (xx) Alternate Port

Figure 13-10. Mis-ordered Ethernet Frames During Reconfiguration

2. Switch A detects that the link between ports A3 and C1 has failed an immediately makes A2 its new forwarding port.

3. Frame F2 is received via port A1 and forwarded from port A2 to Port B1 and then to the FCF via port B2.

4. Frame F1 is forwarded from port C2 to port B3, then to the FCF via port B2 and arrives out-of-order after frame F2.

A similar situation can occur within a Fibre Channel Fabric during a reconfiguration of that Fabric. Whether this results in an error depends upon the implementation of the destination port. In some implementations, whenever an out-of-order condition is detected, the corresponding operation fails. In other implementations, the receiving port may be able to correctly handle the out-of-order condition and no error results.

13.4 Ethernet Duplicate MAC Address Errors

Duplicate MAC addresses can result in a multitude of errors including frames delivered to the wrong port, frames not being delivered to the correct port and forwarding loops. Duplicate MAC addresses can occur as a result of configuration errors, device failures, or malicious behavior.

There are multiple variations of duplicate MAC address conditions:

- Two VN_Ports may have the same MAC address
- A VN_Port and a VF_Port may have the same MAC address
- A VN_Port and a VE_Port may have the same MAC address

- Two VF_Ports may have the same MAC address
- A VF_Port and a VE_Port may have the same MAC address
- Two VE_Ports may have the same MAC address

Some combinations are more likely to occur than others. Assuming that FCoE Forwarders use "burned-in" MAC addresses for the VF_Ports and VE_Ports, it is unlikely that a duplicate address would occur. On the other hand, there are many situations where a VN_Port MAC address is created dynamically, either by the hypervisor in a virtual machine environment or by using Fabric Provided MAC Addressing (FPMA) when Fabrics with the same FC-MAP value are joined.

Finally, a rogue host may attempt to use the MAC address of another entity for malicious purposes. This can result in any of the duplicate MAC address cases listed above.

The following examples illustrate how some these types of situations can occur and how they can be detected and prevented.

13.4.1 Duplicate VN_Port MAC Addresses: Frame Delivered to Wrong Port

Consider the configuration shown in Figure 13-11 on page 199. Assume that initially the two Ethernet networks are not connected. On the left network, Host 1 has MAC address (x) and on the right network, Host 2 also has MAC address (x). As long as the two Ethernet networks remain separate, the fact that both host systems have the same MAC address is not a problem.

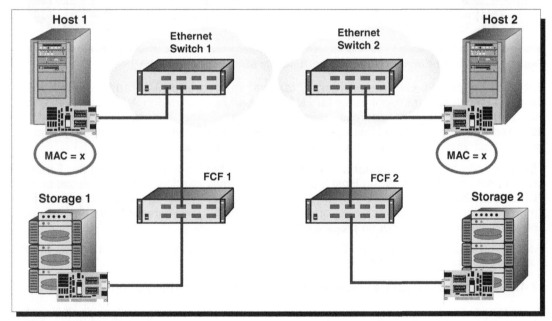

Figure 13-11. Cross-Connect Error Due to Duplicate MAC Addresses (before)

Assume that both systems are running and the two Ethernet switches are connected by the dashed line as shown in Figure 13-12 on page 200. When the cross connect occurs, nothing bad happens immediately. Each Ethernet switch had previously learned which port has MAC address (x) attached and continues to forward frames to the correct destination based on the previously learned MAC address.

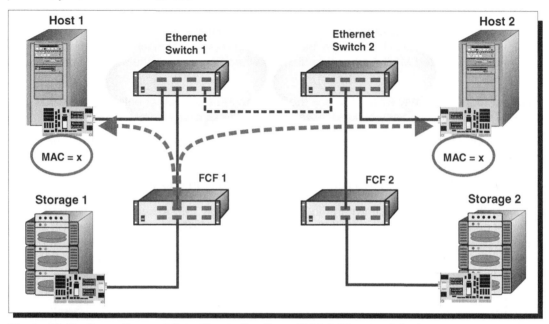

Figure 13-12. Cross-Connect Error Due to Duplicate MAC Addresses (after)

But what happens if Ethernet Switch 1 "forgets" the learned MAC address (x)? When Switch (1) receives a frame intended for Host (1) having a Destination Address of MAC (x), it has "forgotten" where MAC address (x) is and floods the frame. This causes the frame to be delivered to both Host 1 and Host 2. If the frame received at Host 2 just happens to match an existing Exchange, it may result in corruption of the Exchange at Host 2.

This error can readily be detected at Host 2 because the Source Address in the Ethernet frame is not as expected. When Host 2 performed discovery and virtual link initialization with FCF 2, it established a link based on the FCF-MAC address of FCF 2. Receiving a frame from an unexpected source address (i.e., one other than FCF 2) indicates a forwarding problem and that the frame should not be processed.

> NOTE – This example assumes that Direct VN_Port to VN_Port communication is not allowed and that all FCoE traffic is required to flow through an FCF.

13.4.2 Duplicate MAC Addresses (VN_Port, VF_Port): Forwarding Loop

Forwarding loops can also occur as a result of duplicate MAC addresses. Consider the configuration shown in Figure 13-13 on page 201.

Assume that initially the two Ethernet networks are not connected. On the left network in Figure 13-13 on page 201, Host 1 has MAC address (x) and on the right network, FCF 2 also has MAC address (x). As long as the two Ethernet networks remain separate, the fact that both Host 1 has the same MAC address as FCF 2 is not a problem.

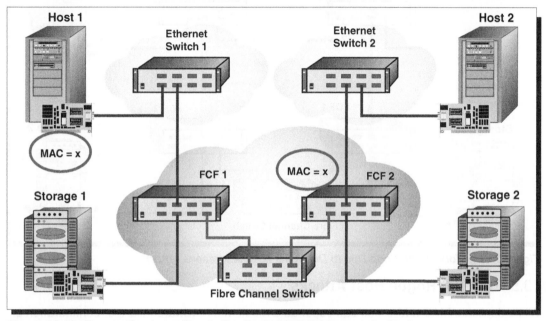

Figure 13-13. Forwarding Loop Due to Duplicate MAC Addresses (before)

Assume that the systems are up and running and the two Ethernet switches are connected by the dashed line. Again, when the cross connect occurs, nothing bad happens immediately. Each Ethernet switch has learned which port has MAC Address (x) attached and continues to forward frames to the correct destination based on the previously learned MAC address.

But, now what happens if Ethernet Switch 1 "forgets" the learned MAC address (x)? Assume that Storage 1 sends a frame to Host 1. When Switch (1) receives the frame intended for Host (1), it has "forgotten" where MAC address (x) is and floods the frame. This causes the frame to be delivered to both Host 1 and FCF 2.

When the frame is received at FCF 2, FCF 2 forwards the frame through the Fibre Channel Fabric to FCF 1 based on the Fibre Channel N_Port_ID in the encapsulated frame (this is the VN_Port in Host 1). The frame arrives at FCF 1 and the frame is now in a loop.

This error can be detected and the loop prevented at FCF 2.

by using Ethernet Access Control lists. Because no FLOGI or FDISC took place between Storage 1 and the FCF 2 port, FCF 2 can recognize this as a forwarding error and not process the frame.

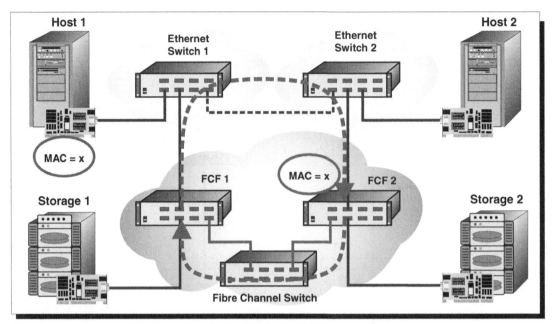

Figure 13-14. Forwarding Loop Due to Duplicate MAC Addresses (after)

13.5 Ethernet Rogue Host Attacks

While duplicate MAC addresses can occur as a result of a hardware failure or configuration errors, this might be expected to be a relatively rare occurrence. However, given the ubiquitous nature of Ethernet and the availability of tools to probe Ethernet environments, the potential for rogue hosts and malicious behavior cannot be ignored.

There are a number of ways in which a rogue host might mount an attack. The following sections explore a number of possibilities.

13.5.1 Rogue Host: Ethernet Switch Learning Attack on VN_Port MAC

This is a variation of the duplicate VN_Port MAC address case. If a rogue host transmits a frame using the source address of another VN_Port it can corrupt the forwarding tables in an Ethernet switch and cause traffic for the other VN_Port to be forwarded to the rogue host.

Consider the example shown in Figure 13-15 on page 203. In this example, the Rogue Host transmits a frame (such as a ping, or multicast or ARP) using the Source Address of Host 1. The Ethernet switch thinks that Host 1 has been moved from Port (1) to Port (7) and updates its forwarding tables to reflect the fact that MAC (x) is now on Port (7).

When the Ethernet switch receives a frame with a destination address of MAC (x), it forwards the frame out Port (7) sending it to the Rogue Host instead of the correct port enabling the Rogue to intercept traffic intended for Host 1. In addition, because one or more frames have been misdirected, one or more Host 1 operations will fail. Whether the intercepted frames re-

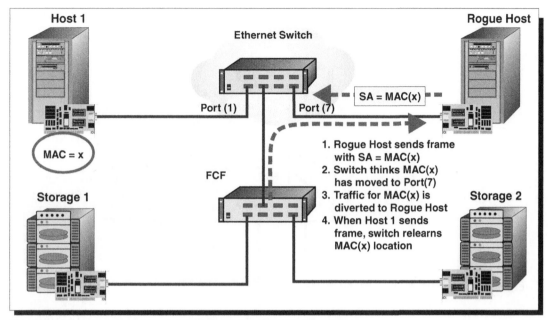

Host 1

Ethernet Switch

Rogue Host

Port (1)   Port (7)   SA = MAC(x)

MAC = x

FCF

1. Rogue Host sends frame
   with SA = MAC(x)
2. Switch thinks MAC(x)
   has moved to Port(7)
3. Traffic for MAC(x) is
   diverted to Rogue Host
4. When Host 1 sends
   frame, switch relearns
   MAC(x) location

Storage 1

Storage 2

Figure 13-15. Learning Attack by Rogue Host on VN_Port MAC

veal sensitive information or not, the attack adversely affects the operations of Host 1 and may culminate in a denial of service at Host 1.

When Host 1 transmits a frame, the forwarding table in the Ethernet switch will be corrected and normal traffic flow resumes.

A Rogue Host can use the same type of attack to redirect or intercept traffic intended for an FCF port by transmitting a frame with the Source Address set to the FCF-MAC address.

This type of attack may not be preventable solely by using Access Control Lists. Depending upon the implementation of the Ethernet switch a frame that is denied by an Access Control List may still cause the forwarding tables to be updated.

13.5.2 Rogue Host: Ethernet Switch Learning Attack on FCF-MAC

This is another variation of the duplicate MAC address case. If a rogue host transmits a frame using the source address of an FCF, it can corrupt the forwarding tables in an Ethernet switch and cause traffic for the FCF to be forwarded to the rogue host.

Consider the example shown in Figure 13-16 on page 204. In this example, the Rogue Host transmits a frame (such as a ping, or multicast, or ARP) using the Source Address of the FCF. The Ethernet switch thinks that the FCF has moved from Port (3) to Port (7) and updates its forwarding tables to reflect the fact that FCF-MAC is now on Port (7).

When the Ethernet switch receives a frame with a destination address of FCF-MAC, it forwards the frame out Port (7) sending it to the Rogue Host instead of the FCF enabling the

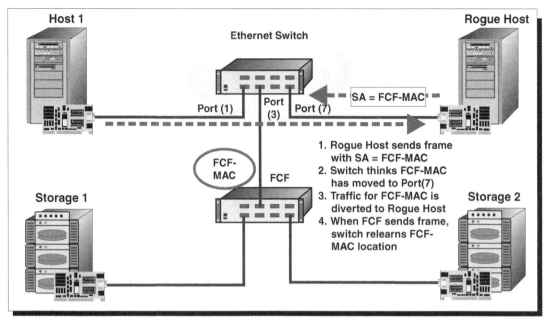

1. Rogue Host sends frame with SA = FCF-MAC
2. Switch thinks FCF-MAC has moved to Port(7)
3. Traffic for FCF-MAC is diverted to Rogue Host
4. When FCF sends frame, switch relearns FCF-MAC location

Figure 13-16. Learning Attack by Rogue Host on FCF-MAC

Rogue to intercept traffic intended for the FCF. In addition, because one or more frames have been misdirected, one or more operations will fail. Whether the intercepted frames reveal sensitive information or not, the attack adversely affects the operations of other devices and may culminate in a denial of service for all devices attached to the FCF.

When the FCF transmits a frame, the forwarding table in the Ethernet switch is corrected and normal traffic flow resumes.

This type of attack may not be preventable solely by using Access Control Lists. Depending upon the implementation of the Ethernet switch a frame that is denied by an Access Control List may still cause the forwarding tables to be updated.

13.6 Fibre Channel Link Error Status Block (LESB)

The Fibre Channel Link Error Status Block provides a means to record link-level errors such as Loss-of-Sync and Loss-of-Signal. The contents of the Link Error Status Block can be read with the Read Link Status (RLS) Extended Link Service. Because FCoE is not using a Fibre Channel link, different link-level errors may be encountered. In order to make this information available, Ethernet link-level errors are mapped to the LESB as shown in Table 13-1 on page 205.

Link Failure Count Field. The Link Failure Count field indicates the number of link failures detected through detection of physical link transitions (i.e., the number of times that the aMed-

LESB Word	FC Description (see FC-LS)	FCoE Description (see below)
0	Link Failure Count	Link Failure Count
1	Loss-of-Synchronization Count	Virtual Link Failure Count
2	Loss-of-Signal Count	Missing FIP Keep Alive or Discovery Advertisement Count
3	Primitive Sequence Protocol Error	Symbol Error During Carrier Count
4	Invalid Transmission Word	Errored Block Count
5	Invalid CRC Count	Frame Check Sequence Error Count

Table 13-1. Link Error Status Block (LESB) Mapping

iaAvailable attribute (see IEEE 802.3-2008 subclause 30.5.1.1.4) changes from the enumeration "available" to any other enumeration.

Virtual Link Failure Count Field. The Virtual Link Failure Count field indicates the number of virtual link failures detected by the Virtual Link maintenance protocol.

Missing FIP Keep Alive or Discovery Advertisement Field. The Missing FIP Keep Alive or Discovery Advertisement field indicates the number of missing Virtual Link maintenance protocol frames. A missing Virtual Link maintenance protocol frame is detected after 1.5 times FKA_ADV_PERIOD since the reception of the last Virtual Link maintenance protocol frame. For an ENode, the Missing FIP Keep Alive or Discovery Advertisement field indicates the number of missing Discovery Advertisements. For a VF_Port, the Missing FIP Keep Alive or Discovery Advertisement field indicates the number of missing FIP Keep Alive frames from an ENode.

Symbol Error During Carrier Count Field. The Symbol Error During Carrier Count field indicates the number of reception errors at the PHY layer that occur during frame reception. The detection procedure is dependant on media and link speed (see IEEE 802.3-2008 subclause 30.3.2.1.5).

Errored Block Count Field. The Errored Block Count field indicates the cumulative count of the events counted by the eight-bit errored blocks counter (see IEEE 802.3-2008 subclause 45.2.3.12.4).

Frame Check Sequence Error Count Field. The Frame Check Sequence Error Count field indicates the number of Ethernet frames received that are an integral number of octets in length and do not pass the FCS check (see IEEE 802.3-2008subclause 30.4.3.1.6).

13.7 Link Incidents

The Link Incident reporting procedure using the Link Incident Report Registration (LIRR) and Registered Link Incident Report (RLIR) Extended Link Services defines link incidents and corresponding incident codes that are based on the Fibre Channel physical layer. A definition of

FCoE Link Incidents and their respective Incident Code values (see Table 13-2 on page 206) are based on the IEEE 802.3 physical layer and the FC0E Virtual Link maintenance protocol.

Bit-error rate thresholding as described in FC-FS defines error intervals as a time period during which Fibre Channel invalid Transmission Words are recognized. For FC0E devices an error interval is a time period during which one or more error blocks (see IEEE 802.3-2008 subclause 45.2.3.12.4) are recognized.

Table 13-2 on page 206 specifies the Link Incidents for FCOE that shall be used in a RLIR ELS request by an FC0E VN_Port, VF_Port, or VE_Port.

Value	Meaning
00h	Reserved
01h	Implicit incident: A condition, caused by an event known to have occurred within the incident port, has been recognized by the incident port. The condition affects the attached link in such a way that it may cause a link incident to be recognized by the connected port.
02h	Bit-error-rate threshold exceeded: The incident port has detected that the Error Interval Count equals the Error Threshold (see FC-FS) where the Error Interval Count is based on errored blocks (see IEEE 802.3-2008 subclause 45.2.3.12.4).
03h	Link Failure - Loss-of-Signal: The aLoseMediaCounter has been incremented for entering an aMediaAvailable state indicating anything other than a remote fault (see IEEE 802.3-2008 subclause 30.5.1.1.4 and IEEE 802.3-2008 subclause 30.5.1.1.5).
04h	Link Failure - Remote fault: The aLoseMediaCounter has been incremented for an aMediaAvailable state being entered indicating a remote fault (see IEEE 802.3-2008 subclause 30.5.1.1.4 and IEEE 802.3-2008 subclause 30.5.1.1.5).
05h	Link Failure - Virtual Link failure: The incident port has detected a Virtual Link failure using the Virtual Link maintenance protocol.
06h to FFh	Reserved

Table 13-2. FCoE Link Incidents

13.8 Chapter Summary

Resource Allocation Timeout Value

- Fibre Channel defines a Resource Allocation Timeout value (R_A_TOV)
  - Specifies when a frame either has been delivered or it is guaranteed that the frame never will be delivered
- R_A_TOV Value =
  - E_D_TOV + (2 * Max. Fabric Transit Time)
- Maximum Fabric Transit Time =
  - (R_A_TOV – E_D_TOV) / 2

Resource Allocation Timeout Value

- Default value for R_A_TOV is 10 seconds
- Default value for E_D_TOV is 2 seconds
- Maximum Fabric Transit Time = 4 seconds (using default values)
- Once R_A_TOV elapses following an error, it is safe to reuse the Sequence and Exchange identifiers (SEQ_ID and OX_ID)
  - There is no possibility of ambiguity or aliasing
  - If a frame were delivered after R_A_TOV, it might appear to be part of a new Exchange that uses the same OX_ID or SEQ_ID
  - This can result in data integrity problems

R_A_TOV Data Corruption (Read)

- Data and Status frames for OX_ID 1234 are delayed due to congestion in the Fabric
- Upon detecting a command timeout, the Initiator aborts the Exchange using ABTS
  - To ensure that all frames associated with the aborted Exchange have flushed out of the Fabric, the Initiator waits a minimum or R_A_TOV before reusing the Exchange ID
- After R_A_TOV has elapsed, Exchange ID value is released and the Initiator reuses the same OX_ID for a new command with the same target
  - The Fabric delivers the frames for the original command
- Initiator interprets frames as belonging to the new command resulting in a data integrity error

R_A_TOV Data Corruption (Write)

- Status frame for OX_ID 1234 is delayed due to congestion.
  - Upon detecting a command timeout, the initiator aborts the Exchange using ABTS.
  - After R_A_TOV has elapsed, the initiator reuses OX_ID 1234 for a new write command to the same target.
- The new write command encounters a write error on the media.
- Before the Check Condition is returned, Fabric delivers Good status for the first command

R_A_TOV Enforcement

- Fibre Channel standards do not specify how R_A_TOV is enforced
- A frame may go through multiple switches on its way from the source to destination
  - There are no mechanisms defined in the standards to enable switches to communicate how much of allowed time has been used
  - There is no "time-to-live" field in the Fibre Channel frame header
- Implementations today enforce R_A_TOV by limiting the number of switches in the path and allocating a portion of R_A_TOV to each switch

R_A_TOV Enforcement

- An implementation may limit the maximum number of switches in path (nothing is specified by the standards)
- Each switch is allocated 1/n of "Maximum Fabric Transit Time" to forward or discard frame
  - Typically 500 msec. per switch (1/8 of 4 seconds)
- *See: Figure 13-4 on page 192*

FCoE and R_A_TOV Agreement

- FCoE data integrity must be at least as good as Fibre Channel's
  - Fibre Channel cannot guarantee data integrity if a frame's transit time is greater than $(R\_A\_TOV - E\_D\_TOV) / 2$
  - If this requirement is violated, undetectable data corruption is possible
- FC standards require a Fabric ensure frames are delivered within this time frame, or not at all
  - Standards are silent on how this is realized
- Best practice is to discard frames that do not transit a switch within a certain period of time
  - 500ms is typical for Fibre Channel switches

Proposed R_A_TOV Solution

- Require Ethernet switches in FCoE environments to enforce R_A_TOV behavior
  - Limit switch forwarding delay to < 500 msec.
  - If a frame can't be forwarded within this time, discard it
  - Same behavior as required for Fibre Channel switches
- Limit maximum path length to ensure no more than eight hops
  - A configuration constraint, not enforced by the switches

FIP Keep Alive

- It may not be possible for the VN_Port or VF_Port to determine when an intermediate Ethernet link fails
  - This is different than native Fibre Channel
- Periodic Discovery Advertisements and FIP Keep Alive messages provide a way to see if a VN_Port or VF_Port is still accessible
  - If three times FKA_ADV_Period elapses without a FKA or Advertisement, the virtual link is considered to be down
  - FKA_ADV_Period value is still under discussion (30 sec. vs. 5 sec.)

FIP Keep Alive: FCF Behavior

- FCoE controller associated with each VF_Port MAC periodically transmits Discovery Advertisements
- When a periodic Discovery Advertisement is sent by the VF_Port capable FCF MAC:
  - The destination MAC address is set to the "ALL ENodes" group address
  - The source MAC address is set to the FCF's MAC address.
  - The Solicited bit (S) is set to zero to indicate the Discovery Advertisement is not being sent in response to a Discovery Solicitation.
- Enables VN_Port to determine that the VF_Port is reachable

FIP Keep Alive: ENode Behavior

- FCoE Controller associated with each VN_Port transmits a FIP Keep Alive message on a periodic basis
  - Notifies the VF_Port's FCoE Controller that the VN_Port is functional
- If a VF_Port's FCoE Controller fails to receive a FIP Keep Alive message from a VN_Port within 2.5 times FKA_ADV_Period
  - It terminates the login session with the VN_Port and frees up associated resources

FIP Keep Alive: Snooping Switches

- Intermediate Ethernet switches may snoop Discovery Advertisements and FIP Keep Alive messages
- Enables switch to identify broken virtual links
  - Switch can remove Access Control list entries for the broken path
  - Switch can remove static forwarding table entries for the broken path

FCoE/Ethernet Specific Errors

- FCoE introduces the potential for additional Ethernet-specific errors and malicious behavior
- Three different categories of errors have been discussed:
  - Cross connect: traffic swap between two VN_Port/VF_Port sessions,
  - Association: a VN Port logs into the wrong VF_Port, and
  - Forwarding loops
- Many of these are the result of duplicate MAC address conditions

Duplicate MAC Addresses

- Duplicate MAC addresses can result in a multitude of errors including:
  - Frames delivered to the wrong port
  - Frames not being delivered to the correct port
  - Forwarding loops
- Duplicate MAC addresses can occur due to device failures, configuration errors, or malicious behavior
- There are many variations of duplicate MAC address conditions:
  - Two VN_Ports have the same MAC address
  - A VN_Port and a VF_Port have the same MAC address, etc.

Duplicate MAC Addresses

- Some combinations are more likely than others.
  - Assuming that FCoE Forwarders use "burned-in" MAC addresses, it is unlikely that a duplicate address would occur
- There are situations where a VN_Port MAC address is created dynamically and duplicates might occur,
  - Hypervisor in a virtual machine environment
  - When using Fabric Provided MAC Addressing (FPMA) and Fabrics with the same FC-MAP value are joined
- A rogue host may attempt to use the MAC address of another entity for malicious purposes

Duplicated Ethernet Frames

- During a spanning tree reconfiguration, duplicate frames may be received
  - This is due to the learning behavior used by Ethernet switches
  - If the destination is unknown, the frame is forwarded out all other switch ports
  - This results in the frame being propagated to the destination, if it exists
- During reconfiguration, a switch may change the path it is using
  - A frame sent via more than one path may arrive multiple times at the destination

Mis-Ordered Ethernet Frames

- During a spanning tree reconfiguration, frames may be received out-of-order
  - A frame has been forwarded down one path
  - That path fails and a switch begins using an alternate path
  - The time down the new path is shorter than the time down the old path
  - A second frame is received and forwarded via the new path and arrived before the earlier frame sent via the old path
- This is no different than what can occur in a native Fibre Channel environment

14. Ethernet Access Control

In a storage environment, it is important to ensure that host systems or servers are prevented from accessing storage resources that they are not authorized to access. Fibre Channel provides a rich set of access control capabilities through zoning, LUN masking and access control lists. In an FCoE environment, considerations must be given to providing appropriate levels of access control to protect against unauthorized access attempts or rogue hosts or devices.

In a native Fibre Channel environment, switches are generally assumed to be trusted devices that control access to the fabric and other Fibre Channel devices. End devices connect directly to a Fibre Channel switch with a physical cable and are unable to communicate with other devices until Fabric Login (FLOGI) has been successfully completed.

Following completion of Fabric Login, communication with other devices is controlled based on Fibre Channel zoning. Zoning is a set of authorizations (zones) set up by an administrator specifying which communication is permitted or denied. A zone specifies a set of devices that are authorized to communicate. A device may belong to one or more zones, each specifying allowed communications.

Zones may be grouped into zone sets, each specifying a specific configuration of the Fabric. By changing the active zone set (configuration), allowable communications within the Fabric can be changed without the need for physical cabling changes.

Zoning may be enforced by limiting information made available in response to Name Server queries or via Registered State Change Notifications (RSCNs). While limiting information prevents discovery of devices, it does not prevent access. This type of zoning enforcement is referred to as "soft zoning".

Zoning may also be enforced by the forwarding mechanisms in Fibre Channel switches. In this case, the switch examines each frame, on a frame-by-frame basis, to determine if the frame should be forwarded. This type of zoning enforcement is referred to as "hard zoning".

Zoning provides protection at the perimeter of the Fabric. Frames are either allowed, or prevented, entry into the based on zoning. Zoning is not enforced on inter-switch links.

14.1 What's Different with Ethernet?

One of the objectives of FCoE was to provide the same level of security as provided in a native Fibre Channel environment. This requires addressing a number of the fundamental differences between a native Fibre Channel environment and an FCoE environment.

14.1.1 Virtual Links vs. Physical Links

The first difference that appears in an FCoE environment occurs because FCoE end devices (ENodes) are not required to connect directly to an FCoE Forwarder (they may access an FCF through one or more intermediate Ethernet bridges). As a result, the FCF cannot serve as the absolute gatekeeper for FCoE communications. When intermediate Ethernet bridges exist between an end device and FCoE Forwarder, those bridges need to participate in the enforcement of access controls in order to provide a level of access control comparable to native Fibre Channel.

14.1.2 Ethernet Bridge Learning vs. Fibre Channel

A second difference between native Fibre Channel and Ethernet arises due to the "learning" behavior associated with Ethernet bridges.

In a native Fibre Channel environment, the switches control addressing by assigning addresses during FLOGI or NPIV FDISC. If a Fibre Channel device attempts to use an address other than what the switch assigned, the switch can block that traffic to prevent address spoofing.

In an Ethernet environment, bridges learn the Ethernet addresses of attached devices by examining received frames. Based on the Source Address in the received frame, the bridge learns which devices are attached to (or accessible via) which bridge ports. There is no protection against rogue devices using the address of another device. This creates the potential for a rogue device to use the address of another device to corrupt the bridge forwarding table and divert traffic from the intended device to the rogue.

Due to this behavior, one cannot trust the Ethernet addressing and must protect against address spoofing by rogue hosts.

14.1.3 Assumptions of Trust

In native Fibre Channel, switches are assumed to be trusted devices that control addressing (via Fabric Login or NPIV FDISC) and enforce access control as defined by zoning.

With soft zoning, host systems and end devices are considered trusted to the extent that they will not attempt communication with devices other than those they discover when querying the Name Server.

With hard zoning, host systems and end devices are not consider trusted and the Fibre Channel switch examines each frame to determine whether the frame should be forwarded.

Because zoning membership is often specified using the device's Port Name, Fibre Channel provides optional cryptographic-based authentication protocols that enable switches and devices to authenticate another entity.

In an FCoE environment, FCoE switches are assumed to be trusted (they are, after all, Fibre Channel switches in disguise). Ethernet bridges, host systems and end devices, in general, are not assumed to be trusted.

14.2 Access Control in the Ethernet Realm

To provide a secure environment, safeguards need to be put in place in an FCoE environment. These safeguards need to protect against unauthorized access, address impersonation, misdirection of traffic through "learning" attacks and denial-of-service attacks.

Ethernet provides two access control method that can be used by FCoE, and those methods are via Ethernet Access Control Lists (ACLs) and static forwarding table entries. When used together, these mechanisms can greatly enhance the robustness of an FCoE environment.

Ethernet bridges that are likely to be used in FCoE data center environments will normally support Access Control Lists. The bridge implements a multi-field classifier, or comparator, that enables selection of frames based on specified fields or combinations of fields (e.g., source address, destination address, EtherType, etc.). The comparator is normally a hardware function within a bridge and implemented using a ternary comparator (compare on "0", "1", or "don't care" conditions).

The Access Control List is a list of directives specifying the action that is to be taken when a comparator condition is met. Typical actions are to "deny" a frame (prevent it from being forwarded) or "permit" a frame (allow it to be forwarded). Based on the comparator, a frame may also be intercepted and directed to the bridge supervisor or control plane for additional processing. An access control list is processed from top to bottom until a compare condition is satisfied. At that point, processing of the ACL for that frame is done.

Access control should be enforced at the perimeter of an Ethernet network carrying FCoE traffic and may be enforced in the interior on inter-bridge links. The actual Access control list entries vary depending the location of a bridge port within the configuration. Locations used in the following discussions are shown in Figure 14-1 on page 214.

An Ethernet bridge may create a set of default access control list entries to provide a level of protection for FCoE traffic. Additional entries may be created manually by an administrator or automatically as a result of FIP operations detected by a bridge.

14.3 Perimeter Protection: ENode Port ACL Entries

A bridge port may be connected to an FCoE ENode, or unconnected but potentially connected to an FCoE ENode later, as shown in Figure 14-2 on page 215.

The entries in this section describe how appropriate Access Control List entries can be constructed in order to provide perimeter protection. These entries are designed so that they can be included ahead of any other, non-FCoE, Access Control List entries without affecting non-FCoE behavior.

The Access Control List entries begin with a set of default entries that are sufficient to permit Discovery but otherwise limit prevent FCoE traffic. Additional entries can be added dynamically based on operations detected by a bridge through examining the FIP protocol.

ACL Starting Point: "All Shields Up". The initial starting point to protect against unauthorized traffic is for Ethernet bridge ports attached to ENodes to simply prohibit all FCoE traffic. This can be accomplished using the following default access control list entries:

```
deny    type    8906h       ; Initially, deny all FCoE traffic
deny    type    8914h       ; Initially, deny all FIP traffic
```

Prevent Rogue Use of FPMA MAC Addresses. When using FPMA, VN_Port MAC addresses are predictable and fall within a pre-determined range defined by the FC-MAP prefix.

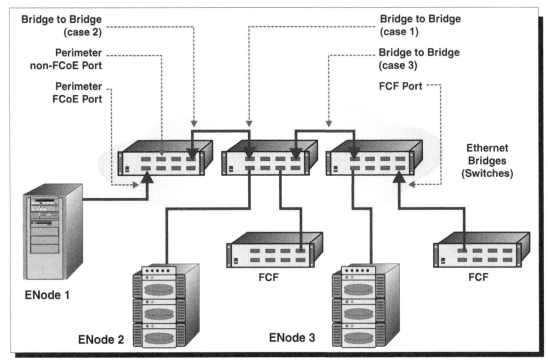

Figure 14-1. FCoE Access Control List (ACL) Locations

An ACL can take advantage of this to prevent duplication of FPMA MAC addresses by non-FCoE devices by including the following entry:

```
deny      Prefix  FC-MAP         ; Deny all addresses beginning with the FC-MAP

deny      type    8906h          ; Initially, deny all FCoE traffic
deny      type    8914h          ; Initially, deny all FIP traffic
```

Enabling FIP Discovery. In order to perform discovery, it is necessary to enable selected FIP operations (EtherType 8914h). ENode Solicitations may be sent to the All-FCF-MACs group address. Because access control lists are processed from top to bottom, the entry is added at the top of the default ACL to enable multicast Solicitations (note: this also enables FIP Keep Alive messages):

```
permit  DA     ALL-FCF-MACs ; Permit FIP to the All-FCFs group address
        type   8914h

deny    Prefix FC-MAP       ; Deny all addresses beginning with the FC-MAP

deny    type   8906h        ; Initially, deny all FCoE traffic
deny    type   8914h        ; Initially, deny all FIP traffic
```

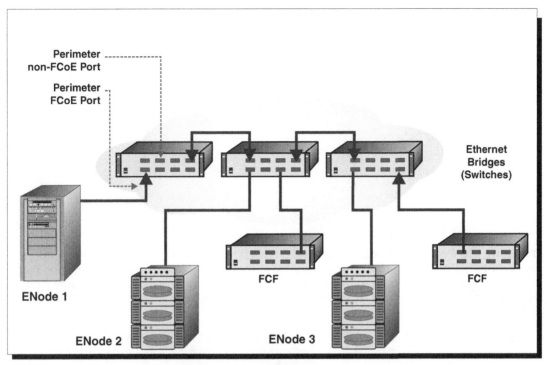

Perimeter
non-FCoE Port

Perimeter
FCoE Port

Ethernet
Bridges
(Switches)

ENode 1

ENode 2

FCF

ENode 3

FCF

Figure 14-2.   Access Control List Entries: Perimeter Port

A Solicitation may also be sent as a unicast frame directly to the FCF-MAC address discovered upon receipt of an Advertisement from the FCF. The following prevent usage of the
FCF's MAC address as a source address and permit unicast frames to the FCF. These entries
can be added automatically by a bridge as a result of snooping FIP Advertisements or manually by an administrator (note: these entries are repeated for each enabled FCF):

```
deny     SA       FCF-MAC        ; Prevent ENode from using FCF's MAC address

permit   DA       FCF-MAC        ; Permit FIP to the FCF's MAC address
         type     8914h

permit   DA       ALL-FCF-MACs   ; Permit FIP to the All-FCFs group address
         type     8914h

deny     Prefix   FC-MAP         ; Deny all addresses beginning with the FC-MAP

deny     type     8906h          ; Initially, deny all FCoE traffic
deny     type     8914h          ; Initially, deny all FIP traffic
```

Enabling VN_Port Traffic. Upon successful completion of Fabric Login (FLOGI) or NPIV
Fabric Discover (FDISC), it is necessary to enable VN_Port traffic using the FCoE protocol. An
Ethernet bridge can automatically create the necessary entry by examining ("snooping") the

---

FIP protocol and adding the following entry upon detection of an LS_ACC to FLOGI or FDISC (this entry will be repeated for each VN_Port):

```
permit   DA       FCF-MAC        ; Must be to the FCF-MAC, and
         SA       VN_Port_MAC    ; From the (assigned) VN_Port MAC address
         type     8906h          ; and FCoE protocol

deny     SA       FCF-MAC        ; Prevent ENode from using FCF's MAC address

permit   DA       FCF-MAC        ; Permit FIP to the FCF's MAC address
         type     8914h

permit   DA       ALL-FCF-MACs   ; Permit FIP to the All-FCFs group address
         type     8914h

deny     Prefix   FC-MAP         ; Deny all addresses beginning with the FC-MAP

deny     type     8906h          ; Initially, deny all FCoE traffic
deny     type     8914h          ; Initially, deny all FIP traffic
```

Disabling VN_Port Traffic. Upon successful completion of Fabric Logout (LOGO to address FF:FF:FEh), a FIP Clear Virtual Links operation to the VN_Port, or as a result of a timeout due to missing VN_Port FIP Keep Alive messages, an Ethernet bridge can automatically remove the ACL entry for the VN_Port. Removing the following statement removes the virtual link and prevents associated FCoE traffic.

```
permit   DA       FCF-MAC        ; Must be to the FCF-MAC, and
         SA       VN_Port_MAC    ; From the (assigned) VN_Port MAC address
         type     8906h          ; and FCoE protocol

deny     SA       FCF-MAC        ; Prevent ENode from using FCF's MAC address

permit   DA       FCF-MAC        ; Permit FIP to the FCF's MAC address
         type     8914h

permit   DA       ALL-FCF-MACs   ; Permit FIP to the All-FCFs group address
         type     8914h

deny     Prefix   FC-MAP         ; Deny all addresses beginning with the FC-MAP

deny     type     8906h          ; Initially, deny all FCoE traffic
deny     type     8914h          ; Initially, deny all FIP traffic
```

Perimeter Prevention of FCoE Traffic. It may be desirable to prevent FCoE traffic of any kind on certain perimeter bridge ports (e.g., those known to connect to links that are not loss-less or outside the FCoE domain. In addition, it may be desirable to prevent usage of address-es know to be specific to FCoE by non-FCoE entities (this prevention may only be possible when using FPMA). This perimeter location is also shown in Figure 14-2 on page 215.

Prevention of FCoE traffic can be provided by the following Access Control List entries:

```
deny     type     8906h          ; Deny FCoE frames
deny     type     8914h          ; Deny FIP frames
deny     Prefix   FC-MAP         ; Deny addresses with FC-MAP (FPMA only)
```

14.3.1 ENode to Enode Traffic

ENode-to-ENode traffic is not permitted by the current FCoE standard. The access control list entries described in this section prevent this traffic by only permitting an ENode to communicate with one or more FCFs.

14.4 Interior Protection: Bridge-to-Bridge ACLs

Access Control Lists can also be used to provide protection on bridge-to-bridge links. The actual Access Control List entries vary depending on the traffic being carried on the link.

14.4.1 Bridge-to-Bridge Link Receiving ENode-to-FCF Frames (Case 1)

A bridge-to-bridge link may receive FCoE frames only from an ENode (i.e., no FCF-to-ENode or FCF-to-FCF traffic) as shown in Figure 14-3.

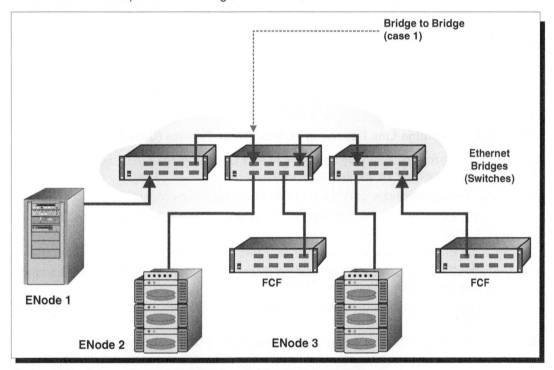

Figure 14-3. Access Control List Entries: Bridge-to-Bridge (Case 1)

In this case, the ingress bridge port should perform the following checks:

1. Verify the Ethernet DA of all FIP frames (EtherType 8914h) is an FCF-MAC address or the ALL-FCF-MACs group address.

---

2. Verify the Ethernet DA of all FCoE frames (EtherType 8906h) is an FCF-MAC address or the ALL-FCF-MACs group address.

3. Verify the Ethernet DA of all FCoE frames is a VN_Port MAC address (may only be possible when using FPMA addressing).

4. Prevent FCoE frames from one FCF to another FCF (by definition no FCF-to-FCF traffic should occur on this link).

The restrictions can be enforced using the following Access Control List entries:

```
permit  DA      ALL-FCF-MACs ; Permit FIP to the All-FCFs group address
        type    8914h

permit  DA      FCF-MAC      ; Permit FIP a specific FCF's MAC address
        type    8914h        ; (repeat this entry for each FCF-MAC address)

deny    type    8914h        ; Deny any FIP traffic not explicitly allowed

permit  DA      FCF-MAC      ; Permit FCoE to FCF having FC-MAP (FPMA only)
        Prefix  FC-MAP       ; must have correct FC-MAP
        type    8906h

deny    DA      FCF-MAC      ; Prevent FCF to FCF traffic
        SA      FCF-MAC      ; (repeat for each FCF-FCF pairing)

deny    type    8906h        ; Deny any FCoE traffic not explicitly allowed
```

14.4.2 Bridge-to-Bridge Link Receiving FCF-to-ENode Frames (Case 2)

A bridge-to-bridge may receive only frames from an FCF to an ENode (i.e., no ENode-to-FCF or FCF-to-FCF frames) as shown in Figure 14-4.

In this case, the ingress bridge port should perform the following checks:

1. Verify the Ethernet SA of all FIP frames (EtherType 8914h) is an FCF-MAC address and the DA is not an FCF-MAC address.

2. Verify the Ethernet SA of all FCoE frames (EtherType 8906h) is an FCF-MAC address.

3. Verify the Ethernet DA of all FCoE frames (EtherType 8906h) is an ENode MAC address (may only be possible when using FPMA).

4. Prevent FCoE frames with a Ethernet DA of an FCF (by definition, this link is receiving only FCF to ENode traffic).

The restrictions can be enforced using the following Access Control List entries:

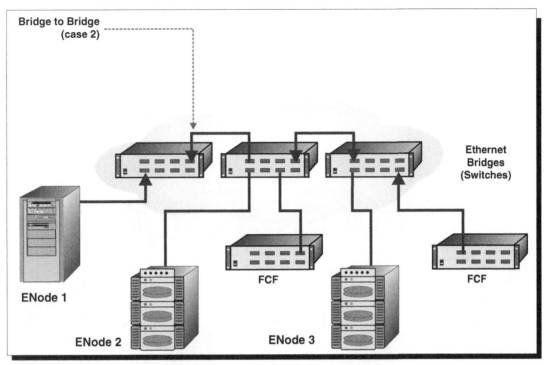

Figure 14-4. Access Control List Entries: Bridge-to-Bridge (Case 2)

```
deny      DA       FCF-MAC          ; deny FIP frames to an FCF's MAC address
          type     8914h            ; (repeat entry for each FCF-MAC address)

permit    DA       ALL-ENODE-MACs;  allow FIP frames to ALL-ENODE-MAC address
          type     8914h            ; (see text below for discussion)

permit    SA       FCF-MAC          ; permit FIP frames from FCF's MAC address
          type     8914h            ; (repeat entry for each FCF-MAC address)

deny      type     8914h            ; Deny any FIP frames not explicitly permitted

permit    SA       FCF-MAC          ; Permit FCoE from FCF with FC-MAP (FPMA only)
          Prefix   FC-MAP           ; must have correct FC-MAP (FPMA only)
          type     8906h

deny      type     8906h            ; Deny FCoE frames not explicitly permitted
```

The second entry in this list (the one permitting frames to the 'ALL-ENODE-MACs' group address) should only be included if it is known and trusted that only FCFs are able to introduce frames destined to the 'ALL-ENODE-MACs' group address. Inclusion of this entry permits automatic creation of entries for FCFs. If this cannot be trusted, this entry should not be included and the administrator should manually configure the appropriate FCF entries in the Access Control Lists.

14.4.3 Bridge-to-Bridge Link Receiving Both FCF and ENode Frames (Case 3)

A bridge-to-bridge link may receive frames from both FCFs and ENodes as shown in Figure 14-5 on page 220.

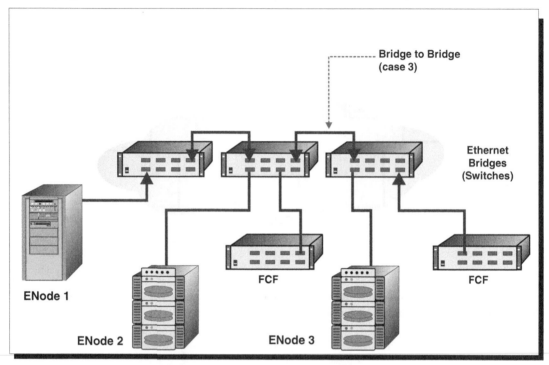

Figure 14-5. Access Control List Entries: Bridge-to-Bridge (Case 3)

In this case, the ingress bridge port should perform the following checks:

1. Verify all FIP frames are either sourced by an FCF or sent to an FCF.
2. Verify all FCoE frames are sourced by an FCF and destined for an ENode, or sourced by an ENode and destined for an FCF.
3. Verify all FCoE frames are either sourced by, or destined for, an FCF.

These restrictions can be enforced using the following Access Control List entries:

```
permit   DA       ALL-FCF-MACs  ; allow FIP frames to an ALL FCF's address
         type     8914h         ;

permit   DA       FCF-MAC       ; allow FIP frames to FCF's MAC address
         type     8914h         ; (repeat entry for each FCF-MAC address)

permit   SA       FCF-MAC       ; permit FIP frames from FCF's MAC address
         type     8914h         ; (repeat entry for each FCF-MAC address)

permit   DA       ALL-ENODE-MACs; permit multicast FIP frames ENodes group
         type     8914h         ; (see discussion below)

deny     type     8914h         ; Deny any FIP frames not explicitly permitted

permit   DA       FCF-MAC       ; Permit FCoE from FCF with FC-MAP (FPMA only)
         Prefix   FC-MAP        ; must have correct FC-MAP (FPMA only)
         type     8906h

permit   SA       FCF-MAC       ; Permit FCoE from FCF with FC-MAP (FPMA only)
         Prefix   FC-MAP        ; must have correct FC-MAP (FPMA only)
         type     8906h

deny     type     8906h         ; Deny FCoE frames not explicitly permitted
```

The fourth entry in this list (the one permitting frames to the 'ALL-ENODE-MACs' group address) should only be included if it is known and trusted that only FCFs are able to introduce frames destined to the 'ALL-ENODE-MACs' group address. Inclusion of this entry permits automatic creation of entries for FCFs. If this cannot be trusted, this entry should not be included and the administrator should manually configure the appropriate FCF entries in the Access Control Lists.

14.5 Chapter Summary

Ethernet Access Control Lists (ACLs)

■ Ethernet provides an access control method that can be used by FCoE
  - That method is via Ethernet Access Control Lists.
  - Ethernet switches that are likely to be used in FCoE data center environments will typically support Access Control Lists
■ The switch implements a multi-field classifier (MFC)
  - Enables selection of frames based on specified fields (e.g., source address, destination address, EtherType, etc.)
  - This is usually a hardware function within the switch
  - Implemented using a ternary comparator (compare on "0", "1", or "don't care" conditions)

Access Control List Processing

■ An Access Control List is a list of directives
  - Specifies the action to be taken when a comparator condition is met
  - Typical actions are to "deny" a frame (prevent it from being forwarded) or "permit" a frame (allow it to be forwarded).
  - A frame may be intercepted and directed to the switch supervisor for additional processing.
  - An access control list is processed from top to bottom until a compare condition is satisfied.
  - At that point, processing of the ACL for that frame is done

15. Data Center Bridging (DCB) Ethernet

Several enhancements have been developed for Ethernet intended for deployment in data center environments. These enhancements improve the delivery reliability, add quality of service attributes and address the issue of congestion notification and management. Together, these enhancements are referred to as Data Center Bridging (DCB) Ethernet.

NOTE – Before the term Data Center Bridging (DCB) Ethernet was agreed upon, different vendors used the terms Data Center Ethernet (DCE) and Converged Enhanced Ethernet (CEE) to identify these enhancements.

15.1 Traffic Classification

In a converged network environment, it is likely that many different types of traffic (each having its own unique delivery requirements) will share the same Ethernet NIC, links and bridge ports. There may be a combination of traditional LAN traffic mixed in with storage traffic (FCoE and/or iSCSI) and inter-processor communication. Ethernet provides several capabilities that enable different traffic classes to be subjected to different delivery policies. These capabilities are:

- 802.1Q VLAN Tag Priority
- Per-Priority Flow Control (PFC) - 802.1Qbb
- Enhanced Transmission Selection (ETS) - 802.1Qaz
- Congestion Notification (CN) - 802.1Qau

Fundamental to all of these functions is traffic classification. Traffic classification segregates frames into different traffic classes based on specified attributes. Once traffic has been segregated into different traffic classes, each traffic class can be subjected to a different delivery policy.

Traffic classification can be performed by software or hardware depending on the implementation. Hardware classification may be done through the use of a ternary comparator (one, zero or don't care) that performs classification based on the values of designated fields. Some examples of attributes that might be used for traffic classification include the following (obviously there are many other possibilities):

- All frames carrying traffic for a single TCP connection
- All frames associated with a specific process running in an end station
- All frames that are transmitted to a particular destination MAC address
- All frames with the same Source and Destination IP addresses

- All frames with the same Source and Destination IP addresses and TCP port number
- All frames that produce the same value when a hash function is applied to specified fields

A high-level illustration of traffic classification, and subsequent selection of frames for transmission is shown in Figure 15-1 on page 224. In this example, a series of undifferentiated frames are subjected to traffic classification that segregates the frames into different traffic classes where they are queued for subsequent transmission.

Different traffic classes are handled as if each is assigned its own logical transmit queue. Based on the delivery policies for the different traffic classes, frames are selected for transmission on the physical link. Ethernet provides several different methods for controlling the selection of frames for transmission as described in the following sections.

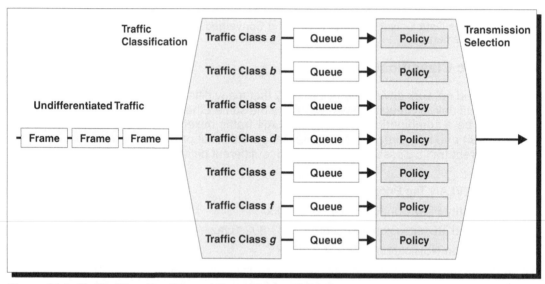

Figure 15-1. Traffic Classification and Transmission Selection

IEEE 802.1Q VLAN Tag Priority. The IEEE 802.1Q standard defines a priority function for Ethernet traffic. During traffic classification, each frame is assigned to a priority level in the 802.1Q VLAN Tag Priority field.

Frames are selected for transmission, or forwarding, based on their priority value. Frames having higher priority take precedence over frames having lower priority. If there happens to be a large volume of high-priority traffic, there may be insufficient bandwidth available to deliver lower-priority traffic in a timely manner.

Per-Priority Pause Flow Control (PFC). Ethernet provides an optional Pause flow control mechanism. A receiver can signal the sender at the opposite end of the link to suspend frame transmission by transmitting a Pause frame. Pause causes all frame transmission to be suspended for a specified period and does not allow different traffic classes to be subject to different delivery policies (i.e., it is a strict Stop/Go mechanism).

The Per-Priority Pause Flow Control (PFC) described in *Per-Priority Pause Flow Control (PFC)* on page 226 enables flow control to be asserted individually on each priority level (or on some levels, but not others). Traffic that must be protected against frame loss due to buffer overflow can be assigned to one or more priority levels that have PFC enabled. Other traffic, that may tolerate lossy delivery can be assigned to other priority levels that are not subject to PFC.

Enhanced Transmission Selection (ETS). It is desirable to expand the concept of providing different delivery policies for different traffic classes to include bandwidth management. This ensures that each traffic class receives at least a minimum specified portion of the link's bandwidth, even in the event of heavy link utilization. The details of Enhanced Transmission Selection are described in *Enhanced Transmission Selection (ETS)* on page 227.

Congestion Notification and Management (CN). (Congestion notification and management add another enhancement to available Ethernet delivery policies. When congestion notification is used and congestion is detected in the network, a Congestion Notification Message is sent to direct the source to reduce the rate of frame transmission.

Congestion notification and management may apply to some traffic classes (as identified using the VLAN Tag priority value), but not others. If Congestion notification applies to a given VLAN Tag priority, that priority value is referred to as a Congestion Notification Priority Value (CNPV). A traffic flow that is being subjected to congestion management is referred to as a Congestion Controlled Flow (CCF).

Congestion notification and management is described in *Quantized Congestion Notification (QCN)* on page 230.

15.1.1 Traffic Class and Flow Identification

It is necessary to be able to identify which frames belong to each traffic class in order to apply different delivery policies to different traffic classes. While the different traffic classes could be identified by using the same traffic classification function in each bridge and end station, this approach has limitations. If any of the attributes used to identify a traffic class are altered while a frame is in transit, it may be impossible to identify the frames associated with that traffic class. For example, if the IP address is one of the parameters used for traffic classification and an IP datagram is forwarded through a router that performs Network Address Translation (NAT), the IP address may be changed and no longer reliable for identifying a given traffic class.

The 802.1Q VLAN Tag priority field is often used to identify a given traffic class, but the limited number of priority values limits the granularity of identification. Multiple traffic streams, or flows, may share the same VLAN Tag priority value. For example, FCoE traffic between multiple initiators and targets may share the same VLAN Tag priority, even though that traffic may consist of unrelated flows.

In some applications, the VLAN Tag priority value may be combined with information from other fields to identify a given traffic flow within a traffic class (e.g., a source or destination address or the EtherType value). This provides a more specific identification of a given flow than is provided by using the priority value alone.

Ethernet Congestion Notification adds an optional Congestion Notification Tag (CN-TAG) that can be used to provide explicit identification of a specific traffic flow.

15.2 Per-Priority Pause Flow Control (PFC)

In a data center environment, the simple pause flow control mechanism provided by the current Ethernet standard (described in *Frame Loss and Ethernet Flow Control* on page 86) may be inadequate because it provides only a "stop and go" mechanism. Either all frame transmission is paused, or all frame transmission is allowed to resume. There is no way to selectively pause certain traffic while allowing other traffic to continue.

In a converged network environment, an Ethernet link may be carrying multiple traffic classes such as FCoE for storage, TCP/IP for networking, iWarp for clustering and, perhaps, others as well (e.g., VOIP). In this type of environment, it is desirable to provide flow control independently for each different traffic class. This is accomplished by performing traffic classification to map the different traffic classes to 802.1Q VLAN Tag priority levels and then controlling each priority level using Per-Priority Pause flow control (PFC). Per-Priority Flow Control requires the use of 802.1Q VLAN tagged frames because the VLAN Tag priority value provides the means to identify a particular traffic class and its associated frames.

An implementation supporting Per-Priority Pause flow control provides transmit and receive queues for each supported priority level. By using independent transmit and receive queues, frames for each supported priority level can be paused or resumed independently as shown in Figure 15-2.

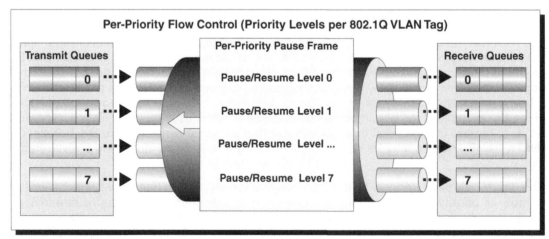

Figure 15-2. Ethernet Per-Priority Pause Flow Control

It is not necessary to support Priority Flow Control for all eight priority levels. Some priority levels may be controlled using PFC while other priority levels may operate without using flow control (as might be normal in a typical Ethernet environment).

As with the basic Ethernet Pause frame, the Per-Priority Pause frame is a MAC Control frame that uses one of the Group MAC Addresses reserved for Ethernet link-level functions as the destination address. Frames sent to this destination address are not forwarded by Ethernet bridges thereby limiting the scope of the Pause frame to the associated link. The format of the Per-Priority pause frame is shown in Figure 15-3 on page 227.

A single Per-Priority Pause frame can assert flow control on one or more priority levels at the same time. The frame contains a Class Enable Vector, which is a 16-bit bitmap, that specifies which VLAN Tag priority levels are affected by the pause frame. The format of the Class-Enable Vector is:

'00000000'b T0 T1 T2 T3 T4 T5 T6 T7

Where T0 is a single bit indicating the frame affects Priority Level 0, T1 is a single bit indicating the frame affects Priority Level 1, etc. By setting one or more bits in the Class Enable Vector, a single Per-Priority Pause frame can control one or more priority levels.

Destination MAC Address (01:80:C2:00:00:01)	
Source MAC Address	
EtherType = 0x8808	OpCode = 0x0101
Class Enable Vector	Pause_Time (0)
Pause_Time (1)	Pause_Time (2)
Pause_Time (3)	Pause_Time (4)
Pause_Time (5)	Pause_Time (6)
Pause_Time (7)	Pad = 0x0000
Pad = 26 bytes of 0x00	
Ethernet FCS	

Figure 15-3. Per-Priority Pause Frame Format

The Per-Priority Pause frame provides a separate Pause_Time field for each priority level. Each field specifies how long frame transmission should be paused for the associated priority level. As with the basic Pause frame, the Pause_Time is specified in units of 512-bit increments at the associated physical link. This provides a Pause_Time range of 0 to 33.6 msec. on a 1 gigabit link (or, 0 to 3.36 msec. on a 10 gigabit link). A Pause_time value of zero means resume transmission for the associated priority level.

When Per-Priority flow control is being used, use of the standard Ethernet Pause flow control on the same link is prohibited.

15.3 Enhanced Transmission Selection (ETS)

Per-Priority Pause flow control (PFC) provides a way to manage individual traffic classes based on 802.1Q VLAN Tag priority levels, but PFC does not provide a way to associate the different traffic classes with 802.1Q VLAN Tag priority levels, prioritize traffic, or limit the bandwidth consumed by a given priority level. Ethernet Enhanced Transmission Selection (ETS) provides a way to specify the traffic classification and mapping to priority levels along with enabling bandwidth management and traffic prioritization.

The goals of ETS are to:

- Classify frames to be transmitted, assign them to Traffic Class Groups (TCGs), and map each TCG to an 802.1Q VLAN Priority level.
- Allow the available bandwidth to be configured among the supported Traffic Class Groups (with the exception of Traffic Class Group 15 which is used for traffic having strict priority with no bandwidth limiting).
- Schedule transmission of frames based on attributes associated with the corresponding Traffic Class Group.
- Allow more than one traffic class per Traffic Class Group.

ETS involves the three key functions that were shown earlier in Figure 15-1 on page 224 (Traffic Classification, Transmit Queueing, and Transmission Selection).

Traffic classification (referred to as Flow Classification and Metering in ETS) maps frames to be transmitted to one or more Traffic Class Groups (TCGs). Traffic classification may be based on the Destination MAC Address, VLAN ID, Priority, Ethertype, or other parameters contained in the Ethernet frame. The actual parameters used during flow classification are not specified by the standard and may be administratively configured or communicated using the DCBX protocol (see *IEEE DCBX Protocol* on page 253). In addition to classifying frames, the Flow Classification and Metering function may also meter the frames to perform traffic shaping or bandwidth management.

Each supported Traffic Class Group has a separate (logical) transmit queue used for frames having similar transmission behavior with regard to attributes such as bandwidth limiting, priorities and use of flow control. Each Traffic Class Group (and its associated transmit queue) ultimately maps to an 802.1Q VLAN Priority level.

The Transmission Selection schedules frames from the transmit queues for transmission by the Ethernet MAC and PHY. Within each Traffic Class Group, frames are processed in order. Depending on the transmission attributes, frames in different transmit queues may by processed out of order relative to the other queues (e.g., a higher-priority frame in one queue may be processed before a lower-priority frame in a different queue, even if the higher-priority frame arrived later).

15.3.1 Traffic Class Groups (TCGs)

Each traffic class or subclass may be mapped to one or more Traffic Class Groups (TCGs). The Traffic Class Group is associated with attributes that determine the scheduling of frames associated with that TCG. Each Traffic Class Group has a four-bit Traffic Class Group ID (TCGID) and (with the exception of TCGID 15) is limited to an administratively configured percentage of the link's available bandwidth. This bandwidth is called the Traffic Class Group Bandwidth (TCG%). The available bandwidth is defined as the bandwidth remaining after all frames associated with Traffic Class Group ID 15 have been processed. Use of the TCGIDs is shown in Table 15-1 on page 229.

NOTE – Traffic Class Group ID 15 is used to provide strict priority scheduling and is not managed by ETS.

Traffic Class Group (TCGID)	Traffic Class Use	Traffic Class Group Bandwidth (TCG%)	Maps to VLAN Priority Level
0	Available for ETS bandwidth allocation	Configurable	Configurable
1	Available for ETS bandwidth allocation	Configurable	Configurable
2	Available for ETS bandwidth allocation	Configurable	Configurable
3	Available for ETS bandwidth allocation	Configurable	Configurable
4	Available for ETS bandwidth allocation	Configurable	Configurable
5	Available for ETS bandwidth allocation	Configurable	Configurable
6	Available for ETS bandwidth allocation	Configurable	Configurable
7	Available for ETS bandwidth allocation	Configurable	Configurable
8 - 14	Reserved	n/a	n/a
15	Strict Priority (not scheduled by ETS)		Configurable

Table 15-1. Traffic Class Group ID Bandwidth Limit Example

When a frame is presented for transmission, the Flow Classification and Metering function maps the frame to one of the supported Traffic Class Groups (identified by the TCGID). The frame transmission selection function schedules the frame for transmission based on the TCGID and available bandwidth and inserts the appropriate VLAN priority level in the 802.1Q VLAN tag, if necessary.

An ETS device is required to support at least three Traffic Class Groups. This enables the following minimum behaviors to be supported:

- Priorities with Priority Flow Control enabled
- Priorities with Priority Flow Control disabled
- Priorities with no Enhanced Transmission Selection behavior

The actual number of Traffic Class Groups (and associated queues) supported by a given implementation is indicated by the Traffic Classes Supported parameter. Each Traffic Class Group ID is mapped to a 802.1Q VLAN Tag Priority Level to provide traffic prioritization and flow control as shown in Figure 15-4 on page 230.

15.3.2 Transmission Selection Algorithm

Prior to the definition of ETS, Ethernet had previously defined two transmission selection algorithms.

- IEEE 802.1Q defined a priority-based transmission selection policy using the 802.1Q VLAN Tag priority value.
- IEEE 802.1Qav defined a credit-based traffic shaper policy for use with audio and video information.

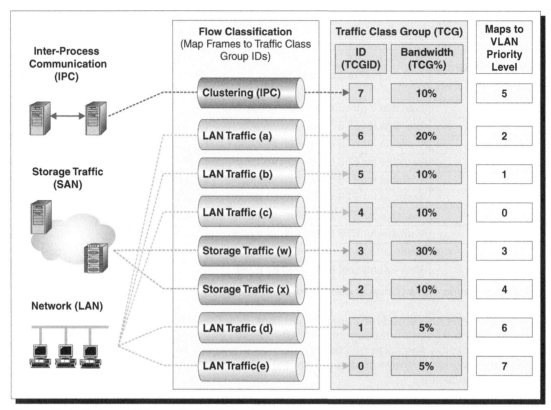

	Flow Classification (Map Frames to Traffic Class Group IDs)	Traffic Class Group (TCG)		Maps to VLAN Priority Level
		ID (TCGID)	Bandwidth (TCG%)	
Inter-Process Communication (IPC)	Clustering (IPC)	7	10%	5
	LAN Traffic (a)	6	20%	2
Storage Traffic (SAN)	LAN Traffic (b)	5	10%	1
	LAN Traffic (c)	4	10%	0
	Storage Traffic (w)	3	30%	3
	Storage Traffic (x)	2	10%	4
Network (LAN)	LAN Traffic (d)	1	5%	6
	LAN Traffic(e)	0	5%	7

Figure 15-4. Enhanced Transmission Selection

The inclusion of ETS results in three different transmission selection algorithms defined by the Ethernet standards plus potential vendor-specific methods. The Transmission Selection Algorithm identifiers listed in Table 15-2 indicate which transmission selection algorithm is being used (or is supported) by a bridge or end station port. Depending upon the implementation, the behavior of a port may be configurable (if the port supports more than one transmission selection algorithm) or the behavior may be fixed by the design.

15.4 Quantized Congestion Notification (QCN)

While link-level flow control mechanisms, such as Ethernet's Pause and Per-Priority Pause or Fibre Channel's Buffer-to-Buffer flow control, prevent frame loss due to buffer overflow conditions, the use of flow control may result in congestion. If a faster device sends frames to a slower destination, the destination may be unable to keep up with the incoming frames. To prevent frame loss, the receiver asserts link-level flow control to cause frame transmission to be suspended on the link. The sender is unaware of this condition and continues to send frames to the destination. This causes traffic to back up along the path, potentially creating congestion.

Identifier	Transmission Selection Algorithm
0	Strict Priority (*see 802.1Q Priority*)
1	Credit-based shaper (*see 802.1Qav*)
2	Enhanced Transmission Selection
3 - 255	Reserved for future standardization
Vendor Specific	The identifier consists of a four-byte value. The three most significant bytes are an OUI that identifies the vendor. The least-significant byte identifies a vendor-specific behavior defined by that vendor.

Table 15-2. Transmission Selection Algorithms

Figure 15-5 on page 231 shows how congestion can occur, and then spread to other points within the network.

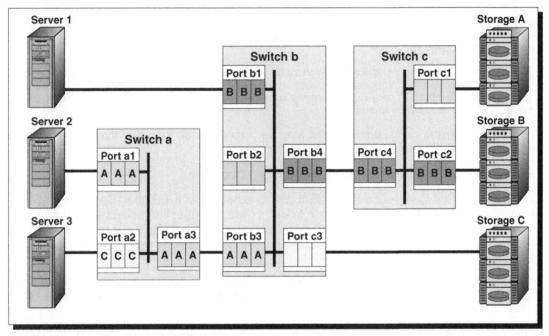

Figure 15-5. Congestion Spreading

1. *Server 1* is sending a series of frames to *Storage b*. *Storage b* is unable to process the frames as quickly as they arrive and uses link-level flow control to suspend frame transmission from *Switch Port c1*.

2. *Server 1* is unaware of *Storage b's* action and continues to send frames for *Storage b*. Because *Switch c* is prevented from forwarding the frames due to flow control, the frames are queued in *Switch c*.

3. When the buffer space in *Switch Port c4* has filled, *Switch Port c4* uses link-level flow control to suspend transmission from *Switch Port b4*. The congestion condition caused by *Storage b* has now spread to the link between *Switches b and c* and is blocking traffic from *Switch b* for *Storage a* and *Storage c*.

4. As a result of the congestion on the link between *Switch Port b4* and *Switch Port c4*, frames from *Server 2* to *Storage a* begin to backup at *Switch b*. When all of the available buffer space has been used, *Switch port b3* uses link-level flow control to suspend frame transmission from *Switch Port a3* further spreading the congestion to the link between *Switch Port a3* and *Switch Port b3*.

5. Frames from *Server 3* to *Storage c* have become victims of the congestion that originated at *Storage a*, then spread to *Switch Port c4* and finally spread to *Switch Port b3*.

Congestion manifests itself through poor performance and timeout conditions. Referring back to the example shown in Figure 15-5 on page 231, when *Storage b* processes a frame, frees up space in its receive queue and is able to accept another frame, frames that had been blocked by the congestion may be able to advance. However, if additional frames for *Storage b* are received, its receive queue may again become full causing the congestion to return almost immediately.

> NOTE – The situation is not unlike a slow truck on a busy two lane highway. Traffic backs up behind the slow truck resulting in congestion. As oncoming traffic allows, one or more cars may be able to pass the truck, temporarily relieving the congestion. As subsequent cars move up behind the truck, the congestion returns almost immediately.

In the case of severe congestion, frames may be blocked for so long that they are eventually discarded by switch ports.

15.4.1 Quantized Congestion Notification (QCN) Objectives

Ethernet Quantized Congestion Notification (QCN) is defined in IEEE 802.1Qau. The objective of Quantized Congestion Notification are to detect when congestion occurs at a Congestion Point (CP) located in a bridge or end station and notify the source of the frames causing the congestion (the Reaction Point, or RP) to reduce the transmission rate of the frames that are causing the congestion.

> NOTE – The Ethernet Congestion Notification mechanism is referred to as "Quantized Congestion Notification (QCN)" because the Congestion Notification message contains a feedback quantity that is quantized to a six-bit value.

In the example shown in Figure 15-6 on page 233, a Congestion Point at *Switch Port c2* detects congestion and signals a Reaction Point (at the end station that is the source of the frames) to limit the frame transmission that is causing the congestion.

15.4.2 Congestion Controlled Flow (CCF)

Some traffic classes may be subject to congestion notification and management while other traffic classes may be excluded from congestion management. Because different traffic classes are mapped to 802.1Q VLAN Tag priority values, this means that some priority values may be subject to congestion management while other priority values are not. If a particular 802.1Q

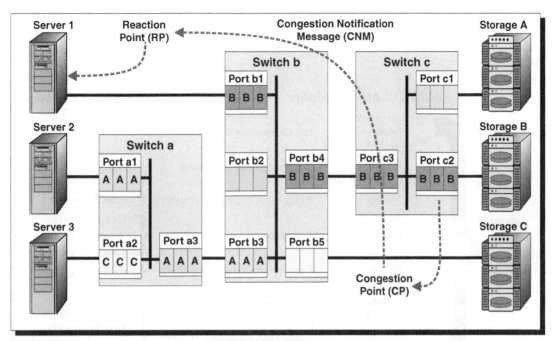

Figure 15-6. Backward Congestion Notification (BCN)

VLAN tag priority value is subject to congestion management, it is referred to as a Congestion Notification Priority Value (CNPV). End stations and bridges use the 802.1Q VLAN tag priority value to determine whether to apply Congestion Notification.

Multiple traffic flows may exist within the same Congestion Notification Priority Value. For example, a single priority value may be used for all FCoE traffic. Within the FCoE traffic may be multiple individual flows that could represent traffic between different initiators and targets. While congestion control could be applied to all traffic associated with the FCoE priority value, it may be desirable to apply congestion control to the specific flow, or set of flows, within that priority value that are causing the congestion.

A Congestion Controlled Flow (CCF) consists of all of the frames that pass through a single flow queue in an originating end station. A Congestion Controlled Flow could be all of the frames for a given VLAN Tag priority value, or a defined subset of those frames. The standard not specify the attributes that an end station uses to associate frames with a specific Congestion Controlled Flow. A particular flow may be determined based on existing fields (or combinations of fields) within a frame, such as the destination MAC address or information in the encapsulated Fibre Channel frame header. All of the frames that belong to a given Congestion Controlled Flow are sent using the same VLAN Tag priority value.

Figure 15-7 on page 234 shows how different VLAN Tag priority values can be associated with Congestion Notification (thereby becoming CNPVs) while other priority values on the same link are not associated with Congestion Notification. In this example, VLAN Tag priorities 1, 3,

4 and 5 are Congestion Notification Priority Values (CNPVs) while priorities 0, 2, 6 and 7 are not CNPVs. Within each Congestion Notification Priority Value, there may be one or more Congestion Controlled Flows (CCFs) depending upon the source(s) of the frames and the implementation of each source.

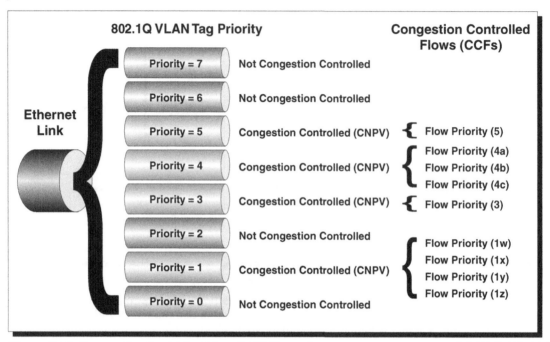

Figure 15-7. Congestion Controlled Flow (CCF) Example

Because it may be difficult to identify which frames are associated with a specific Congestion Controlled Flow, an end station may insert a Congestion Notification Tag (CN-TAG) in frames that it transmits on a CNPV. If an end station inserts CN-TAGs in transmitted frames, and those frames result in congestion, the Congestion Point that detects the congestion will return the CN-TAG in the Congestion Notification Message. This enables an end station to associate the Congestion Notification Message with the correct flow.

The CN-TAG consists of a two-byte tag identifier (indicating that this is a CN-TAG) followed by a two-byte Flow Identifier as shown in Figure 15-8 on page 235. The standard does not specify how an end station selects the value to use for the Flow_ID in the CN-TAG.

15.4.3 Congestion Point (CP)

A Congestion Point (CP), at either an end station or bridge, detects congestion by sampling incoming frames associated with a given Congestion Notification Priority Value (CNPV) queue (see Figure 15-9 on page 236).

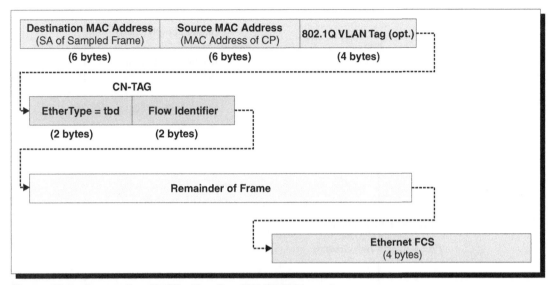

Figure 15-8. Congestion Notification Tag (CN-TAG) Format

The Congestion Point attempts to maintain the each Congestion Notification Priority Value (CNPV) queue at a nominal value called the Queue Equilibrium point (Qeq). The Queue Equilibrium point establishes the threshold for deciding when to initiate congestion management and is selected to provide a balance between utilized queue space and available queue space. If the Queue Equilibrium point is set too high, the queue may fill and result in congestion (due to flow control) or frame loss (due to queue overflow). If the Queue Equilibrium point is set too low, the feedback mechanism may result in poor queue utilization and under-utilized bandwidth.

NOTE – Simulation has suggested that a Queue Equilibrium point of 20% (of a 150KB queue) yields good results.

The Congestion Point maintains a set of parameters that reflect the state of each Congestion Notification Priority Value (CNPV) queue (refer to Figure 15-9 on page 236).

- The Queue Length (Qlen) is the current depth of the queue.

- The Queue Offset (Qoff) is the difference between the Qlen and Qeq (note that this can be either a positive or negative value).

- The Queue Delta (Qdelta) is the difference between the current Queue Length and the previous Queue Length and reflects the rate of change in the Queue Length.

Incoming frames are sampled with a probability factor *(P)* that is dependent on the severity of the congestion (*P* increases linearly from 1% at no congestion to 10% at maximum congestion). This factor is set to adjust the rate of sampling and resultant generation of Congestion Notification messages (sampling too frequently generates excessive Congestion Notification message traffic, sampling too seldom increases to potential for queue full conditions).

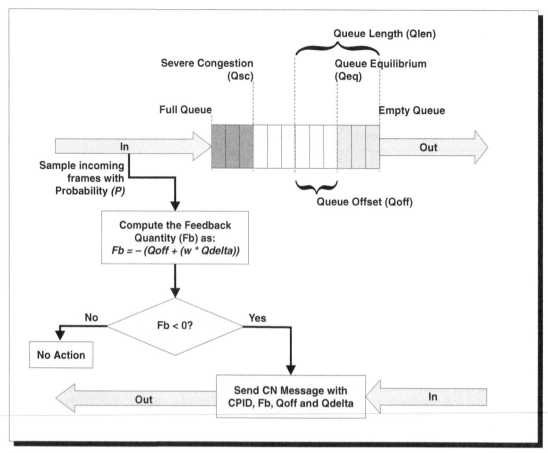

Figure 15-9. Congestion Point (CP) Queue Model

Whenever an incoming frame is sampled, the Congestion Point (CP) computes a Feedback quantity *(Fb)* using on the following formula:

$$Fb = -(Qoff + (w * Qdelta))$$

Where *w* is a non-negative constant that controls the sensitivity to the rate of change.

The Feedback quantity (Fb) reflects both the degree of excess queue utilization (the Qoff parameter) and the relative rate of change (the Qdelta parameter).

If *Fb* is less than zero, the Congestion Point (CP) generates a Congestion Notification Message (CNM) addressed to the source of the sampled frame. The Congestion Notification Message identifies the sending Congestion Point (CP) via a Congestion Point ID (CPID) field, provides the Feedback quantity *(Fb)* and information regarding the severity of the congestion, and returns a portion of the sampled frame to in order to identify the flow associated with the

---

congestion. The Congestion Notification Message is an indication to reduce the transmission rate of the identified flow.

If *Fb* is greater than or equal to zero, no Congestion Notification Message (CNM) is sent.

15.4.4 Congestion Notification Message (CNM) Frame Format

While the CNM frame and message format has not yet been formally standardized, Figure 15-10 on page 237 shows the proposed format.

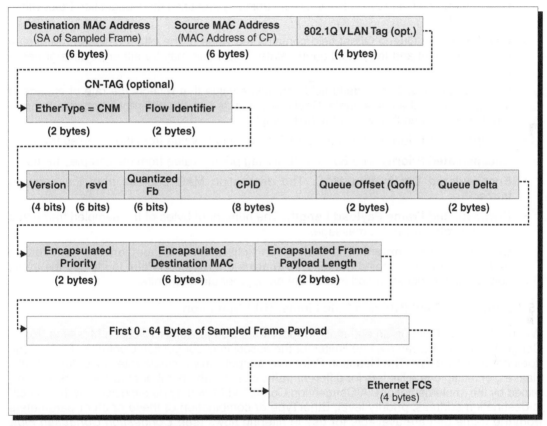

Figure 15-10. CN Message (CNM) Frame Format

The Congestion Notification Message (CNM) is generated by a Congestion Point (CP) when congestion is detected. The destination address set to the source address of the sampled frame source address is set to the MAC address of the Congestion Point.

If the sampled frame contained an 802.1Q VLAN tag, it is copied into the CNM frame. If the sampled frame contained a CN-TAG, it is also copied into the CNM frame.

Parameters contained within the Congestion Notification Message (CNM) include the CPID, the Fb, Qoff, Qdelta, and the first 0 to 64 bytes from the sampled frame (the actual number of sampled frame bytes returned depend on the implementation). Information from the sampled frame is provided so that the Reaction Point (RP) can identify the appropriate flow (if a CN-Tag is not used).

- **Quantized Fb.** The computed Fb value is quantized to six bits before transmission in a Congestion Notification Message.

- **CPID Field.** The Congestion Point ID field uniquely identifies the Congestion Point within the network.

- **Qoff Field.** The Queue Offset field contains the value of the offset between the Queue equilibrium point and the actual queue state. This value may be either positive or negative.

- **Qdelta Field.** The Queue delta field contains a value that reflects the rate of change in the queue since the last sample. Qdelta is computed as the difference between the current Qoff value and the Qoff at the last sample.

- **Encapsulated Priority.** The 802.1Q VLAN Tag priority value from the sampled frame.

- **Encapsulated Priority.** The 802.1Q VLAN Tag priority value from the sampled frame.

- **Encapsulated Destination MAC.** The destination MAC address from the sampled frame.

- **Encapsulated Frame Payload Length.** The number of bytes of the sampled frame that are being returned in this message.

- **Sampled Frame Content.** The Congestion Notification Message contains from zero to 64 bytes from the sampled frame. This enables the Reaction Point to identify the traffic flow causing congestion and implement an appropriate rate limiter.

15.4.5 Reaction Point (RP) and Rate Limiter (RL) Operation

When a Reaction Point (in an end station) receives a Congestion Notification Message from a Congestion Point, it creates a rate limiter for the associated Congestion Controlled Flow (if one does not already exist). The Reaction Point may support only a single rate limiter for all traffic classes, or multiple rate limiters for different traffic classes (the number of rate limiters is determined by the implementation). A Congestion Controlled Flow may be associated with a specific destination address, priority level, EtherType or combination of these or other parameters from the frame that are available for use in filtering flows (see *Congestion Controlled Flow (CCF)* on page 232). Figure 15-11 on page 239 shows a Reaction Point with multiple rate limiters, each associated a different Congestion Controlled Flow.

The Reaction Point rate increase computations use the following parameters:

- **Rate Limiter Current Rate (CR).** The Current Rate is the transmission rate of the Rate Limiter at the present time.

- **Rate Limiter Target Rate (TR).** The Target Rate was the transmission rate of the Rate Limiter immediately prior to receipt of the last Congestion Notification Message.

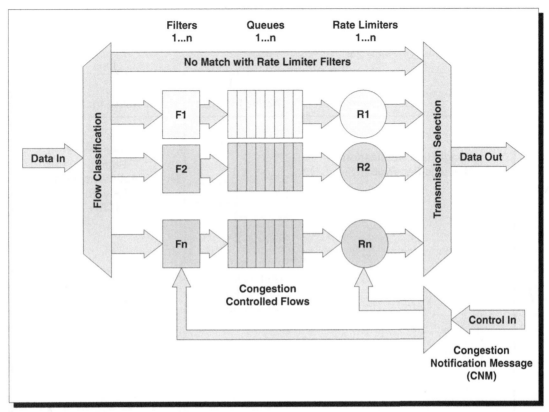

Filters 1...n   Queues 1...n   Rate Limiters 1...n

No Match with Rate Limiter Filters

Flow Classification

Data In

F1   R1

F2   R2

Fn   Rn

Transmission Selection

Data Out

Congestion Controlled Flows

Control In

Congestion Notification Message (CNM)

Figure 15-11. Reaction Point (RP) Rate Limiting

- **Rate Limiter Byte Counter.** The Reaction Point counts the number of bytes transmitted by the Rate Limiter. The Rate Limiter Byte Counter is one of the factors that triggers rate increases by the Rate Limiter.

- **Rate Limiter Timer.** The Rate Limiter Timer is a clock at the Reaction Point that is also used for triggering rate increases. The primary use of the Rate Limiter Timer is to trigger rate increases when the transmission rate is very low.

Rate Decrease Computation. When a Congestion Notification Message is received, the Reaction Point updates sets the Target Rate (TR) equal to the existing Current Rate (CR) and updates the Current Rate using the following formula:

$$CR = CR * (1 - Gd \times |Fb|), \text{ where Gd is selected such that } Gd * |Fb_{max}| = \frac{1}{2}$$

NOTE – The selection of Gd limits the maximum amount that the transmission rate can decrease as the result of a single Congestion Notification Message to no more than 50%.

Rate Increase Behavior. The Reaction Point is not given a rate-increase message. There are no Ethernet acknowledgments or Congestion Notification Messages that direct the Reac-

---

tion Point to increase the transmission rate for a Congestion Controlled Flow. The Reaction Point increases the rate based Rate Limiter Byte Counter and Rate Limiter Timer. Rate increases occur in three phases, Fast Recovery, Active Increase and Hyper-Active Increase as shown in Figure 15-12 on page 240.

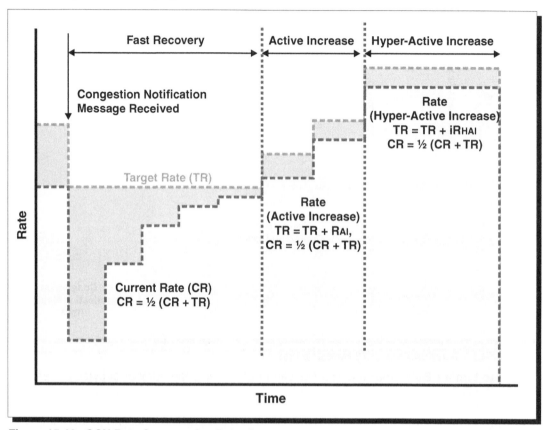

Figure 15-12. QCN Rate Computation Behavior

- **Rate Limiter Byte Counter Fast Recovery.** Rate Limiter Byte Counter Fast Recovery attempts to recover the bandwidth that was lost as a result of the last Congestion Notification Message by counting the number of transmitted bytes. Rate Limiter Byte Counter based Fast Recovery is done in a series of five cycles, each cycles completing after the transmission of 150KB (one hundred 1500 byte frames). At the end of each cycle, the transmission rate is increased as described in *Rate Increase Computation* on page 241.

- **Rate Limiter Byte Counter Active Increase.** After five cycles of Rate Limiter Byte Counter based Fast Recovery have been completed without receiving a Congestion Notification Message, the Reaction Point enters the Active Increase phase and probes for additional bandwidth. During Active Increase, the rate may be increased after 50 frames have been transmitted without receipt of a Congestion Notification Message.

- **Rate Limiter Timer Fast Recovery.** Rate increases based on the number of bytes (or frames) transmitted provide satisfactory results when a large number of bytes are being transmitted. If the number of bytes to be transmitted is very low, it may take an excessive amount of time to recover bandwidth that was lost as the result of a Congestion Notification Message (e.g., if there are only 100KB to be transmitted while in Fast Recovery, the current cycle would not complete and a rate increase would not occur). The accommodate cases where the number of bytes to be sent following a Congestion Notification Message is very low, there is a timer-based rate increase mechanism.

  When a Congestion Notification Message is received, the Rate Limiter Timer is reset, enters the Rate Limiter Timer Fast Recovery state and counts out five cycles of "T" milliseconds duration each.

  Note: "T" was equal to 10 milliseconds in the baseline simulation.

  At the end of each cycle, the transmission rate is increased as described in *Rate Increase Computation* on page 241.

- **Rate Limiter Timer Active Increase.** After completion of five Rate Limiter Timer Fast Recovery cycles, the Rate Limiter Timer enters the Active Increase state and probes for additional bandwidth. During Rate Limiter Timer Active Increase, the rate is increased as described in *Rate Increase Computation* on page 241.

Rate Increase Computation. If *both* the Rate Limiter Byte Counter and Rate Limiter Timer are in Fast Recovery, the Rate Limiter is in Fast Recovery. Each step of either the Rate Limiter Byte Counter or Rate Limiter Timer increases the Current Rate according to the following formula (Fast Recovery):

$$CR = \frac{1}{2} (CR + TR)$$

The rationale for using 150KB (one hundred 1500-byte frames) per Fast Recovery step is based on the assumption that the Congestion Point is sampling incoming frames with a minimum probability of 0.01. Therefore, if the Congestion Point has not generated a Congestion Notification Message within 100 frames, it can be assumed that congestion is no longer occurring and the transmission rate can be increased.

NOTE – The assumption regarding 150KB being equal to 100 frames does not take into consideration the use of jumbo frames. When jumbo frames are used, it may make sense to adjust the above parameters accordingly.

If *either* the Rate Limiter Byte Counter or Rate Limiter Timer is in Active Increase, the current rate is updated whenever either competes a cycle using the following formula (Active Increase):

$$TR = TR + R_{AI}, \text{ where } R_{AI} \text{ is a constant that represents the size of each increase, and}$$
$$CR = \frac{1}{2} (CR + TR)$$

If *both* the Rate Limiter Byte Counter and Rate Limiter Timer are in the Active Increase state, the current rate is updated after the *ith* time that either completes a cycle using the following formula (Hyper-Active Increase):

$TR = TR + iR_{HAI}$, where R_{HAI} is a constant that represents the size of each increase, and $CR = \frac{1}{2} (CR + TR)$

The Rate Limiter goes to the Hyper-Active Increase state only after at least 500 (1500-byte) frames have been transmitted and at least 50 milliseconds have passed since the last Congestion Notification Message. This ensures that the network has had ample opportunity to sample the flow and report any congestion.

15.4.6 Bridge Priority Regeneration

Bridge devices may alter the VLAN Tag priority value in a frame before forwarding the frame. This is controlled by the bridge's priority regeneration table. Because Congestion Notification uses the VLAN Tag priority value to identify frames subject to Congestion Notification, it is essential that a bridge device does not map non-congestion controlled priority values to a Congestion Notification Priority Value or vice-versa.

15.4.7 Congestion Notification Domain

In an ideal configuration, the entire network and all end stations would support congestion notification and rate limiting. In reality, a network may consist of bridges and end stations that support congestion notification intermixed with bridges and end stations that do not support congestion notification (see Figure 15-13 on page 243 for an example). Incorrect configuration may result in the failure of Congestion Notification to operate properly.

- Congestion Notification cannot operate properly if a Congestion Point is not configured to recognize the Congestion Controlled Flows it receives. Congestion Controlled Flows map to specific VLAN Tag priority values, called Congestion Notification Priority Values (CNPVs). If the Congestion Point is not configured to recognize the correct CNPVs, or the VLAN Tag priority values are remapped before reaching the Congestion Point, the Congestion Point may not associate the frames with a Congestion Controlled Flow, or may erroneously associate frames from an end station that does not support Congestion Notification with a Congestion Controlled Flow.

- Congestion Notification cannot operate properly if a Congestion Point receives frames on a CNPV from an end station that does not support Congestion Notification. If congestion occurs as a result of those frames, any Congestion Notification Message sent to that end station won't be recognized. Frames from an end station that does not support Congestion Notification become part of the sampled frame set and may interfere with the sampling of frames from end stations that do support Congestion Notification.

- Frames transmitted from an end station that have a CN-TAG cannot be understood by a bridge or end station that is not Congestion Notification aware.

To prevent these conditions, congestion-aware bridges construct a Congestion Notification Domain (CND) within which a particular CNPV is supported. A Congestion Notification Domain is a connected subset of bridges and end stations that support a particular CNPV value. A

       Chapter 15. Data Center Bridging (DCB) Ethernet

Congestion Notification Domain simply identifies the set of interconnected end stations and bridge ports that support the same Congestion Notification Priority Value. A Congestion Notification Domain does not limit the ability of one device to communicate with another device, it only establishes the domain of devices over which Congestion Notification is operable for a given priority value.

Multiple Congestion Notification Domains may exist within a given LAN, each associated with a specific CNPV. Congestion Notification Domains for different CNPVs may be overlapping, or non-overlapping as shown in Figure 15-13 on page 243.

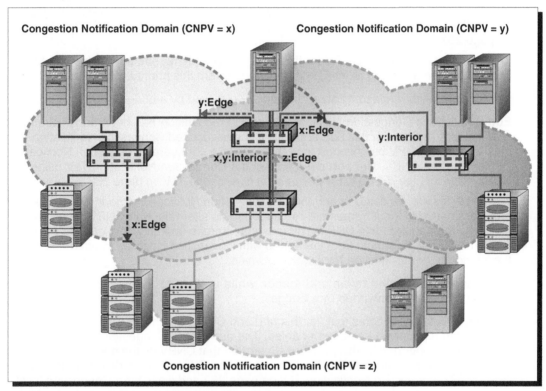

Figure 15-13. Congestion Notification Domains

15.4.8 Congestion Notification Domain Defense

Incorrect configuration can interfere with the correct operation of the Congestion Notification protocol, It is necessary to ensure that only frames associated with a given Congestion Controlled Flow are sent using a Congestion Notification Priority Value in the VLAN Tag.

Congestion Notification Domains can be created manually by configuring bridges and end stations, or automatically using the Data Center Bridge Capability Exchange protocol and the Congestion Notification TLV (see *IEEE DCBX Congestion Notification TLV* on page 262). Automatic Congestion Domain recognition enables congestion notification aware bridges and end stations to automatically determine Congestion Notification Domain boundaries. Congestion Notification Domain recognition is performed on a per-port and per-CNPV basis.

For each port and priority value, the automatic Congestion Notification Domain recognition function can be in one of four states, whether determined by administrative configuration or parameters communicated using the DCBX protocol. The four states are:

- **Disabled.** Automatic Congestion Notification Domain recognition has been administratively disabled for this port. While in this state, the end station or bridge port operates in the same manner as a non-congestion aware port. The port does not send a Congestion Notification TLV using the DCBX protocol (see *IEEE DCBX Congestion Notification TLV* on page 262.

  This priority value is not a CNPV for this port. The priority regeneration table in a bridge controls the remapping of frames on this port to or from this priority value.

  CN-Tags are neither added by an end station or removed by a bridge.

- **Edge.** Automatic Congestion Notification Domain recognition has been administratively disabled for this port. For this port and CNPV, the associated Congestion Notification Priority Value is a CNPV but this port is at the edge of a configured Congestion Notification Domain for that CNPV. The port does not send a Congestion Notification TLV using the DCBX protocol (see *IEEE DCBX Congestion Notification TLV* on page 262.

  While in this state, for this port and for this Congestion Notification Priority Value, the priority parameters of input frames are remapped to an alternate, non-CNPV, value and no priority is remapped to this CNPV. This prevents frames entering from outside the Congestion Notification Domain from interfering with Congestion Notification operation within the interior of the Congestion Notification Domain.

  CN-Tags are not added by an end station while in this state and are removed from frames before being forwarded by a bridge.

- **Interior.** This state indicates that, for this port and CNPV, automatic Congestion Notification Domain recognition has been enabled. The associated Congestion Notification Priority Value is supported by this port, but support for that CNPV by the neighbor port is not yet known. The port sends a Congestion Notification TLV using the DCBX protocol (see *IEEE DCBX Congestion Notification TLV* on page 262 and waits for a Congestion Notification TLV from the neighbor port.

  While in this state, for this port and for this Congestion Notification Priority Value, the priority parameters of input frames are not remapped to another value and no priority value is remapped to this CNPV, regardless of a bridge's priority regeneration table.

  CN-Tags are not added by an end station and are removed from frames before being forwarded by a bridge.

- **Interior Ready.** This state indicates that, for this port and CNPV, the associated Congestion Notification Priority Value is supported by both this port and the neighbor port (as indicated by a Congestion Notification TLV received from the neighbor port).

While in this state, for this port and for this Congestion Notification Priority Value, the priority parameters of input frames are not remapped to another value and no priority value is remapped to this CNPV, regardless of a bridge's priority regeneration table.

CN-Tags can be added by an end station and are not removed from frames before being forwarded by a bridge.

A single Congestion Notification TLV can be inserted into LLDPDUs transmitted from a bridge or end station port that is configured to support a Congestion Notification Priority Value. The Congestion Notification TLV contains two fields that enable automatic control of the Congestion Notification Domain defenses (see *IEEE DCBX Congestion Notification TLV* on page 262 for the format of the TLV):

- Eight per-priority CNPV indicators, one for each priority level, indicating whether that priority level is a CNPV on the port.
- Eight per-priority Ready indicators, one for each priority level, indicating whether priority remap defenses are disabled on the port.

The automatic Congestion Notification Domain recognition protocol is shown in Figure 15-14 on page 245. The CNPV Capable bits in the Congestion Notification TLV indicate priority levels are CNPVs at the sender. The Ready bits indicate for which priority levels the sender is ready to perform the Congestion Notification protocol.

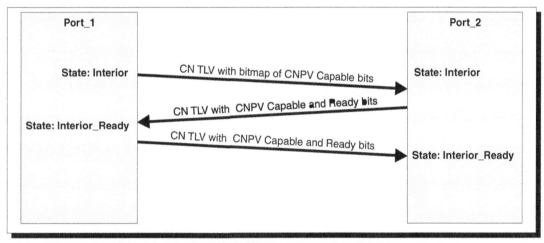

Figure 15-14. Automatic Congestion Notification Domain Recognition Protocol

For every Congestion Notification Priority Value configured on a port, if LLDP finds exactly one remote neighbor, and if that neighbor has sent a Congestion Notification TLV with that CNPV's bit set in the per-priority CNPV indicators, then that CNPV is know to be configured on the remote port. This condition is indicated by the *cnpdRcvdCnpv* variable. In a like manner, the *cnpdRcvdReady* variable indicates whether the remote neighbor has or has not turned off its priority remapping defense.

Multiple instances of LLDP (the protocol that transports DCBX) can run on a single port. Each instance can use a different destination address and, therefore, have a different reach within the LAN. Because automatic Congestion Notification Domain recognition is concerned with the capabilities of the neighbor port, only the instance of LLDP using the Nearest Bridge Address (01-80-C2-00-00-0E) is used for domain recognition. This limits the reach of LLDP and the risk that a non-congestion aware bridge is present.

If a port has multiple neighbors (e.g., it is attached to a shared media LAN), or if the neighbor port is not congestion aware, CN-Tags are removed from any frames prior to transmission on a Congestion Notification Priority Value (CNPV). This prevents propagation of the CN-Tag to non-congestion aware ports.

15.5 Chapter Summary

Data Center Bridging (DCB) Ethernet

- Several enhancements to Ethernet have been developed for data center environments
  - While not required for FCoE, likely will be used in FCoE environments
- The key enhancements are:
  - Per-Priority Pause flow control (PFC)
  - Enhanced Transmission Selection (ETS)
  - Congestion Notification (CN)
  - Data Center Bridge Capability Exchange Protocol (DCBX)
- Previously referred to as Data Center Ethernet (DCE) or Converged Enhanced Ethernet (CEE)

Traffic Classification

- These enhancements support different delivery policies
  - Traffic is classified into different traffic classes
  - Each traffic class can then have different delivery policies applied
- Classification can be based on a variety of attributes:
  - MAC address(es)
  - IP address(es)
  - EtherType or Protocol type
  - Result of hash function applied to specified fields
  - etc....

Transmission Selection

- Once traffic classification has been done, frames can be selected for transmission
  - Multiple transmission selection algorithms have been defined for Ethernet
- Transmission selection may be based on:
  - Priority
  - Flow Control (PFC))
  - Bandwidth constraints (ETS)
  - Congestion (CN)

Traffic Class and Flow Identification

- Need a way to identify different traffic classes and flows
- Could use same classification function in each bridge and end station
  - Maintaining consistency in multiple places is difficult
- If any of the attributes used for classification changes, flow identification fails
  - For example, if using IP address and a datagram goes through router that does Network Address Translation (NAT), the IP address may be changed
- Can use VLAN Tag Priority value (perhaps along with other attributes)

Per-Priority Pause Flow Control (PFC)

- In May 2007, a new variant of Ethernet flow control was proposed
  - Extension of the existing pause mechanism using a new MAC Control frame format
  - Allows flow control to be asserted on a per-priority level basis
  - Can be selectively used on a per-priority level basis (some levels subject to flow control while others are not)
- Requires use of 802.1Q VLAN tagged frames
  - Tag provides the 3-bit priority field that is used to identify the traffic class

"Per-Priority" Pause Frame

- PFC defines a new Pause frame format
  - MAC control frame intended to be processed by the hardware
- Class-Enable bit for each 802.1Q priority level
  - Identifies the priority levels affected by this pause frame
  - Format = 00000000:T0T1T2T3T4T5T6T7
  - T0 indicates frame affects Priority level 0, T1 indicates frame affects Priority level 1, etc.
- Pause_Time field for each 802.1Q priority level

Enhanced Transmission Selection

- Different traffic classes may have different "urgency" and bandwidth requirements
  - Attributes commonly associated with Quality of Service (QoS)
- Need a way to identify different traffic classes
  - Traffic Classification maps different traffic classes to 802.1Q priority levels
  - Enables each traffic class to be handled differently
- May want to limit the bandwidth consumed by specific traffic classes to Prevent starvation of lower-priority traffic
- This is the area being addressed by Enhanced Transmission Selection (ETS)

Enhanced Transmission Selection

- The goals of ETS are to:
  - Classify frames to be transmitted, assign them to Traffic Class Groups, and map each Traffic Class Group to a VLAN Priority level
  - Allow available bandwidth to be configured among the Traffic Class Groups
  - Schedule transmission of frames based on attributes associated with each Traffic Class Group
  - Allow more than on traffic class per Traffic Class Group

Flow Classification and Metering

- Flow Classification and Metering function maps frame to a Traffic Class Group (TCG)
  - This is the Traffic Classification function
- Transmission Selection function schedules the frame for transmission
  - Scheduling is based on the Traffic Class Group (TCG) and available bandwidth
  - Transmission Selection inserts an 802.1Q VLAN Tag, if necessary (the priority value identifies the traffic class)
  - Standard does not specify the scheduling algorithm - only the end result

Traffic Class Group (TCG)

- Each traffic class, or subclass, may be mapped to one or more Traffic Class Groups
  - Traffic Class Group is associated with the attributes that determine scheduling of frames for transmission
  - Each Traffic Class Group has a 4-bit identifier called the Traffic Class Group ID (TCGID)
  - Each Traffic Class Group is limited to a configured percentage of the link's available bandwidth (with the exception of TCGID 15)
- TCGID 15 is used for frames with priority
  - Other traffic classes are sent after any frames for TCGID 15 have been sent

Congestion Notification

- While link-level flow control can prevent buffer overrun conditions, it may lead to congestion
  - A receiver is unable to hold additional frames and throttles the sender using flow control
  - Frames continue to arrive at the sender which eventually throttles the next upstream sender
  - Traffic backs up all the way to the source, eventually throttling the source of the traffic
- Receive buffers along the path have been filled with frames, creating congestion
  - May block other traffic from being delivered
- This is the problem addressed by Congestion Notification (802.1Qau)

Congestion Notification Overview

- Detect when congestion occurs at a Congestion Point (CP)
  - A Congestion Point can be in a bridge or end station
- Notify the source of the frames that are causing the congestion using a Congestion Notification Message (CNM)
  - The Congestion Notification Message tells the source to "slow down"
- The source of the frames (the Reaction Point, or RP) creates a Rate Limiter
  - Rate Limiter limits the rate of frames that are causing the congestion

Congestion Controlled Flows (CCFs)

- Congestion control is applied selectively
  - Some flows may be subject to Congestion Notification while others are not
  - All of the frames that pass through the same congestion-controlled queue are called a Congestion Controlled Flow (CCF)
- The number of congestion-controlled queues (and therefore Congestion Controlled Flows) is implementation dependent
  - May be a single queue for all congestion-controlled traffic
  - May be multiple queues for congestion-controlled traffic

Congestion Notification Priority Value

- Congestion Controlled Flows map to specified VLAN Tag priority values
  - If a specific priority value is subject to congestion management, it is called a Congestion Notification Priority Value (CNPV)
  - End stations and bridges use the priority value to decide whether Congestion Notification applies or not

Congestion Notification Tag (CN-TAG)

- A given Congestion Notification Priority Value (CNPV) may carry more than one traffic flow
  - e.g., traffic from an initiator to multiple targets
  - Flow identification can be difficult
- Congestion Notification Tag enables the originating end station to tag each CCF frame
  - Use of the CN-TAG is optional
  - CN-TAG can help end station identify to correct flow
  - When present, the CN-Tag is returned in a Congestion Notification Message

Congestion Point (CP)

- Congestion Point maintains a queue for each Congestion Notification Priority Value (CNPV)
  - Congestion Point detects congestion by monitoring the associated frame Queue
  - If the Queue is too full, a Congestion Notification Message (CNM) is sent to the source
- Incoming frames are sampled with a probability factor *(P)*
  - Sampling every frame (and potentially generating a Congestion Notification Message) could result in excessive Congestion Notification Message traffic
  - *(P)* is selected to balance congestion detection with Congestion Notification Message traffic

Congestion Point Queue Parameters

- Congestion Point attempts to maintain Queue at a Queue Equilibrium (Qeq) point
  - Leaves room for additional incoming frames
  - Has frames awaiting transmission
- Queue Length (Qlen) indicates how much of the Queue is currently utilized
- Queue Offset (Qoff) is the difference between the Qlen and Qeq
  - Qoff may be positive or negative (queue is fuller or less full than desired)
- Qdelta is the rate of change in queue utilization

Congestion Notification Message

- Whenever a CP samples a frame, it computes a Feedback quantity *(Fb)*
  - $Fb = -(Qoff + (w * Qdelta)$
  - Where "w" is a constant that controls the sensitivity to the rate of change
- If the Feedback quantity is < 0, the CP sends a Congestion Notification Message to the source of the sampled frame
- Congestion Notification Message contains:
  - Current Queue Offset (Qoff)
  - Queue Delta
  - Computed Feedback quantity (Fb)
  - First "n" bytes from the sampled frame

Rate Limiter

- When the Reaction Point receives a Congestion Notification Message, it instantiates a Rate Limiter (if one does not already exist)
  - A Rate Limiter is associated with a specific Congestion Controlled Flow
  - Limits the associated traffic flow to alleviate the congestion
- Frames to the Rate Limiter are selected based on a filtering criteria
  - Determined by the Congestion Notification Message sent from the CP
  - Criteria may be based on Source Address, Destination Address, Ethertype, CN-Tag or other factors

Rate Limiter Decrease Computation

- When a Congestion Notification Message is received, the transmission rate for the associated CCF is reduced.
  - Objective is to alleviate the congestion
  - New rate = Current Rate * (1-Gd * |Fb|)
  - Where Gd is selected such that the maximum reduction = 1/2 the current rate
- The Feedback quantity (Fb) reflects both the queue utilization and rate of change

Rate Limiter Increase Computation

- There are no Rate Limiter increase Congestion Notification Messages
  - The Rate Limiter increases its rate based on a rate increase algorithm
  - Rate increases occur as a result of the number of bytes transmitted and/or the time elapsed since the last Congestion Notification Message
- Rate increases occur in three phases
  - Fast Recovery
  - Active Increase
  - Hyper-Active Increase

Fast Recovery Rate Increase

- During Fast Recovery rate increase:
  - The Target Rate (TR) is set to the Current Rate at the time the most recent Congestion Notification Message was received
- After 150KB have been transmitted, or the Rate Limiter timer has expired, the new rate is set to:
  - CR = 1/2 (CR + TR)
  - This recovers 1/2 the difference between the Current Rate and the rate in effect when the most recent Congestion Notification Message was received

Active Increase

- If 5 cycles of either the Byte Counter or Rate Limiter Timer have completed without a Congestion Notification Message, the rate limiter enters Active Increase.
- In Active Increase, the new Target Rate is set to:
  - $TR = TR + R_{AI}$
  - Where R_{AI} is the size of the increase
- After 150KB have been transmitted, or the Rate Limiter time has expired, the new rate is set to:
  - CR = 1/2 (CR + TR)
  - This represents 1/2 the difference between the current rate and the new Target Rate (TR)

Hyper-Active Increase

- If 5 cycles of both the byte counter and Rate Limiter Timer have completed without a Congestion Notification Message, the rate limiter enters Hyper-Active Increase
- After the *ith* cycle in Hyper-Active Increase, the new Target Rate is set to:
  - $TR = TR + iR_{HAI}$
  - R_{HAI} is the size of the increase per cycle
- After 150KB have been transmitted, or the Rate Limiter time has expired, the new rate is set to:
  - CR = 1/2 (CR + TR)
- This represents 1/2 the difference between the current rate and the new Target Rate (TR)

Congestion Notification Cooperation

- Congestion Notification requires cooperation between a Congestion Point and Reaction Point
- Congestion Notification doesn't operate correctly if:
  - a Congestion Point receives frames on a CNPV that were sent from an end station that does not support CN
  - A Congestion Point is not configured to recognize the correct CNPVs
  - An end station or bridge that does not support CN receives a frame with a CN-TAG
- Congestion Notification aware bridge or end station needs to understand the capability and configuration of its neighbor

Congestion Notification Domain

- Configurations Notification Domain (CND) is a subset of connected bridges and end stations that support a particular CNPV value.
  - Identifies the scope of Congestion Notification for that specific CNPV
  - Congestion Notification Domains for different CNPVs may be overlapping or non-overlapping
  - Congestion Notification Domain does not affect or limit the ability of devices to communicate
- Domains can be configured manually or determined automatically

VLAN Tag Priority Regeneration

- Bridges may alter the priority value before forwarding a frame
  - Enables mapping between values used in one LAN to those used in another LAN
  - Controlled by the Priority Regeneration Table
- Congestion Notification uses priority values to identify Congestion Controlled Flows
- Must ensure that priority regeneration in a bridge does not break Congestion Notification

Domain Recognition

- For each port and CNPV, the Congestion Notification Domain recognition can be in one of four states:
  - Disabled
  - Edge
  - Interior
  - Interior Ready
- The state determines whether
  - Congestion Notification Messages are sent for that CNPV
  - CN-TAGs are added or removed
  - Frames are mapped to a different priority value

Domain Recognition: Disabled

- Automatic domain recognition has been administratively disabled for this port.
  - This priority value is not a CNPV for this port
  - The priority regeneration table in a bridge controls remapping of priority values
  - Congestion Notification Messages are not transmitted by this port
  - CN-Tags are neither added or removed by the port
- This behavior is essentially that of a non Congestion Notification aware port.

Domain Recognition: Edge

- Automatic domain recognition has been administratively disabled for this port.
  - This port is administratively configured to be at the edge of a Congestion Notification Domain
- For this port and CNPV:
  - Priority values of input frames are remapped to an alternate non-CNPV value regardless of the priority regeneration table
  - CN-Tags are not added by an end station
  - Congestion Notification Messages are not transmitted by this port
  - CN-Tags are removed by a bridge port before transmitting a frame

Domain Recognition: Interior

- Automatic domain recognition is enabled for this port and priority value.
  - This port *may* be inside a Congestion Notification Domain
  - The state of the neighbor port has not yet been determined
- For this port and CNPV:
  - Priority values of input frames are not remapped to an alternate value and no priority value is remapped to this CNPV
  - CN-Tags are not added by an end station
  - CN-Tags are removed by a bridge port before transmitting a frame
  - The port transmits the Congestion Notification TLV indicating its configuration

Domain Recognition: Interior Ready

- Automatic domain recognition is enabled for this port and priority value.
  - This port is in the interior of a Congestion Notification Domain and both this port and the neighbor support this CNPV
- For this port and CNPV:
  - Priority values of input frames are not remapped to an alternate value and no priority value is remapped to this CNPV
  - CN-Tags can be added by an end station
  - CN-Tags are not removed by a bridge port before transmitting a frame
  - Congestion Notification Messages may be transmitted

16. IEEE DCBX Protocol

The IEEE Data Center Bridge Capability Exchange (DCBX) protocol provides a way for attached ports to discover DCB features supported by a peer and to communicate parameters associated with those features. DCBX is implemented by extensions to the Link-Level Discovery Protocol (LLDP). The key objectives of the DCBX protocol are to:

- Enable discovery of Data Center Bridging features supported by a peer device.
- Detect mis-configuration or incompatible settings associated with those features.
- Distribute feature settings from a configured device to a peer device.

Features included in the DCBX protocol include Priority Flow Control (PFC), Enhanced Transmission Selection (ETS) and Congestion Notification (CN). It is anticipated that implementations will use a set of default parameters at power on (local parameters), or wait to receive parameters from the peer (remote parameters). Depending upon the implementation, parameters may be configured using a vendor-specific management interface, or through the use of the Simple Network Management Protocol (SNMP) and associated Management Information Bases (MIBs).

IEEE has defined a standardized version of the DCBX protocol as part of the Enhanced Transmission Selection work. There are also vendor-specific implementations of the DCBX protocol that have been used in some products and are described in *Vendor-Specific DCBX Implementations* on page 275.

16.1 Link-Level Discovery Protocol (LLDP)

The Data Center Bridge Capability Exchange Protocol (DCBX) is based on Ethernet standard 802.1AB-2005 (Station and Media Access Control Connectivity Discovery) that defines the Link Level Discovery Protocol, or LLDP. The protocol provides a method for entities to communicate link-level parameters. LLDP is a one-way protocol that enables an entity to advertise connectivity and management information, but does not enable an entity to solicit information from another entity.

16.1.1 LLDP Protocol Data Unit (PDU)

LLDP Protocol Data Units (PDUs) are transferred in standard Ethernet frames with the Ether-Type field set to 88CCh. The destination MAC address is set to 01-80-C2-00-00-0E, which is one of the reserved Ethernet Group MAC addresses (see Table 7-1 on page 72). Frames with this destination MAC address are not forwarded by Ethernet bridges and provide a way to communicate parameters between the two devices attached to a physical link.

The maximum length of the LLDP Protocol Data Unit (LLDPDU) is the maximum information field length allowed by the particular transmission rate and protocol. In IEEE 802.3 Ethernet

---

MACs, for example, the maximum LLDPDU length is the maximum data field length for the basic, untagged MAC frame (1500 bytes).

The LLDP protocol transfers parameters using a "Type, Length, Value" (TLV) format. The 7-bit Type field identifies the parameter type, the 9-bit Length field specifies the size of the parameter information (up to 511 bytes) and the Value field contains the associated parameter value or information. The general format of an Ethernet frame containing an LLDP PDU is shown in Figure 16-1 on page 254.

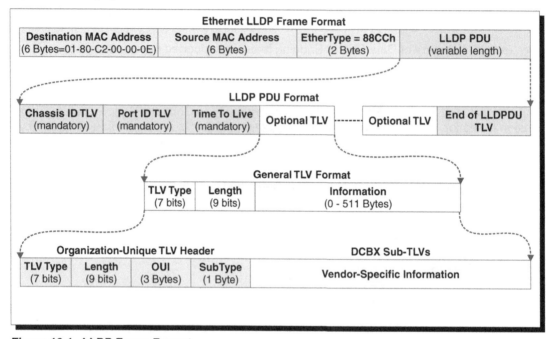

Figure 16-1. LLDP Frame Format

The Chassis ID, Port ID, Time To Live and End of LLDPDU objects are mandatory and required in every LLDP PDU. Zero, or more, optional TLVs may occur between the Time To Live field and the End of LLDPDU. Table 16-1 on page 255 lists the assigned Type values and provides a cross-reference to the associated IEEE standard defining each TLV.

Time To Live Field. The Time To Live field specifies how long (in seconds) the recipient should consider parameter information is the received PDU to be valid. If the "Time To Live" value in a received PDU is zero, the recipient deletes all LLDP parameter information associated with that sender.

The LLDP agent transmits a frame upon expiration of a transmission countdown timer (the recommended default value is 30 seconds) or upon detection of a change in the status or value of associated LLDP parameter information (a link becoming operational is considered a status change and results in an LLDP frame transmission).

TLV Type	TLV Name	Usage	Reference
0	End Of LLDPDU	Mandatory	IEEE 802.1AB-2005, Clause 9.5.1
1	Chassis ID	Mandatory	IEEE 802.1AB-2005, Clause 9.5.2
2	Port ID	Mandatory	IEEE 802.1AB-2005, Clause 9.5.3
3	Time To Live	Mandatory	IEEE 802.1AB-2005, Clause 9.5.4
4	Port Description	Optional	IEEE 802.1AB-2005, Clause 9.5.5
5	System Name	Optional	IEEE 802.1AB-2005, Clause 9.5.6
6	System Description	Optional	IEEE 802.1AB-2005, Clause 9.5.7
7	System Capabilities	Optional	IEEE 802.1AB-2005, Clause 9.5.8
8	Management Address	Optional	IEEE 802.1AB-2005, Clause 9.5.9
9 - 126	reserved		
127	Organizationally Specific TLVs	Optional	IEEE 802.1 TLV set, Annex F IEEE 802.3 TLV set, Annex G

Table 16-1. LLDP TLV Type Values

16.1.2 Accelerated Initial LLDP Transmission Countdown Time

When a PHY completes initialization, the LLDP agent is started. Due to differences in the relative initialization timings between two entities or as a result of a transmission error, it is possible that the initial LLDP parameter transmission is not recognized by the other entity. If this occurs, the parameter information will not be recognized by the peer until a subsequent transmission (typically following expiration of the transmission countdown timer). This means that there may be a period of up to 30 seconds between the link coming active and a successful parameter transfer. Figure 16-2 on page 256 illustrates how this situation can arise.

In order to avoid the extended time that may be required to successfully complete the initial parameter transfer that was shown in Figure 16-2 on page 256, it has been proposed that the first five LLDP transmissions after completion of the PHY initialization occur at one second intervals. The increases the probability of the initial transfer completing successfully in a timely manner as shown in Figure 16-3 on page 256.

16.1.3 Use of Optional TLV by DCBX

The DCBX protocol is implemented through the use of organizationally unique TLVs (Type = 127). The Length field specifies the length of the DCBX information contained within the organizationally unique TLV.

- For the IEEE standard version of the DCBX protocol, the Organizationally Unique Identifier (OUI) field is set to a value assigned for IEEE 802.1 standards (00-80-C2).

- For pre-standard implementations, the OUI field is set to 0x001B21. For DCBX version 1.00, the SubType field is set to 1 and for DCBX version 1.01, the SubType field is set to 2. Following the SubType field are one or more DCBX defined sub-TLVs that communicate feature information and the DCBX protocol state.

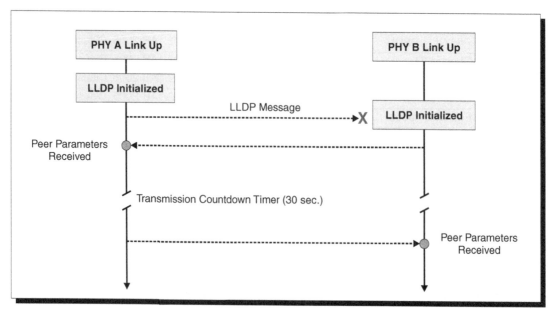

Figure 16-2. LLDP Parameter Transfer Miss at Link Up

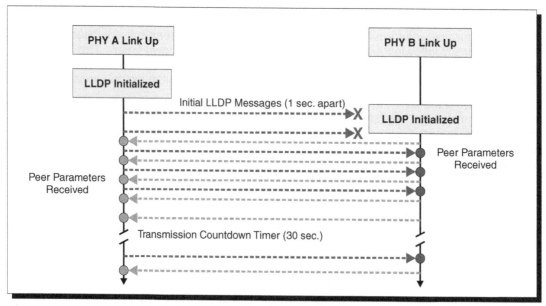

Figure 16-3. LLDP Accelerated Initial Parameter Transfer Proposal

16.2 IEEE Standard DCBX Protocol

IEEE has defined a standardized version of the DCBX protocol that is used to communicate parameters associated with the various DCB Ethernet capabilities. Parameters are passed using LLDP organization-specific TLVs (i.e., the Type field in the TLV header is set to 127). In addition to the IEEE specified DCBX protocol, there are also vendor-specific versions of DCBX that have been implemented in some products. To distinguish the IEEE version from earlier, vendor-specific versions, the Organizationally Unique Identifier (OUI) field in the TLV header is set to a value assigned for IEEE 802.1 standards (00-80-C2).

DCBX uses three sets of parameter information:

- **Local Parameters (LocalAdminParam)** are the locally configured parameters. They may be configured by an administrator or reflect a set of default parameters.

- **Operating Parameters (OperParam)** are the parameters currently in use by a port. If a port has accepted parameters from a peer port, the OperParam may be different than the LocalAdminParam.

- **Remote Parameters (RemoteParam)** are parameters that have been received from the peer port.

DCBX also uses the following controls;

- **Local Willing (W)** indicates that the local port is willing to accept parameters from the peer. When the willing bit is set, it is assumed that the local port will accept any configuration received from the remote port and approximate the received configuration to the best of its capability.

- **Remote Willing** indicates whether the remote port is willing to accept parameters from this port (rwTrue) or not (rwFalse). When Remote Willing bit is set, it is assumed that the remote port will accept any configuration received from the remote port and approximate the received configuration to the best of its capability. If no parameters have been received from the remote port, this control is set to rvNull).

- **Recommendation Valid (RV)** when a port transmits a set of parameters, the parameters may either be informative (rvFalse) or intended to become the operating parameters (rvTrue). If no parameters have been received from the remote port, this control is set to rvNull).

DCBX defines two types of parameter passing mechanisms; Asymmetric Parameter Passing and Symmetric Parameter Passing.

16.2.1 IEEE DCBX Asymmetric Parameter Passing

Asymmetric parameter passing is used to communicate parameter information to the attached peer or between the two attached ports. When asymmetric parameter passing is used, the resulting configuration may be different between the two connected peer ports and the parameters in one port may or may not match the parameters in the peer port.

Two types of TLVs are communicated using asymmetric parameter passing:

- The Configuration TLV (see *IEEE DCBX Configuration TLV* on page 260) is used to communicate the current operational state and the Willing bit. If the Willing bit is set to one, it indicates that the sender is willing to accept configuration parameters from the peer.

- The Recommendation TLV (see *IEEE DCBX Recommendation TLV* on page 260) is used to transfer a recommended set of operational parameters to the remote port. This TLV is only transmitted if a port is configured to make configuration recommendations. When a port is configured to make recommendations, this TLV is transmitted regardless of the willingness of the peer to accept parameters. When the Recommendation Valid (RV) bit is set to zero, it enables communication of parameter information without affecting the operational state. When the Recommendation Valid (RV) bit is set to one, it is assumed that a willing peer will use the provided parameters as it operational parameters (to the best of its capability).

Figure 16-4 on page 258 shows the protocol used for asymmetric parameter passing.

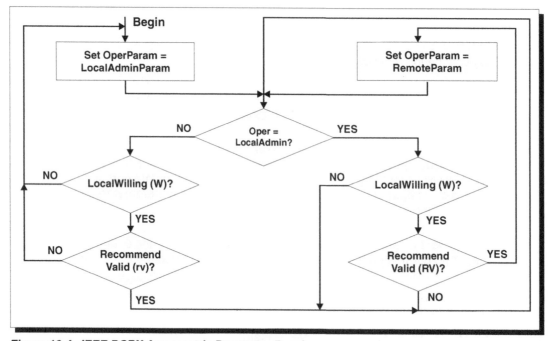

Figure 16-4. IEEE DCBX Asymmetric Parameter Passing

16.2.2 IEEE DCBX Symmetric Parameter Passing

Symmetric parameters are passed with the objective that both peer ports will end up with the same configuration. Figure 16-5 on page 259 shows the protocol associated with symmetric parameter passing.

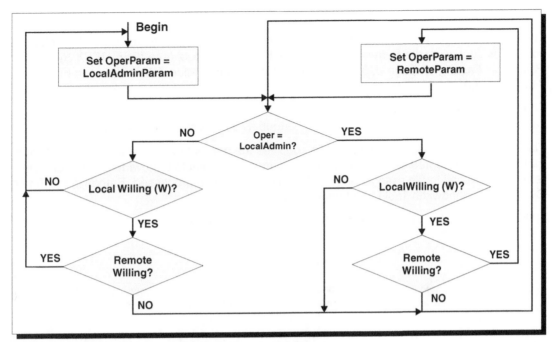

Figure 16-5. IEEE DCBX Symmetric Parameter Passing

16.2.3 IEEE DCBX Traffic Classes Supported TLV

The Traffic Classes Supported TLV is sent by a port to indicate the number of different traffic classes supported by the sender. This information may help the recipient in the allocation of resources that are traffic-class dependent (e.g. number of queues to allocate for Priority Flow Control).

The format of the IEEE DCBX Traffic Classes Supported TLV is shown in Figure 16-6 on page 259. A value of zero in the Traffic Classes Supported field indicates that eight traffic classes are supported.

DCBX Traffic Classes Supported					
Type = 127 (7 bits)	Length = 6 (9 bits)	OUI = 00-80-C2 (3 Bytes)	SubType = ? (1 Byte)	rsvd (5 bits)	Traffic Classes Sup. (3 bits)

Figure 16-6. IEEE DCBX Traffic Classes Supported TLV Format

16.2.4 IEEE DCBX Configuration TLV

The DCBX Configuration TLV is sent to indicate the current ETS configuration. The Configuration TLV is sent using the Symmetric Parameter Passing protocol (see *IEEE DCBX Symmetric Parameter Passing* on page 258). The format of the Configuration TLV is shown in Figure 16-7 on page 260.

The Priority Assignment Table consists of one four-bit entry for each 802.1Q VLAN tag priority value. Each entry specifies the Traffic Class Group ID associated with that priority value.

The Traffic Class Group Bandwidth Table specifies the percentage of the available bandwidth that has been allocated to each Traffic Class Group ID.Available bandwidth is the bandwidth remaining after all traffic associated with TCGID 15 has been processed. Entries in the Traffic Class Group Bandwidth Table must total 100%.

NOTE – The Configuration TLV and Recommendation TLVs may be sent in the same message or in different messages depending upon the implementation.

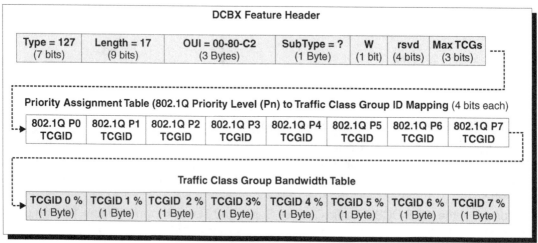

Figure 16-7. IEEE DCBX Configuration TLV Format

16.2.5 IEEE DCBX Recommendation TLV

The DCBX Recommendation TLV is similar to the Configuration TLV except that it is used to communicate a proposed or recommended configuration to the peer port. The format of the Configuration TLV is shown in Figure 16-8 on page 261.

When the Recommendation Valid (RV) bit is set to one, the Recommendation RLV contains the recommended configuration (it is expected that this will become the operational configuration of the other port, if the other port is willing to accept configuration information). When the RV bit is set to zero, the Recommendation TLV contains a proposed set of parameters (that may or may not become the recommended parameters).

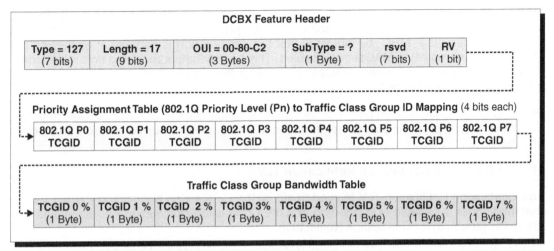

Figure 16-8. IEEE DCBX Recommendation TLV Format

The Recommendation TLV is transferred using the Asymmetric Parameter Passing protocol described in *IEEE DCBX Asymmetric Parameter Passing* on page 257.

> NOTE – The Configuration TLV and Recommendation TLVs may be sent in the same LLDP message or in different messages depending upon the implementation.

16.2.6 IEEE DCBX Priority Flow Control (PFC) Configuration TLV

The IEEE DCBX Priority Flow Control TLV identifies the 802.1Q VLAN tag priority levels PFC for which PFC is enabled. An implementation may choose to support the use of PFC for some priority levels (to provide lossless delivery) but not for other levels.

The format of the IEEE PFC TLV is shown in Figure 16-9 on page 261. The Priority Flow control TLV is passed using the Symmetric Parameter Passing protocol (see *IEEE DCBX Symmetric Parameter Passing* on page 258).

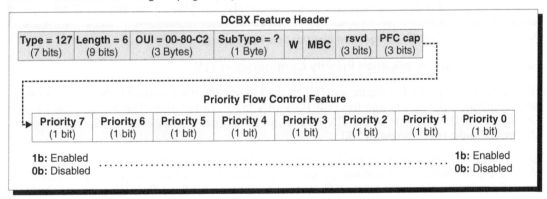

Figure 16-9. IEEE DCBX Priority Flow Control Feature TLV Format

---

MACsec Bypass Capability (MBC) bit. When set to one, the "MBC" bit indicates that the sending port is not capable of bypassing MACsec processing when MACsec is disabled. When set to zero, the "MBC" bit indicates that the sending port is capable of bypassing the MACsec processing when MACsec is disabled. This bit may help a receiving port in determining when to send a Pause frame (MACsec processing may add an additional delay associated with pausing frame transmission).

PFC cap field. This three-bit field indicates the maximum number of traffic classes that may simultaneously support PFC. A value of zero indicates that PFC may be enabled on all eight priorities.

16.2.7 IEEE DCBX Congestion Notification TLV

The Congestion Notification TLV is used to signal the Congestion Notification Priority Values that the sender is capable of supporting and the Congestion Notification Priority Values that are ready (enabled) for Congestion Notification.

The format of the Congestion Notification TLV is shown in Figure 16-10 on page 262.

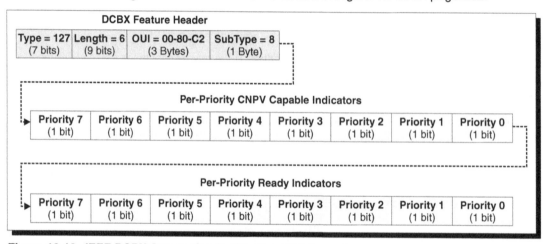

Figure 16-10. IEEE DCBX Congestion Notification TLV Format

16.2.8 IEEE DCBX Application Priority Configuration TLV

The Application Priority Configuration TLV is used to specify the mapping between an application protocol, or protocols, and the 802.1Q VLAN tag Priority value. The Application Priority Configuration TLV consists of the TLV header and one or more Application Priority Tables as shown in Figure 16-11 on page 263.

Each protocol is identified through a combination of the SEL and Protocol ID fields. For example, the FCoE protocol is identified by setting the SEL filed to '000'b and the Protocol ID to 0x8906 for the FCoE Encapsulation Protocol and 0x8914 for the FCoE Initialization Protocol (FIP).

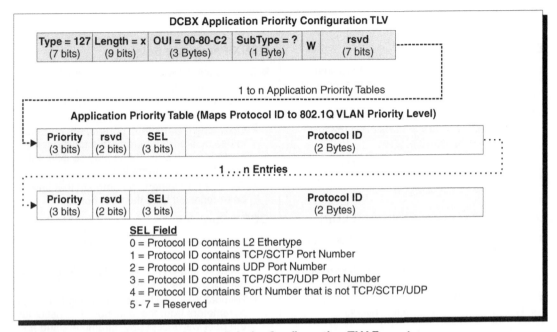

Figure 16-11. IEEE DCBX Application Priority Configuration TLV Format

16.3 Chapter Summary

IEEE DCBX Protocol

- IEEE Data Center Bridge Capability Exchange protocol (DCBX) enables devices to exchange link-level feature parameters
  - Per-Priority Pause Flow Control (PFC)
  - Enhanced Transmission Selection (ETS)
  - Congestion Notification (CN)
  - Application (e.g., FCoE) parameters
- DCBX is a based on extensions to the Link Level Discovery Protocol (LLDP)

Link Level Discovery Protocol (LLDP)

- LLDP enables devices to exchange link-level parameters
  - Originally intended to exchange device identification information (chassis ID, etc.)
- LLDP is a one-way protocol
  - Device sends its information blindly
  - No acknowledgements
  - Cannot request information from the attached device
  - LLDP Parameters sent every 30 seconds or upon a change
- Parameters are communicated in a Tag, Length, Value (TLV) format

LLDP Link-Up Problem

- Devices may miss the initial LLDP message due to link-up timing conditions
  - PHY A completes initialization and sends an LLDP message
  - PHY B is not ready and misses the message
- PHY sends LLDP messages every 30 seconds
  - PHY B receives parameters on a subsequent transmission
  - Time to receive parameters is too long for data center environments
- LLDP Link-Up Problem Proposed Fix:
  - PHY sends 1st five LLDP messages at one second intervals
  - Minimizes time to receive parameters

DCBX Parameter Sets

- DCBX uses three sets of parameter information
  - Local Parameters: locally configured parameters, may be configured by administrator or the default parameters
  - Operating Parameters: parameters currently in use by a port. If parameters have been accepted from a peer, these may be different than the Local Parameters
  - Remote Parameters: parameters that have been received from the peer port.

DCBX Controls

- Three controls are associated with parameter passing:
  - Local Willing (W): The local port is willing to accept parameters from the peer.
  - Remote Willing: The peer is willing to accept parameters from the local port. It is assumed the peer will accept any parameters and approximate the received configuration to the best of its ability.
  - Recommendation Valid (RV): This is a set of recommended parameters (versus informative parameters).

Parameter Passing Modes

- With Asymmetric parameter passing, the two ports may finish with different parameters
- There are two types of TLVs used:
  - A Configuration TLV communicates the current operational state and the Willing (W) bit
  - A Recommendation TLV transfers a recommended set of parameters
  - If the Recommendation Valid (RV) bit is set, it is assumed the peer will use the recommended parameters
- With Symmetric parameter passing, the objective is that both peers end up with the same configuration
  - Which port's parameters are used depends on the state of each port's Willing bit.

A. Summary of FCoE vs. FC Changes

While one of the goals of FCoE is to "transparently and seamlessly" transport encapsulated Fibre Channel frames via Ethernet, some changes are inevitable. This chapter summarizes where FCoE differs from native Fibre Channel.

A.1 Physical Link (FC-0)

FCoE uses Ethernet as its physical link rather than Fibre Channel. Consequently, the standards defining Fibre Channel physical link behavior and characteristics do not apply to FCoE Ethernet links.

For a definition of Ethernet physical links, refer to the appropriate Ethernet standards.

A.1.1 Fibre Channel Speed Negotiation

Fibre Channel defined speed negotiation is not used on FCoE links. For a definition of Ethernet speed negotiation, refer to the appropriate Ethernet standards.

A.2 Fibre Channel FC-1 Differences

Fibre Channel's FC-1 level defines encoding and link-level protocols. This level is replaced by the corresponding Ethernet functions.

A.2.1 Encoding/Decoding

Encoding of data on FCoE links is defined by the Ethernet standards. For a definition of Ethernet encoding for various physical links, refer to the appropriate Ethernet standards.

A.2.2 Link Initialization

FCoE Ethernet links follow the initialization steps and protocols defined by Ethernet.

The Fibre Channel Port State Machine (PSM) defined in the Fibre Channel standards does not apply to FCoE links.

The Link Reset, Link Initialization and Link Failure link-level protocols defined in the Fibre Channel standards do not apply to FCoE Ethernet links. The corresponding LR, LRR, OLS and NOS Ordered Sets are not used on Ethernet links.

A.2.3 Ordered Sets

Fibre Channel defined Ordered Sets are not used on FCoE links.

A.2.4 Start of Frame and End of Frame Delimiters

Fibre Channel SOF and EOF frame delimiters are identified within the FCoE Encapsulation Header and Trailer. A single byte value specifies the corresponding SOF and EOF. The SOF and EOF Ordered Sets used on native Fibre Channel links are not present in the encapsulated frame.

Ethernet SOF and EOF delimiters are defined by the Ethernet standards.

A.2.5 Inter-Frame Gap (IFG)

Fibre Channel links require a minimum of six words between frames. Fibre Channel links also define requirements for IDLEs/Fill Words preceding and following Primitive Signals.

Ethernet physical links do not impose the same inter-frame gap requirements. For a description of the Ethernet requirements, refer to the appropriate Ethernet standards.

A.2.6 Arbitrated Loop is Not Supported

The Arbitrated Loop topology is not supported on Ethernet links. FCoE devices can communicate with native Fibre Channel devices on an Arbitrated Loop via an FCoE Forwarder (FCF) and/or Fibre Channel switch.

A.3 Fibre Channel FC-2 Differences

Other than the items listed below, it is not anticipated that there will be any changes to FC-2 operation of behavior as a result of FCoE.

A.3.1 Flow Control

Fibre Channel's Buffer-to-Buffer flow control (R_RDY flow control) is not used on Ethernet links. An equivalent function is provided by the Ethernet Pause or "Per-Priority Pause" flow control.

Likewise, Fibre Channel's VC_RDY flow control is not used on Ethernet Inter-Switch Links (ISLs).

A.3.2 Class-1 Service Not Supported

Class-1 service is not supported by FCoE.

A.4 Fibre Channel FC-3 Differences

It is not anticipated that there will be any changes to FC-3 operation of behavior as a result of FCoE.

A.5 Fibre Channel FC-4 Differences

It is not anticipated that there will be any changes to FC-4 protocol mappings or operation as a result of FCoE.

A.6 Upper-Level Protocol (ULP) Differences

It is not clear whether Upper-Level Protocols will be affected by the presence of FCoE.

The SCSI architecture defines protocol-specific mode pages and protocol-specific log pages for various physical interfaces that carry the SCSI protocol. The intent is that SCSI-FCP operate the same whether on a native Fibre Channel link or an FCoE Ethernet link. However, more investigation is needed to determine whether the SCSI level needs to be aware of the presence of an FCoE Ethernet link.

A.7 Link Services (ELS and SW_ILS) Differences

The intent of FCoE was to leave operations of the Link Service unchanged wherever possible. It appears that this goal has been largely achieved with the exception of the following.

A.7.1 Path Establishment and Removal Link Services

Extended Link Service requests and replies associated with the establishment of FCoE virtual links are performed using the FCoE Initialization Protocol (FIP). Examples of operations performed using the FIP protocol include:

- Fabric Login (FLOGI) and its associated LS_ACC or LS_RJT
- NPIV Fabric Discover (FDISC with an S_ID of 00:00:00h) and its associated LS_ACC or LS_RJT
- Fabric Logout (LOGO with a D_ID of FF:FF:FEh and its associated LS_ACC or LS_RJT
- Exchange Link Parameters (ELP) Switch Internal Link Service and its associated SW_ACC or SW_RJT

A.7.2 Read Link Status (RLS) ELS

At the time of writing, it is unclear whether this Extended Link Service will be affected by FCoE. RLS returns the content of the Link Error Status Block (LESB). The LESB maintains counters of various link-level error conditions. These counters may not be available on Ethernet links, and/or Ethernet links may have different error conditions to report that cannot be reported via the LESB.

B. 2nd Generation FCoE

B.1 Obsolete SPMA

At the August 2009 T11 meeting, a straw poll was taken regarding the removal of Server Provided MAC Addressing (SPMA). The result of the poll was unanimous agreement to proceed in this direction. This was confirmed by a formal vote at the October 2009 meeting.

With the removal of SPMA, the following items are affected:

- The MAC Address descriptor is no longer required in the FLOGI or NPIV FDISC request or their associated LS_ACC replies. For backward compatibility, it remains unchanged.
- The FP and SP flags are no longer required in the FIP header. For backward compatibility, the FP flag remains and the SP flag is obsoleted.
- The VN_Port MAC address is inherently known once the Fibre Channel N_Port_ID and FC-MAP values are known. The FC-MAP is provided in the FIP Advertisement.

NOTE – These items may be left as is to preserve backward compatibility with FCoE-1.

B.2 Direct VN_Port to VN_Port Communication?

The proposed Discovery and Virtual Link Initialization protocols enable an ENode to discover available FCFs, establish virtual links and the VF_Ports and VN_Ports associated with those links. The Discovery and Virtual Link Initialization protocols also enable an FCF to discover other FCFs, establish virtual ISL links and the VE_Ports associated with those links.

One topic that has been raised is whether VN_Ports should be allowed to communicate directly with other VN_Ports without the VN_Port traffic being required to go through an FCF.

NOTE – At the time of writing, Direct VN_Port to VN_Port communication via a "lossless" Ethernet network was not supported. The current proposals require all communication between VN_Ports to go through an FCF.

Consider the configuration shown in Figure B-1 on page 270. In this configuration, should Host 2 be allowed to communicate with Storage 2 directly through the Ethernet network or should the communication be required to pass through the FCF?

If the frames between Host 2 and Storage 2 are required to go through the FCF, the frames will traverse a path having a total of six hops and travel through seven switches (twice through each "lossless" Ethernet switch and once through the FCF). On the other hand, it the frames were allowed to travel directly through the Ethernet network without having to go through the FCF, the path would have two hops and traverse a single Ethernet switch.

Allowing direct VN_Port to VN_Port communication not only reduces frame delivery latency, but may also help avoid congestion on interswitch links leading to the FCF. In the example in Figure B-1, if all frames are required to go through the FCF, frames between Host 2 and

---

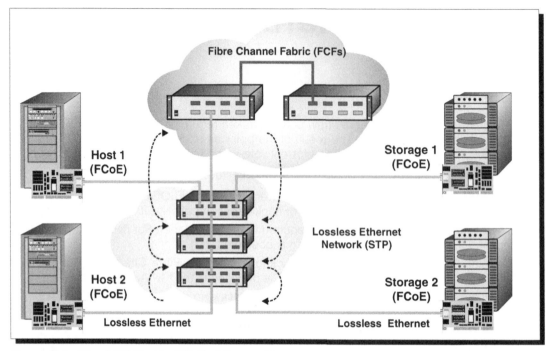

Figure B-1. Direct VN_Port to VN_Port Forwarding

Storage 2 must contend for use of the same link to the FCF as do frames between Host 1 and Storage 1 (and in fact, any communicating FCoE devices connected to the Ethernet network.

If direct VN_Port to VN_Port communication is to be allowed, it raises some interesting questions:

- How does Host 2 discover the MAC address of Storage 2 in order to communicate directly with Storage 2?
- How is zoning (or some other means of access control) enforced?

B.2.1 Direct VN_Port to VN_Port Communication

If an ENode supports direct VN_Port to VN_Port communication, it must maintain a lookup table that associates Fibre Channel Destination_IDs with Ethernet destination MAC addresses. For this discussion, it is assumed that well-known addresses are not contained within the lookup table. Steps that are required to support direct VN_Port to VN_Port operation are shown in grey in the figures in this section.

NOTE – At the time of writing support for direct VN_Port to VN_Port communication had not been determined. No proposals have been made regarding how a VN_Port would discover the MAC address of another VN_Port. For completeness, the diagrams and discussion in this section assume direct VN_Port to VN_Port communication is supported.

If direct VN_Port to VN_Port communication is supported, it is further assumed that a VN_Port can determine the MAC address of another VN_Port by querying the Name Server or querying a yet to be defined sub-function of the Directory server.

Once a VN_Port had determined the Fibre Channel Destination_ID and MAC address of another VN_Port, it enters the values in a lookup table that is used during the encapsulation process to determine the destination MAC address of the resulting Ethernet frame.

B.3 Supporting Point-to-Point Configurations

The FCoE Initialization protocols and operations (and the first generation of the FCoE standard) were developed based on a switched-fabric configuration. When an ENode initializes, it sends a FIP solicitation to discover reachable FCFs (or, it may simply wait for periodic FIP Advertisement from one or more FCFs). When the ENode receives an Advertisement, it knows the MAC address of the FCF(s) and can perform FLOGI with one or more discovered FCFs.

In a point-to-point configuration, there are no FCFs to transmit Advertisements and an ENode has no way to discover the MAC address of the other ENode.

NOTE – While no FCFs are present, it is possible that one or more Ethernet switches may present between the two FCoE ENodes.

B.3.1 Point-to-Point Discovery (Solicitations and Advertisements)

When operating in a point-to-point configuration, one possible solution is for one of the two ENodes to recognize the "All FCoE Forwarders" group address and respond to received Solicitations with Advertisements. This discussion assumes that the host system recognizes the "All FCoE Forwarders" group address, performs certain roles that would normally be performed by an FCF and that the device behavior is unchanged from what it would be in a normal FCF environment.

Additional roles assumed by the host are:

- Recognition of the "All FCoE Forwarders" group address,
- Responding to received Solicitations with Advertisements,
- Using its ENode MAC address wherever an FCF-MAC address is required,
- Transmitting periodic Advertisements, and
- Recognizing received FIP Keep Alive messages as an indication that the device and virtual link are operational

NOTE – While this procedure described in this section assumes an asymmetrical behavior with specific roles for the host and device, these roles could be assumed by both the host and device to create a symmetrical protocol.

An illustration of the point-to-point discovery and initialization process described in this section is shown in Figure B-2 on page 272.

When the host ENode operating in point-to-point mode receives a Solicitation, it responds with an Advertisement having the Solicited (S) bit set to one and the FCF (F) bit set to one. The FCF-MAC address returned in the Advertisement is the ENode's MAC address (normally, this

---

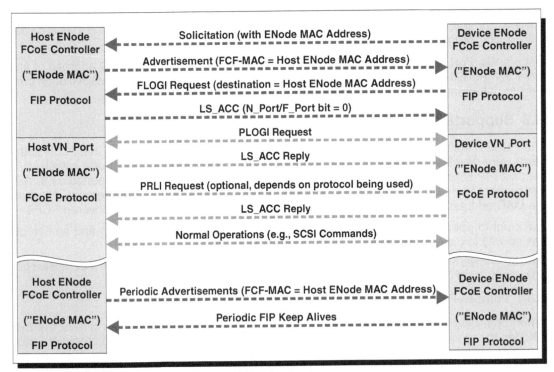

Figure B-2. Point-to-Point Discovery and Initialization?

would be the FCF-MAC address). This enables the device ENode to discover the host ENode MAC address.

In addition to responding to Solicitations, the host ENode must also transmit periodic Advertisements. This is necessary in case the device ENode does not transmit a Solicitation, or the Solicitation is corrupted or lost due to a transmission error. When a periodic Advertisement is sent, the Solicited (S) bit is set to zero, the FCF (F) bit is set to one and the FCF-MAC descriptor address is set to the host ENode's MAC address.

> NOTE – When intervening Ethernet switches are present, default access control lists must be configured as if the host ENode were an FCF. This is necessary to enable the discovery process to function.

B.3.2 Point-to-Point FLOGI and PLOGI

Once the device ENode has discovered the MAC address of the host ENode from the received Advertisement, it can continue with the normal Fibre Channel point-to-point initialization by sending Fabric Login (FLOGI).

When the device ENode sends FLOGI, it is encapsulated as a FIP operation. In a switched Fabric configuration, the FLOGI would be received and processed by the FCF. In a point-to-point configuration, the FLOGI is received and processed by the host ENode.

When the host ENode receives FLOGI, it sends LS_ACC (using the FIP protocol) if the service parameters are acceptable. The host ENode indicates that the LS_ACC came from an ENode rather than an FCF by setting the N_Port/F_Port bit in the common service parameters to zero. This is the same behavior a Fibre Channel node port would follow in a native Fibre Channel point-to-point configuration. When the FLOGI LS_ACC is sent or received, a VN_Port is instantiated by each ENode.

> NOTE – The LS_ACC to FLOGI may be examined by intervening Ethernet switches in order to setup access control list and static forwarding table entries. The behavior of the Ethernet switches is the same as it would be when an FCF is present.

After comparing its Port_Name with the Port_Name in the FLOGI or LS_ACC, the node port with the higher Port_Name proceeds to send N_Port Login (PLOGI) to continue the initialization process.

> NOTE – In SCSI environments, the host (initiator) always sends PLOGI and PRLI, regardless of the Port_Names.

B.3.3 Point-to-Point Keep Alive

Because an FCoE virtual link may span multiple Ethernet physical links, the ENodes may not have a direct indication of the state of the virtual link. To determine if the virtual link is functional and the other ENode reachable, the host ENode operating in point-to-point mode must transmit periodic FIP Advertisements (normally, this would be done by an FCF).

The device ENode must periodically transmit FIP Keep Alive to the host ENode. This enables the host and any intervening Ethernet switches to properly determine the state of the virtual link and remove access control list and static forwarding table entries if the ENode is removed or the virtual link fails.

C. Vendor-Specific DCBX Implementations

Prior to the adoption of the IEEE standardized version of the DCBX protocol a number of products had implemented vendor-specific versions of DCBX. These versions are described in this appendix for reference.

C.1 Vendor-Specific DCBX Version 1.00

DCBX parameters are transferred using an organizationally unique TLV with a Type field value of 127, an OUI field of 00:1B:21h and a Subtype field of 1 (see Figure 16-1 on page 254 for the format of the DCBX TLV). This version may have been replaced by version 1.01 (see *Vendor-Specific DCBX Version 1.01* on page 283) in some implementations.

> NOTE – The information is this section is taken from the "DCB Capability Exchange Protocol Specification Rev 1.0" available online at: "download.intel.com/technology/eedc/dcb_cep_spec.pdf"

Contained within the organizationally unique DCBX TLV is a DCBX Control sub-TLV and zero or more DCBX Feature sub-TLVs. The DCBX Control sub-TLV transfers information associated with the operation of the DCBX protocol itself, while the Feature sub-TLVs transfer parameter information. Remember that the DCBX TLVs are contained within the organizationally unique TLV and are, therefore, referred to as sub-TLVs (i.e., TLVs within a TLV).

C.1.1 DCBX Version 1.00 Control Sub-TLV

The DCBX Control sub-TLV contains information associated with the operation of the DCBX protocol itself. The DCBX Control sub-TLV format is shown in Figure C-1 on page 275.

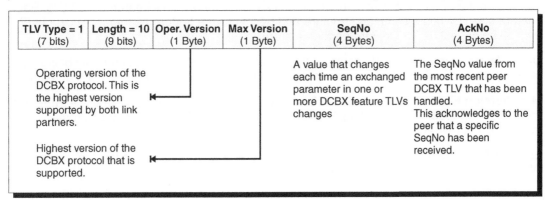

Figure C-1. DCBX Control TLV

Oper_Version Field. This field contains the version of the DCBX protocol that is currently being used between the two entities. If represents the highest mutually-supported version of the DCBX protocol.

Max_Version Field. The Max Version field specifies the highest version of the DCBX protocol that the sender is capable of supporting. Version numbers begin with zero and are incremented as the protocol is revised.

SeqNo Field. The Sequence Number (SeqNo) is a 32-bit value that changes each time an exchanged parameter in one or more DCBX feature TLVs changes. This value provides a way for the entities to identify and track a particular parameter transfer.

AckNo Field. The Acknowledge Number (AckNo) contains the SeqNo value from the most recent peer transfer that has been handled. It acknowledges to the peer entity that a specific SeqNo has been received.

C.1.2 DCBX Protocol Flow

The DCBX protocol is used to transfer parameters, provide sequence numbering and acknowledgements, and detect a protocol timeout. The flow can be modeled as a continuously running function as shown in Figure C-2 on page 277. This example is intended to illustrate the operation of the protocol and does not necessarily represent an implementation.

The main body of the protocol is involved with maintaining the state of the protocol, transferring feature information (both initially and in the event that a feature parameter changes) and receiving feature and control information from the peer device.

Protocol state information is transferred using the DCBX Control TLV (shown in Figure C-1 on page 275). The three control parameters transferred are the OperVersion, SeqNo and AckNo. Feature information is communicated using one or more DCBX Feature Sub-TLVs as described in the next section.

C.1.3 DCBX Version 1.00 Feature Sub-TLV Format

Parameters for specific features are communicated in one or more Feature sub-TLVs. Each Feature sub-TLV has a common structure and begins with a feature header as shown in Figure C-3 on page 278. The feature parameters are

Oper_Version Field. This field contains the version of the feature that is currently being used between the two entities. If represents the highest mutually-supported version of that feature.

Max_Version Field. The Max Version field specifies the highest version of the feature that the sender is capable of supporting. Version numbers begin with zero and are incremented as the protocol is revised.

Enabled Bit. When set to one, this bit indicates that the corresponding feature is enabled. When set to zero, the feature is not enabled.

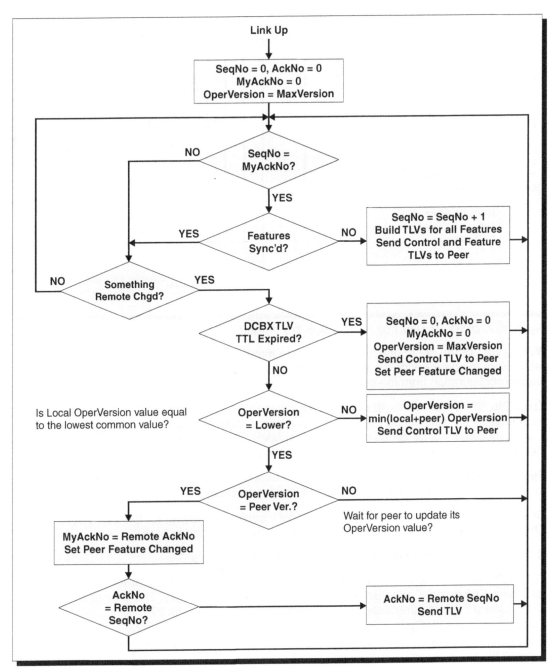

Figure C-2. DCBX Protocol Flow Example

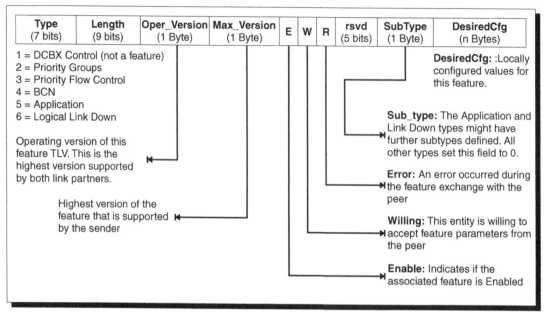

Figure C-3. DCBX Version 1.00 Feature Sub-TLV Format

Willing Bit. When set to one, this bit indicates that the sender is willing to accept its configuration from the peer entity. An entity that sets this bit must be capable of accepting any valid feature configuration from the peer.

Error Bit. When set to one, the error bit indicates that an error occurred during the parameter exchange for the associated feature. This can occur when the operating configuration and operating mode cannot be set as the protocol requires. This bit is also set if both entities are willing to accept feature configurations from the other and the DesiredCfg fields and incompatible.

SubType Field. TLVs for the Application and Link Down types may have multiple subtypes associated with different applications or link down conditions.

DesiredCfg Field. This field contains the locally configured values for the associated feature. The values for each feature type are described in the following sections.

C.1.4 DCBX Version 1.00 Traffic Class Group (PG) Feature

The Traffic Class Group Feature specifies bandwidth allocation and priority handling parameters (see *Enhanced Transmission Selection (ETS)* on page 227). The format of the Traffic Class Group Feature parameters are shown in Figure C-4 on page 279.

> NOTE – The terminology used in the DCBX specification is currently not consistent with that used in the Enhanced Transmission Selection proposal. It is expected that the terminology will be reconciled during the standardization process.

Chapter C. Vendor-Specific DCBX Implementations

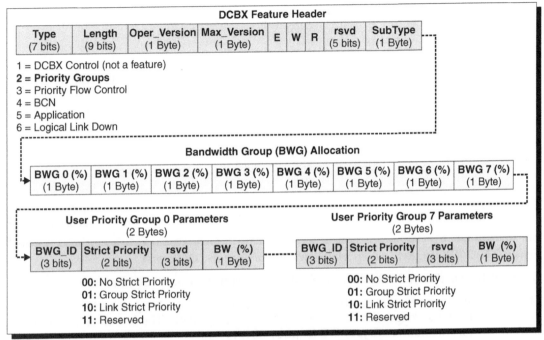

Figure C-4. DCBX Version 1.00 Traffic Class Group Feature TLV Format

All parameters must match between the local and peer nodes. If they do not match, a configuration error is indicated by the "Error" bit and the feature is disabled.

BWG_Percentage Field. The BWG_Percentage field specifies the percentage of the link's bandwidth (0% to 100%) allocated to each Bandwidth Group.

Strict Priority Field. The Strict Priority field within each User Priority Allocation specifies if priority applies to this User Priority Allocation, and if so, the priority type.

User Priority Percentage Field. This field specifies the percentage of the BWG bandwidth allocated to this User Priority Allocation.

C.1.5 DCBX Version 1.00 Priority Flow Control (PFC) Feature

The Priority Flow Control feature parameter is used to indicate support for Per-Priority Flow control (see *Per-Priority Pause Flow Control (PFC)* on page 226). The value is a one-byte bitmap indicating which levels are enabled or disabled as shown in Figure C-4 on page 279. All parameters need to match for Priority Flow Control to be available.

Legacy implementations that do not support Priority Flow Control set this parameter to indicate all priority flow control levels are disabled (00h) and revert to the basic Pause flow control as defined in 802.3x.

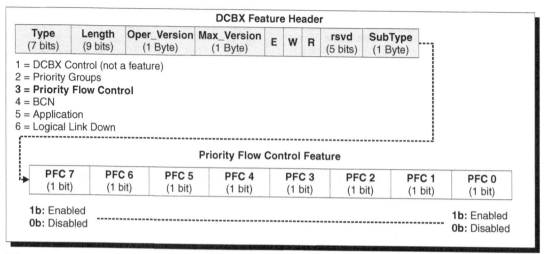

DCBX Feature Header

Type (7 bits)	Length (9 bits)	Oper_Version (1 Byte)	Max_Version (1 Byte)	E	W	R	rsvd (5 bits)	SubType (1 Byte)

1 = DCBX Control (not a feature)
2 = Priority Groups
3 = Priority Flow Control
4 = BCN
5 = Application
6 = Logical Link Down

Priority Flow Control Feature

PFC 7 (1 bit)	PFC 6 (1 bit)	PFC 5 (1 bit)	PFC 4 (1 bit)	PFC 3 (1 bit)	PFC 2 (1 bit)	PFC 1 (1 bit)	PFC 0 (1 bit)

1b: Enabled
0b: Disabled

1b: Enabled
0b: Disabled

Figure C-5. DCBX Version 1.00 Priority Flow Control Feature TLV Format

C.1.6 DCBX Version 1.00 Backwards Congestion Notification (BCN) Feature

The BCN feature parameters establish values for the Backwards Congestion Notification feature (see *Quantized Congestion Notification (QCN)* on page 230). The format of the BCN feature parameters is shown in Figure C-6 on page 281.

> NOTE – The terminology used in the DCB specification differs in some areas from that being proposed for the 802.1Qau standards activity. It is anticipated that terminology will be reconciled as the standard is approved.

BCNA Field. This field contains the BCNA (Congestion Point ID) value passed from a switch to the host.

CP Admin Mode Bit. When set to one, this bit indicates this device is capable of generating BCNs. It is used by the peer to determine if it needs to forward BCN tagged frames or strip the BCN (RLT) tag.

RP Admin Mode Bit. When set to one, this bit indicates this device is capable of responding to BCN messages.

RP Oper Mode Bit. This bit is set for an edge switch if the attached end station does not support Rate Controllers. If RP Admin Mode is true, this bit is set to false. If RP Admin Mode is false, then this bit is set to true.

Remove Tag Oper Mode Bit. The RLT tag needs to be removed before data is sent out via this port. Set based on the CP Admin Mode bit of the peer port. If peer CP Admin Mode bit is false, then set this bit to true, else set this bit to false.

Rp Gd Field. This field contains the Reaction Point decrement coefficient.

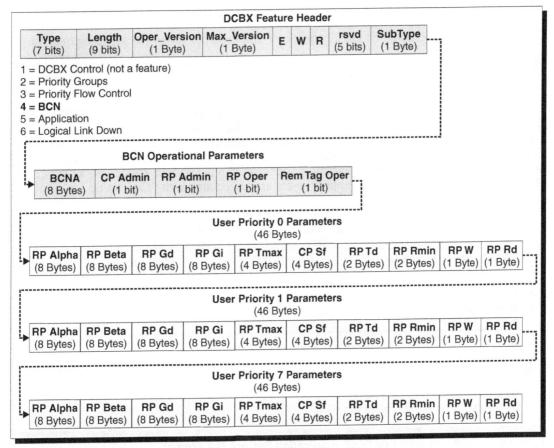

Figure C-6. DCBX Version 1.00 BCN Feature TLV Format

Rp Gi Field. This field contains the Reaction Point increment coefficient.

Rp W Field. This field contains the Reaction Point derivative weight.

Rp Ru Field. This field contains the Reaction Point rate unit.

Rp Tmax Field. This field contains the Reaction Point maximum time to backoff after BCN0.

Rp Rmin Field. This field contains the Reaction Point default rate to resume after first BCN0.

Rp Alpha Field. This field contains the Reaction Point maximum decrease factor.

Rp Beta Field. This field contains the Reaction Point maximum increase factor.

Rp Td Field. This field contains the Reaction Point drift interval.

Rp Rd Field. This field contains the Reaction Point drift factor.

Cp Sf Field. This field contains the Congestion Point fixed portion of the sampling interval.

Cp Sr Field. This field contains the Congestion Point random portion of the sampling interval.

C.1.7 DCBX Version 1.00 Application Feature

DCBX can be used to communicate application-specific information using the DCBX Application Feature sub-TLV with the Type field value set to five. The only application-specific information currently proposed is for the FCoE protocol application (this is identified by setting the SubType field value to zero). The format of the FCoE Application Feature TLV is shown in Figure C-7 on page 282. The feature parameter consists of a single byte containing a bitmap that identifies which 802.1Q VLAN tag priority levels are associated with FCoE traffic.

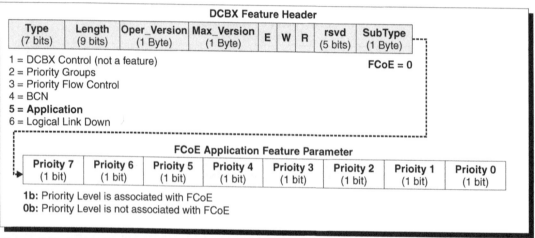

Figure C-7. DCBX Version 1.00 FCoE Application Feature TLV Format

C.1.8 DCBX Version 1.00 Logical Link Down Feature

Logical Link Down is a mechanism that enables an entity to indicate the state of a logical link. For example, the virtual link used by FCoE may be logically down, even if the associated Ethernet physical link is operational and carrying LAN traffic. A device may want to take a logical link down in order to force multipathing software to use a different logical link or to enforce policies such as security.

The format of the Logical Link Down Feature TLV is shown in Figure C-8 on page 283. The feature parameter consists of a single byte containing one bit that indicates the state of the associated logical link.

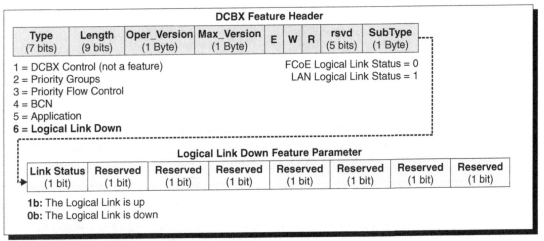

DCBX Feature Header

Type (7 bits)	Length (9 bits)	Oper_Version (1 Byte)	Max_Version (1 Byte)	E	W	R	rsvd (5 bits)	SubType (1 Byte)

1 = DCBX Control (not a feature)
2 = Priority Groups
3 = Priority Flow Control
4 = BCN
5 = Application
6 = Logical Link Down

FCoE Logical Link Status = 0
LAN Logical Link Status = 1

Logical Link Down Feature Parameter

Link Status (1 bit)	Reserved (1 bit)	Reserved (1 bit)	Reserved (1 bit)	Reserved (1 bit)	Reserved (1 bit)	Reserved (1 bit)	Reserved (1 bit)

1b: The Logical Link is up
0b: The Logical Link is down

Figure C-8. DCBX Version 1.00 Logical Link Down Feature TLV Format

C.2 Vendor-Specific DCBX Version 1.01

DCBX version 1.01 reduced the number of different feature TLVs and changed the format of some of the feature TLVs. Only the DCBX Control Sub-TLV, Traffic Class Groups TLV, Priority Flow Control and Application features are supported. The Traffic Class Groups and Application Feature formats are changed from version 1.00 and the Backwards Congestion Notification and Logical Link State TLVs are not supported at all.

Version 1.01 is identified by a value of 2 in the SubType field of the Organization-Unique TLV header.

> NOTE – The information is this section is taken from the "DCB Capability Exchange Protocol Base Specification" available online at: http://www.ieee802.org/1/files/public/docs2008/az-wadekar-dcbx-capability-exchange-discovery-protocol-1108-v1.01.pdf

C.2.1 DCBX Version 1.01 Control TLV

The DCBX Control Sub-TLV and associated DCBX protocol state machine remain unchanged from version 1.00 as described in *DCBX Version 1.00 Control Sub-TLV* on page 275.

C.2.2 DCBX Version 1.01 Traffic Class Groups (PG) TLV

The DCBX Traffic Class Groups Sub-TLV has been significantly changed from version 1.00. The purpose of the Traffic Class Groups feature is to map 802.1Q Priority values to Traffic Class Groups. Each Traffic Class Group is limited to a percentage of the link bandwidth to protect against starvation of other traffic classes.

The format of the Traffic Class Groups Sub-TLV is shown in Figure C-9 on page 284.

Following the DCBX Feature Header, there is an eight-entry 802.1Q VLAN Tag Priority value to Traffic Class Group ID mapping table. Each entry in the table is four bits allowing an 802.1Q

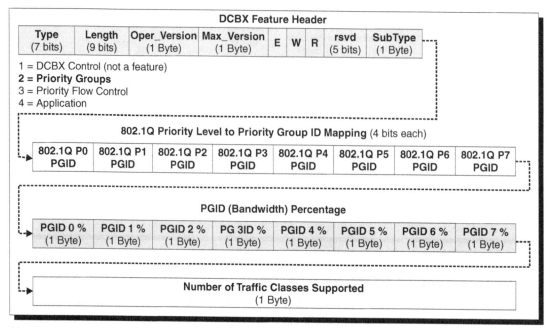

Figure C-9. DCBX Version 1.01 Traffic Class Groups Feature TLV Format

Priority value to be mapped to one of 16 possible Traffic Class Group IDs. PGIDs from 0 to 7 are available for mapping up to eight different bandwidth-limited traffic classes. Values from 8 to 14 are reserved and a value of 15 is used to indicate strict 802.1Q link priority not subject to bandwidth limiting.

The Traffic Class Group (Bandwidth) Percentage table specifies the percentage of the link bandwidth available to each Traffic Class Group ID. The bandwidth percentage is not an allocation of bandwidth, but rather a bandwidth limitation in the presence of other traffic. If other traffic is not present, the Traffic Class Group may receive more bandwidth than what is specified by this parameter.

The Number of Traffic Classes Supported field specifies the number of different traffic classes that are supported.

C.2.3 DCBX Version 1.01 Priority Flow Control (PFC) TLV

The Priority Flow Control Sub-TLV maintains the same format as in version 1.00 (see *DCBX Version 1.00 Priority Flow Control (PFC) Feature* on page 279) except for the addition of an additional parameter, "Number of Traffic Class PFCs Supported" as shown in Figure C-10 on page 285.

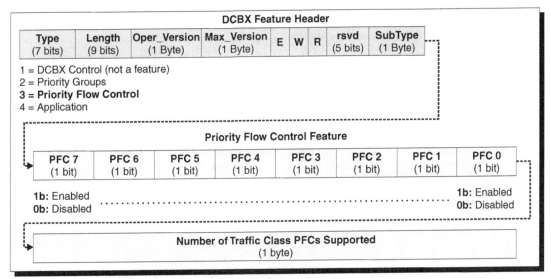

Figure C-10. DCBX Version 1.01 Priority Flow Control Feature TLV Format

C.2.4 DCBX Version 1.01 Application Protocol Feature

The Application feature is used to specify the application protocol, or protocols, associated with an 802.1Q VLAN tag Priority value. The Application Protocol Feature sub-TLV consists of the feature header and one or more Application Protocol Descriptors as shown in Figure C-11 on page 286.

Each protocol is identified by the use of an Organizationally Unique Identifier (OUI) and Protocol ID. For example, FCoE implementations currently use an OUI value and Protocol IDs of 0x8906 for the FCoE Encapsulation Protocol and 0x8914 for the FCoE Initialization Protocol (FIP).

> NOTE – Intel has offered the use of OUI 0x001b21 for pre-standard implementations. Once the DCBX standard is approved it is expected that implementations will use a standard-defined OUI value. The cur rent IEEE draft uses an OUI value of 0x0080C2 which is an OUI assigned to 802.1.

There are two bits in the OUI field that are not commonly used within an OUI (they correspond to the Universal/Local and Individual/Multicast bits). These bits are identified as the SF field and are used to further specify the type of Protocol ID contained in the descriptor as shown in the figure.

The UP Map field specifies the 802.1Q VLAN Tag Priority Field value that is associated with the specified protocol.

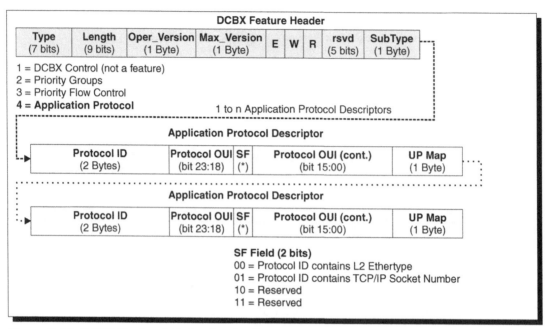

Figure C-11. DCBX Version 1.01 Application Protocol Control Feature TLV Format

C.3 Chapter Summary

DCBX Protocol

- Data Center Bridge Exchange protocol (DCBX) enables devices to exchange link-level feature parameters
  - Per-Priority Pause Flow Control parameters
  - Enhanced Transmission Selection parameters
  - Congestion Notification parameters
  - Application (FCoE) parameters
- DCBX is a based on extensions to the Link Level Discovery Protocol (LLDP)

Link Level Discovery Protocol (LLDP)

- LLDP enables devices to exchange link-level parameters
  - Originally intended to exchange device identification information (chassis ID, etc.)
- LLDP is a one-way protocol
  - Device sends its information blindly
  - No acknowledgements
  - Cannot request information from the attached device
  - LLDP Parameters sent every 30 seconds or upon a change
- Parameters are communicated in a Tag, Length, Value (TLV) format

LLDP Link-Up Problem

- Devices may miss the initial LLDP message due to link-up timing conditions
  - PHY A completes initialization and sends LLDP message
  - PHY B is not ready and misses the message
- PHY sends LLDP messages every 30 seconds
  - PHY B receives parameters on a subsequent transmission
  - Time to receive parameters is too long for data center environments
- LLDP Link-Up Problem Proposed Fix:
  - PHY sends 1st five LLDP messages at one second intervals
  - Reduces time to receive parameters

Traffic Class Groups Feature Sub-TLV

- Traffic Class Group Feature transfers Bandwidth Group (BWG) parameters
  - Percentage of link bandwidth allocated to each Bandwidth Group
- And, Traffic Class Group (UPG) parameters
  - Associated Bandwidth Group (BWG)
  - Priority behavior
  - Percentage of BWG bandwidth available to this UPG
- *See Figure C-4 on page 279*

DCBX and LLDP

- DCBX uses a vendor-unique TLV to communicate parameters
  - Actual parameters are communicated using sub-TLVs within the vendor-unique TLV
- DCBX implements a higher-level protocol on top of LLDP
  - Provides Sequence Numbering and Acknowledgements
  - Higher-level protocol is controlled using a DCBX Control sub-TLV

DCBX Control and Feature TLVs

- Control TLV controls the state of the DCBX protocol
  - Provides version co-ordination
  - Provides Sequence Numbers
  - Provides Acknowledgements
  - Protocol control is done using a Control TLV
- DCBX feature information is communicated using one or more Feature sub-TLVs
  - Each Feature sub-TLV begins with a common feature header

FCoE Application Feature Sub-TLV

- DCBX can be used to communicate application-specific information
  - Uses the DCBX application TLV (a DCBX Feature sub-TLV with the Type field value set to five)
- The only application-specific information currently proposed is for the FCoE protocol application
  - The format of the FCoE Application Feature TLV is shown in *Figure C-7 on page 282*
  - The feature parameter consists of a single byte containing a bitmap that identifies which priority levels are associated with FCoE traffic

Logical Link Down Feature Sub-TLV

- Logical Link Down is a mechanism that enables an entity to indicate the state of a logical link
  - For example, the virtual link used by FCoE may be logically down, even if the associated Ethernet link is operational
  - A device may want to take a logical link down in order to force multipathing software to use a different logical link
- *See Figure C-8 on page 283*

Priority Flow Control Sub-TLV

- Priority Flow Control Feature indicates which Per-Priority Flow control levels are supported
  - One-byte bit map with one bit for each priority flow control level
- *See Figure C-5 on page 280*

DCBX BCN Feature Sub-TLV

- The DCBX BCN Feature parameters includes:
  - A set of common parameters
  - A set of parameters for each User Priority (per the 802.1Q VLAN tag Priority field)
- *See Figure C-6 on page 281*

Bibliography

Fibre Channel and FCoE Related Books

[1]   Kembel, Robert W. *The Fibre Channel Consultant: Fibre Channel A Comprehensive Introduction,* Northwest Learning Associates, 12 Water Street, Hingham, MA 02043, telephone 781-626-4746, FAX 781-626-4751, www.NLAbooks.com.

[2]   Kembel, Robert W. *The Fibre Channel Consultant: Fibre Channel Arbitrated Loop,* Northwest Learning Associates, 12 Water Street, Hingham, MA 02043, telephone 781-626-4746, FAX 781-626-4751, www.NLAbooks.com.

[3]   Kembel, Robert W. *The Fibre Channel Consultant: Fibre Channel Switched Fabric,* Northwest Learning Associates, 12 Water Street, Hingham, MA 02043, telephone 781-626-4746, FAX 781-626-4751, www.NLAbooks.com.

[4]   Gai, Silvano and DeSanti, Claudio *I/O Consolidation in the Data Center,* Cisco Press, 800 East 96th Street, Indianapolis, IN 46240, www.cicsopress.com.

Approved Fibre Channel Standards

Copies of ANSI and INCITS approved standards are available from the INCITS Online Standards store at www.incits.org.

Framing and Signaling:

[5]   INCITS 424:2007. *Fibre Channel Framing and Signaling - 2 (FC-FS-2)*

[6]   INCITS 424:2007 AM 1:2007. *Fibre Channel - Framing and Signaling - 2 AMENDMENT 1 (FC-FS-2/AM1)*

[7]   INCITS 373:2003[R2008] *Fibre Channel Framing and Signaling Interface (FC-FS)*

Protocol Mappings:

[8]   INCITS 416:2006. *SCSI Fibre Channel Protocol - 3 (FCP-3)*

[9]   INCITS 374:2003[R2008] *Fibre Channel Single - Byte Command Set-3 (FC-SB-3)*

[10]   INCITS 374:2003 AM 1:2007. *Single-Byte Command Set - 3 (FC-SB-3) Amendment 1 (FC-SB-3/AM1))*

[11]   INCITS 356:2002[R2007] *Fibre Channel Audio-Video (FC-AV)*

[12]   INCITS 357:2002[R2007] *Fibre Channel Virtual Interface Architecture mapping (FC-VI)*

Services:

[13]   INCITS 433:2007. *Fibre Channel - Link Services (FC-LS)*

[14] INCITS 427:2007. *Fibre Channel Generic Services-5 (FC-GS-5)*

Topologies:

[15] INCITS 418:2006. *Switch Fabric - Generation 4 (FC-SW-4)*

[16] ANSI X3.272:1996. *Fibre Channel Arbitrated Loop (FC-AL)*

[17] INCITS 332:1999[R2009] *Fibre Channel Arbitrated Loop (FC-AL-2)*

[18] INCITS 332:1999 AM 1:2003[R2008] *Fibre Channel Arbitrated Loop (FC-AL-2) Amendment 1 (Supplement to INCITS 332:1999)*

[19] INCITS 332:1999 AM 2:2006 *Fibre Channel Arbitrated Loop 2nd Generation (FC-AL-2) Amendment 2 (Supplement to INCITS 332:1999)*

Technical Reports:

[20] INCITS/TR-36:2004[R2009] *Fibre Channel Device Attach (FC-DA)*

[21] INCITS/TR-39:2005. *Fibre Channel Methodologies for Interconnects -2 (FC-MI-2)*

Fibre Channel Standards Under Development

Copies of iNCITS Fibre Channel standards under development are available from the T11 web site at www.T11.org.

[22] INCITS Project 1861-D. *Fibre Channel - Framing and Signaling - 3 (FC-FS-3)*

[23] INCITS Project 1822-D. *Fibre Channel - Switch Fabric - 5 (FC-SW-5)*

[24] INCITS Project 2103-D. *Fibre Channel - Link Services - 2 (FC-LS-2)*

[25] INCITS Project 1833-D. *Fibre Channel - Generic Services 6 (FC-GS-6)*

[26] INCITS Project 2204-D. *Fibre Channel - Generic Services - 7 (FC-GS-7)*

[27] INCITS Project 2159-D. *Fibre Channel - Backbone - 6 (FC-BB-6)*

[28] INCITS Project 1871-D. *Fibre Channel - Backbone - 5 (FC-BB-5)*

[29] INCITS Project 1870-D. *Fibre Channel - Device Attach - 2 (FC-DA-2)*

Ethernet Standards

[30] IEEE 802.1AD. Station and Media Access Control Connectivity Discovery (LLDP)

[31] IEEE 802.1D. IEEE Standard for Local and metropolitan area networks: Media Access Control (MAC) Bridges

[32] IEEE 802.1Q. IEEE Standard for Local and metropolitan area networks: Virtual Bridged Local Area Networks

[33] IEEE 802.3. IEEE Standard for Local and metropolitan area networks

[34] IEEE 802.3ad. IEEE Task Force for Ethernet Link Aggregation (see 802.3 clause 43)

Ethernet Standards Under Development

[35]   IEEE 802.1Qau. Congestion Notification (CN)

[36]   IEEE 802.1Qaz. Enhanced Transmission Selection (ETS)

[37]   IEEE 802.1Qbb. Priority Based Flow Control (PFC)

On-Line Resources

There are a number of World-Wide Web and FTP sites providing convenient access to Fibre Channel information and standards under development. There are also a number of reflectors facilitate the on-line discussion of standards related activities and discussion. Finally, various provides of Fibre Channel equipment and components maintain on-line sites that provide information about their specific products or services. Several sites that the reader may find to be of interest are listed below.

World-Wide Web Sites:

http://www.fibrechannel.org - Home page for the Fibre Channel Association, a trade group established to promote the use of Fibre Channel technology.

http://www.IEEE.org - Home page for IEEE - the organization that develops Ethernet standards.

http://www.iol.unh.edu/consortiums/fc/index - University of New Hampshire interoperability testing site.

http://www.incits.org - Home page for the InterNational Committee for Information Technology Standards (INCITS). Information regarding standards under development.

http://www.Open-FCoE.org - Open-FCoE is the home of the Fibre Channel over Ethernet implementation for the Linux operating system.

http://www.SNIA.org - Home page for the Storage Network Industry Association. A trade association formed to advance the use of Storage Area Networks.

http://www.T11.org - Home page for the National Committee for Information Technology Standards (NCITS) T11 committee. Fibre Channel, HiPPI, and IPI related working drafts, proposal, presentations in regards to standards under development. Also meeting schedule and minutes for NCITS technical committee T11.

http://www.T10.org - Home page for the National Committee for Information Technology Standards (NCITS) T10 committee. SCSI, SSA, ATAPI related working drafts, proposal, presentations in regards to standards under development. Also meeting schedule and minutes for NCITS technical committee T10.

USENET News Groups:

comp.periphs.scsi - Discussion of SCSI peripherals

IEEE Organizational Unique Identifier (OUI):

For information regarding IEEE assignment of organizational unique identifiers (used in Fibre Channel names and Ethernet MAC addresses), see the following Web site:

http://standards.ieee.org/regauth/oui/index.html

IEEE Standards Department
Iris Ringel
445 Hoes Lane
P.O. Box 1331
Piscataway, NJ 08855-1331
Phone: (908) 562-3813, Fax: (909) 562-1571
email: i.ringel@ieee.org

Glossary

A

Active   The state of a Sequence at a Sequence Initiator between transmission of the first and last frames of a Sequence. The state of a Sequence at a Sequence Recipient between receipt of the first and last frames of a Sequence.

Active Zone Set   The active zone set is the zone set definition currently in use and being enforced.

Address Assignment   A process whereby addresses are assigned to switches and switch ports.

Address Identifier   A 24-bit address value used to uniquely identify the source (S_ID) and destination (D_ID) of Fibre Channel frames.

Adjacent Switch   A remote switch that can be reached without traversing intermediate switches.

AL_PA   Arbitrated Loop Physical Address.

Alias address identifier   An address identifier recognized by a port in addition to its Native Address Identifier. An alias address identifier may be shared by multiple N_Ports.

Arbitrated Loop   A Fibre Channel topology structured as a loop and requiring a port to successfully arbitrate prior to establishing a circuit to send and/or receive frames.

Arbitrated Loop Physical Address (AL_PA)   A one-byte value used to identify a port in an arbitrated loop topology. The value of the AL_PA corresponds to bits 7:0 of the 24-bit Native Address Identifier.

Area   The second level in the three-level addressing hierarchy originally defined in FC-FG.

Area Identifier   An eight-bit value that identifies an area. The area identifier corresponds to bits 15-8 of an address identifier.

Attenuation   A reduction in signal strength or power through a transmission medium or connectors, usually expressed in units of dB.

Available BB_Credit   A value used by a transmitter to determine permission to transmit frames and if so, how many. The transmitter may transmit a frame when available BB_Credit is greater than zero.

Available_receive_buffers   The current number of buffers in a receiving port which are available for receiving frames at link rate.

Arbitration Wait Timeout Value (AW_TOV)   The minimum time that an L_Port waits while arbitrating before originating a loop initialization.

Average power The optical power measured by an average reading power meter when a specified code sequence is being transmitted.

AW_TOV Arbitration Wait Timeout Value.

B

B_Port Fibre Channel Bridge Port.

Bandwidth The maximum information carrying capacity of a system.

Bandwidth Group A object used to represent to allocation of a percentage of an Ethernet link's bandwidth to one or more traffic classes.

Baud The encoded bit rate per second.

BB_Credit Buffer-to-Buffer Credit.

BCN An acronym for Backward Congestion Notification.

Beginning running disparity The disparity present at the transmitter when the special character associated with an ordered set is encoded. The disparity present at the receiver when the special character associated with an ordered set is decoded.

Bit error rate (BER) The probability that a transmitted bit will be received in error. The bit error rate is expressed as the ratio of error bits to total number of bits.

Bit synchronization The state when the receiver is delivering correctly clocked bits at the required bit error rate.

BNC An acronym for Bayonet Neil Councilman. A coaxial connector specified by EIA/TIA 403-A and MIL-C-39012.

Block Upper-level application data assigned a single information category and transferred within a single sequence.

Bridge Port (B_Port) A Fibre Channel inter-element port used to connect bridge devices with E_Ports.

Broadcast Link A WAN or LAN segment with two or more interfaces. A WAN broadcast link can be ATM, SONET, and a LAN broadcast link can be Gigabit Ethernet.

Buffer-to-Buffer Credit A Fibre Channel link-level flow control mechanism.

BWG see BandWidth Group

Byte A group of eight data bits.

C

C-Band Optical transmission in the range of 1530-1562 nm.

Cable plant The passive interconnection between a transmitter and receiver consisting of cables, connectors, patch panels, splices, etc.

CCF see Congestion Controlled Flow

CFW   An acronym for Current Fill Word.

Circuit   1. An arbitrated loop circuit as described in *Loop Circuit*. 2. A Class-4 bidirectional circuit consisting of two unidirectional virtual circuits.

Cladding   The part of an optical fibre that surrounds the core and keeps the light confined to the core.

Class of service   A frame delivery scheme exhibiting a specified set of delivery characteristics and attributes.

Class-1   A class of service providing a dedicated connection between two ports with confirmed delivery or notification of non-deliverability (now obsolete).

Class-2   A class of service providing a frame-switching service between two ports with confirmed delivery or notification of non-deliverability.

Class-3   A class of service providing a frame-switching datagram service between two ports or a multicast service between a multicast originator and one or more multicast recipients.

Class-4   A class of service providing a fractional bandwidth virtual circuit between two ports with confirmed delivery or notification of non-deliverability (now obsolete).

Class-6   A variation of Class-1 service providing a multicast connection between a multicast originator and one or more multicast recipients with confirmed delivery or notification of non-deliverability (now obsolete).

Class-F service   A connectionless, frame-multiplexed service used between Fibre Channel E_Ports and B_Ports for coordination of the internal behavior of the Fabric.

Class-N service   A generic reference to any class of service other than Class-F.

CNPV   *see Congestion Notification Priority Value.*

Close   An arbitrated loop protocol used to terminate a loop circuit.

Code balance   The ratio of 1 bits to the total number of bits in a transmitted bit stream.

Code violation   An error that occurs when a received transmission character does not conform to the 8b/10b coding rules.

Comma   The seven bit sequence 0011111b or 1100000b in the encoded data stream.

Comma character   A special character containing the comma pattern.

Congestion Aware System   An end station or bridge the supports Ethernet Congestion Notification.

Congestion Controlled Flow (CCF)   A sequence of frames, all having the same 802.1Q VLAN tag priority value, that use a single Reaction Point to support congestion notification.

Congestion Notification Domain (CND)   A set of Ethernet end stations and bridges that are compatibly configured to support Congestion Notification.

Congestion Notification Priority Value (CNPV)   A value of the priority parameter that a congestion aware system uses to support Congestion Notification.

Congestion Notification Message (CNM) A message sent by a Congestion Point to a Reaction Point containing congestion information used by the Reaction Point to reduce its transmission rate.

Congestion Notification Tag (CN-TAG) a tag that contains a Flow Identifier.

Connection initiator The node port that initiates a Class-1 dedicated connection and receives a valid response.

Congestion Point (CP) An Ethernet end station or bridge port that monitors a single queue serving one or more Congestion Notification Priority Values and can generate Congestion Notification Messages and remove Congestion Notification Tags.

Connection recipient The node port that receives a Class-1 dedicated connection request and transmits a valid response.

Connector A mechanical device mounted at a signal source or receiver or on the end of a cable.

Conversation A series of frames between a given source and destination. Frame delivery order is preserved within a conversation by link aggregation or trunking techniques.

Core The part of an optical fibre that carries the light.

Credit Permission given by a receiving port to a sending port to send a specified number of frames.

CT_HDR Common Transport Header. An information unit header defined by the Fibre Channel Common Transport (FC-CT) protocol.

CT_IU Common Transport Information unit. An information unit defined by the Fibre Channel Common Transport (FC-CT) protocol.

Current Fill Word (CFW) The fill word that the LPSM uses when a fill word is to be transmitted.

D

DA Ethernet Destination Address.

dBm Decibels below 1 mw.

DCB Data Center Bridge. The term used to identify Ethernet implementations that support Priority Flow Control (PFC), Enhanced Transmission Selection (ETS) and Congestion Notification (CN). This term has replaced the earlier usage of Data Center Ethernet (DCE) and Converged Enhanced Ethernet (CEE).

DCBX Data Center Bridge Capability eXchange protocol (see *"IEEE DCBX Protocol"* on page 253).

Distributed Services Timeout Value (D_S_TOV) The maximum time that a requestor will wait for a response to an FC-CT distributed services request.

Domain The highest level in the three-level addressing hierarchy defined in FC-FG.

Domain Address Manager A switch responsible for assigning addresses to other switches outside of domain.

Domain_ID An eight-bit value that identifies a domain. The Domain_ID corresponds to bits 23:16 of a Fibre Channel address identifier.

Domain_ID List A list in which each record contains a Domain_ID and the Switch_Name of the switch that has been assigned that Domain_ID.

Downstream Principal ISL An inter-switch link over which a switch has received one or more requests intended for the principal switch.

DMA An acronym for Direct Memory Access. A hardware function providing direct access to memory for reading or writing data.

D_S_TOV Distributed Services Time-Out Value.

E

E_D_TOV Error Detect Time-Out Value.

E_Port Fibre Channel Expansion Port.

E_Port Identifier 1) An address identifier assigned to an E_Port. 2) An identifier used by the FSPF routing protocol to identify an E_Port within a switch.

E_Port Name A 64-bit identifier assigned to an E_Port and following the name format specified in FC-PH and FC-FS. Each E_Port must provide a unique E_Port name within the Fabric.

EFP Exchange Fabric Parameters Switch Internal Link Service.

ELP Exchange Link Parameters Switch Internal Link Service.

ELS see Extended Link Service.

ENode An FCoE Node.

Entry Switch A switch that receives an FC-CT request directly from a node port. The entry switch may forward to request to other switches for processing.

Error Detect Timeout Value (E_D_TOV) The minimum time that a node port waits for sequence completion before initiating recovery.

ESC Exchange Switch Capabilities Switch Internal Link Service.

EtherType A field in an Ethernet frame used to identify the protocol carried within the frame.

ETS Enhanced Transmission Selection (see *"Enhanced Transmission Selection (ETS)"* on page 227).

Exchange A Fibre Channel mechanism for identifying and tracking a set of related Sequences between two node ports.

Exchange_ID A 16-bit identifier assigned to a specific operation.

Exchange Fabric Parameters (EFP) A switch internal link service (SW_ILS) used during selection of a principal switch.

Exchange Link Parameters (ELP) A switch internal link service (SW_ILS) used to exchange service parameters between switch ports.

Exchange Switch Capabilities (ESC) A switch internal link service (SW_ILS) used to converge on a common routing protocol between switches.

Expansion Port (E_Port) A Fibre Channel switch port that is connected to another switch port with an inter-switch link.

Extended Link Services A set of protocol independent Fibre Channel services.

F

FCoE Initialization Protocol The FCoE Initialization Protocol is used to perform link services that establish or remove FCoE virtual links and ports. Examples of operations performed using the FCoE Initialization Protocol include Discovery, Fabric Login (FLOGI) and NPIV Fabric Discover (FDISC). The FCoE Initialization Protocol is identified using the EtherType field.

FIP FCoE Initialization Protocol.

F_Port Fibre Channel Fabric Port.

F_S_TOV Fabric Stability Timeout Value.

Fabric 1) As defined in FC-FG, an interconnection topology that connects Nx_Ports and is capable of routing frames using only the D_ID information in the frame header. 2) As commonly used, a topology consisting of one or more interconnect Fibre Channel switches.

Fabric Controller 1) As defined in FC-FG, the entity responsible for operation of the Fabric. 2) The entity at well-known address FF:FF:FDh.

Fabric Element As defined in FC-FG, the smallest unit of a Fabric that meets the definition of a Fabric. From the perspective of attached Nx_Ports a Fabric consisting of multiple Fabric elements is indistinguishable from a Fabric consisting of a single Fabric element.

Fabric F_Port The entity at well-known address FF:FF:FEh.

Fabric Login (FLOGI) A Fibre Channel Extended Link Service command used to establish a session between a node port and the Fabric. When Fabric Login is accepted, the fabric assigns an N_Port_ID to the node port.

Fabric_Name A 64-bit unique identifier assigned to each Fibre Channel Fabric. The Fabric_Name is communicated during the login and port discovery processes.

Fabric Port (F_Port) A switch port that is not capable of arbitrated loop operations and is connected to a single N_Port.

Fabric Provided MAC Address (FPMA) An FCoE MAC address based on the concatenation of an FC-MAP value and assigned VN_Port_ID.

Fabric Shortest Path First (FSPF) A protocol used to distribute routing information.

Fabric Stability Timeout Value (F_S_TOV)   A timeout value used for various reasons, including during Fabric initialization and principal switch selection.

FC Entity   The interface between an FC Switching Element or an FC stack and the FCoE Entity. Each FC Entity contains a single instance of either a VE_Port, a VF_Port, or a VN_Port.

FC-AL   The Fibre Channel Arbitrated Loop standard, ANSI X3.272-1996.

FC-AL-2   The Fibre Channel Arbitrated Loop standard - 2, ANSI X3.332-199x.

FC-GS-2   The Fibre Channel Generic Services standard - 2, ANSI X3.288-1999.

FC-FG   The Fibre Channel Fabric Generic, ANSI X3.289-1996.

FC-MAP   A 24-bit value that may be supplied by an FCoE Forwarder and used to form a VN_Port MAC address.

FC-PH   The Fibre Channel Physical and Signalling standard ANSI, X3.230-1994.

FC-PH-2   The Fibre Channel Physical and Signalling standard - 2, ANSI X3.297-1997.

FC-PH-3   The Fibre Channel Physical and Signalling standard - 3, ANSI X3.303-1998.

FC-SW   The Fibre Channel Switched Fabric standard, NCITS 321-1998.

FCF (FCoE Forwarder)   A Fibre Channel Switching Element (see FC-SW-4) with one or more "lossless" Ethernet MACs, each coupled with an FCoE Controller. An FCF forwards FCoE frames addressed to it based on the D_ID of the encapsulated FC frames.

FCoE Controller   A functional entity, coupled with a "lossless" Ethernet MAC, instantiating new VE_Ports, VF_Ports, and VN_Ports, and/or creating new FCoE_LEPs.

FCoE Entity   The interface between the FC Entity and a "lossless" Ethernet MAC. Each FCoE Entity contains one or more FCoE_LEPs.

FCoE Link Endpoint (FCoE_LEP)   The data forwarding component of an FCoE Entity that handles FC frame encapsulation/decapsulation, and transmission/reception of encapsulated frames through a single Virtual Link.

FCoE Node (ENode)   A Fibre Channel Node (see FC-FS-2) with one or more "lossless" Ethernet MACs, each coupled with an FCoE Controller.

FCP   The Fibre Channel Protocol for mapping SCSI-3 operations to Fibre Channel.

FIFO   A First-In, First-Out data buffer.

Fill Word   A transmission word that is either an IDLE or ARB ordered set.

FIP Keep Alive (FKA)   An FCoE link keep alive message.

FKA   *see FIP Keep Alive.*

FL_Port   A switch port that is capable of arbitrated loop operations and is connected to one or more NL_Ports in an arbitrated loop topology.

FLOGI   see Fabric Login (FLOGI).

Flooding   To cause information to be sent to all switches within a Fabric.

Flow Identifier (Flow ID)   A unique identifier assigned by a congestion aware end station that can be used to associate Congestion Notification Messages with a Reaction Point that rate controls the associated Congestion Controlled Flow.

FPMA   *see Fabric Provided MAC Address (FPMA).*

Frame   A data structure used to transport information from one Fibre Channel port to another.

FSPF   Fabric Shortest Path First (FSPF).

G

GS   Fibre Channel Generic Service. A service, such as the Name Server, defined by the Fibre Channel standards and existing at a well-known address.

FC-CT_IU   Fibre Channel Common Transport information unit. An information unit defined by a Fibre Channel Service using the FC-CT protocol.

FC-CT Accept   Fibre Channel Services Accept. An information unit indicating acceptance of a Fibre Channel Services request.

FC-CT Reject   Fibre Channel Services Reject. An information unit indicating a Fibre Channel Services request could not be processed.

FC-CT Request   Fibre Channel Services Request. An information unit requesting a specific Fibre Channel Services function be performed, or providing notification of a specific event or condition.

Full-Duplex   A mode of communications allowing simultaneous transmission and reception of data frames.

Fx_Port   A Fibre Channel switch port capable of operating as either an F_Port or FL_Port.

H

Half-Duplex   A mode of communications allowing either transmission or reception of data frames at any point in time, but not both (link control frames are always permitted).

Hard Address   The AL_PA which an NL_Port attempts to acquire in the LIHA Loop Initialization Sequence.

Hello   A service used by routing protocols to determine neighbor switch relationships and verify bidirectional communications. Hello is also used to sense when a link to a neighbor switch has failed.

HBA   An acronym for Host Bus Adapter.

Host Bus Adapter (HBA)   A hardware facility in a node that provides an interface attachment.

I

IN_ID   Initial Identifier. A field in the CT_HDR used to indicate the N_Port_ID of the client originating a Fibre Channel Services request.

Information Unit (IU)   A unit of information defined by an FC-4 mapping. Information Units are transferred as a Fibre Channel Sequence.

Interject   The process of interleaving Class-F frames onto an existing Class-1 connection within the Fabric.

Intermix   An optional feature that allows Class-2 and Class-3 frames to be interleaved onto an existing Class-1 connection.

Inter-Switch Link (ISL)   A link directly connecting an E_Port of one switch to an E_Port of another switch.

IP   Internet Protocol.

IPA   Initial Process Associator. An identifier associated with a process at an N_Port.

ISL   Inter-Switch Link.

Isolated   A condition in which no Class-n frames may be transmitted across an inter-switch link.

IU   An acronym for Information Unit.

iWARP   Internet Wide Area RDMA Protocol. iWARP is a superset of the Virtual Interface Architecture that permits zero-copy transmission over legacy TCP.

J

JBOD   Acronym for 'just a bunch of disks" referring to a number of disks connected to one or more controllers.

L

L-Band   Optical transmission in the range of 1570-1610 nm.

L_Port   A Fibre Channel node or fabric port capable of performing arbitrated loop functions and protocols. NL_Ports and FL_Ports are examples of loop-capable ports.

LAN   An acronym for Local Area Network.

Link   A connection between two Fibre Channel ports consisting of a transmit fibre and a receive fibre.

Link Level Discovery Protocol (LLDP)   An Ethernet protocol that enables connected devices to exchange link level information.

Link Services   A set of Fibre Channel protocols for performing link-related actions such as establishing sessions or retrieving error or status information.

Link State Update (LSU)   An FSPF SW_ILS used to communicate routing table update records.

LIP   Loop Initialization Primitive Sequence.

LIS_HOLD_TIME   The maximum time allowed for each node to forward a loop initialization sequence.

LM_TOV   Loop Master Timeout Value.

LLDP   see Link Level Discovery Protocol (LLDP)

Local Area Network (LAN)   A network connecting devices within a single building or campus.

Local Switch   A switch directly attached via one or more inter-switch links to the originating switch. Frames may be sent from the originating switch to the local switch without passing through any intermediate switches.

Login BB_Credit   On an arbitrated loop, a value equal to the number of receive buffers that a receiving NL_port guarantees to have available when a loop circuit is established. Login BB_Credit is communicated in the FLOGI, PLOGI, or PDISC link services.

LOGO   A Fibre Channel Extended Link Service command to terminate a session between two node ports or a node port and the fabric.

Loop Circuit   A temporary point-to-point like path that allows bidirectional communications between loop-capable ports. The loop circuit begins when the arbitration winner port enters the Open state and ends when that port receives a CLS while in the transfer or transmitted close states, or sends a CLS while in the received close state.

Loop_ID   Seven-bit values numbered contiguously from zero to 126 and representing the 127 legal AL_PA values on a loop (not all of the 256 hex values are allowed as AL_PA values per FC-AL).

Loop Initialization Primitive Sequence   A primitive sequence used to begin the arbitrated loop initialization process.

Loop Fabric Address   An address identifier used to address a loop for management purposes. The loop fabric address consists of the Domain+Area+00h of the associated FL_Port.

Loop Failure   Loss of synchronization for greater than R_T_TOV or loss of signal.

Loop Master Timeout Value (LM_TOV)   The minimum time that the loop master waits for a loop initialization sequence to return.

Loop Port   A Fibre Channel node or fabric port capable of performing arbitrated loop functions and protocols. NL_Ports and FL_Ports are examples of loop-capable ports.

Loop Port State Machine (LPSM)   A logical entity which performs the arbitrated loop specific protocols.

Loop Tenancy   The period of time between when a port wins arbitration and when it returns to the monitoring state.

Lossless Ethernet MAC   A full duplex Ethernet MAC implementing extensions to avoid Ethernet frame loss due to congestion (e.g., the Pause mechanism, see IEEE 802.3-2005).

Lossless Ethernet Bridging Element   An Ethernet bridging function supporting the minimum required capabilities of "lossless" Ethernet MACs.

Lossless Ethernet Network   An Ethernet network composed only of full duplex links, "lossless" Ethernet MACs, and "lossless" Ethernet Bridging Elements.

LPSM   Loop Port State Machine.

LSU   Link State Update Switch Internal Link Service.

M

MAN   An acronym for Metropolitan Area Network.

Metropolitan Area Network (MAN)   A network that connects devices within a metropolitan area.

MFC   Multi-Field Classifier.

Multicast_Group_ID   An address identifier in the range of FFFB00h to FFFBFF that references a Multicast Group.

Multicast_Group_number   A single-byte value that identifies the multicast group. This byte corresponds to bits 7-0 of the Multicast_Group_ID.

Multi-Field Classifier   A function, usually consisting of a ternary comparator, that enables classification of traffic based on one or more fields.

N

N_Port   A Fibre Channel port within a node that is not using the arbitrated loop protocol.

N_Port Identifier   An address identifier assigned to a node port (either N_Port or NL_Port).

NAA   Network Address Authority. An identifier indicating the format of a network address, especially when used as a Fibre Channel name.

Name_Identifier   A 64-bit identifier assigned to a node, port, switch or Fabric and following the format defined in FC-PH and FC-FS. Names within the Fabric must be unique within their associated name type (i.e., Node_Name, Port_Name, Switch_Name).

NAS   An acronym for Network Attached Storage.

Neighbor   A domain that can be reached by traversing one inter-switch link.

Network Operating System (NOS)   An operating system designed to support network communications between nodes.

NL_Port   A Fibre Channel port within a node that is using the arbitrated loop protocols.

Node   An entity that controls one or more N_Ports or NL_Ports.

Node_Name A 64-bit unique identifier assigned to each Fibre Channel node. The Node_Name is communicated during the login and port discovery processes.

Node Port A Fibre Channel port within a node. The port may capable of either point-to-point or arbitrated loop operations.

Non-L_Port A Node or Fabric port that is incapable of performing the arbitrated loop functions and protocols. N_Ports and F_Ports are examples of loop-incapable ports.

Non-Participating Mode A mode within an L_Port that inhibits that port from participating in loop activities. L_Ports in this mode continue to retransmit received transmission words but are not permitted to arbitrate or originate frames. An L_Port in the non-participating mode may or may not have an AL_PA.

Non-Zero Domain_ID List A Domain_ID list that contains at least one record.

Nx_Port A Fibre Channel port within a node operating as either an N_Port or NL_Port.

NOS 1. Network Operating System. 2. The Not Operational Sequence Primitive Sequence.

O

Open An arbitrated loop protocol used to establish a loop circuit.

Open Originator The L_Port on an arbitrated loop that won arbitration, sent an OPN ordered set, and entered the OPEN state.

Open Recipient The L_Port on an arbitrated loop that received an OPNy ordered set and entered the OPENED state.

Originator Exchange_ID (OX_ID) A 16-bit identifier assigned by the exchange originator to a specific operation.

OX_ID Originator Exchange_ID.

P

Participating Mode A mode within an L_Port that allows the port to participate in loop activities. A port must have a valid AL_PA to be in participating mode.

Path A route through the topology between a source and destination.

Path Selection The process whereby a path is selected.

PDU Protocol Data Unit.

PLDA Fibre Channel Private Loop Direct Attach Technical Report.

Point-to-Point Link 1) A link connecting two N_Ports. 2) A link connecting to E_Ports.

Port 1) A generic reference to an N_Port, NL_Port, F_Port, FL_Port, E_Port, or other type of Fibre Channel port. 2) In some protocols, a reference to a software access point within the protocol stack.

Port_Identifier As defined by FC-FG, bits 7-0 of an address identifier.

Port Mode   1) When applied to a switch port, a generic reference to E_Port, F_Port, or FL_Port operation. 2) When applied to a node port, a generic reference to N_Port, or NL_Port operation.

Port_Name   A 64-bit unique identifier assigned to each Fibre Channel port. The Port_Name is communicated during the login and port discovery processes.

Preferred Address   The AL_PA which an NL_Port attempts to acquire first during loop initialization.

Preferred Domain_ID   A Domain_ID previously granted to a switch by the domain address manager.

Previously Acquired Address   During arbitrated loop initialization, the AL_PA which was in use prior to receipt of LIP. Immediately following power-on and between the time one loop initialization is completed and the next one begins, an NL_Port may not have a previously acquired address unless it remembers it while power is removed.

Principal ISL   An inter-switch link used to communicate with the principal switch.

Principal Switch   A switch selected to perform certain functions, including managing the assignment of Domain_IDs to other switches.

Private Loop Direct Attach (PLDA)   A technical report which defines a subset of the relevant standards suitable for the operation of peripheral devices such a disks and tapes on a private loop.

Private NL_Port   An NL_Port that does not attempt login with the Fabric and only communicates with other NL_Ports on the same loop.

PRLI   A Fibre Channel Extended Link Service command used to establish a session and exchange service parameters between two instances of an FC-4 process.

PRLO   A Fibre Channel Extended Link Service command used to remove a session between two instances of an FC-4 process.

Protocol   A defined convention defining communication between two entities.

Protocol Data Unit (PDU)   A unit of information defined by an upper level protocol, such as the Internet Protocol (IP).

Public NL_Port   An NL_Port that attempts login with the Fabric (FLOGI) and can observe the rules of either public or private loop behavior. A public NL_Port may communicate with both private and public NL_Ports.

R

R_A_TOV   *see Resource Allocation Timeout Value.*

RAID   Acronym for Redundant Array of Independent Disks; referring to a collection of disk drives containing redundant data.

RDI   *see Request Domain Identifier (RDI).*

Reaction Point (RP) A port function that controls the transmission rate of frames for one or more Congestion Controlled Flows.

Registered Link Incident Report A Fibre Channel Extended Link Service command that contains information associated with a link incident.

Registered State Change Notification (RSCN) A Fibre Channel Extended Link Service command that transfers information about one or more state change events.

Reliable Flood Flooding where all switches are guaranteed to receive the flooded message.

Remote Switch A switch that may be reached via one or more inter-switch links. A remote switch may be adjacent to the local switch or reached via one or more intermediate switches.

Request Domain Identifier (RDI) A switch internal link service (SW_ILS) used by a non-principal switch to request a Domain_ID from the principal switch.

Request Rate The rate at which requests are arriving at a servicing entity.

Resource Allocation Timeout Value (R_A_TOV) 1) Minimum time that an L_Port waits before reinstating the Recovery Qualifier. 2) The maximum amount of time that a frame may be in transit in the topology. If a frame has not been delivered within this amount of time, the topology guarantees that it never will be delivered.

Resource Recovery Timeout Value (RR_TOV) Minimum time that the Private Loop Direct Attach technical report requires a Target to wait for an ADISC or PDISC extended link service following a LIP before it is allowed to implicitly log out a SCSI Initiator.

Responder Exchange_ID (RX_ID) A 16-bit identifier assigned by the exchange responder to a specific operation.

RLIR see Registered Link Incident Report.

Router An entity within a switch responsible for routing connectionless frames.

Routing The process of transmitting frames toward the destination port.

RR_TOV see Resource Recovery Timeout Value.

RSCN see Registered State Change Notification (RSCN).

RSTP An acronym for the Ethernet Rapid Spanning Tree Protocol.

RX_ID Responder Exchange ID.

S

S-Band Optical transmission in the range of 1485-1520 nm.

SA An acronym for Ethernet Source Address.

SAN 1. Storage Area Network. 2. System Area Network.

SCSI Small Computer System Interface.

Server Provided MAC Address (SPMA) An addressing method in FCoE-1 that has been obsoleted.

Service Rate   The rate at which an entity is able to service requests (e.g., the rate at which an arbitrated loop is able to service arbitration requests).

SI   Sequence Initiative.

SNMP   Simple Network Management Protocol.

Small Computer System Interface (SCSI)   An interface designed for attaching peripheral devices to small computer systems.

Simple Network Management Protocol (SNMP)   A protocol defined for providing network management and monitoring functions.

SONET   Synchronous Optical Network (SONET).

SPMA   Server Provided MAC Address (obsolete).

Storage Area Network (SAN)   A configuration allowing multiple systems and storage devices to be interconnected using storage command protocols.

STP   An acronym for Spanning Tree Protocol.

SW_ACC   A reply sequence indicating that the corresponding switch internal link service request was accepted and is now complete. SW_ACC may return requested information in the payload.

SW_ILS   Fibre Channel Switch Internal Link Services.

SW_RJT   A reply sequence indicating that the corresponding switch internal link service request was not accepted. SW_RJT returns a reason code and explanation in the payload.

Switch   A Fabric element consisting of three or more switch ports and a switching construct that conforms to the FC-SW-x standard.

Switch Construct   An entity within a switch that transports frames between switch ports.

Switch Internal Link Services (SW_ILS)   A set of switch-specific link services for configuring and managing the Fabric address space. Switch internal link services use protocol type=22h.

Switch_Name   A 64-bit unique Fibre Channel name assigned to a switch. The Switch_Name is used during selection of a principal switch.

Switch_Priority   A value used during selection of a principal switch. The Switch_Priority may cause one switch to take precedence over another switch during the principal switch selection process.

Synchronous Optical Network (SONET)   An optical network widely used for metropolitan area networks.

T

TCG   *see Traffic Class Group (TCG).*

TCGID   *see Traffic Class Group ID (TCGID).*

TLV   An acronym for Tag, Length, Value or Type, Length, Value. A data format consisting of the three identified fields.

TNC   An acronym for Threaded Neil Councilman. A coaxial connector specified by MIL-C-39012 and MIL-C-23329.

Topology   An interconnection scheme that allows multiple Fibre Channel ports to communicate. For example, point-to-point, arbitrated loop, and switched Fabric are all Fibre Channel topologies.

Traffic Class Group (TCG)   A group of 802.1Q VLAN Tag priority levels bound together for the purpose of bandwidth management. All priority levels within the same TCG are expected to have similar traffic handling requirements with respect to latency and flow control.

Traffic Class Group ID (TCGID)   A four-bit value that identifies a Traffic Class Group.

Transfer   An optional procedure that may be used by an L_Port in the OPEN state to establish a series of sequential circuits with other L_Ports without re-arbitrating for each circuit.

Transmission Character   A 10-bit character encoded according to the rules of the 8B/10B algorithm.

Transmission Word   A 40-bit group consisting of four 10-bit transmission characters.

U

UDP   An acronym for User Datagram Protocol.

ULP Process   A function executing within an FC node which conforms to Upper Layer Protocol (ULP) defined requirements when interacting with other ULP processes.

ULP_TOV   Upper Level Timeout Value.

UPG   *see Traffic Class Group (UPG).*

Upper Level Timeout Value   The minimum time that a SCSI ULP process waits for SCSI Status before initiating ULP recovery.

Upstream Principal ISL   An inter-switch link over which the local switch will send one or more requests intended for the principal switch.

User Datagram Protocol (UDP)   A protocol defined as a part of the Internet Protocol (IP) suite.

Traffic Class Group (UPG)   An Ethernet construct identifying transmission attributes associated with a traffic class.

V

VC_RDY   A Fibre Channel Primitive Signal used to provide flow control on a specific virtual channel.

VE_Port_Name   The Name_Identifier of a VE_Port.

VF_Port_Name   The Name_Identifier of a VF_Port.

Virtual E_Port (VE_Port)   The data forwarding component of an FC Entity that emulates an E_Port and is dynamically instantiated on successful completion of an ELP Exchange. The term virtual indicates the use of a non Fibre Channel link connecting the VE_Ports.

Virtual F_Port (VF_Port)   The data forwarding component of an FC Entity that emulates an F_Port and is dynamically instantiated on successful completion of an FLOGI Exchange. The term virtual indicates the use of a non Fibre Channel link connecting a VF_Port with a VN_Port.

Virtual Link   The logical link connecting two FCoE_LEPs over a "lossless" Ethernet network and is identified by the pair of MAC addresses of the two link end-points.

Virtual N_Port (VN_Port)   The data forwarding component of an FC Entity that emulates an N_Port and is dynamically instantiated on successful completion of an FLOGI or FDISC Exchange. The term virtual indicates the use of a non Fibre Channel link connecting a VN_Port to a VF_Port.

VN_Port_Name   The Name_Identifier of a VN_Port.

W

WAN   An acronym for Wide Area Network.

Wide Area Network (WAN)   A network connecting devices beyond a single metropolitan area.

World Wide Name (WWN)   A 64-bit worldwide unique identifier assigned to Fibre Channel entities.

Z

Zero Domain_ID List   A Domain_ID list that is empty.

Zone   A group of devices that are able to communicate with one another.

Zone Definition   The parameters that define a zone including the zone name, number of zone members and zone member definitions.

Zone Member   A device that is a member of a zone.

Zone Member Definition   The parameters that identify a zone member. A zone member may be identified by a port on a switch (especially, Domain_ID and port number), and/or worldwide Port_Name.

Zone Name   An ASCII string assigned to a zone.

Zone Set   A set consisting of one or more zones.

Zone Set Name   An ASCII string assigned to a zone set.

Zone Set State   The current state of a zone set (Activated or Deactivated).

Zoning Configuration   A set of zoning configuration data including the Zone Set state and Zone definitions.

Index

Symbols

Numerics

10GBASE-CU 83
10GSFP+CU 83
802.1AB-2005 (Station and Media Access Control Connectivity Discovery) 253

A

A Flag 138
AckNo Field 276
Active Increase 240, 241
Active zone set 293
Address
    alias address identifier 293
    assignment 293
    Identifier 293
    preferred 305
    previously acquired 305
Adjacent switch 293
Alias
    address identifier 293
Arbitrated Loop
    circuit 302
    defined 293
    fabric address 302
    failure 302
    port 302
    tenancy 302
Area 293
    Identifier 293
Available BB_Credit 105, 293
Avionics Environment project 25

B

B_Port, *see Bridge Port (B_Port)*
Backwards Congestion Notification (BCN) 232
BB_Credit 293

available 293
login 302
N_Port ID Virtualization (NPIV) 105
BCNA Field 280
Bits
    CP Admin Mode 280
    Enable 276
    Error 278
    Remove Tag Oper Mode 280
    RP Admin Mode 280
    RP Oper Mode Bit 280
    Willing 278
bits
    MBC 262
BNC 294
Bridge Port (B_Port) 294
Broadcast Link 294
Buffer-to-Buffer flow control 85
BWG_Percentage Field 279

C

C-Band 294
CCF 294
Class Enable Vector 227
Class-F 295
Class-n 295
Close 295
cnpdRcvdCnpv 245
cnpdRcvdReady 245
Comma character 295
Command Descriptor Block (CDB) 25
Congestion Controlled Flow (CCF) 232, 295
Congestion Notification
    Frame Format 237
Congestion Notification Domain (CND) 295
Congestion Notification Message (CNM) 296
Congestion Notification Priority Value (CNPV) 225, 233, 295
Congestion Notification Tag (CN-TAG) 234
Congestion Point (CP) 234, 296